THE EARLY MEDITERRANEAN VILLAGE

What was daily life like in Italy between 6000 and 3500 BC? This book brings together the archaeological evidence on a wide range of aspects of life in Neolithic Italy and surrounding regions (Sicily and Malta). Exploring how the routines of daily life structured social relations and human experience during this period, it provides a detailed analysis of how people built houses, buried their dead, made and shared a distinctive cuisine, and made the pots and stone tools that archaeologists find. This book also addresses questions of regional variation and long-term change, showing how the sweeping changes at the end of the Neolithic were rooted in and transformed the daily practices of earlier periods. It also links the agency of daily life, and the reproduction of social relations, with long-term patterns in European prehistory.

John Robb has lectured on archaeological theory and the European Neolithic at Southampton University, and, since 2001, at Cambridge University. He has conducted archaeological fieldwork on Neolithic and Bronze Age sites in Italy and research on prehistoric Italian skeletal remains. He is also the editor of the *Cambridge Archaeological Journal*

CAMBRIDGE STUDIES IN ARCHAEOLOGY

Cambridge Studies in Archaeology aims to showcase the very best in contemporary archaeological scholarship. Reflecting the wide diversity and vigour of archaeology as an intellectual discipline, the series covers all regions of the world and embraces all major theoretical and methodological approaches. Designed to be empirically grounded and theoretically aware, and including both single-authored and collaborative volumes, the series is arranged around four highlighted strands:

- Prehistory
- Classical Archaeology
- Medieval Archaeology
- Historical Archaeology

Titles in series

The Archaeology of Class in Urban America
Stephen A. Mrozowski

Archaeology, Society, and Identity in Modern Japan
Koji Mizoguchi

Death and Memory in Early Medieval Britain
Howard Williams

THE EARLY MEDITERRANEAN VILLAGE

AGENCY, MATERIAL CULTURE, AND SOCIAL CHANGE IN NEOLITHIC ITALY

JOHN ROBB
Cambridge University

CAMBRIDGE UNIVERSITY PRESS

CAMBRIDGE
UNIVERSITY PRESS

32 Avenue of the Americas, New York NY 10013-2473, USA

Cambridge University Press is part of the University of Cambridge.

It furthers the University's mission by disseminating knowledge in the pursuit of education, learning and research at the highest international levels of excellence.

www.cambridge.org
Information on this title: www.cambridge.org/9781107661103

© John Robb 2007

This publication is in copyright. Subject to statutory exception and to the provisions of relevant collective licensing agreements, no reproduction of any part may take place without the written permission of Cambridge University Press.

First published 2007
First paperback edition 2014

A catalogue record for this publication is available from the British Library

Library of Congress Cataloguing in Publication data
Robb, John, 1962 Mar. 18–
The early Mediterranean village / John Robb.
p. cm. – (Cambridge studies in archaeology)
Includes bibliographical references and index.
ISBN-13: 978-0-521-84241-9 (hardback)
ISBN-10: 0-521-84241-7 (hardback)
1. Neolithic period – Italy. 2. Antiquities, Prehistoric – Italy. 3. Italy – Antiquities.
I. Title. II. Series.
GN772.22.I8R63   2007
937 – dc22   2006101937

ISBN 978-0-521-84241-9 Hardback
ISBN 978-1-107-66110-3 Paperback

Cambridge University Press has no responsibility for the persistence or accuracy of URLs for external or third-party internet websites referred to in this publication, and does not guarantee that any content on such websites is, or will remain, accurate or appropriate.

CONTENTS

List of Figures	*page* xiii
List of Tables	xix
Preface	xxi
ONE: THEORIZING NEOLITHIC ITALY	1
A Sense of Loyalty	1
Some Necessary Concepts	4
Social Reproduction	4
Material Normality	8
Frameworks and Orientations: Time, Space, Landscapes, and Histories	9
Tools of Thought: Bodies, Habitus, Identity, and the Senses	11
Fields of Action and Projects of the Self	13
From the Point of View of Things	18
Making History: Creativity, Commitment, and Gulliver's Dilemma	20
The 1st of September, 5000 BC: A Note on Methodology	22
Time Travel	24
Neolithic Beginnings	24
The World at 5000 BC	27
Neolithic Italy: The Rough Guide	28
TWO: NEOLITHIC PEOPLE	35
Ideal Lives	35
Refractions of the Neolithic Body	36

Bodies Themselves: Skeletal Evidence of Social Biology	36
Presencing the Living Group: Model Demography	40
The Represented Body	43
The Corporeal Corpus	43
The Materiality of Figurines	46
Gendered and Ambiguous Bodies	50
Abstracting the Body: Communities of Figurine Practice	52
People in Death	56
Neolithic Italian Burial	56
Burial, Status, and Identity	61
A Meaningful Burial Programme	63
Being Neolithic	65
The Human Career	65
Gender and Its Limits	67
Politics and Difference	70
The Road Ahead	73
THREE: THE INHABITED WORLD	75
Places of Life: Houses and Villages	76
Houses and Households	77
The House as Embedded Technology	81
Houses and Meaning	85
The Lifespan of Houses	87
From Houses to Villages: Settlement Size and Boundedness	90
Houses, Sites, and the Dead	95
Heads in Houses	95
Burial at the Boundaries?	96
Villages as Ancestral Places	96
The Microgeography of Dwelling	98
Economy and Frequentation	98
The Perception of Time in the Landscape	102
Macrogeography: Cultural Landscapes, Regional Identities, and Translocal Action	107
Cult Sites, Cosmology, and Gender	107
Gendered Spaces?	110
Natural Places and the Inhabitable World	112
People Create Spaces; Spaces Create People	116

FOUR: DAILY ECONOMY AND SOCIAL REPRODUCTION	119
The Archaeology of Foodways: From Calories to Cuisine	120
Cuisine	120
The Italian Neolithic Food Economy	122
Not on the Menu	122
Grains and Legumes: The World of Starches	129
Notes of Flavour	133
Animal Choices	137
The Sociality of the Food Economy	142
The Sociality of Herds	142
Eating: Rhythms and Tastes	144
Cooking	148
Culinary Prehistory: Neolithic Cuisine as Habitus and Taskscape	152
FIVE: MATERIAL CULTURE AND PROJECTS OF THE SELF	159
Archaeological Classics	159
Pottery and Meaning	161
Italian Neolithic Pottery: A Social History	161
A Bit of Historiography	161
The Genealogy of Pottery Traditions	163
Skill, Orientation, and the Layering of Local Knowledge	172
The Social Geography of Italian Neolithic Pottery	178
Fractal Styles and Impressionist Maps	178
Creative Process and Archaeological Patterning	181
Difference, Situated Perception, and Local Knowledge	184
Foreshadowing Patterns of Social Action	185
Obsidian and Flint	186
The Lithic Economy in Neolithic Italy	186
The Obsidian "Trade"	192
Obsidian and Cultural Practices: The Alternative View	197
Axes and Their Life-Paths	204
Axe Basics	204
Contexts of Axe Deposition	208
Axe Biographies and Agency	214
A Methodological Note on Artefact Analysis	218

SIX: NEOLITHIC ECONOMY AS SOCIAL REPRODUCTION 219
  People at the Center of a Decentered Narrative 219
    A Quick Recapitulation 221
      Bodies 221
      Places 222
      Food 223
      Artefacts 225
  The Social Senses 226
  Unfinished Business: Space, Time, Projects 230
  Projects of the Self 237
  Difference and the Organization of Value 239
  The Commonwealth of People and Things 245

SEVEN: NEOLITHIC ITALY AS AN ETHNOGRAPHIC LANDSCAPE 250
  Spatial Demography 252
  Travel, Trade, Warfare 254
  Culture Areas and Differing Lifeways 260
    Village Farmers 261
    Dispersed Farmers 264
    Mixed Mountaineers and Lake Villages 265
    Interpreting Regional Differences 267
  Social Networks: The Calabrian Stentinello World 269
  The Social History of Unique Places: Lipari 275

EIGHT: THE GREAT SIMPLIFICATION: LARGE-SCALE CHANGE AT THE END OF THE NEOLITHIC 286
  Practice and History 290
    Historical Practice: Life without a Primum Mobile 290
    Temporal Scale, Regional Analysis, and Patterns of History 291
  The Late Neolithic and Copper Age in Peninsular Italy and Sicily 295
    Material Culture and Exchange 295
    Settlement and Productive Economy 300
    Burial, the Body, and Politics 305
  The Great Simplification 311
    Social Production and Intensifying Pastoralism 311

Place and Relatedness	313
Gendered Bodies	315
Agency, Aesthetics, and the Organization of Value: A New Synaesthesia	317
Processes of Change	320
Always in Transition	320
Re-Reading the Sequence	322
Causality and Spread	326
Coda: Malta – The Road Less Taken	329
Wandering through Tribespace: The Social Foundations of Prehistoric Italy	334
Notes	343
Bibliography	347
Index	373

LIST OF FIGURES

1	Italy: landscape features.	page 29
2	Administrative regions of Italy.	30
3	Selected Neolithic sites discussed in the text.	31
4	Neolithic body modifications. (a) Catignano: mature female with two trepanations following a serious cranial fracture; (b) Fonteviva: intentional removal of front teeth in life in females.	39
5	Figurines from Neolithic Southern Italy. (a) Grotta di San Calogero; (b) Penitenzeria; (c) Favella; (d) Favella; (e) Favella; (f) Baselice; (g) Passo di Corvo; (h) Rendina.	47
6	Figurines from Neolithic Central and Northern Italy. (a) Catignano; (b) Ripoli; (c) La Marmotta; (d) Vhò; (e) Arene Candide; (f) Riparo Gaban.	49
7	Single burial in village contexts: Passo di Corvo Tomb 5.	57
8	Anomalous burials. (a) Young adult male exposed in village ditch, Ripa Tetta; (b) Young adult woman at bottom of well, Passo di Corvo Tomb 11; (c) Mass burial, Diga di Occhito; (d) Headless burial, Madonna di Loreto.	59
9	Articulated versus disarticulated skeletons in Neolithic burials.	61
10	The normal lifespan in Neolithic Italy.	63
11	Burial pathways.	65
12	Neolithic houses. (a) Collapsed daub, Balsignano; (b) Catignano; (c) Acconia; (d) Superimposed foundation	

LIST OF FIGURES

	ditches from rebuilding episodes, Ripa Tetta; (e) Capo Alfiere, note monumental stone wall and stone-paved floor.	78–79
13	Burnt (fired) daub with impressions from sticks and reeds of house frame. (a) Penitenzeria, Calabria; (b) Masseria La Quercia, Puglia.	80
14	Ditch section, Ripa Tetta, a small Early Neolithic village on the Tavoliere.	91
15	Ditched village layouts. (a) Posta Villano, Tavoliere; (b) Masseria Acquasalsa, Tavoliere; (c) Passo di Corvo, Tavoliere; (d) Murgia Timone, Matera.	92–93
16	Reconstructed land use for Penitenzeria and Umbro.	99
17	The social landscape around Penitenzeria. (a) Possible paths, resources, and landmarks; (b) View southeast from Penitenzeria, showing general size and possible location of gardens and limit of territory exploited for gardening, pasture, and foraging.	103
18	Accumulated frequentation areas over 30 years around the site of Penitenzeria, Bova Marina, Calabria.	104
19	Midden, Penitenzeria, Bova Marina, Calabria. Dark, rocky stratum in lower half of section is dense midden deposition from occupation several centuries long. Approximate depth of trench 1.5 m.	105
20	Grotta Scaloria, Manfredonia, Puglia: cult site in lower cave, with fine vessels placed to catch dripping water.	109
21	Spatiality of gender: some possible relations.	111
22	The shape of land without high mountains.	115
23	Neolithic landscape: zones and places around a Neolithic habitation.	117
24	Carnivore canines, probably used as ornaments.	125
25	The household's food source, and hours of labor: Grinding stone for preparing grain, Malerba, Puglia.	133
26	Zoomorphic pottery vessel probably representing a pig or a cow, Colle S. Stefano, Abruzzo.	137
27	(a) *Struttura di combustione*, Mileto, showing layer of charcoal and ash underlying burnt rocks; (b) Earth oven	

	from ethnoarchaeological reconstruction, showing rocks, coals, and food buried under earth during cooking.	151
28	Genealogy of Neolithic pottery traditions.	164
29	Typical Neolithic vessel forms.	165
30	Approximate distribution of pottery styles through the Neolithic.	166
31	Examples of regional pottery styles. (a) Impressed wares from Lagnano da Piede; (b) Matera scratched wares from Grotta dei Pipistrelli (left) and Tirlecchia (right); (c) Stentinello wares from Capo Alfiere; (d) Bichrome painted wares from Passo di Corvo; (e) Trichrome painted wares from Grotta delle Felci, Capri; (f) Serra d'Alto wares from Serra d'Alto; (g) Diana wares from Contrada Diana, Lipari.	168–169
32	Penitenzeria, Bova Marina, Calabria. Stentinello style decorated bowl probably made by a learner.	175
33	Penitenzeria Stentinello bowls. (a) Basic design pattern summarizing principles found in most decorated bowls; (b) Variation in actual vessel designs.	179
34	Examples of recombinant pots. (a) Mixing of painting and impressing in Lagnano da Piede style, Fonteviva; (b) Use of the microrocker decorative technique in Impressed Ware assemblage, Masseria Mastrodonato, Bisceglie; (c) Scratched rendition of "impressed" c-motif, Serra d'Alto; (d) Impressed rendition of trichrome-style motif, Passo di Corvo.	183
35	Neolithic use of obsidian and flint. (a) Obsidian core for producing small blades, Castellaro Vecchio, Lipari; (b) Core for producing long blades from honey-coloured Gargano flint, Passo di Corvo; (c) Waste flakes from reducing obsidian nodules, Gabellotto Gorge obsidian source, Lipari; (d) Obsidian and flint bladelets and expedient flakes, Umbro, Calabria; (e) Formal tools of local flint, Gargano flint and obsidian, Arpi, Puglia.	187
36	Neolithic use of sourceable geological raw materials.	194–195
37	Working axes from habitation sites; note breakage and edge damage. (a) Umbro, Calabria; note partial	

	refashioning and re-use as a hammerstone; (b) Penitenzeria, Calabria; (c) Pizzica Pantanello, Basilicata; (d) Passo di Corvo, Puglia.	209
38	"Campignano" style flaked bifacial axe from Masseria Schifata, Puglia.	210
39	Cache of axes beneath house floor at Capo Alfiere, Crotone, Calabria.	211
40	Axes from ritual sites. (a) Hal Saflieni Hypogeum, Malta; (b) Grotta Scaloria, Puglia.	212
41	Surface finds of axes, as represented in antiquarian collections, Parma.	213
42	Axe reduction and miniature axes. (a) Broken axe butt, Umbro, Calabria; (b) Axette, Umbro, Calabria; (c) Hypothetical sequence of reduction of axe to "axe-amulet" or axette; (d) Miniature axe replica of phyllite, Umbro, Calabria.	215
43	Axe biographical pathways.	217
44	The color red. (a) Red ochre stain on grinding stone from ritual site, Grotta delle Felci, Capri; (b) Red ochre fragment, Umbro, Calabria.	227
45	Material flows in space and time. (a) Houses and villages; (b) Food; (c) Animals and herds; (d) Axes; (e) Pottery; (f) Obsidian.	232–233
46	Cumulative material flows in space and time.	237
47	Spatiality of exchange: a Tavoliere example.	257
48	Early Neolithic canoe from "La Marmotta," Lake Bracciano.	267
49	Calabria, Eastern Sicily, and adjacent areas.	273
50	The Lipari archipelago during the Neolithic.	277
51	Copper Age pottery. (a) Pontecagnano, Campania; (b) Maccarese, Lazio; (c) Conelle di Arcevia, Marche.	297
52	Copper Age weaponry. (a) Flint daggers and arrow points, Pontecagnano; (b) Burial assemblage containing metal dagger, stone daggers, and arrow points, Spilamberto; (c) Knives and arrow points, Moletta Patone di Arca; (d) Flint dagger, Remedello.	301

LIST OF FIGURES

53 Neolithic or Copper Age hunting and weapon art. (a) Cemmo statue-menhir, Valcamonica, note that this represents a palimpsest of imagery, probably including Bronze Age (plough motif); (b) Naquane rock carvings, Valcamonica; (c) Hunting scene, Porto Badisco cave paintings, Puglia. 302–303

54 Copper Age burials. (a) Final Neolithic introduction of collective burials in stone cists, Masseria Bellavista, Taranto; (b) Transitional Neolithic–Copper Age burials in small chamber tombs, Piano Vento, Sicily; (c) Copper Age burials in small shaft-and-chamber tombs, Pontecagnano, Campania; (d) Single burial with status-related grave goods, Remedello. 305

55 Copper Age human representations. (a) Stone statue from final Neolithic tomb, Arnesano, Puglia; (b) Large male clay figurine from ritual deposition, Piano Vento, Sicily; (c) Male figurine, Ortucchio, Fucino basin, Abruzzo; (d) Male and female statue-stelae, Lunigiana; (e) Menhir-stela, Bagnolo, Valcamonica; (f) Female statue-stela, Lagundo; (g) Male statue-stela, Lagundo. 309

56 Malta and Gozo: megalithic temple plans. (a) Skorba; (b) Ta Hagrat; (c) Ggantija. 330

57 Malta and Gozo: human representations. (a) Female figurines, Skorba temple; (b) Statue, Hagar Qim temple; (c) "Sleeping Lady" figurine, Hal Saflieni hypogeum; (d) Carved stone phalli, Tarxien temples. 332–333

58 Possible pathways for intensification. 341

LIST OF TABLES

1	Model demography of Neolithic communities, assuming 50 percent child mortality and life expectancy of 25 years at age fifteen.	page 41
2	Life events in a five-year period, based upon demographic reconstructions in Table 1.	42
3	Human body imagery in prehistoric Italian art, Neolithic through Iron Age.	44
4	Some figurine groupings.	54
5	Figurine oppositions.	55
6	Raw materials for typical Neolithic huts.	81
7	Middle–Late Neolithic burials excavated in previously occupied Neolithic habitation sites.	97
8	Land use needs and possible population levels with selected Neolithic economies.	101
9	Faunal data from Neolithic sites in Central and Southern Italy (percentages of NISP bones in assemblages).	126
10	Palaeobotanical samples from selected Neolithic sites in Italy.	130
11	Some characteristics of domesticated animals.	138
12	Neolithic sheep, goats, cattle, and pigs at Lagnano da Piede, Passo di Corvo and the Grotta Pacelli.	141
13	Spatial differences in sheep/goat and cattle bones at Passo di Corvo.	147
14	Summary of possible Neolithic food resources.	153
15	Neolithic cuisine as a generative map.	155

LIST OF TABLES

16	Ceramic chronology.	167
17	Operational sequence for producing pottery at Umbro and Penitenzeria.	173
18	Lithic raw material use in selected areas.	188
19	Some possible motives for the obsidian trade.	198
20	Axes from different contexts.	214
21	The possible Neolithic color world.	229
22	Archaeological approaches to material agency.	234
23	Spectrum of settlement definition.	261
24	Neolithic sequences from Lipari, Southern Calabria/Sicily, and Northern Calabria/Campania.	279
25	Overview and possible interpretation of the Lipari sequence.	284

PREFACE

This book has three audiences, to each of which it will seem unsatisfactory in different ways. Theoretical archaeologists in the Anglophone tradition may wish for the theoretical agenda to be pursued further and, perhaps, with less encumbering detail. Italian prehistorians, on the other hand, may lament the great mass of data on the Italian Neolithic that I have glossed over in the interests of synthesis and social interpretation. To each of these communities, I ask for tolerance, and, hopefully, to each I can offer some compensation. The theoretical archaeologist may appreciate the chance to see a theoretical agenda worked through systematically across the entire spectrum of archaeological data. For Italian prehistorians, I would hope to offer some interesting interpretations to pursue empirically, in places convergent with ideas arising within the Italian prehistory community. The third audience will be theoretically minded European prehistorians who share the author's desire to see prehistoric Europe neither reduced to one-size-fits-all theoretical frameworks nor left faceless and uninterpreted. To this audience, I can only say that the more ambitious a book is, the more likely it is to fall short, and nobody knows a book's limitations like the author.

This project has been in the making for about a decade. In that time, I have discussed aspects of archaeological theory and Mediterranean prehistory with many friends and colleagues. Many of them will disagree with the ideas and interpretations put forth here; many were unaware that their innocently offered piece of advice or information held great significance for this project as it gestated; all were generous with what they thought and knew.

I am particularly grateful to many colleagues and students at Cambridge and Southampton who have discussed these ideas with me over many years; I have had particularly helpful discussions with Elizabeth DeMarrais, Mark Edmonds, Clive Gamble, Yannis Hamilakis, Lila Janik, Yvonne Marshall, Preston Miracle, and Marie Louise Stig Sørensen. I have learnt much about agency theory from Marcia-Anne Dobres. My colleagues in the Bova Marina Archaeological Project (Umberto Albarella, Gianna Ayala, Marina Ciaraldi, Lin Foxhall, Helen Farr, Hamish Forbes, Paula Lazrus, Kostalena Michelaki, Doortjè Van Hove, and David Yoon) have been a source of ideas and support for many years, and I am grateful to Dr. Elena Lattanzi, Dr. Emilia Andronico, and Dr. Annalisa Zarattini of the *Soprintendenza Archeologica della Calabria* for supporting our excavations in Southern Calabria. Among American colleagues, I have benefited from discussions with Rob Tykot, Nerissa Russell, and Katina Lillios, and Dan Evett introduced me to the Italian Neolithic many years ago; while at Michigan I learned much from John Cherry, John Speth, Bob Whallon, Milford Wolpoff, Henry Wright, and Norm Yoffee. The members of our informal, peripatetic (but generally London-based) seminar on the Italian Neolithic have provided a knowledgeable and critical audience for many of my ideas. I am particularly grateful to Keri Brown, Caroline Malone, Mark Pearce, Mark Pluciennik, Robin Skeates, Simon Stoddart, and especially to Ruth Whitehouse for her detailed comments on the manuscript.

Many of my Italian colleagues, raised in a different archaeological tradition, will be bemused by my interpretations. Every tradition defines its own cardinal sins; Italian prehistory places more emphasis upon the particularity of data and less upon generalisation and social inference. I hope that this work will be read in a spirit of charitable tolerance and that it may even provide an idea or two worth being empirical about. In any case, I owe particular gratitude to the many Italian prehistorians I have met who have proven unfailingly generous with their time and knowledge, particularly Giovanni Boschian, Alessandro Canci, Alberto Cazzella, Andrea Dolfini, Alfredo Geniola, Alessandra Giampietri, Alessandro Guidi, Maria Rosa Iovino, Laura Longo, Brian McConnell, Francesco Mallegni, Laura Maniscalco, Giorgio Manzi,

PREFACE

Domenico Marino, Italo Muntoni, Giuseppe Nicoletti, Giovanna Radi, Mary Anne Tafuri, Santo Tinè, Vincenzo Tinè, Carlo Tozzi, Alessandro Vanzetti, Barbara Zamagni, and Annalisa Zarattini. Elsewhere in the Central Mediterranean, I am grateful to Stašo Forenbaher and Reuben Grima. None of these colleagues should be held responsible for the limits of my local knowledge or the interpretation I put it to.

Chapter 5 draws extensively upon discussions with Kostalena Michelaki and Helen Farr, and some ideas in Chapter 3 were worked out in collaboration with Doortje Van Hove. I thank Graham O'Hare for sharing his axe data generously, and the many colleagues and institutions listed below who have very generously granted permission to reproduce their figures: A. Ammerman, E. Anati, M. Cavalier, A. Cazzella, M. A. Fugazzola Delpino, U. Irti, M. Langella, J. Mallory, A. Manfredini, G. Bailo Modesti, G. O'Hare, G. Radi, F. Radina, S. Tinè, V. Tinè, L. Todisco, C. Tozzi, and D. Van Hove, as well as the Museo Archeologico Eoliano, the Museo Nazionale Preistorico/Etnografico "L. Pigorini", the Soprintendenza Archeologica della Basilicata, and the Soprintendenza Archeologica della Puglia. J. Skinner provided the original drawings, and J. Meadows drew some of the maps. I am also grateful to A. Sherratt for help accessing collections in the Ashmolean Museum, Oxford, and to J. Carter for the opportunity to view prehistoric collections from University of Texas work in the Metaponto area.

I am grateful to have been able to work with Jon Morter; his unexpected and tragic death in 1997 cut off a wonderfully stimulating collaboration which, like all of his colleagues, I remember with great regret.

Financial support for early stages of writing came from a Leverhulme Foundation Research Fellowship for 2001–2002. The prehistoric research of the Bova Marina Archaeological Project has been supported by the British Academy, the Arts and Humanities Research Board, the Cotton Foundation for Mediterranean Archaeology, the Mediterranean Archaeological Trust, the University of Southampton, and the McDonald Institute for Archaeological Research (Cambridge University).

I am grateful to Starr Farr for help and support throughout this project. This book is dedicated to my children Johanna and Nicholas. Raising them has been an education in itself.

ONE:
THEORIZING NEOLITHIC ITALY

> O body swayed to music, O brightening glance,
> How can we know the dancer from the dance?
> William Butler Yeats, *Among School
> Children* (Yeats 1962, p. 117)

> He neglected friend and relatives, and when he met one of them in the street (going to or from his office) he found it hard to carry on a sensible conversation. He grew more and more appalled at how little people knew of the 1st of September 1973.... The Subject turned out to be just about inexhaustible. Who would have guessed that so much had happened on exactly the 1st of September 1973?
> Tor Age Bringsvaerd, "The Man Who Collected the First of September, 1973" (Bringsvaerd 1976, p. 79)

A Sense of Loyalty

I became an archaeologist because I wanted to study *people*. All too often, however, I find myself writing about *things*. Sometimes it's things for their own sake: "This field season we dug up 20,000 undecorated potsherds and 3 decorated ones...." Sometimes I write about people, but with the usual tacit proviso that people are important only as far as they can be related to the corpus of 20,003 potsherds.

As a way of seeing the past, this is unsatisfactory. Our archaeological bookshelf is littered with the textual equivalents of nineteenth-century museums, display cases with rows of rigidly positioned arrowheads with faded labels: humanity subordinated to the geometry of the glass box. Even our attempts to escape the mental prison of artefacts often result merely in lifelike, frozen dioramas with only the surfaces of people. Lifelike, not living: caricatures of people, ancient shadows driven by single winds of tradition, food, sex, power, or identity. Do the people in our works act with a subtlety and a complexity that we recognise in ourselves? Infrequently. Do these works allow us to truly recognise the cultural differences of the past? Almost never.

Southern Italy between 6000 and 3500 BC is completely unremarkable. It is neither dynamic nor rapidly changing. It is not megalithic or monumental. There are no "high-status" burials. There is very little in the way of "hot technologies" – the metalwork, exotic goods, cult gear, or monuments which we have traditionally endowed with archaeological *mana*. It is a past of people simply getting on with their own lives. People like this often do not furnish helpful fodder for our stories about adaptation, inequality, or meaning – and in consequence, they are normally relegated to negative, residual categories such as "tribes" and almost completely left out of archaeological narratives.

Human *ordinariness* is an extraordinary accomplishment: it is the sheer ability of humans to believe and to act. This book is motivated by a sense of loyalty to the ordinary past. Throughout human history, most people have not been the scheming political elites, profoundly religious megalith users, or the other categories of actors who populate the pages of archaeological theory. If we do not theorise about ordinary people, if we assume that they are mere bricks in the fabric of society, we leave the great bulk of our subject uninvestigated. Similarly, ordinary material culture – the undecorated body sherd, the casual flake – forms the vast bulk of all archaeological collections. If we theorise only about "hot technologies" rather than about everything that the archaeological record affords us, we are throwing away most of our data. Ordinary life provides an extraordinary impetus to theory, a cliff-face which affords few handholds: if we can understand the agency of ordinary life, we can understand anything in the past.

One ambition of this work, thus, is to tell the story of the ordinary past – of the women, men, and children whose life stories make up the substance of remote millennia. I attempt to provide a systematic introduction to the Italian Neolithic – systematic not in the sense of covering every archaeological manifestation of this long and diverse period, but in attempting to think about as many dimensions of human experience as possible. If, in the process, this book also provides an entrée into this fascinating time and place, I will be pleased. Beyond this, the goal of archaeology is not to discover what social theorists knew yesterday, nor to rewrite the last good ethnography that we have read against a dimmed, distant backdrop. No other discipline commands our time, depth, and ability to see long-term general patterns – few other fields take material culture as seriously – and we stand increasingly alone in our ability to study nonstate societies. Hence, the second goal of this book is to trace the linkages between ordinary life and long-term history, between people acting in the short term and the larger patterns of both change and conservatism which we see unfolding across entire regions and down through the millennia. I hope to trace how humans make their history on a scale beyond experience of a single lifetime.

Finally, with theory as with cooking, the proof of the pudding is in the eating. This book presents an interpretation of early Mediterranean villages; the theoretical agenda outlined here is grounded in ideas about agency, material culture, and social change which are summarised briefly in this chapter. The title of this book also pays homage to Flannery's *The Early Mesoamerican Village* (Flannery 1976). I first encountered Flannery's book in 1984, as an ex-student of Middle English literature trying to understand what archaeology was all about. The theoretical landscape has shifted immensely over the last three decades. I have tried to avoid the sterile polemics which afflicted archaeology in the 1980s and 1990s, and Flannery's research agenda contained the precocious seeds of many current concerns. Still, much of what follows would probably look equally alien to the Real Mesoamerican (or Mediterranean) Archaeologist, the Great Synthesizer, and the Skeptical Graduate Student (who no doubt has since been afflicted with skeptical graduate students of his own). Yet one of the principal lessons of *The Early Mesoamerican Village* was that archaeological theory benefits more from studies which road-test ideas on the ground than from purely theoretical manifestos, and, if the goal of theory is to help us to understand the past, good theory will always be self-effacing.

So this book is an experiment in writing, an attempt to write about the past differently to reach and to understand a different kind of past. Fulfilling these ambitions completely is impossible – but I have learned a lot in trying.

Some Necessary Concepts

Social Reproduction

All interpretations of the past rely upon some general idea of human nature. Sometimes it lurks buried beneath deep strata of archaeological minutia; sometimes it occupies center stage with the archaeology as a coda to the philosophical meditation; but it is always there. Much of the 1960s and 1970s debate between culture historical and processual archaeology, for example, revolved around whether it is more useful to conceptualise humans as passive reproducers of tradition or as ecological organisms, just as much of the 1980s and 1990s theory wars between processualism and post-processualism hinged on whether we must theorise that humans are motivated by universal concerns, such as prestige or survival, or by the particular symbols of their own culture.

Although theory is omnipresent, it is also a tool; and one yardstick for a theory is whether it helps us to understand a particular archaeological problem. In this book, I address the relationship between agency and daily life – a challenge succinctly stated by Yeats in the poem *Among School Children*. To answer this question, we have to consider the relationship between action and actor, between long-term structures and fleeting moments. Precisely because this philosophical ground is so fundamental, it has been worked over many times. In this chapter, I do not review the many different points of view on this issue in social theory but briefly summarise the basic principles underlying the interpretation presented in this book.

Social theorists prior to Marx and Engels essentialised human nature. It was assumed either that people acted in accordance with their universal nature as humans, or in accordance with their particular fixed nature as savages, civilised Europeans, and so forth. Such views did not vanish instantly with the publication of *The German Ideology*, of course; indeed, in Victorian social evolution and culture history these views continued to be influential until well into the twentieth century. But what Marx and Engels did was to put human action and consciousness systematically into relation to social context:

> The model of production of material life conditions the social, political, and intellectual life process in general. It is not the consciousness of men [sic] that determines their being, but, on the contrary, their social being that determines their consciousness. (Marx 1978, p. 4)

People develop their capacity for acting through participating in social and economic relations. Human activity, therefore, changes two things: it produces a product or effect in the external world, and it shapes the actor's consciousness as a specific kind of being capable of acting within particular social and economic relationships.

The insight that social life must be understood dialectically was left neglected or considered to be implicit through much of twentieth-century social theory. In the 1970s, however, both Giddens (1979) and Bourdieu (1977) returned to this theme in reaction to models dominated by system and structure (cf. Ortner 1984; Sahlins 1981). Giddens begins with a critique of classical sociology centered upon role, rules, and institutions. If it is true that people act in accordance with structures, where do these structures come from? How do people vary them? How do the structures change? To answer these questions, Giddens proposes a dialectical approach in which action is the outcome of rules which it recursively organises. Bourdieu, reacting principally against structuralism, based his work on a parallel insight. Humans act in accordance with learned cultural structures which Bourdieu calls *habitus*, an ingrained system of dispositions which provide the basis for regulated improvisation. Reciprocally, habitus is never formulated rigidly; people infer its basic principles from a multitude of disparate cultural behaviours. Even though habitus has considerable inertia, changes in cultural behaviour have the potential eventually to change it. Note that, although a naïve reading would equate *structures* with social restraint and determination and *action* with individual intention and freedom, for both Bourdieu and Giddens, structures are not only restrictive but are also productive; structures enable one to act. Put another way, one cannot exist as an undifferentiated, essential specimen of humanity, but only as a specific kind of person in a specific social situation.

In social and archaeological theory, humans' capacity to act is often discussed under the rubric of "agency" (Barrett 2001; Dobres 2001; Dobres and Robb 2000; Dobres and Robb 2005, Dornan 2002; Flannery 1999; Gardner 2004; Gell 1998; Giddens 1979; Johnson 1989; Joyce and Lopiparo 2005; Ortner 1984; Sewell 1992; Shanks and Tilley 1987). Agency should be construed in terms of the dialectics of social reproduction rather than being equated narrowly with the self-interested efforts of political actors to accomplish their individual ambitions, as is sometimes done in archaeological discussion of ancient social change. In our own experience as agents, intention is often the most salient part of our experience of action. But human action also embodies and reproduces the totality of conceptual structures and social relations within which such an act is possible. To take a poignant example, consider the painful irony of a solemn academic seminar on racial and class exclusion conducted entirely by university-educated, middle-class white people (McCall 1999, pp. 18–19). The earnest intention is to confront social exclusion, but the occasion inherently perpetuates a system in which, as McCall notes, conventionally agreed practices of language, space, bodily demeanor, and deference

> serve to delineate the linguistic territory of academic discourse, complete with all the nuances of race, gender, and class that language carries.... These structural relations are not concerned with the validity of what a particular speaker says but with the institutional legitimacy of events such as this, positioned in places such as this. Our participation, our agency, constitutes the social through these arrangements independently of the trajectory of our intentions. Indeed, often our intention is to militate against the very system whose structures we reproduce in speaking and acting – note, for instance, academic forums on and against racism within our system of higher education, which through its

deployments of cultural authority continually reproduces the privileges associated with acting, speaking, and thinking "white." (McCall 1999, pp. 18–19)

Intentions are mobilised within specified fields of discourse, and they cannot result in action until they are localised within recognised and rule-bound genres of behaviour. Genres of action are woven from external and internalised rules, norms, layers of prescription, obligation, habit, assumption, and belief. Tracing this line of thought further, any intended action presupposes a multitude of structures, arrangements, and conditions which must be true, or provided, or in conformity with a norm, for the action both to exist as a possibility and then be brought to pass. It follows that one effect of action, and quite possibly the principal one, is to reproduce these conditions and structures which enable it (Barrett 2001, p. 62).

Social reality, thus, is continuously generated through individual action – through ordinary actions whose proximate aim is to accomplish some specific task at hand. Agency, thus, exists neither as a quality of agonistic individuals nor of determining settings and structures, but in the "grey zone" (Levi 1988) of action between them. The intentional pursuit of goals is possible only through complicity with power structures, cultural ideas, and ways of behaving – parameters of a situation that people enter into and normally accept as part of the situation. This has two general implications for agency theory. First, agency is a relational quality; the concept of agency really applies not to actors in isolation but to the social relations within which they act. Second, we do not act with a universal, reified "agency"; we act with the historically situated agency particular to those relationships. Language affords a parallel: although language is a universal and defining human capability, we do not speak Language but rather English, Italian, Iroquois, or Walbiri. Similarly, although we can discuss human agency in the abstract, when we interpret a social world it makes sense only to speak of particular, contextualised forms of agency – the agency of an early twenty-first-century Western male, or a seventeenth-century Iroquois female, or a Neolithic Italian child. These modes of existence differ and, therefore, make specific forms of agency important objects for archaeological interpretation.

Material Normality

All human relationships are necessarily material relationships. People know and define themselves and others through their bodies, orient themselves in a material world, carry out physical actions in tangible contexts, communicate through gestures, sound, and visual clues, and participate in a continued flow of substances – food, images, things, substances, work, and so forth. Even transcendental contact with the immaterial normally requires particular places, bodily attitudes, and paraphernalia. Materiality is fundamental to social life (Miller 2005). Moreover, we cannot think in isolation from the material world, which provides both sensory information and an extended cognitive system (Malafouris 2005), and cultural ideas must be expressed in material things to be deployed politically (DeMarrais, Castillo, and Earle 1996).

"The most important vehicle of reality maintenance is conversation" (Berger and Luckmann 1967, p. 172). Yet, conversation itself is a material process. We talk to others about things and actions we understand as materially existing; even when discussing the immaterial, we talk in particular material contexts, using apparatus (books, images, dress, gestures) and often with material referents for the intangible. Moreover, conversation, broadly speaking, is a chain of action through which understandings of the world are shared, checked and validated, transacted, and modified, and such chains of action are as much material as linguistic. If I make a pot by using techniques learned from other potters and idioms shared with others, in the expectation that they will see it, use it and understand it in certain ways, I am effectively conducting a material conversation with them.

Beyond material conversations, social reality is a material construction. "The reality of everyday life is organised around the "here" of my body and the "now" of my present" (Berger and Luckmann 1967, p. 36), and these are physical orientations of the body, space, and time. Moreover, as Bourdieu points out in his discussion of doxa, the undiscussed, silent, enduring presence of material things can be a powerful force in granting these things the status of immanent realities. Material things possess duration and spatial extension which may pre-exist any particular project and which renders them settings and conditions for any planned action. Perceiving and negotiating the material world is an inescapable part of action. Finally, the material world contains inescapable processes which involve fundamental ambiguities which must be theorised. It is not surprising that many of the central loci of social reproduction involve necessary and inevitable transformations: the development of bodily difference in sex and age; the transformation of physical matter into bodies via social foodways; work and production as the transformation and circulation of physical world; and death as transformation of bodies into other material states and kinds of beings.

Because social reality is a material construction, there are many ways in which archaeologists can investigate it fruitfully. What follows is a brief, and necessarily selective, review of some avenues of investigation which will be pursued in this case study.

FRAMEWORKS AND ORIENTATIONS: TIME, SPACE, LANDSCAPES, AND HISTORIES: "Place" rather than "space" has become almost a theoretical cliché, yet the central points are important. To summarise a vast literature briefly (Barrett 1994; Leone 1984; Parker, Pearson, and Richards 1994; Shanks and Tilley 1987; Tilley 1994):

1. People orient themselves and act within culturally constituted landscapes built up of places, general zones, and networks of paths. These landscapes are heterogeneous and discontinuous: they contain places created by the actors themselves and known intimately, places frequented periodically or under unusual circumstances, and places inaccessible from personal experience. The same is true for temporalities (Bradley 1991; Gosden 1994). Knowledge of landscapes is built up of equally heterogeneous materials, from daily practices, architectural structuring, and depositional practices, through long-distance travel, second- or third-hand report, story, legend, rite, or prejudice.
2. *Space* and *time* are understood materially, and are rarely separated. Other places are understood as possessing different temporalities and vice versa (Lowenthal 1985). Places are often understood experientially in terms of the time needed to reach them or traverse them. Time is made material via *time marks* or *memory anchors* which make the passage of time visible in the

perceived landscape (Gathercole and Lowenthal 1990). Moreover, the alternative major metaphor for understanding temporality, processes of growth and development (such as seasonal rhythms and the human lifespan) also have spatial referents – annual rhythms of activities, points of memory for human life stories, and historical moments fixing and synchronizing many human lives. Hence, memory and landscape are mutually constructed (Edmonds 1999). The "temporality of the landscape" is eloquently expressed in Ingold's concept of taskscape, the congealed sum of the activities carried out in a landscape over time (Ingold 2000).

3. Although such cultural landscapes can sometimes be summarised synoptically (Bourdieu 1977; Ortiz 1969), because spatial and temporal orders are produced in practices, cultural landscapes are situated. Agents with different regimes of activity may possess different understandings of landscape and timescape. Such differentials in spatial enabledness form a component of the agencies needed to practice specific activities.

4. Space and time may also become a political resource, through differential knowledge (Helms 1983), or through acts of reference such as intentional exoticism, the rejection of difference, conscious anachronism, and the reinvention of tradition (Hobsbawn and Ranger 1993), or the rejection of it.

Because spatiality and temporality are built up from heterogeneous concepts and practices, archaeologically, we must investigate them through the convergence of multiple analyses. No single field of practice such as ritual, trade, travel, or work can bring to light an encompassing sense of order such as Foucault's (1977) concept of discipline. Investigation must extend across fields of practice and require a range of tactics. In the following analysis, these investigations include discussion of how people created fixed points through the placement of settlement and architecture, how enduring human marks provided histories and memories for the past, and how particular uses of landscapes provided sources of knowledge and meaning. A central concept is "frequentation," the sedimentation of daily experience in particular places, which draws upon both Ingold's concept of the *taskscape* and the idea of time–space embeddedness and rhythms pioneered by Hagerstrand (1977) and developed by Giddens (1984).

TOOLS OF THOUGHT: BODIES, HABITUS, IDENTITY, AND THE SENSES: The body is a key theme in recent theory, not only in Bourdieu's practice theory and Foucault's cultural analysis, but also in phenomenology (Merleau-Ponty 1962), feminism (Butler 1993), anthropology (Csordas 1999), and other strands of recent thought (Shilling 2003). Indeed, the huge literature on the body makes clear the centrality of embodied experience to social action and social reproduction. These have had important echoes in archaeological thought (Hamilakis, Pluciennik, and Tarlow 2002; Meskell and Joyce 2003). The common strand is the rejection of the Cartesian model of a self-sufficient intellect contained within the neutral, natural, and self-evident vessel of a material body. Rather, the body is the locus of experience and social reproduction: humans' ability to think and act emerges from the embodied organism. The body is the locus of habituated and routinised action and of much non-discursive action. For example, skill involves an inculcation of bodily experience (Dobres 2001; Ingold 2000). Moreover, it is through the body that one interacts with, understands oneself, and is understood by other people.

The link between bodies and thought is well-encompassed in Bourdieu's most enduring contribution, the concept of habitus. Habitus is the deeply instilled generative principles which provide the cultural logic according to which agents negotiate their ways through both old and new situations (Bourdieu 1977). Habitus provides the agent's unquestioned tools of thought, the values and oppositions which shape our thinking, the terms of identity and personhood which make us who we are, and the emotional currencies we live through.

Archaeologists have developed two lines of investigation for approaching habitus and the body – iconographic and structural analysis. The former focuses upon representations and upon "key symbols" (Ortner 1972), the handful of central symbols that recur in many contexts and that summarise fundamental components of meaning. Although key symbols can potentially be anything (one would hardly predict that a bizarre, infrequently used Roman torture device would become a major European religious symbol), they frequently invoke bodily substances and symbolisms, transactional valuables, or symbols linking human lives to larger cosmological narratives. For example, Treherne's (1995) discussion of the warrior's body in Bronze Age Europe isolates weapons, armor, and related paraphernalia as material components of male personhood. Similarly, Russell (1998) discusses cattle as a social valuable, and many analyses of the Western European Neolithic isolate monuments as key symbols of an experienced cosmological order. Sensory qualities such as colors may have strong symbolic connotations, for example, stone color in Aboriginal Australia (Jones 1989; Morphy 1992; Taçon 1991). The same is true for visually distinct styles, which may be used to represent meanings applicable across domains of experience (e.g., Modernist blockiness or Victorian Gothic in historical architecture). Iconographic analysis of contextual associations may help bring forth meanings such as the use of the color white to create a sense of purity.

The second tactic, structural analysis, involves putting symbols in relationship to each other to investigate patterns of difference. *Doxic* belief has an emergent logic which crosses fields of activity, which is brought to light by analysis of cross-domain patterning. Although there has been widespread criticism of structuralism, it is clear that structuralism is a bad master but a useful servant. As in Bourdieu's own work, much of the most interesting work in post-structuralist archaeology uses structural analysis as an encapsulated, tactical methodology; for example, burial analyses commonly oppose whole skeletons and integral individuals to fragmented skeletons and composite or collective social beings. As I have discussed, this may be a necessary methodological reflection of social reality, in which people need fixed reference points, even if only as fulcrums for acts of opposition or dissent.

Habitus bridges abstract value structures and personal identities. It provides an extension of the body outwards as a cosmological classifier and operator. It also provides a means for understanding one's own identity. Self-defining acts often involve the experience and expression of bodily idioms – *hexis* in Bourdieu's (1977) terms, or performativity in Joyce's (2000) somewhat different approach. Thus, personhood can be both a cultural norm and an always unfinished project (Fowler 2004; Sørensen 2000). One implication is that personal identities are neither relatively fixed essences such as rank or status, gender, and age, nor are they entirely negotiable, unconstrained, and emergent. Rather, they are integrated into biographical narratives. The human biography, as a narrative life story appropriate to a particular kind of body, provides a sequence of identities for acts of self-fashioning (Johnson 2000). Such identities can be seen in the traditional archaeology of status (Wason 1994), gender (Nelson 1997; Nelson 2002), and age (Sofaer 2000) through patterns of adornment and dress, burial treatment and accompaniments, and representations. Moreover, the culturally defined biography or life story includes prescribed concepts of the appropriate "good death" (Gnoli and Vernant 1982) which summarises or fulfills a life story. The life story is often evaluated and defined retrospectively through ritual acts of closure (Turner 1988); this forms a useful basis for approaching mortuary behaviour.

Growing out of phenomenological approaches to the past, the "archaeology of the senses" (Hamilakis 1998; Hamilakis 1999) presumes that there is a reciprocal relationship between sensory perception and experience and social context. People are taught to experience the world sensorally in culturally appropriate ways, and, conversely, their sensory experiences validate and, unquestionably, make the social order of which they form a part. This line of thought has been developed extensively for vision in landscape-oriented studies. There is also an increasingly well-developed archaeology of color (Jones and MacGregor 2002). For other senses, Hamilakis has emphasised how taste and smell are linked to social rhythms and to the construction of memories of an occasion or celebration. Archaeologically, architectural and landscape settings can be investigated to see how they were designed to structure visual (Tilley 1994) and auditory (Watson 2001) experiences, and the possibilities for an archaeology of taste and cuisine have only been sampled.

FIELDS OF ACTION AND PROJECTS OF THE SELF: Fields of action are central to the interpretation of the Italian Neolithic presented in this book and are central to much of the archaeological analysis, in general. Yet, archaeologists have tended to focus either upon high-level meanings, such as habitus, or upon individual practices; fields of action have rarely been problematised either theoretically or methodologically.

Agency is not a generalised or unspecified quality of action but rather is particular to a field of discourse within which it is constituted (Barrett 2001; Dobres and Robb 2005; Dobres and Robb 2000; Dornan 2002; Fowler 2004; Gardner 2004; Gillespie 2001; Joyce and Lopiparo 2005). In this sense, the "agency of why" is conditioned and encapsulated by the "agency of how": the enabling structures and limiting conditions, the ways in which things have to be done. Thus, agency must be localised not in a simple, easily expressed abstract goal but rather in the emergent practical logic of the projects through which this goal is understood, defined, and can be pursued. Fields of action are the key to the materiality of agency. Values are immaterial abstractions (Rappaport 1979); enacting a value in a particular field of action means translating it into material practices. However, in contrast to a top-down Platonism, translating a value into a material practice transforms it to create something new, rather than creating a thin derivative of dogma. For example, hunting or sport may be anthropologically interpretable as an ideological drama about class or gender, but this does not mean that we can access, experience, or dispute these values without the medium of the drama. Moreover, fields of action are social networks as well; each defines a community of practice within which material conversations can take place.

Activities within fields of action are human projects: chains of events involving response to chance and contingency, dramas with defined beginnings, narrative forms, and conclusions which shape the unfolding of action (Turner 1974, 1988). The dramatic quality of the material encounter of doing is well-expressed by Ingravallo:

> the anthropocentric illusion founders when material culture puts it face to face with the unforeseeableness of the material, obliging humans to negotiate its tricks and resistances. It is a bodily struggle which puts in check the traditional dualistic visions of the world which assigns matter inertness and predictability and humans' freedom and invention. In reality, in the moment in which brain, hands and feet measure themselves all together against a world believed to be

docilely manipulable, that world is negated with an arbitrary act of unforeseeableness, eventuality and subjectivity. (Ingravallo 1999, p. 16, translation J. Robb)

A genre of action is a potential reality coming in to being (Barrett 2001, p. 153). Knowledge and actions are things we exercise; reproducing knowledge is a social act (Barth 2002); and practical skill is laden with meanings of identity, efficacy, and the production of certainty.

Participating in a field of action requires belief, commitment, a continued involvement in long-term projects, social relations of co-behaviour, public identity claims and associated attitudes, memories and emotions, and even a willingness to change oneself (e.g., by acquiring knowledge or experience). The upshot of this argument is that exercising a field of action is also a project of self-formation. During their lives, people participate in many projects of different kinds, and with different kinds of agency; in a sense, personhood, "the condition of being a person as conceptualized by a given community" (Fowler 2004, p. 155) refers to the most encompassing and generalised life project, and one which may involve a variegated *cursus honorum*. Moreover, if action results from a palimpsest of agencies both within and among actors, some of which have important collective dimensions, the question of how multiple agencies are organised becomes a significant one. Simple models of hierarchy presume a singular kind of agency in which individuals are distinguished only by the degree to which they possess an undifferentiated power. Where this is, manifestly, not the case, we must consider a heterarchy (Ehrenreich, Crumley, and Levy 1995) of qualitatively distinct agencies, existing in balance, in tension, or in contradiction.

Traditionally, archaeologists have studied activities rather than projects. But there are a number of important questions which can be raised about fields of action. Much of these have to do with the cultural definition of the material world; the physical item itself is always only the skeleton of an "extended artefact," the social artefact constituted by these beliefs and practices (Robb 2004).

- What is being done (as a defined kind of cultural activity)? Although in some cases this may be self-evident, in others definitions may be subtle. For example, the interment of bodies in tombs may not always involve "burial" whose principal purpose is the permanent disposal of the dead; trade or food preparation may involve quite distinct social activities depending on context, scale and occasion; even making pottery may be distinguished into several quite distinct fields of activity (such as studio pottery, fine art, industrial production of kitchenware, and industrial production of nonculinary ceramics).

- What are the key symbols and central artefacts for this genre of action?
- Who are the appropriate people for doing it and in what circumstances? What knowledge is involved, and how is it acquired and maintained? What are the social implications of skill, and how does skill form part of a discourse of identity (Dobres 2001; Sinclair 1995)? How is this knowledge distributed geographically as part of the definition of space? How does this prescribe a long-term programme of identity (e.g., being a potter, rather than simply making a pot)?
- How it must be done technologically, bearing in mind that technology is not only a functional means to an end but a fundamental source of social representations and meanings (Dobres 2001; Lemonnier 1992; Pfaffenberger 1992)?
- What are the rules and practices for correct usage of these techniques and artefacts? "Correct usage" should be understood here not as rigid prescription but in the sense of a constitutive definition or truth conditions. For example, there is often a close correspondence between a kind of occasion, a food or beverage, and a form of vessel to use to consume it. This does not mean that one cannot drink wine from a coffee cup, soup bowl, or margarine tub, but the choice to do so would itself be part of the definition of what was being done (e.g., holding a formal dinner versus an informal occasion with friends, a holy communion, or a dinner alone at home).
- What are appropriate spatial and temporal contexts for doing it? How are these constructed to provide stage management for the performance of meaning? How does the sense of occasion form part of a spatiotemporal fabric of composed places, recurrent activities, periodicities, and dramas?

- What are the concomitant artefacts which form an assemblage related to it? What material resources are necessary, and what chains of entanglement and material provision do they entail or incur? What program of long-term planning, maintenance, commitments, and social relationships are involved?
- How do the definition, association, and social role of the field of action relate to its long-term history? For example, do the conditions in which the relevant knowledge is reproduced affect its historical trajectory (Barth 1987; Barth 2002)? Is the field of action redefined throughout its history?

Fields of action form useful units for long-term historical analysis, as they often form material trajectories traceable through long time-spans. Archaeologically, what we see as cultural change – the rise of a new burial rite, the spread of an assemblage, a dramatic shift in economic production – is often moments of genre formation, where an existing variant practice is proclaimed as a new orthodoxy, often with a new uniformity of practice and material culture, a rearrangement of social relations, and a new elaboration of ancient symbols.

Fields of action are constituted through individual actions, and unless we consider individual action, genres of behaviour merely add another layer of determinism. In acting within a field of action, people act creatively, varying what they do to accomplish a proximate intention. This is the level of context-specific maneuver, tactic, practice, and performance, discursively understood and taught. What makes a good pig sacrifice or a good fox hunt? How can a ritual utterance be striking without breaching the limits of sanctity? Like speech acts, material acts have a great range of play: often the intention is simply to execute the basic purpose with efficacy or with distinction, but one can also do it excessively, intentionally, carelessly or badly, ironically, innovatively, or differently. Such variation encompasses individual strategies of competition, emulation, innovation, redefinition, resistance, and subversion. Archaeologically, one standard analytical tactic has been to contrast norms and variations in material production in terms of enabling structures and individual expression (Hegmon and Kulow 1995). Another has been to dissect the temporally ordered structure of action, looking at the *chaîne opératoire* not only as a collective social representation but also as providing space for individual choice (Dobres 2001).

From the Point of View of Things

Material culture is fugitive; the harder we try to interpret it, the more we simply reduce it to a sign of something else. Most archaeological investigations of material culture, like the interpretive strategies above, assume the primacy of either humans or systems of meaning. A radically different strategy is to decenter humans, effectively viewing them as creations of things rather than the converse.

Although this has idea been poorly developed in archaeology practice, this sweeping reorientation is nevertheless suggested by several lines of thought. Foucault's idea of individual subjectivities as the creations of decentered systems of power certainly leads in this direction. Within material culture studies particularly, the focus upon artefact biographies (Appadurai 1988; Gosden and Marshall 1999), particularly of heirlooms which may span many human lifespans (Lillios 1999), raises the possibility of parallel, interacting, but distinct histories for people and things. Chapman (2000) similarly raises the idea of material flows which are distributed among and which bind together many contexts and actors in his concepts of enchainment and fragmentation. Malafouris (2005) has characterised material culture as an externalised cognitive system in which material things possess an enactive logic. This implies that one can view systems of material culture as possessing an emergent cognition to some degree autonomous of the people forming one component of them, much as a nervous system possesses a functionality that is distinct from that of its constituent neurons. The most explicit suggestion in this direction is Gell's (1998, p. 153) discussion of how things reference each other to form an "art production system" transcending their makers. Because every instance of an action – carrying out a kula exchange, making a painting, building a Maori meeting house – is generated via mental consideration of other actions which have gone before, other actions which exist, and a host of possible, impossible and contingent hypothetical instances, and because these representations and their interrelations exist in an intersubjective public consciousness lasting over a long span, it follows that the totality of a given kind of actions – the whole kula system, an artist's oeuvre, all Maori meeting houses – can be considered a cognitive process happening over decades and independently of the individuals within it. In effect, the kula thinks itself through the actions of people carrying it out.

Things thinking people: to many archaeologists this concept will raise the prospect of a brave new world of material determinism, and I have no desire to erase humans from our vision. Yet, the convergence of such disparate thinkers demonstrates that it is a vision to be taken seriously. Material agency derives neither from the mastery of an inert material world by the human intellect, nor from the determination of human consciousness by the material conditions of existence. Rather, it is inherent in the relationship between humans and material things, and in relationships between humans as mediated by material things. We must therefore look, at the very least, at human and material histories which unfold in parallel and which exert profound influences on each other. Rhetorically, in jarring loose our vision from purely human concerns, it can be useful to aim at a distanced, creative bewilderment, to see human history strangely as a creation of things. In what ways is the Internet thinking, when a whole discipline writes on keyboards or conducts an integrated professional life via email? In what sense are the university's thousand classrooms, with their embodied discipline of space, ironbound timetabling, and inherent discourse of authority via certification by examinations, teaching students more than the lecturers posed rigidly at their podiums? In what sense do Neolithic pots create their potters, or do games of exchange play their players?

Getting at such insights archaeologically requires a different range of tactics. One approach may be to trace variation and creativity within a kind of material production over long spans of time – to see how far a material tradition can be read as an "art production system." A second is to trace the networks of cognition involved in carrying on tasks of social reproduction, for example, the ways in which material contexts and projects orient people, structure their sensory experiences, and prompt them to solve problems of daily existence with solutions at hand. Third, we can look for ways in which artefacts link people – through transactions and obligations, through operational sequences fragmented among many participants which create people with identical or complementary bodies of knowledge. Finally, a fourth approach may be to start with fields of action and work outwards until they converge in an ensemble of interlocking projects, bound together by mutual programs of action, complementary obligations, or places within a taskscape.

Making History: Creativity, Commitment, and Gulliver's Dilemma

Where does this discussion leave the individual and his or her ability to act creatively, to innovate, or to resist? And how do we understand history as a human production? These issues will be explored in Chapters 7 and 8, but it is worth touching upon them here briefly.

Individual action and history are inextricably linked. Launching a study of social reproduction in terms of time means that we see a historical sequence as a succession of tomorrows, each of which possesses a prospective indeterminacy to be negotiated. If we are to avoid viewing history teleologically as retrospectively inevitable, we must theorise spaces for alternative actions, for ambiguities, for ways the world could have been, or could have been understood, otherwise. In some cases, new worlds emerge from the collision of circumstances and people trying to perpetuate normality. In other cases, equally important for archaeology, it is stability we need to understand. By implicitly equating agency with social change, archaeologists have effectively deprived people in centuries or millennia of apparent cultural stability – the Formative, the Archaic, the Neolithic, the Paleolithic – of social agency.

A practice-theory answer to these questions is readily stated, if difficult to implement systematically. History emerges from situated human action. As Marx and Engels stated (Marx and Engels 1978), humans make their own history, but in conditions imposed upon them by the past. These conditions, of course, encompass not only the physical and social settings of action, but its cultural givens as well. In turn, action results in reproducing these structures, positions, and resources – some changed, some maintained, some reproduced without question.

The result is history as an unfolding series of conjunctures of the structure, in Sahlins's terms (Sahlins 1981, 1985). Historical process is the long-term working out of practice (Pauketat 2001).

One of the most important implications of this, and one particularly relevant to prehistory, is the inextricability of continuity and change. Any particular action draws upon a great multiplicity of structures, positions, and resources. Humans require fixed points of leverage to act; in a world where everything is fluidly negotiable or invented for present need, humans would resemble astronauts floating ineffectually in space. Moreover, these tools of thought and deed impose a commitment to the project and its supporting propositions: immersed in society for any length of time, one cannot operate under the assumption that symbols and attitudes are real and meaningful, rather they become real and meaningful to the actor through participation, through the process of acting socially.

Hence, paradoxically, one can act creatively, even revolutionarily, only through the medium of the status quo. To act strikingly in one way, one must implicitly accept the working parameters of the situation – other usages, techniques, bodies of knowledge, and social relations. Voters can vote bad politicians out of office but only at the cost of validating the electoral system which created them. Workers can display status through ostentatious consumption but only by participating in an encapsulating economic system which may make other statuses entirely unattainable. Striking out for the horizon with bold originality requires conforming rigidly to other parameters of a field of action – its semantics, material provision, and social relationships. This is neither to argue that change never occurs, nor to argue pessimistically that human attempts to change things are futile. Akhenaton's attempt to reform Egyptian religion was abandoned after his death, but Martin Luther's Reformation changed the shape of Christianity. Campaigns for social justice in the twentieth century have necessarily worked within existing political, economic, and cultural structures but have had crucial effects on race and gender equality. But social change is situated within an existing present. We wind up like Gulliver, tied down by the Lilliputians by a hundred thin threads.[1] The dilemma is that struggling to be free in one direction binds the threads more tightly in other directions; only a major wrench or rupture – colonial encounters, for instance – will change many at once. And only analysis on all levels at once will reveal this network of threads.

The 1st of September, 5000 BC: A Note on Methodology

In "The Man Who Collected the First of September, 1973," Tor Age Bringsvaerd describes a man who, in fear of losing his grip on reality, decides to collect all the information available on his everyday world. Quickly overwhelmed by the size of the task, he limits himself to learning all possible facts about one day. Even this quickly takes over his life: there is so much to know. His apartment fills up with boxes and files, its walls shaggy with papers. He becomes increasingly myopic, fixated, and unable to communicate. Finally, verging on solipsism, madness, and disease, he dies.

This is the strategy adopted here, though hopefully with less drastic consequences.

My method, in this project, is simply to tease apart a normality of the past, strand by strand. It is extraordinary how rich the detail is and how much there is to know about the 1st of September, 5000 BC. Virtually all archaeological records are massively under-interpreted. Perhaps (though I doubt it) we have now said all one can possibly say about Lascaux Cave, or Ötzi, or Cahokia. But generally, we have subjected our archaeological material to only a very limited range of questions and to questions which highlight our fixations rather than where the material leads us.

As discussed above, the foremost locus of social reproduction is in "small things forgotten," in Deetz's (1977) memorable and accurate phrase: in the thousand minutiae of daily life rather than monumental edifices and heroic endeavour. In Chapters 2–5, I try to draw out the dimensions of daily life in the Italian Neolithic – bodies, landscapes, food, objects – thrusting each one firmly back into the realm of human action. Each is a field of action in which we can see ancient people carrying out projects which were important to them. Nothing is more tedious than the butterfly-collecting of pottery decorations; nothing is more exciting than watching humans direct their fingers at work on the clay of their lives.

The goal of this strategy is, in some ways, a "thick description" of Neolithic life, as Geertz (1973) terms the act of ethnography. This is not simply the accumulation of detail; the vocabulary and ideas outlined above provide the unifying terms of discourse, and, in Chapter 6, I try to bring these separate domains of life together by discussing the organizing textures of social reproduction in Neolithic Italy.

The reader is forewarned with three caveats. First, even this strategy of saturation does not say everything there is to say; unlike Bringsvaerd's protagonist, I want to survive the project! I have had to be selective rather than encyclopedic, and to marshal interpretations according to my particular interests. Thus, I make no pretense at a definitive interpretation and last word upon the Italian Neolithic.

Second, in the interests of interpretation, in Chapters 2–6, I treat my area – the Italian peninsula, Sicily, and Malta, with occasional forays into adjacent areas such as Northern Italy, Dalmatia, or Sardinia – as possessing a homogeneous culture. Similarly, I assume basic continuity throughout the Neolithic, from about 6000 BC through about 4000 BC, with occasional forays into the Late Neolithic and even the Copper Age. On a practical level, this facilitates analysis; the data are often sparse, and it helps to be able to put a site or artefact from Toscana at 5500 BC into relation to one from Puglia at 4500 BC. However, such a ploy would be worse than useless if there were not in fact some important cultural elements shared throughout this broad area over such a long time spans. Clearly, assuming a homogeneous culture area is an analytical fiction – but so are all such decisions of analytical scale (Knauft 1993; see also Chapter 7 in this book). Rather than arguing whether all culture must be interpreted locally or not, it makes sense to work back and forth between scales. Only by trying to formulate the general principles of Neolithic social relations can one see how specific regions varied. Here Chapters 2–6 present Neolithic Italy as a generalised and synchronic world, with occasional mentions of how places and times varied. In Chapters 7 and 8, I turn to regional difference and long-term change.

Finally, an analysis such as this runs the inevitable perils of cultural analysis. Tacit practices rely upon silent efficacy; they usually sound trivial, shallow, and arbitrary when verbalised. Here, the strategy is to not only pick apart the texture of Neolithic life, but also, hopefully, to stitch it back together, to show how many interlocking practices and institutions created not a seamless whole free from internal tensions, but rather a strong, figured and self-perpetuating texture of agreements and tensions, a world in which Neolithic creativity and inevitability were the prospective and retrospective of the same action of weaving time into history.

TIME TRAVEL

Neolithic Beginnings

Between 6500 and 6200 BC, people in Italy undertook the Neolithic project. Exactly how this happened is debated. A social history of the Neolithic has to start by affronting a monumental discourse, Neolithic origins, which has overshadowed almost all other aspects of Neolithic research. For Europe, the four major models have been the wave of advance model of mass migration driven by population increase (Ammerman and Cavalli-Sforza 1984; Runnels 2003); the enclave model of rapid, leapfrogging migrations driven by social or cultural forces (Bogucki 2000; Zilhão 2003); the forager adoption model stressing cultural and social choices (Thorpe 1996; Whittle 1996); and the political-strategy model in which individual foragers adopted domesticates as supplementary resources to deploy for political ends (Bender 1978; Hayden 1990). Within Europe, in general, traditionally the Neolithic has been seen as reaching the Balkans and inland Central Europe through migration, and the Atlantic lands, Scandinavia, and the Alps through forager acculturation. But recent work has tended to complicate this picture. Such migrations as may have occurred seem to have been enclave movements, not waves of advance (Bogucki 2000), with little evidence of population pressure. Even at the smallest regional scale, Neolithicisation was a mosaic happening through many different processes (Whittle and Cummings 2007). Most strikingly, it is seriously misleading to dichotomise the process into "migration versus acculturation": the social relations involved were likely to have been far more complex (Robb and Miracle 2007).

The process in Italy is surprisingly ambiguous. Chronologically, based upon a Bayesian calibration of all available radiocarbon dates for the first 500 years of the Neolithic, Alexander (2005) concluded that Puglia was Neolithicised several centuries before the rest of Italy, before 6000 BC, a conclusion supported by conventional interpretation of dates as well (Skeates 2003). The Neolithic appears to have spread rapidly but patchily after 6000 BC to enclaves in the upper Adriatic, Sicily, Lazio, Liguria, and Sardegna. It probably spread gradually outward from these enclaves, for example, spreading regularly down the Ionian coast from Puglia to Southern Calabria between 6000 and 5700 BC. Another enclave migration bore the Cardial Ware up the Ligurian Coast (Barfield et al. 2003).

However, the social mechanism is far less clear. Conventional wisdom favors an initial immigration from northwestern Greece across the Adriatic to Puglia, followed by a mixture of coastal enclave migration and forager adoption (Bagolini and Cremonesi 1987). It has generally been assumed that the precocious Neolithic in Puglia, which appears full-fledged with no local precursors, represents migration across the Adriatic from northwest Greece and Albania, and this indeed seems possible. Within Italy, things are less clear. Biagi (2003) argues that there is very little evidence at all for late Mesolithic occupation in Italy, and, hence, that the Neolithic spread through migration into a virtually empty environment. But arguments have also been made for solely acculturation models (Donahue 1991; Whittle 1996). There are other reasons why the terminal Mesolithic record may be sparse, and in areas such as the high Apennines of Central Italy, highland Basilicata, western Sicily (Tusa 1997), and the Alps (Barfield et al. 2003) continuity of occupation may be seen, sometimes accompanied by a mixed foraging-farming economy (Tagliacozzo 1992; Tagliacozzo 1993; Tagliacozzo 1997).

Be that as it may, by about 5700 BC, there were thriving Neolithic communities throughout Southern Italy and in parts of Central Italy By 5500 BC, Sicily and Liguria were considered to be Neolithicised, and by about 5000 BC the Neolithic had reached the fastnesses of the Alps, the swamps of the Po Valley, and islands further offshore, such as Sardinia and Malta. For the next two millennia, Italy was a Neolithic world.

The first Neolithic settlement in Italy is essentially a lowland phenomenon, and in any region it is unclear how the earliest Neolithic settlements related to the invisible forager occupants of surrounding areas. Neolithic migrants may have moved into empty areas; there is virtually no Mesolithic known on the Tavoliere, where the earliest Neolithic sites occur densely. Or Neolithic products and techniques may have proved attractive enough to draw thinly spread foragers together to coalesce in new settlements whose uniformity reflects common new cultural models. Or "migrants" and "natives" may have in fact been closely related and interacting, with the former simply being neighbors who chose the new economic road a little earlier. The coarse data available normally do not let us distinguish between such alternatives (which may be equifinal in any case (Robb and Miracle 2007)). It seems most likely that all of these processes or alternatives occurred in different areas.

But what *is* clear is that in most areas, the Neolithic resulted in a rapid rise in population, a much more stationary population whose movement was anchored by permanent houses and villages, and the abrupt establishment of a way of life with few obvious Mesolithic continuities (the most frequently cited being a persistence of some lithic technologies). Rather than representing a single huge and uniform migration, the first century or two of Neolithic life probably show how an economic choice that was taken for any of a range of reasons rapidly led to a stable and generally homogeneous way of life throughout most of Italy. Effectively, whatever the reason for the introduction of domesticates, the unintended consequences of this choice would progressively exclude alternatives. The key was the choice to rely economically upon domesticates rather than a mixed economy as in areas such as Scandinavia, where there was a protracted "substitution" phase (Zvelebil and Rowly-Conwy 1986). For example, denser food resources lead to rising populations, which in turn outstrip local game and gathered resources; commitment to crops limits mobility, making more distant resources difficult to exploit and cause more distant social networks to atrophy; in a thinly settled landscape the attraction of social aggregation outweighs loss of mobility. Within a few generations (in archaeological time, instantaneously), formerly optional resources and systems of exploitation become obligatory. In terms of theories of historical practice, this supports the model of the funnel-shaped Neolithic, with many roads in and few pathways out. Going Neolithic would thus be a relatively rapid transition between two equilibrium states.

The World at 5000 BC

Seven thousand years ago, Earth was still mostly a green planet of foragers, from the Archaic New World to the Jomon on the opposite shores of the Pacific. Only in a half-a-dozen odd locations between Melanesia and the Mediterranean had people begun to plant, harvest, and store. In Europe, at least half-a-dozen distinct lifeways could be seen. A border to the farming world would have enclosed the Balkans and a swathe of Eastern Europe above the Black Sea, the Hungarian Basin and a great slice of the Northern European Plain from southern Poland to Paris, Italy to the Alps, and much of Iberia and Southern France. All along the Atlantic and Baltic shores there was up to a millennium of forager history yet to run. But it would be a mistake either to stress this arbitrary economic classification too much or to assume that things were homogeneous on either side of it. The foraging world at 5000 BC ranged from sparse and highly mobile groups who created a fugitive archaeological record in much of Central and Northern Europe to pockets of people who lived much of the year in large groups in one place along a favourable river or coastline. Among farmers, the largest communities in Europe were clumped in villages atop Balkan tells like snails living on their shells. Bandkeramik longhouse dwellers kept contact with other loess islands in the forests of Poland, Germany, and France, while trading with foragers, perhaps kin, dwelling in hills, marshes, and coastlands. The thinly scattered farmers in the mountains of Southern France or Central Spain had certainly more contact and probably more common culture with the dense forager groups on the nearby Atlantic coast than with the large villages in the faraway plains of Greece or Anatolia from which their domesticated plants and animals ultimately derived.

There were genuine social and economic differences during this span, and between different regions (even sorting out the many distinct styles of pottery used is a considerable project). Nevertheless, Early and Middle Neolithic societies shared much in common. They stand apart from a new kind of Neolithic society which developed in the later the fifth millennia, variably termed the Late or Final Neolithic and associated with Diana, later Ripoli and Lagozza–Chassey ceramics. It is this Early–Middle Neolithic which is the principal focus in Chapters 2–6.

At first glance, the Italian Neolithic corresponds to the stereotypical image of this period distressingly well. All of the major elements of the "Neolithic package" are present from the very beginning: agriculture and herding, villages and houses, pottery, grinding stone technology, polished stone axes, and even ritual paraphernalia such as figurines. There are major differences with the Neolithic of Atlantic Europe and Scandinavia. The economy was based overwhelmingly upon domesticated plants and animals, there is plenty of evidence for sedentary settlement, and the mundane archaeological record affords no megaliths and few florid ritual sites.[2] To the extent that archaeological theory is consciously or unconsciously shaped by a particular archaeological record, one aim of this volume is to see how successfully some concepts drawn partially from theory informed by the British Neolithic theory can be applied to such a different record and what modifications are required to do so.

Yet, within Italy, life at 5000 BC was diverse too. With its central position, long north–south extension and rich geographical variability, Italy was virtually a microcosm of Europe (Figure 1). The flat lowlands of Puglia, Italy's answer to Thessaly, were filled with ditched villages of a hundred or more people with a millennium of farming at their backs. Across the rest of the peninsula and Sicily, farmers were ubiquitous but thinly spread, often confined to lower altitudes among rugged, eagle-haunted fastnesses. Lake-dwellers paddled canoes between houses built on piles on the lakes of Central Italy, and recently-acculturated foragers in the high Apennines, the Alpine valleys and around the marshy Po Valley practiced a bastard, half-Mesolithic/half-Neolithic way of life. As an ethnographic landscape, a journey from the Alps to Malta would have crossed through many different kinds of societies (Figures 2 and 3).

Neolithic Italy: The Rough Guide

This book deals with the Central Mediterranean, principally Central and Southern Italy, Sicily and Malta, between about 6000 BC and

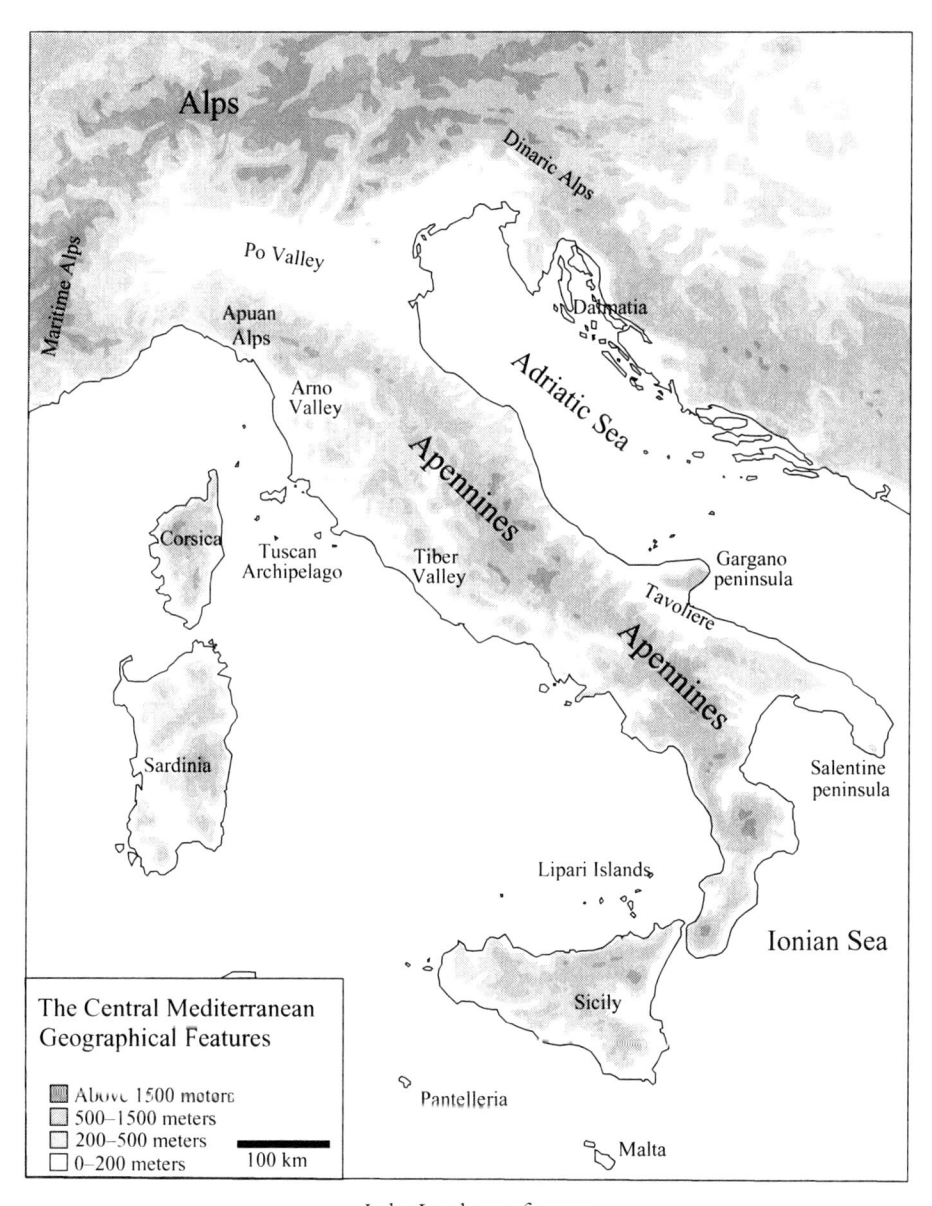

1. Italy: Landscape features.

2. Administrative Regions of Italy.

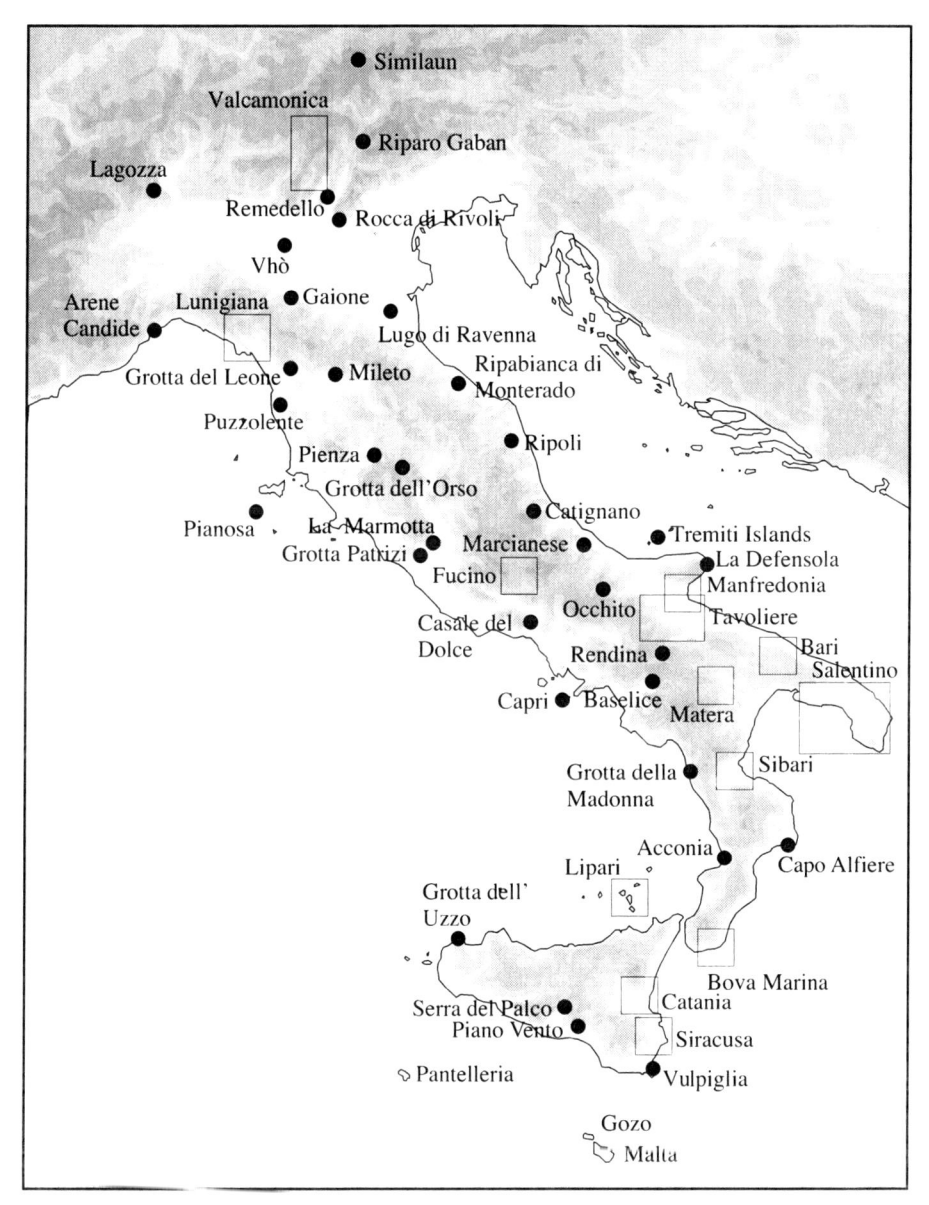

3. Selected Neolithic sites discussed in the text. **Groups of sites** *Fucino:* Grotta Continenza, Ortucchio, Santo Stefano. *Tavoliere:* Passo di Corvo, Ripa Tetta, Foggia, Lagnano da Piede, Fonteviva. *Manfredonia:* Grotta Scaloria, Coppa Nevigata, Masseria Aquilone, Masseria La Quercia, Masseria Candelaro. *Bari:* Balsignano, Ipogeo Manfredi, Cala Scizzo, Grotta Pacelli, Cala Colombo. *Salentino:* Serra Cicora, Porto Badisco, Torre Sabea. *Matera:* Serra d'Alto, Trasano, Tirlecchia, Murgia Timone, Murgecchia. *Sibari:* Favella, Grotta Sant'Angelo, Grotta S. Michele, *Bova Marina:* Umbro, Penitenzeria. *Lipari:* Contrada Diana, Acropolis, Castellaro Vecchio. *Catania:* San Marco, Trefontane, Paternò, Perriere Sottano. *Siracusa:* Stentinello, Megara Hyblaea, Matrensa.

3000 BC. Many readers will have visited or perhaps lived in this area; to most others it will be familiar from books and films. None will have lived in this time.

The first step in any journey is leaving home: figuratively, jarring our mental representation of Italy loose from anything familiar. Some of what our mental anchors drag up is useful; others less so. As today, the area enjoyed a Mediterranean climate with mild, rainy winters and hot, dry summers. The backbone of the landscape remained long, rugged mountain systems, principally the Apennines, which broke up the landscape, made communication difficult, and created great ecological variability: in many places one can move from a subtropical sea level to a sub-Alpine mountaintop in less than 20 km. But to modern eyes, the landscape would also look alien. Unlike modern Italy, the land would have been clothed in forests, relatively open Mediterranean woodlands, predominantly hardwoods. Some familiar landscapes would be completely absent. Level expanses of wheat fields such as the Tavoliere in Puglia were visually and ecologically much more varied, crossed by streams long since filled in (Delano Smith 1983). Productive, featureless farmlands and city sites from the Maremma and Po Valley at sea level to the Fucino basin in the high Abruzzo were undrained, rich wetlands.

The Italy of seven thousand years ago would have been a more varied and richer landscape. Visually, the modern checkerboard of khaki and olive fields and hedges would be gone; there would have been more small areas, more nuances of shade and color. How one sees, of course, is intimately related to how one travels. We inescapably think of Italy either as a synoptic map representation, with all the innate assumptions of abstract Cartesian space, or as a sweeping, open vista, a living landscape painting, taken in from the detached, privileged observation point of an airplane, train, highway, or window – two modes of seeing which have remarkably coalesced in the last decade with the advent of satellite images, a genie imagery which seems magically to confirm what we always knew. In a wooded world negotiated by paths, we move through smaller, more intimate places, and senses of location and orientation may have been completely different. Scale too needs recalibration. Italy is larger than Britain, roughly the size of New England or of Pennsylvania, though long and narrow, over 1,000 km from north to south. Today one can cross it in an hour in an airplane or a day or two in a train or car, whisked through intervening space without involvement. We can make it a whole by seeing it as a whole. On foot, without roads, and through a landscape of constant social negotiation, a day's travel might finish one or two villages over, and travelling to the other end of the country might be a season's project, and a hazardous one.

Neolithic habitations were small places one came upon walking through hills. For example, Penitenzeria, excavated by the Bova Marina Archaeological Project between 2000 and 2003, turned out to be a settlement too small really to be called a village. It is a little terrace, a scrap of level land 50 m across between steep slopes above and below, where the vista is framed by the high rugged mountains of Calabria, the sparkling Ionian Sea and the looming bulk of Mount Etna in the distance. People lived here for between 100 and 400 years, between 5500 and 5000 BC (Robb 2004).

Penitenzeria can stand as a benchmark of the Italian Neolithic to mark some important points for the twentieth century tourist. People lived in small clusters of one-room wattle-and-daub houses. They gardened and ate cereals and legumes. They herded the standard Old World domesticates – sheep, goats, cattle, and pigs. They traded or collected raw materials, some from quite distant places, and made and used pottery, polished stone axes, and flaked stone tools. We find the odd ornament – a shell bead, a pierced fox tooth. Compared with many other European Neolithics, it is long on quotidian material culture and short on "ritual" or "politics." There are no megaliths, few burials, and only a few odd items such as inexplicable figurines. The archaeological record is mundane rather than florid, easily made invisible in archaeological categories such as "lithics" and "ceramics," like a strange x-ray which reveals virtually every bit of broken pottery and hides so much else that was important to people. One has to look carefully to see the human practices, colors, and faces behind it.

Such sites were related in a social geography difficult to imagine, a sparseness of population which would mean that most people lived their lives in residential groups of less than a hundred people. In most areas, people lived in hamlets of small wattle-and-daub huts; in a few areas such as Puglia, Basilicata and eastern Sicily, they dug circular ditches to enclose villages. Even in these places, the largest population estimate for any village puts it at only 200–300 people (Tinè 1983). It would not be uncommon to walk all day without seeing anybody; some areas were probably without permanent inhabitants. It is impossible to estimate the population of a place like Penitenzeria with any precision but there is room on the little hillside terrace that it occupies for no more two or three houses at a time; twenty-five people would be a generous estimate. If the site was occupied for ten generations or less, as the radiocarbon dates suggest, the total population who ever lived there is probably less than the combined field crews of our last decade's fieldwork in Calabria.

As de Certeau (2002) says, any journey is a story, and this is equally true for travels in time. It is impossible to tell the story of Penitenzeria without marking obligatory frames of reference centered upon our own present – the date and the location on a map. A visit to Neolithic Penitenzeria would be disorienting, without our names, landmarks, distances, centralities, and remotenesses. It would not be seven thousand years ago, but a fresh present in a different history. Even the act of visiting would be different: the modern traveler remains disengaged, physically present but apart, his or her needs catered for impersonally and without reciprocal obligation, in a way difficult for even eighteenth century visitors and unthinkable in most traditional societies.

Other places and times, told as a journey, are never free from the image of the traveler with his or her needs and expectations. In this volume, I hope to work back and forth between the archaeological world of Neolithic Italy and the human world of a place defined by human interactions in the present rather than by classifications of the past. Hence, an alternative way of telling this story, less familiar in archaeology, would be to scrap this volume, take a fresh sheet of paper, and write:

One morning a family woke up and went out to the fields to pull weeds and gossip. While they were there, a stranger arrived.

TWO:

NEOLITHIC PEOPLE

A man lives not only his personal life, as an individual, but also, consciously or unconsciously, the life of his epoch and his contemporaries.
Thomas Mann, *The Magic Mountain*. (Mann 1952, p. 32)

Ideal Lives

People are not simply who they claim to be. Indeed, we cannot understand social action simply by taking claims to identity and status at face value; what makes news on Page 1 may be merely a shadow of, or distraction from, subtler, but more important, patterns. But claims and narratives of identity are not irrelevant. As representations of goals and ideals, ideal lives provide targets for self-formation and for the evaluation of others throughout a human lifespan. Ideal lives permit and bracket an agent's participation in life-projects. Paradoxically, they can exercise tremendous power even when they merely provide an ideal narrative, by exerting a creative tension which directs people's energies: in a society of divorced, apartment-dwelling urban single parents believing that "normal" families live in family homes in small towns; in a society in which laws are theoretically ratified by all voters though written and shepherded through legislatures by a few; or in an egalitarian tribal society in which all, theoretically, become elders although in fact mortality, social exclusion, or the vagaries of the *curriculum vitae* prevent all but a few from doing so (Kelly 1993).

Although our goal is to understand people as they are defined through their works, it is useful to start by letting people present themselves, either as individuals or as categories. Aside from the comprehensibility of beginning with familiar archaeological categories such as gender, age, and status, such identities provide to be frameworks around which other cultural patterns were organised and understood.

For the Italian Neolithic, starting with this problem is somewhat like tackling a mountain ascent on the sheerest rock face. Conventional evidence for the "archaeology of identity" is meager. There are few iconographic representations of people in "art" or other media, there are no large cemeteries, and most burials lack status-related grave goods or treatment. However, as we will see, when conventional analyses yield little insight, it is likely that we are asking the wrong questions.

Refractions of the Neolithic Body

Bodies Themselves: Skeletal Evidence of Social Biology

Skeletal evidence is not entirely mute for Neolithic Italy, although it is best used in conjunction with archaeological evidence. The fifty to one hundred skeletons which have been studied by anthropologists provide the most direct witness of Neolithic Italians. The people were small to medium in stature, although well within the modern range of variation; average adult stature was about 156 cm for females and about 166 cm for males. This is a slight reduction from Palaeolithic stature, in keeping with general European trends, and is smaller than any subsequent period (Formicola 1983; Frayer 1981; Robb 1994). This reduction in stature is not necessarily due to malnutrition or illness, but it may indicate a useful adaptation to an activity regime with less mobility than their forager ancestors engaged in and perhaps with periodic food scarcity: a Ford Fiesta model human rather than a Land Rover.

Nevertheless, Neolithic humans endured both hardship and wear and tear. Cribra orbitalia, which indicates an iron-deficient anemia due to diet, illness, or parasites in childhood or early adulthood, is relatively common, affecting 31 percent of juveniles. So are enamel hypoplastic lesions, defects of dental enamel which betray systemic disturbances of some kind in childhood (Robb 1994). From the ages at which hypoplasias occurred, children were stressed throughout their childhoods. Some individuals display several episodes of growth disturbance, and one, Catignano I (Robb and Mallegni 1994), experienced seven distinct episodes between the ages of two and nine years, raising the possibility of annual seasonal stresses. Among the complaints of adult life, the commonest skeletally is dental disease and tooth loss; this is probably a consequence of a cariogenic grain-based diet. Although the process was highly variable, at the least, some individuals started to lose molars in their twenties and older individuals universally lack several teeth. There is little other pathology known in Neolithic skeletons, although this undoubtedly reflects fragmented skeletons and relatively early age at death, rather than a truly healthy population (Wood et al. 1992): the principal indicator of poor health is simply dying young. Estimating demography in skeletal populations is dicey at the best of times and very few Italian Neolithic samples have been reliably aged. However, as a general yardstick, when scattered remains as well as complete burials are counted, juvenile skeletons are almost as common as adults; and death among adults less than 30 years old was also common (Robb 1994).

The few stable isotope samples analyzed show a diet heavily weighted towards plants, presumably domestic crops, and with little use of marine resources (see Chapter 4 in this book). Few skeletal signs of activity are known, but some individuals display squatting or kneeling facets in their ankles and feet. In one sample from Liguria, males had bilateral stress markers in the upper chest suggesting heavy axe use, perhaps for clearing land and working wood (Canci and Marini 2003). Leg bone cross sections reflect the bones' ability to resist bending stresses during locomotion, and sexual dimorphism in leg bone cross section tends to reflect patterns of activity related to an overall way of life. Italian Neolithic femurs and tibiae display relatively high sexual dimorphism, with a dimorphism of 5.7 percent in femur midshaft section and of 4.1 percent for the tibia. This lies at the upper end of ranges reported for agricultural villagers (Brock and Ruff 1988; Robb 1995). Interestingly, sexual dimorphism in mobility is usually ascribed to subsistence activities such as hunting or transhumant herding. Because Italian Neolithic people neither relied extensively upon wild resources nor, apparently, engaged in long-range pastoralism, the skeletal data may imply that males moved around much more than females for a range of other social reasons.

Several types of intentional bodily modification are known. The earliest known tattoos, found in the "Ice Man" mummy from the South Tyrol, come from the very northern limit of Italian territory (Spindler 1994). This find dates to the Neolithic-Copper Age transition, but it at least raises the possibility of tattooing here. Other bodily decoration has been inferred from clay stamps called pintaderas, possibly used to decorate bodies, although these could have been used to create designs on other objects too. Skeletally, about one third of adult female skeletons show front teeth knocked out intentionally during some time before death, and this figure would rise if we included teeth removed close enough to death that the root sockets had not resorbed (Figure 4) (Robb 1997). From one or two cases where a broken root shows signs of wear, the technique appears to have been to break the tooth at the neck, probably by a direct blow. No cases are known among males, and this is clearly gender-related behavior. As there is no particular pattern of facial trauma in females, tooth removal did not result from violence. Whether for cosmetic, ritual, or social reasons, it would have furnished a permanent and visible mark of identity, and carrying out the procedure would have been a public bodily act relating the patient and the operator.

Like tooth removal, trepanation would have been a public, multiperson social intervention. Of the four Neolithic trepanations known (Canci 1998, Germanà and Fornaciari 1992), one case, Catignano I, occurs in a female; her skull shows two episodes of trepanation following a major but healed cranial trauma (Figure 4). The second, a male from Trasano, was found with the roundel of bone, suggesting that he died during or shortly after the operation and that the purpose was not to obtain a roundel of skull for some other purpose. The third case, Grotta Patrizi (Grifoni Cremonesi and Radmilli 2001; Mangili 1954; Patrizi, Radmilli, and Mangili 1954), is a trepanation in a young adult male who suffered from a facial dysplasia which would have been evident in life. He was buried in a ritual cave with the most extensive grave assemblage known from the Italian Neolithic, a collection of idiosyncratic items, and, taken together, his physical appearance, his burial location and

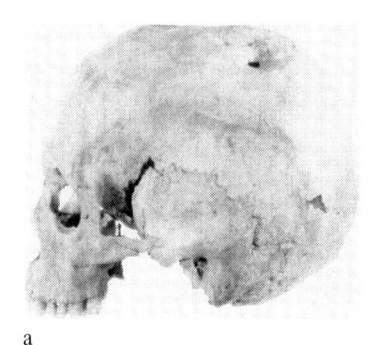

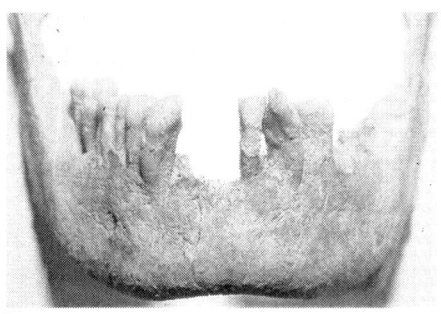

4. Neolithic body modifications. (a) Catignano: mature female with two trepanations following a serious cranial fracture (Robb and Mallegni 1994); (b) Fonteviva: intentional removal of front teeth in life in females (Robb 1997).

treatment, and his trepanation suggest that he held a special ritual status. The trepanation is particularly interesting in that it probably took place in two episodes: the first, which involved scraping the skull, possibly for scarification, was healed, while the second was unhealed and probably resulted in the death of the man, or at least accompanied it (Germanà and Fornaciari 1992). A fourth case, from Arma dell'Aquila in Liguria, is an incomplete, healed trepanation in a woman who survived to old age (Canci 1998). Overall, trepanation is found in somewhere between 2 and 4 percent of Neolithic Italian skulls; this approximate figure suggests that, where it was practiced, perhaps one or two people in any local village network may have been trepanned. The sample is small, but it is suggestive that trepanations occur either in older individuals or in people with unusual ritual status.

Few cases of violence are known, but when this figure is calibrated according to the low number of skeletons examined anthropologically, the Neolithic actually displays quite a high rate of healed cranial traumatic injury (Robb 1997) – higher than in later periods such as the Copper and Bronze Ages, often thought to have been more warlike. There has been little examination of peri-mortem trauma, though peri-mortem skull injuries are alleged in two children buried in an unusual grave at Madonna delle Grazie (Pesce Delfino et al. 1979), and violence may also underlie the yet-unanalyzed mass burial of a dozen people at the Diga di Occhito (Tunzi Sisto 1999). Interestingly, injuries are found in both males and females. For example, healed cranial traumas are known from a young adult male at Ripa Tetta who had received a blow just above the right eye (Robb, Mallegni, and Ronco 1991); a young adult female from Masseria Valente who had also broken her clavicle (Salvadei and Macchiarelli 1983); a young male from Arma dell'Aquila (Canci 1998); the older female from Catignano who had experienced a serious skull fracture; and a young adult woman at Villa Badessa whose skull displayed a healed depressed fracture, probably from a stick or a club (Germanà and Fornaciari 1992). Such injuries suggest direct violence with fists, clubs, or axes; given the state of the skeletal material, we would be able to see arrow injuries only in the most fortunate circumstances (such as in the arrowhead embedded in the Ice Man's torso). Thus, traumatic injury caused by violence was common, it was caused by close-range attack in at least some cases, and it affected both men and women.

Presencing the Living Group: Model Demography

Estimating population size from archaeological sites is an exercise in pure guesswork, but sometimes such exercises can be enlightening. Without committing ourselves dogmatically to rigid models, we can at least sketch in some likely parameters of the situation. The typical Italian Neolithic hut had an area of between 15 and 40 m^2 (see Chapter 3 in this book). By Naroll's (1962) rule, this would correspond to two to four people. Even without with this rigid yardstick, it is hard to imagine such huts housing more than a few individuals or a nuclear family. Although, for various archaeological reasons, we can never know exactly how many houses existed contemporaneously on a site; some sites are very small indeed and sites with more than twenty or so houses in evidence are very rare. It seems probable that most Neolithic Italians lived in residential groups of fewer than 100 people, with many settlements that were substantially smaller.

Table 1 presents the general demography of such a community, reconstructed using Weiss's (1973) model life tables. The life table used here is a general model for premodern populations which is compatible with the high child mortality and low adult age at death in Italian Neolithic skeletal samples. It estimates 50 percent child mortality and a life expectancy at age fifteen of 25 years, and it assumes a stable population and an even sex ratio.

Table 1. *Model Demography of Neolithic Communities, Assuming 50 Percent Child Mortality and Life Expectancy of 25 Years at Age Fifteen*

Group Size		Juveniles (Age 0–15)	Young Adults (Age 15–30)	Adults (Age 30–50)	Old Adults (Age 50+)
25 people	Total	10.65	7.00	5.10	2.25
	Males	5.33	3.50	2.55	1.13
	Females	5.33	3.50	2.55	1.13
50 people	Total	21.30	13.99	10.20	4.51
	Males	10.65	7.00	5.10	2.25
	Females	10.65	7.00	5.10	2.25
100 people	Total	42.59	27.98	20.40	9.02
	Males	21.30	13.99	10.20	4.51
	Females	21.30	13.99	10.20	4.51
200 people	Total	85.19	55.97	40.80	18.03
	Males	42.60	27.99	20.40	9.02
	Females	42.60	27.99	20.40	9.02
500 people	Total	212.98	139.93	102.01	45.08
	Males	106.49	69.96	51.00	22.54
	Females	106.49	69.96	51.00	22.54

This lets us sketch in the rest of the population, even if only tentatively. If we assume that Penitenzeria, at the low end of the population scale, had a population of twenty-five, it would have contained about ten to twelve children and about six adults of each sex. About half of the adults would have been under 30 years old; only a couple of people at any given point would have had memories spanning several generations. Such settlements would have been able to function socially only through close links with other hamlets for enterprises involving numbers of people (such as assembling a raiding party, a boat crew, or a group of elders to conduct rituals). The same is true for periodic events. For example, if males and females underwent separate initiations between the ages of 15 and 20, communities of twenty-five to fifty people would not have been able to assemble an age-grade of initiates of any size without coordination with neighboring villages (Table 2). Similarly, a male or female reaching the age of 20 years in such a community must have married outside it, both due to the sparseness of potential mates in any particular age category as well as to probable close kin links among the residents. Simulating twenty-five-person groups with different marriage rules,

Table 2. *Life Events in a Five-Year Period, Based upon Demographic Reconstructions in Table 1*

Group Size (Number of People)	Births	Juvenile Deaths (0–15 Years Old)	Adult Deaths (Age 15+)	Males or Females Turning 15 Years Old	Males or Females Turning 20 Years Old
25	6.40	3.20	3.20	.80	.68
50	12.80	6.40	6.40	1.60	1.36
100	25.59	12.80	12.80	3.20	2.73
200	51.18	25.59	25.59	6.40	5.46
500	127.96	64.00	64.00	16.00	13.64

Wobst (1974) found that a community needed to be in contact with seven to nineteen other groups (175–475 people total) to form a stable mating network. Moreover, given the demographic fluctuations afflicting small groups, the average lifespan of twenty-five-person groups would have been on the order of 180 years. In contrast, if a Tavoliere-style ditched village or an unditched village such as Catignano or Favella contained 100 people, it offered quite different social possibilities. At 100 people, a village could potentially mount a sex-specific group of twenty to thirty adults for collective tasks such as harvest, hunting, gathering, raiding, or defense. Collective experience and memory would have had a greater time depth, with a dozen or more senior adults.

Demographic reflections have several important implications for the present discussion. Within all Neolithic communities, most or all people would have been related by kinship links, and people would have known each other intimately. Identity would be strongly oriented according to place within a demographic pyramid created by mortality. "Young adults" (15–30 years of age) would already have outlived half of their birth cohort and would constitute the largest adult bloc, while achieving 50 years of age would afford an important status, in itself, as one of a few people with access to precedent, experience of infrequent events, and historical memory. Finally, "communities of practice" were probably very small, and if tasks such as potting, warfare, or gardening were gender-specific, only a handful of adults would have been able to carry them out. This would have conditioned the reproduction of knowledge (Barth 2002), as many activities would have been undertaken at long intervals or by very small groups of knowledgeable individuals (see below on figurines, and Chapter 6). It would also render knowledge of any restricted task an important component of identity.

The Represented Body

THE CORPOREAL CORPUS: Neolithic Italian art offers some fascinating representations of humans (Table 3). Evidence is admittedly patchy, and some of the most important corpuses fall outside of the core area of this study, either in space (Northern Italy) or in time (at the Neolithic-Copper Age boundary or later). However, there are some important general trends.

Both media and themes changed through time, in ways broadly familiar from elsewhere in Europe. Neolithic human representations predominantly are small figurines, often female. A few rock art images may date to this period, but dating is ambiguous both for Alpine rock art and for Porto Badisco. Major changes happen with the end of the Neolithic through the early Copper Age. Figurines vanish almost entirely. Innovations include landscape art, with major rock art complexes at Valcamonica and in other Alpine valleys, at Porto Badisco in Puglia and at Levanzo in Sicily. Human representations move from handheld to landscape in scale, with schematic monumentalised statues found in Lunigiana and in the Alps. Thematically, standardised gender imagery includes weaponry and hunting for males and breasts and ornamentation for females. Such monumental figures may represent ancestors or cosmological beings (Fedele 1990; Keates 2000) or both. This pattern persists through the Bronze Age, although the Alpine cosmological stelae vanish and imagery in general becomes scarcer outside the heartland of Alpine rock art and the Lunigiana area. Towards the Iron Age, we see a resurgence of stelae with several major new groups (the Daunian and the Villanovan), a greater variety of imagery in many media, and the reemergence of figurines, this time in the form of small bronze figures, often of male warriors.[1]

For the bulk of the Neolithic, our main database comes from figurines, which, fortunately, have been systematically reviewed in three

Table 3. *Human Body Imagery in Prehistoric Italian Art, Neolithic through Iron Age*

	Northern Italy	Central Italy	Southern Italy	Sicily	Malta	Sardinia
Early–Middle Neolithic (sixth–fifth mill. BC)	*Figurines*: varied figurines, mostly female *Rock art*: ?a few rock carvings at Valcamonica and elsewhere in the Alps	*Figurines*: varied figurines, mostly female	*Figurines*: varied figurines, mostly female Rock art:?Porto Badisco (poorly dated) Other: a few anthropomorphic images on vessels	*Figurines*: a few figurines, varied		Small volumetric figurines, generally ungendered
Late–Final Neolithic (later fifth–early fourth mill. BC)	*Figurines*: varied figurines, mostly female *Statuary*: Alfaedo statue *Rock art*: Val Camonica rock carvings (plows, "idols," spirals, daggers)	*Figurines*: varied figurines, mostly female	*Figurines*: varied figurines, mostly female *Statuary*: Arnesano statue *Rock art*: Porto Badisco and other painted caves (hunting and nonrepresentational art)		*Figurines*: a few figurines, varied	Small flat, schematic figurines, female
Copper Age (later forth–early third mill. BC)	*Statuary*: Lunigiana stelae, Alpine statue-stelae *Rock art*: Val Camonica and other sites: hunting, geometric, dagger images		*Rock art*: Porto Badisco and other painted caves (hunting and nonrepresentational art)	*Statuary*: a few larger figures (e.g., Piano Vento male) *Rock art*: Levanzo fish and anthropomorphic motifs?	*Figurines*: highly varied female, nongendered and animal/hybrid figurines *Statuary*: monumental "fat person" statues	*Figurines*: small flat schematic figurines, female, in mortuary contexts

44

Bronze Age (later third–second mill. BC)	*Statuary*: Lunigiana stelae *Rock art*: Monte Bego, Val Camonica and other sites: hunting, geometric, dagger images		*Statuary*: Sporadic stelae	*Figurines*: anthropomorphic "frying pans"	*Figurines*: small metal statuary *Statuary*: sporadic stelae
Iron Age (first mill. BC)	*Figurines*: small metal statuary *Statuary*: Lunigiana stelae *Rock art*: Monte Bego, Val Camonica: varied and complex imagery	*Figurines*: small metal statuary *Statuary*: Villanovan stelae, sporadic other stelae	*Statuary*: Daunian stelae, sporadic other stelae		*Figurines*: small metal statuary (*bronzetti*)

recent works (Fugazzola Delpino and Tinè 2003; Giannitrapani 2002; Holmes and Whitehouse 1998). The number of figurines known has at least doubled since Graziosi's first review (Graziosi 1974), and this includes a handful of recent finds (Fugazzola Delpino 2001; Fugazzola Delpino and Tinè 2003; Langella et al. 2003; Robb 2003; Tozzi and Zamagni 2001). Counts differ according to whether one includes fragmentary or poorly-contextualised material, items which may have formed parts of pots rather than free-standing figurines, and representations not clearly human. There are between 60 and 100 figurines known (Figures 5–6).

Italy lies on the western edge of the great Neolithic figurine tradition encompassing the Balkans and Aegean, Anatolia, and the Levant. There are fewer figurines in Italy than in zones further east. However, it is important not to misread the comparison with these much better-known areas: although many single sites in the Balkans have yielded more figurines than all of peninsular Italy has, virtually no Neolithic Italian site has been excavated as extensively as Balkan and Anatolian tells, which often have much greater volumes of sediment shoveled out of them. The most interesting point to emerge from the comparison is really how utterly heterogeneous the Italian corpus is, in comparison with Balkan collections in which clearly defined types exist. As Whitehouse and Holmes (1998) note, attempts to divide the corpus into clear types can isolate a handful of groups with half a dozen exemplars each, but most of the corpus resists classification; virtually each figurine is unique. More than anything else, this heterogeneity suggests that, although deriving from a common tradition, figurines were used in a different way in Italy than in the Balkans.

THE MATERIALITY OF FIGURINES: Figurines are small, rarely more than 10 cm in size. The great majority are made of clay. The materials, the technical knowledge, and the operational sequence for making a figurine draw strongly upon those for making pottery. Informal replication has shown that, once the paste was mixed, it would have taken only a few minutes to model a figurine. Interestingly, the technology and style of figurines also mirrors that of pots. For example, those from Southern Calabria and Sicily tend to be made of rough impasto, sometimes decorated with stamped impressions; the Cala Scizzo and Grotta Pacelli

NEOLITHIC PEOPLE

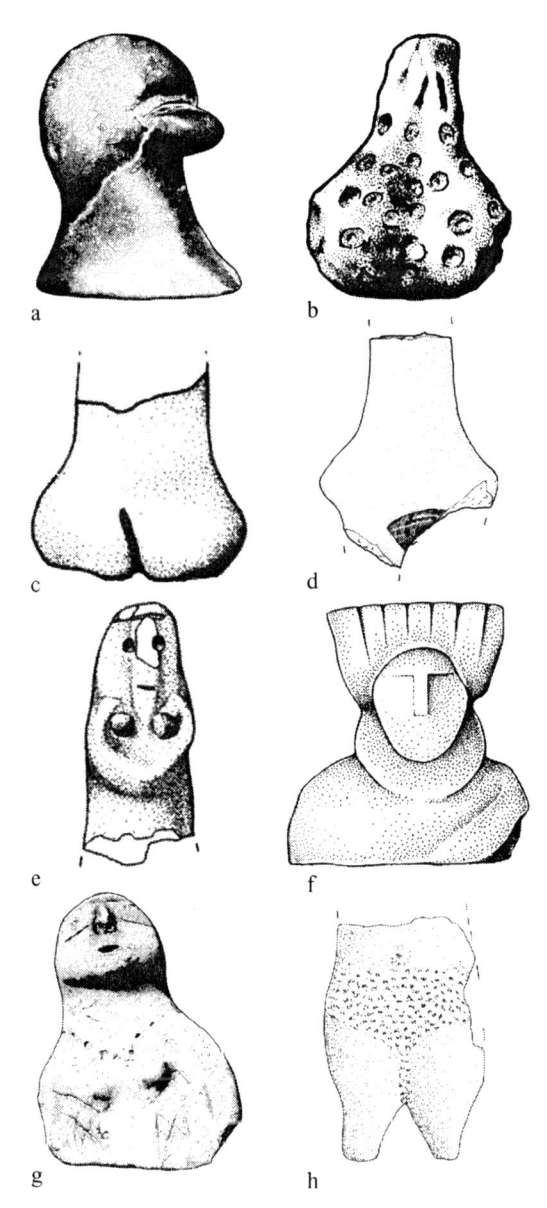

5. Figurines from Neolithic Southern Italy. (a) Grotta di San Calogero (redrawn after Graziosi 1974); (b) Penitenzeria (source: original); (c) Favella (Tinè 2007, courtesy of V. Tinè); (d) Favella (Tinè 2007, courtesy of V. Tinè); (e) Favella (Tinè 2007, courtesy of V. Tinè); (f) Baselice (Langella et al. 2003, courtesy of M. Langella); (g) Passo di Corvo (Tinè 1983, courtesy of S. Tinè); (h) Rendina (redrawn after Cipolloni Sampò 1982). Not to scale.

figurines share the tradition of sophisticated *figulina* modeling found in Serra d'Alto pots, and the Passo di Corvo figurines resemble the dark burnished pots from the site. Similarly, the Catignano figurine and those from nearby Ripabianca di Monterado share a common form, but the former is executed in painted figulina like Catignano wares, the latter in rough impasto like Impressed Wares (Tozzi and Zamagni 2001). These considerations suggest that figurines were made by potters, perhaps at the same time as potting sessions.

Once made, we do not know what figurines were used for, and to some extent this is a fruitless question until there are further studies either of archaeological context or of fragmentation and use-wear. These figurines probably served varied functions. Most clay figurines show little concern for finely detailed modeling or intensive surface finishing, suggesting that status or display was not a major concern, nor was a recognizable representation of a particular individual. The operational sequence dispels any idea of spontaneous play; once modeled, they would have had to dry for an extended period before being fired. Some figurines, such as the flat-based upper torsos found in some Adriatic contexts, were probably intended to stand upright, and others may have rested in a sitting position. Clay figurines tend to be found broken on village sites in ways suggesting casual disposal following use for a particular occasion such as, perhaps, healing rites, initiation rites, or social agreements (Talalay 1993). The most likely function of the small clay figurines seems to be a relatively informal ritual performed around the household. Intriguingly, among durable finds, stone tools and pottery are normally the most common, with axes several orders of magnitude less common, followed by skeletal remains and then figurines. Taking this at face value, it implies that, throughout Italy, figurines were used consistently enough to maintain the tradition, but very infrequently. This seems too infrequent to suggest toys, for example. It may suggest either an event rarely experienced (healing from specific illnesses) or a life transition (birth or initiation perhaps), perhaps relevant to only part of the population. In small communities such events may have been far between (Table 2). One key difference with Balkan Neolithic sites, then, may have been the use of figurines for less frequent purposes or, simply, in much smaller communities.

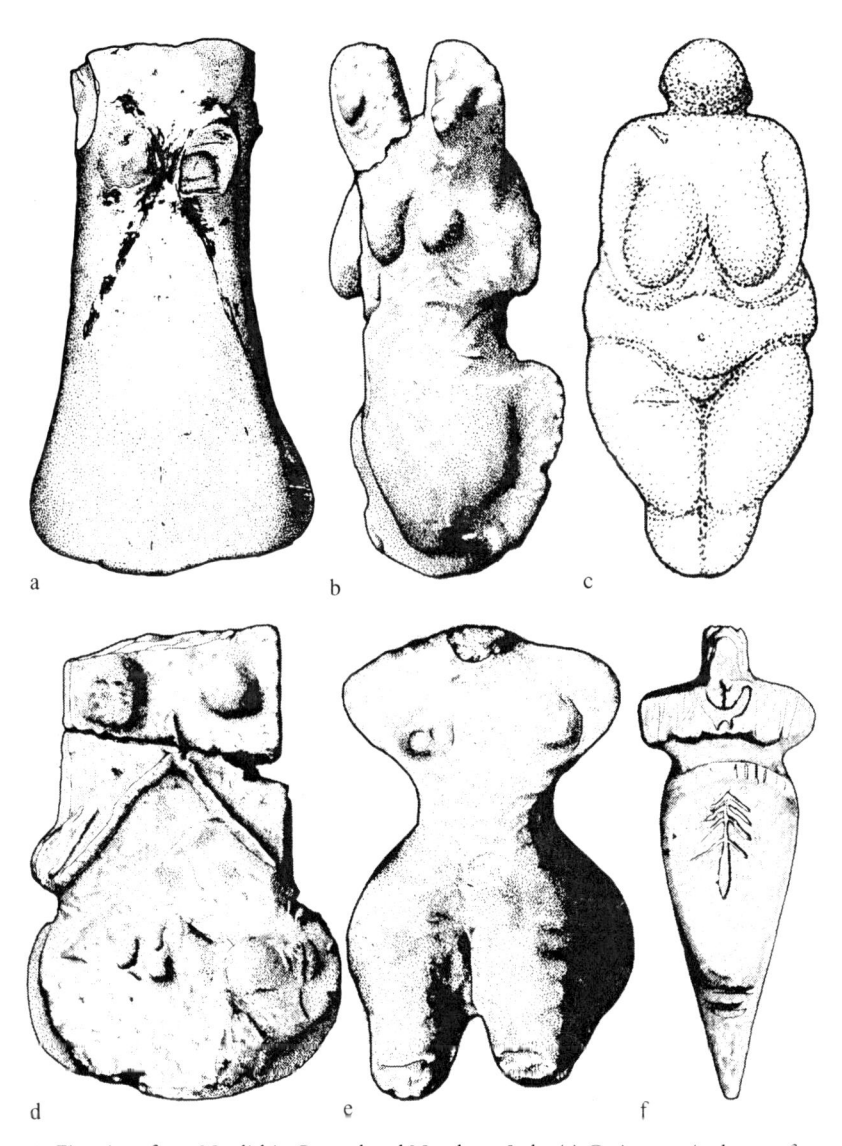

6. Figurines from Neolithic Central and Northern Italy. (a) Catignano (redrawn after Tozzi and Zamagni 2003); (b) Ripoli (redrawn after Graziosi 1974); (c) La Marmotta (Fugazzola Delpino 2001, courtesy of M. A. Fugazzola Delpino. Image copyright Museo Nazionale Preistorico/Etnografico L Pigorini, Roma EUR – by concession of the Ministero per i Beni e le Attività Culturali); (d) Vhò (redrawn after Graziosi 1974); (e) Arene Candide (redrawn after Graziosi 1974); (f) Riparo Gaban (redrawn after Graziosi 1974). Not to scale.

At the end of their lifespan, small clay figurines appear not to have been curated with particular care and seem to have been disposed of without ceremony on habitation sites, either in or around houses (as at Rendina and Catignano), in middens [as at Penitenzeria and at Poggio Olivastro (Bulgarelli, D'Erme, and Pellegrini 2003)] or in ditches. No particular patterns of fragmentation suggest that they were broken intentionally (Chapman 2000) or deposited in any particularly structured way. In contrast, figurines found in other contexts, such as ritual or burial sites, probably served different roles. These figurines are sometimes made of stone rather than clay (Holmes and Whitehouse 1998), a choice which implies different operational sequences and different skills akin to axe-making rather than potting. They depict the body in different ways (see below), and they had different biographies, finishing with their intentional deposition in a ceremonial context.

GENDERED AND AMBIGUOUS BODIES? Figurines reference human bodies. Like all representations of the body, they draw upon the lived human body, as perceived and experienced in a range of ways, for their subject and potential meanings. Conversely, through acts of abstraction and reformulation, they direct how the body is seen and experienced (Bailey 2005).

Discussion of Neolithic Italian figurines has revolved almost exclusively around gender. Do Neolithic figurines depict females? The answer is surprisingly hard to pin down. On one hand, it cannot be doubted that all Neolithic figurines for which obvious sexual features are present are females; the ithyphallic figurines from Piano Vento and from Ortucchio (Figure 55) date to the transitional Final Neolithic/Early Copper Age (Holmes and Whitehouse 1998). However, a closer look makes gender assessment less clear-cut. As genitals are rarely depicted, identification tends to hinge upon the presence of breasts; figurines with prominent buttocks are sometimes considered female, but this seems less self-evident, given how highly stylised and schematic most of the figurines are.[2] Moreover, sexual characteristics are not clear on many figurines, whether because of schematism or because they are fragmented.

Therefore, two positions are possible. Most Italian scholars tend to assume that all figurines represent females, except for a few obvious exceptions such as bird-headed images (see below). In some cases, this attribution is more plausible than it would seem at first sight: although the Penitenzeria figurine (Figure 5b) does not bear clear signs of sex, it can be placed at the abstract end of a continuum of figurines in which a more clearly female figure is represented by strongly flexed lower body with a highly reduced torso. On the other hand, some relatively complete figurines bear no overt sexual features, and there is no basis for assuming that heads with elaborate headdresses (such as the Baselice figurine, Figure 5f) must depict women. The alternative position is that the figurines represent heterogeneous categories of beings, some female, some not (Giannitrapani 2002; Holmes and Whitehouse 1998; Whitehouse 2001). Holmes and Whitehouse point out further that many "female" figurines actually appear quite phallic; perhaps the clearest example is the Favella 1 figurine (Figure 5c) (Tinè 2007), which lacks unambiguous signs of female sex and which has the form of a cylindrical shaft surmounting two globular protuberances. Other ambiguous figurines may include a range of Sicilian variations on a cylindrical shaft with small appliqué breasts and the "mushroom-headed" figurines from the Po Valley. This ambiguity of representation, Holmes and Whitehouse argue, represents a composite model of personhood incorporating both male and female qualities. The "gender ambiguity" interpretation is difficult to assess, as we must avoid confounding an intended ambiguity with our own inability to interpret due to fragmentation and ignorance of schematic codes. And ambiguity, by definition, resists clear and simple construal. The bottom line seems to be that, if we were able to place figurines along a spectrum of ambiguity, two contradictory results would emerge. A few figurines clearly suggest a dual interpretation, although a much greater number appear straightforwardly female. Moreover, the most problematic figurines tend to fall in clusters, particularly in the "cylindrical shaft" clump in Calabria and Eastern Sicily and in the "mushroom-headed" group in the eastern Po Valley.

Figurines do not directly embody master ideologies, but nor are they independent of them. Rather, they show such abstract value systems as recreated in specific fields of action, in ways which may not represent them fully or in ways compatible with other practices (see Chapter 1 in this book). Hence, it is perhaps most accurate to say that, rather than representing directly an abstract, Italy-wide code of gendered personhood, figurines reflect a selection of possible meanings mobilised within a particular context. If so, it is no surprise that they expressed different meanings from one community to another, and, therefore, that patterns of gender ambiguity in figurines are localised.

Why should specifically female figurines predominate? Traditionally, archaeologists have drawn an association between the adoption of farming, the fertility of the soil, female fertility, and figurines as part of ritual practices. In contrast, gender-minded theorists have either criticised this view or maintained a carefully studied silence on the issue. While following the latter line of argument, I would argue for a yet more heretical opinion. Because we have almost no other human representations surviving from the Neolithic, and because figurines have traditionally be classified as "art," we have tended to assign figurines a dominant ideological or theological voice. Consciously or not, we have effectively slotted them into the material culture space of the crucifix or major cult image. But figurines were small, casually made and discarded items probably used in specific, narrowly-defined contexts. Social life must have involved many such objects, portraying many different things in many media. Hence, very likely, it is simply a vagary of archaeological preservation that the one category of small ritual item which was preserved in a durable medium happened to portray females. What is important about figurines, therefore, is not any universal statement privileging the female body they represent, but rather what they show about the process of representing the human body, and the positioned statements about it within their contexts.

ABSTRACTING THE BODY: COMMUNITIES OF FIGURINE PRACTICE: This raises the question of communities of practice and how figurines were made and used in social processes. Here, again, figurine practice strongly resembles pottery practice; the pattern emerging is one of fragmented rather than standardised practice (see Chapter 5 in this book).

Typology gives us a start. Neolithic Italian figurines resist typological classification. Although we can group some figurines into loose assortments, many are unique. Holmes and Whitehouse (1998) note several such groups, and Fugazzola Delpino and Tinè's (2003) recent typological review groups the corpus into well over a dozen categories, many with only one or a few examples. A rough grouping which nevertheless omits many one-off figurines (Table 4) clearly show that figurines were made within regional networks of practice which, intriguingly, were more or less the same scale as pottery styles but which did not necessarily coincide with them. For instance, the Calabrian–Sicilian group crosscuts Stentinello and Impressed Wares, and the Adriatic cylindrical group crosscuts Impressed and painted wares.

In Barth's (2002) anthropology of knowledge, regional and temporal patterns of knowledge are governed by the social conditions in which knowledge is reproduced. Italian Neolithic figurines are reminiscent of Barth's Mountain Ok ritual knowledge: infrequently reproduced by thinly spread, very small groups of practitioners. The result was that a general regional stock of themes and symbols was locally reconfigured into an impressive variety of results. There is no reason to suppose that figurines represent a common pan-Italian dogma; the substance as well as the style would have been reinterpreted and transformed from group to group.

On the smallest scale, each figurine would have been the product of a particular, circumstantial act of reworking elements of a regional tradition. Indeed, close reading of the figurine corpus yields examples of just such a process. The two Passo di Corvo figurines, for example, share elements of the contemporary tradition extending up the Adriatic to the Marche, for example, in depicting only the upper body and head, with the breasts the prominent feature on a rudimentary torso. However, unlike the Catignano and Ripabianca figurines, they flatten the body rather than representing it as cylindrical. Sometimes the results are still more dramatic; the Campo Ceresole (Vhò) figurine takes a Po Valley "mushroom-headed" figurine but idiosyncratically gives it two heads, and there is another two-headed figurine known from Ripoli. Two of the most remarkable examples show the integration of Neolithic tradition with pre-Neolithic history. One is the Riparo Gaban group of figurines, including a female torso carved from the surface of a boar's tooth, an anthropomorphically carved pebble, an anthropomorphic figure carved on a human femur (possibly to form a flute-like musical instrument) and a small, elaborate female body of bone colored with ochre (Figure 6f). These are from the VBQ strata in a site with strong evidence of hunter–gatherer continuities, and represent the fusion of a

Table 4. Some Figurine Groupings (Modified after Holmes and Whitehouse 1998)

	Examples	Material	Regions of Body	Depositional Context	Areas/Periods
Seated female	Rendina?	Clay	Legs, torso, and head	Villages	
Female with folded arms	Arene Candide	Clay	Torso and head	Villages	Liguria and Po Valley (VBQ)
Mushroom-headed female	Vhò	Clay	Torso and head	Villages	Po Valley
Short-armed female	Arene Candide, Chiozza, Pollera	Clay	Torso, head, and truncated arms	Villages	Liguria and Po Valley (VBQ)
Cylindrical female	Catignano, Ripabianca, Sammardenchia	Clay	Torso and head	Villages	
Cylindrical, ambiguous	Favella, Penitenzeria		Lower body, and rudimentary torso	Villages	Calabria, Sicily
Bird-headed	S. Calogero	Stone	Head		
Whole body, larger	Arnesano, Alfaedo	Stone	Head modeled, torso rudimentary	Funerary contexts	End of Neolithic
Head only, elaborate coiffure	Baselice, Gr. Pacelli, Cala Scizzo, Monte Grande	Clay	Head only	Ritual contexts	Serra d'Alto, S. Italy

Table 5. *Figurine Oppositions*

Only Heads or Heads with Rudimentary Bodies	Only Bodies or Bodies with Rudimentary Heads
Clay or stone	only clay
Ritual or funerary contexts	Villages
Ungendered beings	Female beings
Unusual beings (bird-people, coiffed heads)	generalised people

new Neolithic theme, female figurines, with traditional materials such as bone. The other is the La Marmotta figurine (Figure 6c). This figurine was found in a good Neolithic context, within a house structure in a lake village now submerged beneath Lake Bracciano (Fugazzola Delpino 2001). Yet, it is almost identical to some Upper Palaeolithic figurines, such as the examples from Balzi Rossi, both in its style of representing a female body and in its material (steatite, otherwise unknown in the Italian Neolithic figurine corpus). The most likely possibility is that the La Marmotta figurine is *both* an Upper Palaeolithic figurine *and* a Neolithic figurine: it affords a remarkable glimpse of Neolithic people collecting a striking item from a nearby ancient site, assimilating it to their own categories of material production, and integrating it into their ritual practices.

Each figurine had its own history and represents a creative moment in a community of practice. However, amidst the profusion of difference thus created, we can still see some general structuring principles which perhaps represent elements of habitus. One is the use of the color red to mark and adorn the surface of the body; traces of ochre are found on the bodies of a number of figurines in a way which may suggest bodily adornment in life as well as the ochre scattered on some burials.

A second principle is the differential use of body zones to reference different elements of being (Table 5). Although the borders of classifications are necessarily untidy, figurines tend to fall into two general categories. The majority abstract the human body to use the torso to create a generalised female body which is so schematic that it is often to be identifiable as a human representation only by the breasts. However, a minority of figurines ignore the body and use the head: these include a few bird-headed figurines from Sicily, the Arnesano and Alfaedo stone figures, and the three fine ceramic heads with elaborate headdresses from Cala Scizzo, the Grotta Pacelli and Baselice. The latter group is especially interesting; the opposition between generalised female bodies, often apparently unclothed, and ungendered figures with elaborate headdresses is known elsewhere, particularly in Sardinian Middle Neolithic contexts (Lilliu 1999) and in fourth–third millennium BC Malta. It may represent an opposition between women and senior, or supernatural, authority figures of either or both sexes. More generally, this resonates with the centrality afforded the head in practices of trepanation which may have been reserved for prominent or ritually significant people (see earlier discussion of trepanation). It suggests that the body, as a resource for social action, afforded symbolization of both generalised, female bodies via the torso and specific forms of social or supernatural power or authority through the head.

People in Death

Burial is both a physical act and a representation of human lives. Although personal identities, such as gender and status, have formed a traditional staple of burial archaeology, the range of contextual meanings enacted goes far beyond this (Parker Pearson 1999; Ucko 1969). In this section, after a brief description of the Italian Neolithic burial corpus, we look at how burial tied together people, communities, and history.

NEOLITHIC ITALIAN BURIAL: The archaeology of burial in Neolithic Italy has been reviewed systematically several times (Bagolini and Grifoni Cremonesi 1994; Grifoni Cremonesi 2003; Grifoni Cremonesi, Mallegni, and Tramonti 2003; Grifoni Cremonesi and Radmilli 2001; Robb 1994). To date, more than 100 burial sites with the remains of more than 400 individuals have been excavated, and the much smaller sample of well-excavated and well-published burials is growing rapidly.

Burial traditions are complex. For much of the Neolithic, the basic rite was single primary inhumation in a simple pit without durable grave goods (Figure 7); burials were located either in settlements or in caves. However, in all periods, there were alternative treatments. There is significant chronological development: in the later Neolithic (few concrete dates exist but such innovations probably appear in the early fifth millennium BC and increase towards the end of the millennium). Tomb

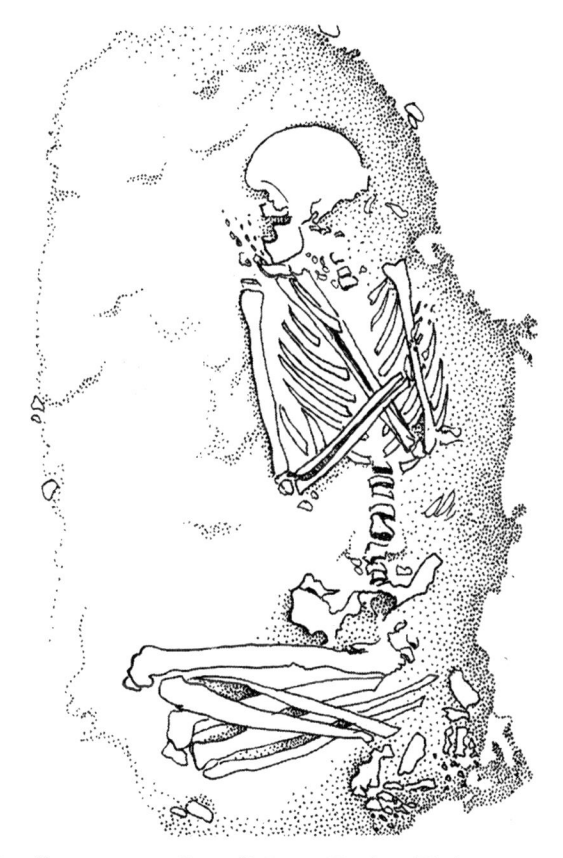

7. Single burial in village contexts: Passo di Corvo Tomb 5 (Tinè 1983, courtesy of S. Tinè).

architecture appears in the form of stone cists, grave goods begin to appear regularly, and formal cemeteries separate from settlements come into use. All of these developments are patchy and do not particularly typify any particular region or ceramic group; even within groups such as the Final Neolithic Diana culture, often characterised as using caves and small collective tomb cemeteries, there was considerable variation.

Even during the Early and Middle Neolithic, single primary inhumation is only part of the story. There are at least five general categories of variant:

> 1. Disarticulation (Figure 8). Although primary inhumation is considered the typical rite, the majority of burials are not in fact articulated skeletons. In fact, 53 percent of skeletons from

open air sites have been found disarticulated and fragmented, and the figure rises to 88 percent for cave sites (Robb 1994).[3] Moreover, this destruction itself was a cultural process. While some is undoubtedly due to post-Neolithic disturbance [e.g., Ripa Tetta I, whose extremities were removed by an Iron Age pit (Robb, Mallegni, and Ronco 1991)], at least some disturbance happened during the Neolithic [e.g., at Casa S. Paolo where isolated bones were found near a hearth (Vinson 1975)]. Moreover, enough semiarticulated or incomplete burials exist at sites such as Passo di Corvo to assure us that much, if not all, "scattered" bone does indeed originate in disturbance of actual burials. Although most archaeologists generally disregard disturbance as simply an inevitable effect of entropy and site destruction, it deserves serious interpretation. It is clear that Neolithic people knew about human bone on sites. They effected some of the disturbance, loose bone on sites still occupied would have been evident, and in some cases, such as Samari, we can document the gathering up and redeposition of loose bone (Grifoni Cremonesi, Mallegni, and Tramonti 2003). At Casale del Dolce, depositions of human bone included a neonate in a pit, a cremation with deposits of grain associated with it, and two instances of loose bones deposited in pits (Manfredini and Muntoni 2003). Disarticulation does not seem to have been a distinct rite *per se*; rather it was probably a known and expected phase of a burial's future. They would not have regarded burial as a permanent deposition but as a stage which would have ended normally in disturbance and scattering of bone after some time.

2. Skull manipulation or curation. Two sites are known where skulls were removed from otherwise complete burials. In one [Madonna del Loreto (Tunzi Sisto 1999)] the body may have been buried headless; in another [Cala Colombo (De Lucia et al. 1977)] the skull was clearly removed from the buried body some time later, presumably by people using the cemetery. There are several other sites where people retained skulls, something more common with multiple burials towards the end of the Neolithic; examples include Girifalco and Masseria

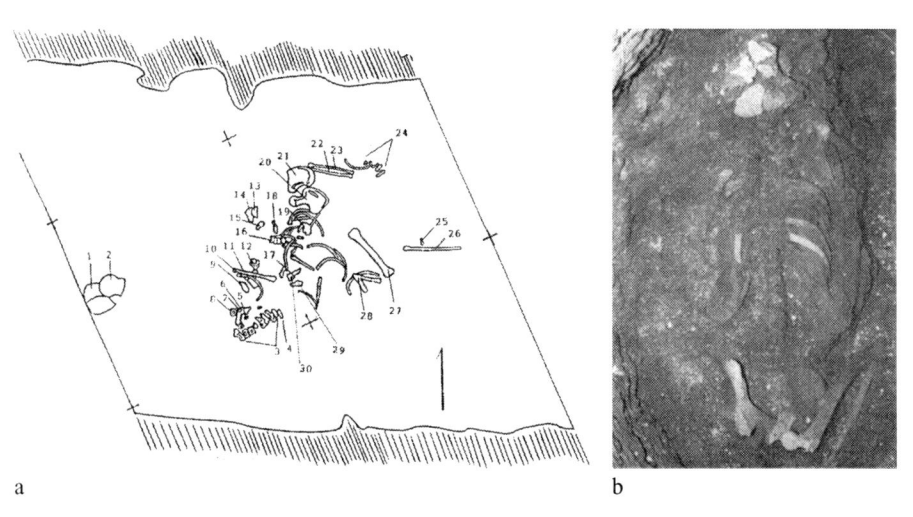

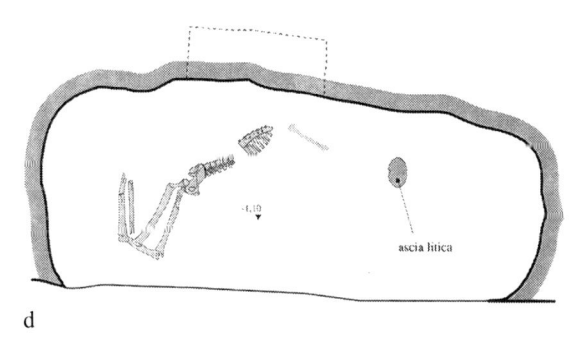

8. Anomalous burials. (a) Young adult male exposed in village ditch, Ripa Tetta (Robb, Mallegni, and Ronco 1991); (b) Young adult woman at bottom of well, Passo di Corvo Tomb 11 (Tinè 1983, courtesy of S. Tinè); (c) Mass burial, Diga di Occhito (Tunzi Sisto 1999, courtesy of Soprintendenza Archeologica della Puglia); (d) Headless burial, Madonna di Loreto (Tunzi Sisto 1999, courtesy of Soprintendenza Archeologica della Puglia).

Bellavista. At Scaloria Cave, amidst about thirty burials, one isolated skull was set upright and decorated with beads (Winn and Shimabuku 1988). In these cases, we have people disturbing burials within cemeteries but recognizing, conserving, and positioning the skull. In another pattern of skull deposition which may be related; three sites are known where skulls were kept around the village (see Chapter 3 in this book). These sites show human bone as potentially an important substance in itself. Among other uses of human bone, Mosso (1908) refers to a ring made from a human femur at Coppa Nevigata, although the details are sketchy. Somewhat further afield, a human femur diaphysis was used to make an engraved tube, possibly a flute-like musical instrument, at the Riparo Gaban in the Alps (Graziosi 1975).

3. Ritual status or circumstances. In a few cases, something was done which bore very little relation at all to the normal burial rite, and the best explanation for this is probably in the ritual status either of the dead person or of the circumstances of burial themselves. For example, at the Grotta Patrizi (Grifoni Cremonesi and Radmilli 2001; Patrizi, Radmilli, and Mangili 1954), a young adult male was buried in a ritual cave with strange assortment of grave goods, including cups, bowls, broken grinding stones, flint blades, pebbles, a bow, a bizarre assortment of small animal bones such as six fox tibias, and a quartz crystal. This man had a trepanation and a facial dysplasia, and he is sometimes interpreted as a spiritual leader. As a second example, at the Grotta Continenza in the mountains of the Abruzzo (Barra et al. 1992), one deposition contained the cremated remains of two children inside a pot daubed with yellow clay, with a cremated adult female scattered on top of them. Cremation is also known at Casale del Dolce (Manfredini and Muntoni 2003). At Madonna delle Grazie in Puglia, two children were buried in a pit with a burnt layer of pebbles above them. One has a possible peri-mortem trauma and an argument has been made for sacrifice here (Pesce Delfino et al. 1979).

4. Exposure. Besides the most famous Italian Neolithic person of all, the Alpine Ice Man (Spindler 1994), there are two known

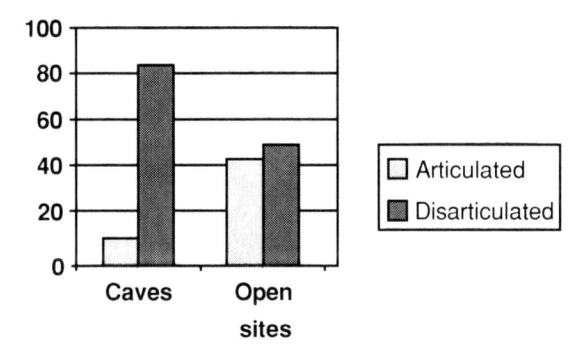

9. Articulated versus disarticulated skeletons in Neolithic burials.

cases of bodies left unburied (Figure 9 a, b). One is Ripa Tetta II, a young adult male left at the bottom of a ditch, probably scavenged by carnivores and burnt in a surface fire (Robb, Mallegni, and Ronco 1991). The second known example is Burial 11 from Passo di Corvo, a young adult woman found face down in a sprawled position at the bottom of a well (Tinè 1983). These depositions clearly represent anomalous denials of the normal rite rather than a regular practice of exposure. Recently, Papadopoulous (2000) has argued, for Classical Greece, that people buried in such strikingly anomalous ways were probably stigmatised individuals. One can imagine various histories for these individuals, as stray warfare victims, perhaps, or as victims of internal politics such as tribal witch executions.

5. Mass burials. At Diga di Occhito in northern Puglia (Tunzi Sisto 1999), about a dozen people were buried together at once (Figure 9c). At Grotta Pavolella in northern Calabria at least twenty people were cremated together *in situ* (Carancini and Guerzani 1987). Unfortunately, neither site has yet been analysed osteologically, but these may represent either epidemic deaths or, more probably, Neolithic massacres as known from the famous sites of Talheim in Germany and Schletz in Austria.

BURIAL, STATUS, AND IDENTITY: Standard archaeological categories of status, so useful in analyzing large cemeteries of single burials, have little relevance for Neolithic Italian burials. Burial was not a way of expressing relative prestige (Whitehouse 1984). Even when grave goods or tomb architecture do appear, they tend to be either uniform or completely idiosyncratic. For example, in an early processual analysis, Barker (1981) attempted to interpret the Grotta Patrizi burial as a chief. However, its very uniqueness makes this interpretation suspect; presumably claims to status through outstanding burial treatment rest upon appeal to a well-established and generally accepted convention that burial treatment can symbolise competitive status, and if this were so, we would presumably see parallel, but less outstanding, assemblages in many other burials (as, in fact, occurs in the Copper Age). Such unusual burials are better treated as expressions of qualitative ritual difference.

Nor is gender particularly marked in burial treatment. In a systematic statistical review (Robb 1994), the only difference between males and females was that males tended to be buried lying on their right side, females on their left. This association has been disputed; Grifoni (Grifoni Cremonesi and Radmilli 2001) argues that the earliest burials all lie on their left, with a subsequent shift later in the Neolithic, and Pluciennik (1998) has queried the nature of a fuzzy gender distinction to which there are many exceptions. Yet, it is a statistically significant nonrandom association and demands interpretation. We must not misconstrue the nature of ritual practice in small, decentralised communities. The fact that we do not observe rigid, exception-free patterns throughout all of Neolithic Italy does not mean that recurrent practices were not structured meaningfully. Rather, actual burial practice reflected local reworkings. A widely shared structure of belief can be ritually enacted in more than one way. For example, Christian churches often relate burial position to the Holy Land in the east, but some churches bury the dead with the head to the east to be near the Holy Land, while others place the dead head west so as to face the Holy Land when resurrected. General symbolic associations can underwrite regional variants in practice. If this is true, we would expect to observe a statistical association between burial position and sex rather than a rigid, absolute correspondence.

In fact, the principal status-related difference in burial treatment distinguishes between adults and children. Children's bones are disarticulated far more often than adults' bones, both in caves and at open-air sites (Robb 1994). Post-Neolithic factors presumably would to affect juvenile and adult graves differently, and the greater fragility of juvenile bones would cause them to be destroyed more readily, not to be

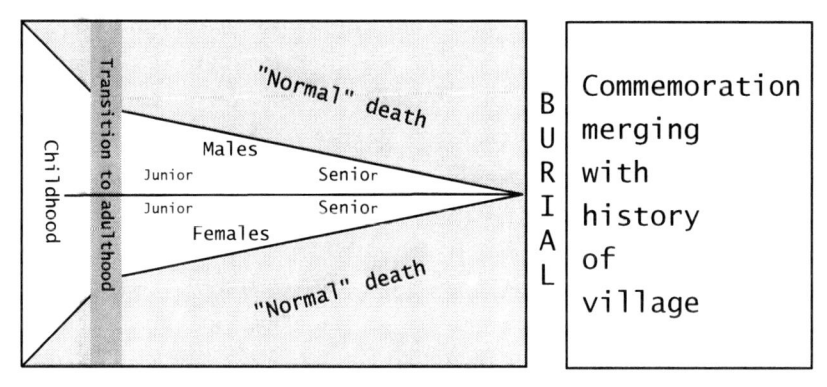

10. The normal lifespan in Neolithic Italy (Robb 2002).

disturbed more often. Rather, this probably reflects the fact that children's graves may not have been marked or remembered to the same degree as were adult's graves; in effect, their depositional history is a result of a cultural judgement that they were less socially important than adults.

A MEANINGFUL BURIAL PROGRAMME: Although the great variety of Italian Neolithic burial treatments does not represent personal status directly, it does not amount simply to a catalogue of oddities. It is only by relating these alternative treatments to each other that we can approach their meaning.

All societies have multiple ways both of dying and of burying. These variegated ways of death are often evaluated with reference to an ideal ending to a particular life story, a concept which Gnoli and Vernant (1982) term the "good death." Moreover, variant burial treatments cope with how people died in relation to central moral values and are interdependent with each other in structured burial programmes. For example, burying criminals or suicides at crossroads has no meaning without the concept of burial in consecrated ground as the normal and correct highway to eternity.

Single burial in a simple pit within villages or inhabited caves marked the normal death in Neolithic Italy (Robb 2002) (Figures 10–11). Theoretically, such simple on-site burials can be understood by considering the role of burial in constructing memory. In the Italian Neolithic, people identified themselves and their group with their houses and resident village (see Chapter 3 in this book). One progressed through a normal lifespan, became a gendered adult, and died in expected circumstances. Burial functioned to facilitate both remembering and forgetting; by reconfiguring what was known about a person, it helped create the social transition triggered by death. Burying people around the village both merged their personal history with the longer-term history of the group and endowed the place with a sense of ancestry. It was not expected that this burial would be maintained integral forever; rather, it was normal for most burials to be disturbed in the future, presumably after the lapse of an interval of appropriate memory. The scattered human bones in the ditches, pits, and middens were general ancestral presences, no longer recognised as individuals but still a testimony of the enduring presence of people and place.

This baseline normal biography could be either abbreviated or prolonged (Figure 11). Juveniles probably had less marked and less remembered graves which were disturbed more readily, effectively hastening their progress towards the end state of disarticulated ancestral substance. Conversely, the social being of the dead was protracted by retaining and manipulating bones; skulls particularly provided foci for the construction of memory, possibly as relics from burials, trophies from enemies, or both. The data are poor for quantification, with every category besides official "burials" underreported; there may also have been archaeologically invisible burial treatments, and the category of "scattered bone" probably lumps quite distinct burial pathways together. But as far as one can tabulate, these "normal" burials, leading to either articulated single burials or to scattered bones, account for half to three quarters of the dead.

Other variants provide at least three alternate routes to eternity – or at least to the twenty-first century. Mass deaths in extraordinary circumstances, probably warfare or epidemics, were given one-off multiple burials. People dying with unusual ritual statuses or circumstances were given equally unique treatments, all different. Finally, a small group of people was denied any burial at all – which is, of course, a burial treatment in itself, and one which excised them from group history and memory.

As a methodological note, this case illustrates how one a burial programme is constructed around a central life narrative. In general,

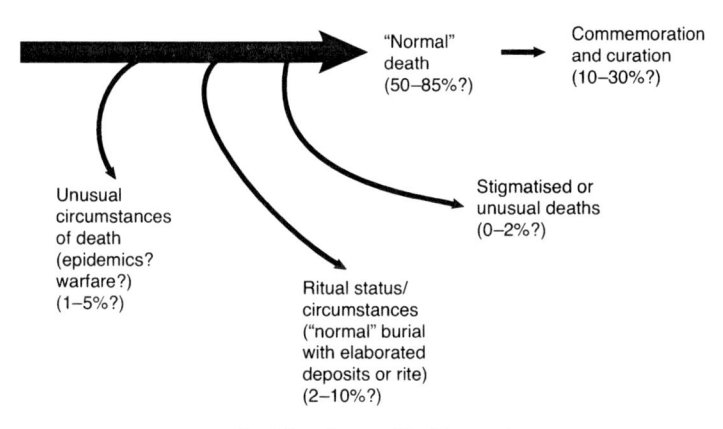

11. Burial pathways (Robb 2002).

there are four tactics: (1) abbreviating the burial pathway for people of lesser social centrality, often children; (2) extending it or elaborating it for people of greater social concern whose remains act as a focus of memory, which may involve keeping and using human bone; (3) opting out of it for completely different pathways for people in qualitatively different statuses and circumstances; and (4) denying it ostentatiously for people excised from moral communities.

Being Neolithic

This chapter has reviewed traditional archaeological evidence on people – skeletal remains, representations of people, and burials. Each of these has its own data, themes, and problems, and they need, first, to be understood in terms of this interpretive context. However, we now need to juxtapose them, to extrapolate humans from varied relations in which they participated. This project requires seeing people on two scales: in terms of the history of individual bodies – a discrete story with a trajectory in time – and in terms of the composite society, always fluctuating and changing as people acted out their lives but projecting itself as a timeless order.

The Human Career

The biography as a narrative provides a framework for living, a concept of the expected course of events, and a guide to self-formation at various stages of life. Moreover, time on the scale of personal biographies merges, via collective memory, with the history of the group, and ultimately with larger origin narratives (Robb 2002).

Children were the most numerous single group in Neolithic Italian society. Dental and cranial evidence suggests that children underwent periodic hardship, from hunger or illness, and death in childhood was common. Although children were accorded burial similar to adults, their graves were more often disturbed and presumably remembered for a shorter span, suggesting that, however affectionately they were regarded, they were not considered equal in status to adults. Childhood was not entirely a time of trouble, however. Occasional artifacts show children learning adult skills such as making pottery (see Chapter 5 in this book). Juvenile handprints in Porto Badisco Cave (Graziosi 1980) demonstrate that children sometimes participated in important rituals, perhaps initiatory (Whitehouse 1992).

With the end of childhood came the ability to participate in adult practices such as tooth ablation. The household was an important unit in village society (Chapter 3), presumably centered around one or several related adults. Growing older meant not only acquiring adult capabilities, knowledge, and experience, but also moving progressively up through the demographic pyramid. A young adult between 20 and 30 years old would have already outlived half of his or her birth cohort, and in a small village would have been an important member of the small group of active adults able to carry out strenuous tasks. However, they would have still limited experience of annual or infrequent events such as trading expeditions, wars, house building, or crop variability. Experience is important; the most successful hunters, for example, are often not athletic young males but are older males who have studied game for years (e.g., Rosaldo 1980). Someone reaching an age above 40 years, such as the Catignano I woman (Robb and Mallegni 1994), would have been one of very few people able to remember her grandparents' generation, kinship ties based upon long-dead kin, or a periodic famines or epidemics. Such pathways through life were not only abstract but were evident in the body. Catignano I, for instance, bore accumulated signs and stigmata of adult female status (with removed front teeth), a lifetime of hard physical work (in stress-related enthesopathies and osteoarthritis), normal tooth loss due to decay, a serious pelvic disorder which may have limited mobility for some time, a small fracture of a toe, a large cranial fracture which must have required a long period of healing, and two distinct trepanations. With scars, healed injuries, aches, adornments, and modifications, the body served as a physical map of the biography as an accumulation of life experience.

When death came, people were buried around villages and in nearby caves. For most of the Neolithic, burials were not kept apart from settlements; rather, the dead were integrated with the fabric of the village, perhaps in liminal locations (Chapter 3). Burials could theoretically remain undisturbed indefinitely. However, the fact that many were in fact subsequently disturbed during the Neolithic suggests that the key concern was not maintaining the body intact beyond a certain interval of memory. Interestingly, following this dehumanising or transitional interval, the human body was consigned to the same depositional pathway as figurines, pots, stone tools, and other detritus of everyday life – the tangible remains of the past evident around the village. The result was the identification of people with the places they inhabited at the horizon of vision, the vanishing point of social attention.

This was the common process; alternative lives were marked by alternative deaths. These included mass burials in exceptional historic circumstances which must have marked the generational memory of the group; idiosyncratic burials perhaps for ritual practitioners or in ritually unusual circumstances; and ways of extending the period of memory by retrieving and manipulating bone, especially skulls.

Gender and Its Limits

Italian Neolithic gender has proven surprisingly controversial (Whitehouse 2001). Italian scholars have rarely seen gender as anything other than a natural consequence of biological difference (Vida Navarro 1992). Ironically, scholars who distrust Anglo-American theorizing as a speculative departure from empiricism blithely take for granted universalizing interpretations of figurines as the *Dea madre* and the gender associations of activities such as pottery-making. For their part, Anglophone theorists willing to construct elaborate castles of hypothesis based upon their favorite ethnography become stubbornly reticent when discussing who actually hunted or made pots. Even Anglophone theorists are surprisingly divided; Skeates (1994) and Pluciennik (1998) have argued for local, contextually-based gender systems, while Robb (1994) and Whitehouse (1992, 2001) have postulated much more general gender systems. In the most far-reaching view, Whitehouse has used Porto Badisco cave to claim a general system of male domination based upon access to secret ritual knowledge. It is probably fair to say that, although both Robb's and Whitehouse's arguments have been based upon generalising patchy evidence in the presumption (drawn from regional studies in Melanesia, Native North America, and other ethnographic areas) that a widely shared gender ideology existed. Skeates and Pluciennik's highly contextual views do not allow us to grapple with those broad trends which are evident (such as skeletal and burial distinctions and the occurrence of figurines).

The assembled evidence is disparate, particularly if Porto Badisco Cave, almost all Alpine rock art, and the Lunigiana stelae are excluded as probably dating to the very end of the Neolithic or later [a dating which to some extent undermines claims for balanced gender complementarity (Morter and Robb 1998)]. To recapitulate some key points:

- Skeletal markers of activity show two sex-related differences. First, a significant number of adult women – probably at least a third – had anterior teeth removed during life, a bodily modification which created a lifelong marker of a particular status. Second, marked dimorphism in long bone shaft architecture suggests that males engaged in a relatively high amount of mobility compared to females.
- The only male–female difference evident in burial treatment was a statistical tendency to bury males on the right side and females on the left side – a systematic formal distinction in the cultural treatment of biologically male bodies and biologically female bodies.
- Female figurines, widely found but in small numbers, were probably paraphernalia for a very specific activity rather than symbolizing an over-arching ideology. At their most minimal, the female body is defined through the diacritical presence of breasts, implying a categorical distinction between, on one hand, females and males, and on the other hand, adult females

and juveniles. This may suggest that becoming a sexually mature adult female was an important transition in which biological development underwrote the social recognition of a new identity.

If we suppose that the final Neolithic evidence from the Valcamonica rock carvings and, probably, from the Porto Badisco cave art can be read back into earlier periods, male and female bodies were represented distinctly in rock art, the former with a phallus and the latter with a round spot between the legs.[4] Moreover, both corpuses attest an association between males, weaponry and hunting. Although this is a widespread Copper Age and Bronze Age symbolic focus both in Italy and elsewhere in Europe, it seems implausible that it would originate ab novo; it seems more probable that males were associated with hunting and weapon use throughout the Neolithic but that this association was symbolically elaborated in archaeologically poorly visible ways before the fourth millennium BC. The only direct evidence for Neolithic weapon use, however, is the probable presence of a bow in the Grotta Patrizi male burial (Grifoni Cremonesi and Radmilli 2001).

A society without gender is impossible to conceive, and enough evidence exists for Neolithic Italy to see consistent categorical gendered distinctions between female bodies (both biological and in representations) and male ones. However, not all aspects of bodies can be related to gender. Adornments in several forms are known, including pendants made from deer canines and carnivore teeth, small beads, and even small axes pierced for suspension. It is not known who wore these ornaments. Nor is there an evident association between the use of ochre to color bodies. A few figurines display traces of ochre on the body (Holmes and Whitehouse 1998), and ochre was used in burials as well, particularly in the Late Neolithic Diana culture. It is commonly found on sites and adorning human bodies with it is one plausible use. But we cannot infer from figurines that it was used to mark female bodies without comparable male representations. The same is true for depictions of hair shown on some figurines. A stronger argument for bodily constitution independent of gender comes from the infliction of violence, which affected both men and women. Similarly, trepanation and, more generally, the use of the head in burial and in figurines to signify unique or important statuses and crosscut male and female genders. In all of these respects, the Neolithic stands in contrast to the Final Neolithic and Copper Age, when gender distinctions snap into a clear focus which suggests the political centrality of gender.

Politics and Difference

Recent archaeological theory has emphasised gender and individual experience to the neglect of politics. With a few exceptions, the last serious consideration of Neolithic Italian political structure was over two decades ago (Barker 1981; Cazzella and Moscoloni 1992; Guidi 2000; Whitehouse 1984). These New Archaeology–influenced works reviewed evidence for political leadership and reached conclusions still valid today. Neolithic Italy lacks virtually all of the canonical indicators of social hierarchy: wealthy burials, elite architecture, centralised administrative places, large-scale constructions, and site hierarchies (Cazzella and Moscoloni 1992; Guidi 2000; Whitehouse 1984). Highly skilled craftspeople certainly existed, but they were not maintained dependents of leaders or elite classes. Long-distance trade was carried on in axes and obsidian, but there is little evidence that leaders used these items as political capital for ostentatious consumption or redistribution to clients. The largest collective works, village ditches, could have been organised collectively or ad hoc by leaders rather than managerial chiefs. The overall pattern, with small-scale houses and settlements and little ritual paraphernalia, was pronounced enough not only to dispel any suspicions of Neolithic "chiefdoms," but even to induce Whitehouse (1984) to suggest Neolithic "bands" – a daring and original conclusion, as applications of Service's typology to Neolithic Europe (Milisauskas 1983, 2002) universally designated early farming societies as "tribes."

For most processual archaeologists, calling Neolithic societies egalitarian "tribes" was essentially a negative conclusion: it characterised them by what they lacked and thwarted further discussion. Fortunately, there have been at least three relevant rethinkings in recent decades. In the early 1980s, the British Neolithic–Bronze Age transition was recast as a shift in the nature of social reproduction from ritual to prestige competition (Braithwaite 1984; Shennan 1982; Thorpe and Richards 1984). This general line of thought culminated in recent visions such as

Barrett's (1994) and Thomas's (1999) works. Although neither ritual nor prestige competition may be especially appropriate themes for Neolithic Italy, the essential point is that social change could be construed not in terms of formal hierarchical structures but as a non-evolutionary shift in cultural frameworks, reflexes, and strategies. Independently, within social anthropology, Godelier's (1986) model of "Great Man" societies brought into question long-standing and influential typological categories such as Sahlins' (1963) "Big Men" and "Chiefs." In "Great Man" societies, Godelier argued, forms of value are qualitatively different and incommensurate. Hence, there are many leaders whose recognition is based upon their different skills at warfare, ritual, oratory, farming, exchange, and many other activities – but prestige at one activity cannot be transacted into other forms of prestige. Although Godelier's concept has been criticised theoretically and empirically (Godelier and Strathern 1991; Roscoe 2000), it usefully punctures the Anglo-American fixation upon structural hierarchy as the only important principle of social organisation. Finally, Crumley's concept of heterarchy provides an alternative to hierarchy in describing political structures (Ehrenreich, Crumley, and Levy 1995). As a description of social organisation, "heterarchy" refers to a situation in which elements may not be ranked, either because they are qualitatively different (e.g., between apples and oranges) or because their relative ranking is ambiguous (e.g., between similar but competing elements). Though primarily a descriptive term, heterarchy has proven a useful concept in discussing complexity within egalitarian societies. Egalitarian leadership, thus, can be organised in many different ways, and how it is organised derives, among other reasons, from cultural values and reflexes, from regimes of social reproduction.

In Neolithic Italy, notable statuses are enigmatic and show little clear semantic concentration; there is no discernable criterion of wealth or status such as a common scale of grave goods. Idiosyncratically conspicuous grave goods and practices probably denote ritual purposes and statuses more than simple consumption and display of valuables. As in ethnographically described Great Man societies (Godelier and Strathern 1991), community size is very small, warfare appears common (see Chapters 3 and 7 in this book), and communication between different community networks was probably low, to judge from the tendency to distinct regional pottery styles (Chapter 5 in this book) and low levels of interregional exchange. The figurine corpus suggests a similar conclusion, with great heterogeneity probably due to small, highly fragmented local communities of ritual practice. Exchange seems to have involved restricted domains of life rather than providing a unitary way for people to transform production into prestige relevant to many contexts. Individuals participated in a wide range of activities which presumably afforded status and recognition – as fields of action, we know of warfare, gardening, parenthood, various forms of craft manufacture, feasting, exchange, and travel – but these do not appear to have been integrated into a united prestige structure such that any one symbolism summed up an individual's social value.

As hypotheses for approaching Italian Neolithic social organisation, thus, I would formulate three principles which, at this point, remain suggestions to be followed up in chapters the to come.

1. Italian Neolithic political organization was egalitarian rather than hierarchical. This is not to exclude the possibility of any hierarchy; all societies combine multiple forms of leadership, and even generally egalitarian societies may have hereditary leaders [e.g., ritual chiefs (Liep 1991)]. But there is no evidence to suggest that hierarchy formed the master discourse organising how people thought and acted, for instance by combining prestige gained in varied activities into a generalised, cross-domain prestige. Hence, it was a heterarchical society, based on defining persons and activities in terms of qualitative difference.

2. For pottery, as we will discuss in Chapter 5, an aesthetic reflex was the creation of difference as a means for actors to position themselves with regard to each other and to the canons of a given field of practice.

3. In terms of the central processes through which people defined themselves and created social relations, there is little sign of competition for prestige in the sense proposed for Copper and Bronze Age societies. However, neither is there evidence that large-scale ritual was an important part of normal social reproduction. The main locus of action in which people experienced the world and their place in it meaningfully was in carrying out the many activities of daily life. The Neolithic

"economy" was more than a means of providing subsistence and shelter. It created Neolithic people; it provided the means through which individual bodies were enabled, differentiated, endowed with biographical histories, and related to groups. Hence, the principal hypothesis elaborated in the following chapters: Neolithic economy as social reproduction.

THE ROAD AHEAD

Neolithic Italy appears intractable; the material reviewed in this chapter raises as many questions as it resolves. As a starting point for an "ethnography of the Neolithic" (Tilley 1996), it resists the meaning-oriented analyses to which archaeological settings saturated with "art" and "ritual" lend themselves (Barrett 1994; Bradley 1998; Edmonds 1999; Tilley 1994; Tilley 1996). It also thwarts the admirably sharp-edged focus upon status, identity, and life stories possible with extensive individual burial data (O'Shea 1996). But the fact that these roads seem blocked should not be regarded simply as an unfortunate defect of the evidence, an archaeological record which does not shape up to what we would like it to be and which is therefore uninterpretable.

The real defect lies in our archaeological imagination. Of course, the data are not ideal; the largest single lacuna, to me, is the lack of clear associations between categories of identity and activities. But archaeological data are *never* ideal, and often when they seem to resist interpretation, it really suggests that the question asked does not fit the contours of the data. Social anthropologists have long debated the extent to which interpretive concepts are relevant and useful within specific culture areas [e.g., whether African concepts of lineage or Melanesia concepts of the body can be transposed to other areas (Strathern and Lambek 1998)]. Archaeological methods and interpretations are context-specific too. Here, the fact that the Neolithic evidence does not supply fodder for clear interpretation using a Bronze Age or an Iron Age concept of political status probably means that this is not the most useful tool. Similarly, elsewhere in Neolithic Europe, systems of meaning were reproduced through the ritualisation of landscapes. The lack of such landscapes here does not mean that Neolithic Italians lived in a meaningless world, nor that meaningful experience is beyond our grasp in the lack of monuments.

Rather, Neolithic social relations created different kinds of persons, and were reproduced through different kinds of processes. Based upon hints from the burial, art, and skeletal evidence, politics may have been heterarchical, based upon the creation of complementary difference rather than the competition for uniform, generalised statuses which could underwrite hierarchy. With all the usual caveats about preservation, it is an unstated tenet of most archaeological interpretation that the archaeological evidence reflects people putting their energy into what was important to them. The Italian Neolithic path leads us not to large-scale ritual, nor to competition for status, but to daily activities, to "economy" as the principal venue for the creation of agency and the locus of social reproduction. Rather than judging a priori, on the basis of our own tacit views about gender, class, and function, that daily economy is an uninteresting and purely practical affair, we should follow where this path leads.

THREE:
THE INHABITED WORLD

> I recently had the experience of acting as host to Indonesian hill tribesmen visiting England. They came from a people long regarded as economically "irrational" in that they sink much of their wealth in buffalo that are then slaughtered in large numbers at their funerals. They, however, found the English staggeringly irrational in the amount of money, proportion of income and amount of effort that they devote to owning their own home. Why, they asked, should anyone spend so much on owning a home he could never be in because he had to go out to work to pay for it?
>
> Nigel Barley, *Native Land*. (Barley 1990, p. 51)

Houses are more than shelter; they embody cultural values, commitment to places, and plans of action. Few things bring home the difference of another culture more strongly than how they inhabit their houses. Houses and villages are a fundamental aspect of culture, both for us and for Neolithic people. One illustration of this is a remarkable pattern found throughout Southern Italy and Sicily. Archaeologists excavating an Early or Middle Neolithic village come across burials dating to much later in the Neolithic – perhaps 500 years or more. One of the best-documented cases, thanks to systematic radiocarbon dating, is Serra Cicora in the Salentino peninsula of Puglia (Ingravallo 2001; Quarta et al. 2005). Here people inhabited a small village in the mid-sixth millennium BCcal, leaving the usual debris as well as burying several of their dead within the village. Some five hundred years later, in the early to mid-fifth millennium BCcal, habitation here had long since ceased. Nevertheless, people returned to the site to bury another dozen people.

Why were living sites important? People and the places they inhabit are inextricable; agency cannot be localised solely in humans or in material places – it must be in the relationship between them. Neolithic villages were more than shelters. Houses and villages were the largest single artefact made at that time and were an institution which structured people's lives as much as it reflected them. They created settings for routinised perceptions and interactions, they categorised people in space, and they provided the anchor for cosmological landscapes. Their houses and villages symbolised the identity of their inhabitants, and when they were no longer inhabited, they were still places of ancestral presence. Hence, houses, villages, and the lives of the people dwelling in them are a good place to begin considering the Neolithic Italian world.

Places of Life: Houses and Villages

To begin with places of life, the constructed spaces where people spent their days: Neolithic sites include habitations, burial sites, ritual sites, and isolated find spots. All kinds of sites occur in both caves and open air sites, though caves occur patchily as large regions lack the necessary bedrock formations. Of these kinds of sites, isolated find spots are virtually uninterpreted, in part because the context is normally lacking. Some (axe finds) are discussed in Chapter 5. Ritual and burial sites are discussed later in this chapter. Most open-air sites are generally assumed to represent habitations.

To the archaeological imagination, the Italian Neolithic is the age of villages. This image took form early in the twentieth century with the excavation of substantial sites such as Ripoli in the Marche, Stentinello in Sicily, and Serra d'Alto near Matera. It received an enormous boost in the 1950s with Bradford's investigation of the hundreds of large ditched villages he had discovered through crop marks while flying an RAF plane over the Tavoliere of northern Puglia during World War II (Bradford 1949). Ditched villages are typical of central and northern

Puglia (Geniola and Ponzetti 1987, Jones 1987), the Matera region (Geniola, Camerini, and Lionetti 1995; Lo Porto 1978; Lo Porto 1989; Ridola 1924; Soprintendenza Archeologica della Basilicata 1976), and southeastern Sicily (Orsi 1890; Orsi 1924), and they occur elsewhere along the Adriatic and in the southern margins of the Po Valley. They are typically between 100 and 300 m in diameter, with a few much larger. This size is deceptive; much of the area inside seems not to have been occupied by houses, and most of the smaller ones may well not have held more than a dozen households. Moreover, ditched villages are far from typical. In many, perhaps most areas of peninsular Italy and Sicily, Neolithic people lived either in open villages or in tiny hamlets of a few houses. These different modes of settlement had important social implications (see Chapter 7).

Houses and Households

Regardless of how they were grouped, the basal unit of settlement was the house (Figure 12). Houses are well-attested, though there are only about a dozen well-excavated examples. The common technique, known from almost all houses, was to build walls by plastering clay daub on a basket-like framework of sticks and reeds lashed to sturdy upright timbers (Figure 13). Sometimes this was set upon a low foundation of a row or two of stones, presumably to raise the clay wall off of damp ground. In other cases, walls were set in postholes within footer trenches. How houses were roofed is unknown, though it is generally supposed that they were thatched. Almost all attested houses consist of a single room, which was square, rectangular, or oval, with a size of 3–5 m wide by 5–7 m long; the larger examples, such as at Casale del Dolce (Bistolfi and Muntoni 1997; Manfredini and Muntoni 2003), range up to 10 m. Often, one end was rounded. There are occasional cases of houses possible made of other materials, for instance, at Campo Ceresole, where the living structure resulted in a thick layer of anthropogenic sediment, apparently without daub (Bagolini et al. 1987).

Neolithic contain many other kinds of structure, less clearly identifiable. Open areas cobbled with small stones are very common. It is assumed that they represent prepared work surfaces, perhaps intended to remain mud-free during the rainy season. Commonly similar surfaces

THE EARLY MEDITERRANEAN VILLAGE

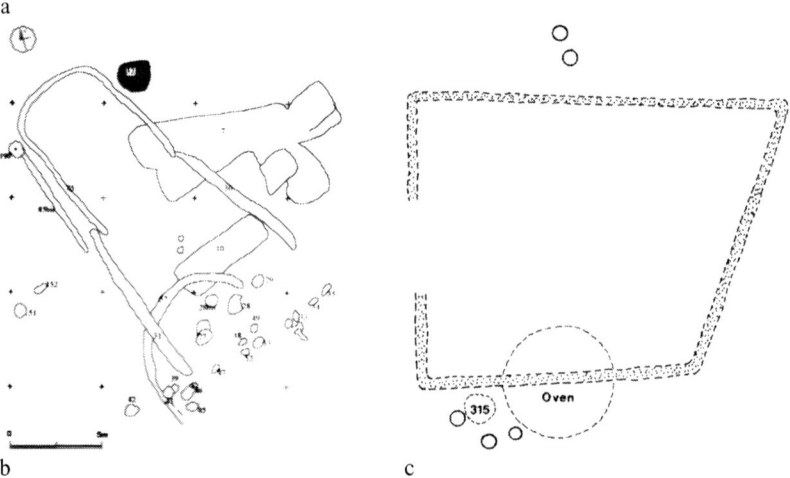

12. Neolithic houses. (a) Collapsed daub, Balsignano (Radina 2003, courtesy of F. Radina); (b) Catignano (Tozzi and Zamagni 2003, courtesy of C. Tozzi); (c) Acconia (Ammerman, Shaffer, and Hartmann 1988, courtesy of A. Ammerman); (d) Superimposed foundation ditches from rebuilding episodes, Ripa Tetta (photo: Robb, used courtesy of C. Tozzi); (e) Capo Alfiere, note monumental stone wall and stone-paved floor (J. Morter excavations; photo: Robb).

78

d

e

12 *(continued)*

plastered with clay are found, such as at Tricalle, where a beaten earth pavement was edged with a small ditch, presumably for drainage (Ducci, Perazzi, and Ronchitelli 1987). Among fire-related structures, hearths are known both inside and outside of houses. In open areas between

13. Burnt (fired) daub with impressions from sticks and reeds of house frame. (a) Penitenzeria, Calabria (photo: Robb); (b) Masseria La Quercia, Puglia (Ashmolean Museum; photo: Robb).

houses, pits filled with charcoal and burnt stones are often found; these are known as *strutture di combustione* (see Chapter 4 in this book for discussion). About half a dozen small ovens have also been found; these circular clay rings or domes were probably used for firing pottery (see Chapter 5). The most intractable finds are pits. Pits of all sizes are known, including some very large ones. Some regularly formed, clay-lined pits are clearly silos for storing crops. Others held burials or were for ritual depositions [such as the shaft containing ochre-painted pebbles and articulated caprovine legs at Masseria Candelaro (Cassano et al. 2003)]. More mysterious are the large, irregularly formed pits [as at Favella (Tinè 2004), Fossacesia (Cremonesi 1988), Catignano (Tozzi and Zamagni 2003), Masseria Candelaro (Cassano et al. 2003), and Marcianese (Geniola 1992)]. These are variously considered as for drainage, quarrying clay, storage or refuse disposal; work surfaces are sometimes found inside them (Tozzi and Zamagni 2003). Finally, there are the smaller, regularly formed oval ones about 30 cm deep and 2–3 m long and wide. Early in the twentieth century, these unfortunately acquired the misleading name *fondi di capanne* ("hut floors"), which belies the fact that their function is entirely conjectural (Cremonesi 1988). They have been variously claimed to be the floors of very small, single-person huts, borrow pits to obtain clay for building, mixing pits where large amounts of house daub were prepared, drainage for huts built over them, or sites of particular, structured depositions.

Table 6. *Raw Materials for Typical Neolithic Huts*

Material	Use	Quantity	Average Distance to Closest Source
Clay	Daub for walls	7,000 kg	120 m
Water	Mixing daub	? several thousand liters (kg)	270 m
Plants, sticks, and reeds	Frame for walls; cordage; mixing in paste	? several cubic meters	270 m
Rocks	Wall "filler"; features such as hearths	100 kg	440–660 m

Source: Shaffer 1985, p. 110–111, with additions.

THE HOUSE AS EMBEDDED TECHNOLOGY: Italian Neolithic houses have never really been studied as material culture, as human creations, as plans and programs for living. Their technology, however, gives a good starting point. Shaffer's work at Acconia (Ammerman 1985; Ammerman, Shaffer, and Hartmann 1988; Shaffer 1983; Shaffer 1985; Shaffer 1993) provides a remarkable example of whole-house archaeology, which can be supplemented by other studies (Mallory 1987; Tozzi and Tasca 1989).

The *chaîne opératoire* for a house began with assembling materials (Table 6). For a small hut, up to 7000 kg of clay would be needed (Shaffer 1985). Sites at Acconia were located an average of 120 m from clay sources. Elsewhere in Italy, sites are often located near clay outcrops; this may be one reason why Tavoliere villages are often located near the edges of terraces where escarpments can give access to clay strata. Quarrying and hauling clay would have required substantial labor – at least seven hundred trips with bucket-sized 10 kilo lumps. Quarrying was presumably done with hands, sticks, and axes; antler mattocks as found in Neolithic Atlantic Europe are unknown. If quarrying a bucket-sized load of clay and carrying it to site took notionally half an hour, providing a house-worth of clay would take 350 person-hours of work – 1–2 weeks work for three or four people. Crushing and grinding such a large heap of quarried clay would probably have been equally time-consuming. Perhaps half again as much weight in water would have to be carried, as well as the stones used for wall bases and fill and for features such as hearths. Leaves, chaff, and chopped straw were mixed in with the daub, and substantial quantities of fibrous plants such as ferns, grasses and sedge for cordage must have been essential (Shaffer 1985, p. 102).

For the frame, wood, sticks and reeds, to about one tenth of the volume of clay would have been needed (Stevanovic 1997, p. 362). Willow, alder, and oak were used, as well as reeds (Shaffer 1985, p. 102). From the impressions left in daub (Mallory 1987; Shaffer 1985; Tozzi and Tasca 1989), it was rare to use timbers larger than 20–30 cm in diameter, and even timbers this large were used only for major beams. Such trunks were adequate to support the structure; cutting larger trunks down to useful dimensions would have been hard and unnecessary work. With occasional exceptions such as the Ripa Tetta house, which seems to have been built substantially of split planks (Tozzi and Tasca 1989), most houses were framed largely of sticks 3–7 cm in diameter, with smaller twigs or reeds used to support daub between these. At a rough estimate, with major supports at the corners, medium-sized supports every meter, and small sticks every 5 cm in between, the walls of a house 4 m by 6 m and 1.5 m tall would have required at least 29 m of large (15–20 cm) timber and 38 m of medium (5–10 cm) timber. The biggest heap on the worksite would have been at least 360 1–2 cm. sticks 1.5 m long – not even counting the roof. Finding large quantities of long straight sticks long would have required careful observation of the surrounding woodlands, particularly recently cleared areas with new growth. Studies of French lake villages have shown that Neolithic house-builders chose wood with care, using different species from different microenvironments (old forests, younger forests, regenerating fields); wood use depended not only upon which trees were available in nearby woodlands, but also upon what role the wood had to play (posts, stringers, planks) and whether or not it had to be split into planks (Petrequin 1996). For wattle-and-daub walls, one obvious strategy which fits well with suggestions that Neolithic people practiced a form of woodland management (Castelletti et al. 1998) would have been to coppice nearby trees of appropriate species a year or two in advance of building.

After digging the postholes and erecting major beams, the smaller sticks would have been woven in or tied on to create an open basket-like framework. String or cordage of vegetable fiber was probably used to tie the stick framework together. Dried, crushed, and ground clay would have been mixed with water and straw, chaff, or leaves in batches as it was used, to keep it from drying out before it was applied. Shallow pits 2–3 m long such as the *fondi di capanne* would have been ideal for mixing large batches of daub. The mixed clay was then plastered liberally on the frame. Walls were usually between 15 and 30 cm thick, although the walls were occasionally much thicker. Their surface appears to have been smoothed by hand. There are rare traces of plastic decoration and one painted fragment is known (Tozzi and Zamagni 2003). Like a newly-made pot, the house would have had to dry gradually, with any drying cracks replastered as they opened up. A roof – probably of reeds or thatch bound with cordage (Shaffer 1985) – may have been put on before plastering the walls to shelter them as they dried, and hearths and similar features would have had to follow the basic construction phase.

The spatiality of house-building represents a balance between a location not too distant from bulky and heavy resources – it is significant that clay is usually the closest resource besides water (Table 6) – and other factors. House location may also have been related to access to land or to varied ecotone resources (Jarman and Webley 1975), position in social networks, and perhaps factors of history or aesthetic preference (Shaffer 1985). Once constructed, houses became focal points for social experience (see next section).

In the temporality of houses, two facts are clear. First, house building was seasonal: houses were probably built in spring and summer. This is suggested both by the vegetation contained in the daub analyzed at Acconia (Shaffer 1985) and by the need for dependable periods of warm, dry weather for the clay walls to dry. As a major task, the timing may also have been governed not only by climate but by the need to dovetail with other work and social schedules – to avoiding the mid- to late-summer harvest, or to take advantage of seasonally available foods such as recently born livestock to host work groups. Second, the actual building event was merely the culmination of an extended process of planning and preparation, including the acquisition not only of all the materials discussed above but of information, experience, and skill as well. Beyond cutting and stockpiling timbers and digging clay, builders no doubt monitored places where reeds and saplings were to be found and perhaps encouraged their growth well before they were needed. Making cordage is very time consuming (Hardy and Sillitoe 2003; Sillitoe 1988); accumulating enough cordage to bind the frame together was probably among the most time-consuming manufacturing tasks and may have been the first step carried out. Tasks involving concerted effort, such as hauling clay and erecting the frame, may have been distributed among groups. Houses were moment in long chains of events linked by planning and by the social relationships through which work was mobilised.

The technological simplicity of these houses is misleading; technology is a social process invoking accepted social representations of how things should be done (Lemonnier 1992). With available materials and tools, Neolithic people could have built a wide range of shelters: skin-covered teepees, rectangular stone roomblocks, massive timber longhouses, or round, partially underground pit-houses – all viable choices pursued elsewhere in the tribal world. The Italian Neolithic hut was a product of social choice. Most of the basic technological components were practiced daily in other contexts – digging, the use of stone axes to cut and trim wood, the use of grinding stones and pounders to prepare clay. One rationale for building such houses was thus that they fit into and made use of a familiar repertory of tools, techniques, and skills: the hands and muscles already knew what to do, and the chains of material provision were already in place. Material provision excluded other possibilities. For example, cattle were important social valuables, infrequently consumed (see Chapter 4 in this book). Given the low consumption of cattle, the largest and commonest skin-bearing animal, skin houses were probably not practical.

At the same time, a social logic of labor was involved. By comparison with housing choices not taken, Neolithic Italian housing suggests a flexible disaggregation of people. The aim was not to create a concentration of people bound by architectural form into a relatively static grouping – a Pueblo or tell-style roomblock of contiguous apartments, an Iroquois, or LBK-style multifamily longhouse. Rather, architecture involved modularity: small separate houses. Even when people aggregated into villages, the population may have consisted of relatively few households, and there continued to be an architectural emphasis on maintaining separating households, which reappears in features such as the "c-ditches" defining a household's area. Moreover, house-building technology was adapted to this flexibility. Erecting an LBK longhouse, for example, requires a collective effort akin to erecting a megalith, due to the massive size of timbers involved. It obligates the house builders to work as an extended group. In contrast, all tasks for building Neolithic Italian houses could have been carried out equally well by a large group in a single concentrated episode or by a small group incrementally. The choice would have been between extending the project temporally or socially. Moreover, many incremental tasks, such as carrying, mixing, and plastering, could have been done by anybody in the community, including children and old people, rather than requiring concentrated bursts of strength. Once a handful of adults sufficient to cut and raise the relatively small major beams was available, the limiting factor on the minimum group able to put up a house would have been experience. If a house lasted a minimum of twenty to thirty years, a community of five households would have built one no more often than every five years or so, and many adult householders would have built themselves only a house or two in their adulthood. To the extent that specific, nongeneric knowledge was involved – knowing how to mix up daub rather than pottery fabrics, or how to apply daub to the frame so as to minimise cracking as it dries – working in mixed-age groups to pool experience would have been essential.

Although the "barn-raising" scenario (Ammerman, Shaffer, and Hartmann 1988) is an attractive one, and we can readily imagine work parties coming together with food and drink, it seems likely that how these tasks were actually carried out would have varied locally according to the available labor force. This flexibility cannot be considered simply as an adaptation to an often sparsely distributed population; thin Neolithic populations in Central Europe and Britain built massive long houses and megalithic monuments. In Italy small, modular houses were the norm even where population was more concentrated and larger constructions such as village ditches were undertaken. It represents a genuine social choice, a tradition embodying an idea of how people should relate. It underlines the autonomy of the nuclear household as the basal unit of society.

HOUSES AND MEANING: The Italian Neolithic daub hut provides scanty material for florid anthropological analysis of houses as social operators saturated in space and meaning (Parker Pearson and Richards 1994). No doubt this may in part be because only one example, at Acconia (Ammerman, Shaffer, and Hartmann 1988), has ever been excavated and published in such a way as to permit household archaeology even as defined three decades ago (Flannery 1976). But it probably also indicates, simply, that we are asking the wrong questions.

What were houses actually *for*?[1] Most activities probably took place outside, in open areas. This is suggested by the limited space inside houses which would preclude many activities and by the spatial distribution of debris at Acconia (Ammerman, Shaffer, and Hartmann 1988), by the existence of a variety of other features around villages, and by the attention given to creating cobbled and plastered pavements as work areas in most excavated villages. Occasionally actual activity areas are excavated, as at Quadrato di Torre Spaccato where an area about 2 m^2 contained a dense concentration of flint and obsidian flakes (Anzidei 1987). Indeed, at many sites, such as Catignano (Tozzi and Zamagni 2003), all of the excavated hearths are outside houses, suggesting that even in winter, most of the basic activities took place in between rather than within houses. We must imagine Neolithic people as spending most of their daylight hours *all'aperto*, in the open spaces between houses and around the villages. There is also little to suggest that houses were an important medium of self-presentation (e.g., variation in size, in architectural elaboration, in decoration, in siting within settlements). As cosmological and social operators [*sensu* (Bourdieu 1977)], we should probably look at the settlement and landscape as a whole rather than the house per se.

Huts probably fulfilled three particular roles. One was shelter from the elements, particularly during cold and rainy weather between October and April. There are hearths known inside several houses (Acconia, Rendina, Lagnano da Piede) and thick clay walls would have had good thermal properties, storing and radiating heat. Some necessary activities would probably also have been carried out in shelter during bad weather, for instance, grinding grain, cooking, and eating. One hut at Serra del Palco, Sicily, destroyed in a conflagration, contained pots, tools, and grain lying upon grinding stones (La Rosa 1987). The second function would have been storage, particularly of valuables. The only known cache inside a house is a deposition of five stone axes under a floor at Capo Alfiere (Morter 1992), but houses would have afforded keeping places both for things kept out of general circulation and things needing protection from the elements. Silos or storage pits, presumably for crops, are known in open areas at several sites (Cremonesi 1988), but houses could have contained foodstuffs such as fat, honey, dried meat or salt stored in pots, tools and ornaments, baskets, and cordage.

But shelter and storage could have been created in other forms. As a highly structured microenvironment, the house also generated the phenomenology of the household, through patterns of vision, sound, movement, knowledge and copresence. Houses divided space into an inside and outside, with discontinuities of sight and hearing. Movement inside houses was channeled by fixtures and doors; outside the house, movement was flexible in an open, multicentric space. Moreover, belonging in a house conferred rights of access and exclusion, knowledge of things hidden and contained, and entry into a separate world of conversations and interactions. Such distinctions may have been important in a world without privacy as we know it. Out of the continuum of possible interactions, the structure of the house effectively created discrete levels of interaction, shared experience and categories of relatedness. The Italian Neolithic hut represented and created the common identity of a small group. Much of its daily life happened in common with others sharing their village space, but the house reserved common rights, access to knowledge and interaction to a smaller, basal units. This small, well-defined unit stands in contrast to the flexible access, movement, perception, and interaction typical of the open, collective areas of the village.

THE LIFESPAN OF HOUSES: Like people, houses had a beginning and end. House construction is relatively well-understood, as discussed above, though we do not know the social trigger to building one. There is some hint of foundation rites. Evidence is scanty (possibly because very few published houses have been excavated beneath the living surface), but isolated skulls in pits beneath houses have been found at Marcianese in the Abruzzo (Geniola 1992) and Balsignano in central Puglia (Radina 1999, Radina 2003), and a dog skull was found beneath a house at Catignano (Tozzi and Zamagni 2003).

Wattle-and-daub houses weather and crack, but, with maintenance, could well be expected to last two or three decades (Ammerman, Shaffer, and Hartmann 1988) – a generation in human terms, and long enough that it would be common for the social unit to break down via death or separation of the household before the architecture did. In this light, the end of a house's lifespan is particularly intriguing.

A surprising number of Neolithic Italian houses were burnt. Daub, if left unfired, will melt back into clay. All archaeologically preserved daub has been heated hot enough to fire it, at least minimally; this requires exposing it to temperatures of at least 400°C for at least a short period. While daub at some sites (at Penitenzeria, for example) remains soft and crumbly and falls at the low-fired end of the scale, at many sites, large, thick chunks of daub are completely and evenly fired, implying a substantial and sustained exposure to heat. Temperatures above 1000°C will likely result in visible vitrification (Stevanovic 1997). At Balsignano, daub was heated to not more than 500°C (Fiorentino et al. 2003). At Favella, daub chunks from the walls were heated to 450–600°, while pots upon the floor of burned houses reached temperatures nearer 900°C; this is consistent with temperatures reached at different heights during experimental burnings of wattle and daub huts (Muntoni 2004).

It is obvious that we have no way of knowing how many daub houses (or other structures) existed which were never exposed to fire, though postholes unaccompanied by daub are occasionally found. But we can say with confidence that well-fired daub is found at most open-air sites which have been excavated to any great extent. Moreover, archaeomagnetic studies at both Acconia (Shaffer 1993) and Balsignano (Fiorentino et al. 2003) demonstrate that house daub was burnt while still standing rather than after collapse; this is also suggested by large chunks of daub fired equally well on both internal and external surfaces at many sites. Thus, extensive burning while a house was still standing was a common fate, if not necessarily the only one, for an Italian Neolithic house. Going one step further, it is probable that houses were burned intentionally. Both Stevanovic for the Balkans and Shaffer (1993) for Italy argue that incidental or accidental burning will not heat large amounts of daub to this temperature. Aside from the roof and crossbeams, much of the flammable part of houses is buried within daub, with little access to oxygen, and accidental fires are likely to wane once exposed beams and roofs have burnt out. Generating enough heat to create a self-sustaining fire which will burn wood embedded within walls and heat 15–30 cm thick walls to low firing temperatures throughout requires fuel and planning (Stevanovic 1997).

Why burn a house? Probably not to harden the clay like pottery and make it more resistant to weathering, as has occasionally been suggested for the Balkans; it makes little sense to use a constructional technique which results in the immediate destruction of the house (Stevanovic 1997). Using fire to eradicate pests and vermin from a house would presumably involve much lower and less destructive temperatures. Shaffer (1993) has argued that old houses were burnt intentionally to fire the daub into permanent nodules which could have been reused as building material for new houses, thus saving the effort of quarrying and carrying clay. However, there are difficulties with this view. Technologically, as Shaffer noted, incorporating many stones in daub walls led to cracking, and this seems a likely result if large nodules of hard-fired daub were built into walls too. It is hard to see how large refired nodules would be fitted into the irregular, close-packed spaces around the basket-like frames. It surely would have been easier to recycle unfired daub simply by immersing it in water to melt it back into clay. Empirically, surely such nodules would be visible in the texture of daub fragments, either as fracture lines or as temper-like inclusions; yet, they have never been noted by daub analysts. Burning resulting from accidents and warfare are possible and no doubt happened sometimes. Yet, it is hard to imagine raiders piling fuel within a house and tending it for several hours to make sure the house burned thoroughly (Stevanovic 1997). It is also questionable whether conflict-related conflagrations should be expected at almost every village which has been extensively excavated.

The conclusion is that many, perhaps most, Italian Neolithic houses were intentionally destroyed by residents of the village itself for social reasons. In the Balkans (Stevanovic 1997; Tringham et al. 1992), house burning has been interpreted as closure following the ending of a household, perhaps for the death of its head or members. Similarly, Brück (1999) has argued that houses in Bronze Age Britain were intentionally destroyed to mark the end of the lifespan of the group occupying them, and Bradley (1998) has argued that LBK longhouses were probably abandoned after one or two decades, well before the end of their useful life. For Neolithic Italy, thus, archaeological evidence suggests that there was considerable cultural emphasis on the household as a bounded, defined unit of society. The house, the largest single investment of labor and a fixed backdrop for many social dramas, was instrumental in defining the membership of this group, in providing it with common rights and sensory experience. In this context, and with such broad parallels elsewhere in Neolithic Europe, it makes sense to envision the destruction of the house as an act of closure marking the death or dissolution of the social group it defined and symbolised.

From Houses to Villages: Settlement Size and Boundedness

Outside of the house, it was an active world: people were knapping stone tools, firing pottery in fires and kilns, cooking, tending and butchering animals, processing skins, and so on, not to mention just sitting and talking. Features on many sites speak of a common and active life in the open: hearths, kilns, pits, prepared work surfaces, and generally dense distributions of debris such as animal bone and stone flakes. Space outside the house was architecturally unchanneled; the pattern of movement, of sight and vision and of interaction, would have been flexible and polycentric.

The number of households that made up a settlement varied. At the lower end of the spectrum are sites such as Penitenzeria, where the physical limits of the site precluded the presence of more than a handful of houses at the most. It is always difficult to judge the absence of structures, but excavations at Casale del Dolce during construction of the Rome–Naples high-speed train line uncovered 60 percent of the site and found two well-preserved houses, which does not suggest dense settlement (Bistolfi and Muntoni 1997; Manfredini and Muntoni 2003; Zarattini and Petrassi 1997). At the upper end are sites such as Passo di Corvo with several dozen house compounds visible on aerial photographs (Tinè 1983), Acconia (Ammerman 1985), with forty-four daub structures located, and Ripoli (Cremonesi 1965). However, these large settlements should be regarded with caution. The archaeological record collapses the site history, and it is unknown how many structures were actually in use at any given time. Although it is common to find

14. Ditch section, Ripa Tetta, a small Early Neolithic village on the Tavoliere (Puglia). Approximate width of ditch is two meters (photo: Robb, used courtesy of C. Tozzi).

villages of several hundred meters diameter in Puglia, Basilicata, and Sicily, much of the space inside of the village actually appears not to have been used for houses. As a generalization, we can perhaps imagine most Neolithic Italians as living in communities of somewhere between one or two and ten huts, with a commensurate population of less than a hundred.

Modes of settlement varied within Neolithic Italy according to how nucleated and bounded "sites" were. In much of Italy and Sicily, people appear to have lived in small clusters of houses, or in neighborhoods of dispersed houses [a pattern first defined in southern Calabria (Ammerman 1985)]. All along the Adriatic lowlands, however, larger villages are found, with more numerous houses, a mode of settlement also known around Matera in lowland Basilicata and south-eastern Sicily. Throughout this range, ditched villages are known, and they were especially common in the Tavoliere of northern Puglia and around Matera (Figure 14). In many Tavoliere villages, the architectural division of space was carried still further with smaller "c-ditches" bounding individual house compounds within the village (Figure 15) (Kem Jones 1987; Tinè 1983).

15. Ditched village layouts. (a) Posta Villano, Tavoliere (Jones 1987); (b) Masseria Acquasalsa, Tavoliere (Jones 1987); (c) Passo di Corvo, Tavoliere (Jones 1987); (d) Murgia Timone, Matera (Ridola 1926). Note the c-ditches in the Tavoliere examples and two entrances at Murgia Timone.

THE INHABITED WORLD

c

d

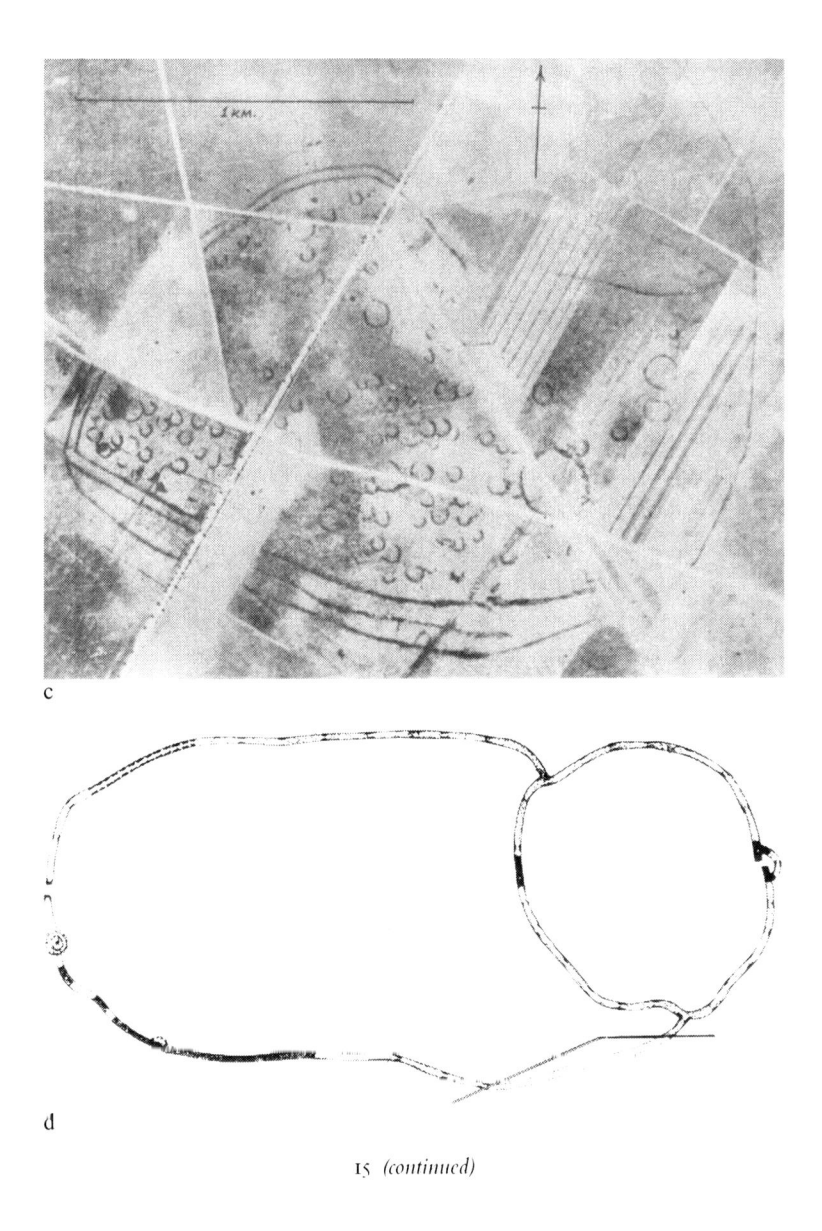

15 *(continued)*

The purpose of village ditches is widely debated (Brown 1991; Skeates 2002). Where they are present, ditches are typically 2–3 m deep and 2–3 m wide, with a curving, level bottom (Figure 14). Various authorities have interpreted their purpose as defense of the village, containing its herds (Jones 1987), collecting water (Gravina 1975), drainage in times of heavy rain (Tinè 1983), and to provide symbolic boundaries for the community (Skeates 2002). They were used as mortuary structures (see section on burials later in this chapter). All interpretations have some difficulty, and the ditches may have been multifunctional too. However, there are several salient points to note here. First, ditches often enclose a relatively large area given the number of houses evident within them, which makes little sense for practical drainage. Second, they are sometimes multiple and/or interrupted (perhaps for access), and some have defensible entryways, which suggests defense or herd containment. A defense interpretation would also agree with mounting evidence for violence and warfare in Neolithic Italy (see Chapters 2 and 7). Finally, posing symbolic boundedness as an alternative to other interpretations is a relict of an unhelpful theoretical opposition between the "practical" and the "symbolic." Practical action originates in cultural logic and reproduces it (see Chapter 1 in this book). If Neolithic Italians felt the need to dig a ditch, they did so through their perception of their social world, their sense of how they related to other people, and the dangers and risks of their landscape. Like a house wall, a defensive barrier partitions continuous space into categorical zones. It effectively creates and fixes an enduring definition of "us" and "them," of inside and outside. It is in this sense that Skeates (2002) perceptively sees village ditches as liminal structures, and in which we should interpret the recurrent deposition of the dead in village ditches (see below). Once created, a ditch would have been a major structuring feature in the perception of the landscape around the village and an agent channeling interaction between and within groups. Moreover, the collective and cooperative labor involved in creating a ditch would have been substantial (Brown 1991). Brown estimates that a c-ditch around a house compound would have needed about 714 construction-hours, or about eighty to ninety person-days. The ditch enclosing a small ditched village would have taken in the range of 3,500–6,000 construction-hours, or perhaps between 500 and 1,000 person-days of work: this might mean full-time ditch-digging for the entire residential community for about a month, whether undertaken all at once or intermittently. If neighboring communities came together to help, it may have taken less time. In either case, creating a ditched village would have been a substantial collective undertaking, an act of commitment to a group and of belonging to a place

Ditches thus were a means of creating spatial boundedness, a symbol of a strongly expressed, oppositional collective identity. The replication of this structure within the settlement with Tavoliere c-ditches seems to express a further segmentation within the group paralleling that between groups and, again, emphasizing the distinctiveness of the household as a modular unit of society.

Houses, Sites, and the Dead

In Chapter 2, it was argued that the simple, on-site burials typical of Neolithic Italy can be understood by considering the role of burial in constructing group memory. Here it is simply worth mentioning several ways in which human bodies were deployed spatially to create this signification.

HEADS IN HOUSES: As noted in Chapter 2, several burials are known in which bodies were either buried headless or had skulls removed some time later, and the skull, and generally the head, was a focus of elaboration in burials, in trepanned individuals, and in figurines depicting unusual, perhaps supernatural personages. Three sites are known where skulls were kept around the village. At Balsignano (Radina 2003) the skull of an adult male was deposited just outside a house before it was constructed. At Marcianese (Geniola 1992), the skull of an adult female was deposited beneath a house, apparently before the house was built, perhaps as a foundation deposit. Neither of these apparently included the mandible or cervical vertebrae, suggesting that disarticulated skulls rather than complete heads were deposited. At Masseria Candelaro (Cassano and Manfredini 1990), a cache of eight skulls is reported from within a village. These skulls may be either trophies or ancestral relics. There has been no detailed contextual and taphonomic analysis of how "sporadic bone" was used in villages, and hence it is unknown whether this reflects general usages. But these examples at least demonstrate that human bone, an important substance, may have been used to empower houses and sites.

BURIAL AT THE BOUNDARIES?: If the house and the settlement were important in how people thought of their own identity, burial gave them time depth and endowed people and places a single, unified history. Burying people around the village both merged their personal history with the longer-term history of the group and endowed the place with a sense of ancestry. The location of burial implies a willingness to have the dead present in the village rather than distanced from life. In this context, one function of village ditches may to serve as repositories of bone and bodies. Although this has never been entertained within Italian archaeology, the use of ditches as places for mortuary processing is familiar from British causewayed enclosures such as Windmill Hill and from LBK sites such as Herxheim.

In the Tavoliere ditched villages, the majority of human bone is found in village or house compound ditches (Robb 1994). Human bone is also known from village ditches in Sicily (Stentinello, Megara Hyblaea) and around Matera and Central Bari (Casa San Paolo, Murgecchia, and Murgia Timone). To some extent, this is not surprising, considering that on many Tavoliere sites the ditch has been the principal focus of excavation. Yet, enough nonditch areas have been excavated at sites such as the Candelaro group, Passo di Corvo and elsewhere to suggest that this is not the only reason why burials are found in ditches. As I have argued, ditches were artificially constructed lines dividing different categories of space, an inside from an outside, a community from its social and cosmological environment. Ditches, as liminal places and as collective undertakings, may have been considered appropriate for burial depositions (Skeates 2002), and ancestral presence, if a positive force, may have been interposed between the community and the external world.

VILLAGES AS ANCESTRAL PLACES: Burial was the linkage between place and history, and both were important for the identity of the group. This is the key to the striking pattern of Late Neolithic burials at Middle Neolithic villages. At more than a dozen sites in the Italian peninsula and Sicily, burials apparently dating to the later phases of the Neolithic have been found at habitation sites from the Early and Middle Neolithic (Table 7). Strikingly, the sites represent all areas of Southern Italy and crosscut cultural groups.

Table 7. *Middle–Late Neolithic Burials Excavated in Previously Occupied Neolithic Habitation Sites*

Sicilia	Piano Vento	Initial Copper Age Cemetery on Stentinello Village
Sicilia	Matrensa	Diana cist tomb in Stentinello village
Sicilia	Megara Hyblaea	Diana cist tomb near Stentinello village
Sicilia	Vulpiglia	Serra d'Alto burials in Stentinello village
Calabria	Corazzo di Soverito	Diana burials overlying Stentinello habitation
Basilicata	Murgecchia	Diana–Bellavista burial in painted-ware village
Basilicata	San Martino	Diana tomb on Serra d'Alto village
Basilicata	Serra d'Alto C	Possible Serra d'Alto/ Diana tomb in Serra d'Alto village
Basilicata	Tirlecchia	Two probable Late Neolithic tombs on Serra d'Alto village
Basilicata	Trasano	Serra d'Alto burials in Matera Scratched Ware village
Puglia	Cala Tramontana	Diana cemetery near red-painted ware village
Puglia	Fontanarosa Uliveto	Diana tomb resting on top of filled-in ditch
Puglia	Malerba	Serra d'Alto pozzetto tombs in earlier ditched village
Puglia	Masseria Candelaro	Serra d'Alto burials in red-painted ware village, from time when ditch was open
Puglia	Serra Cicora	Serra d'Alto burials in Impressed Ware village
Abruzzo	Villa Badessa	Ripoli burials in Middle Neolithic village

Source: Ingravallo 2001; Robb 2001.

What caused this pattern? There are several possibilities. A few superpositions of later burials and earlier villages may be coincidental, but surely not this many. As another null hypothesis, one might argue that we find Late Neolithic burials at Middle Neolithic villages simply because these villages have been the subject of considerable archaeological attention. However, if this were the case, we should also expect to find burials, or occupations, of other periods, including earlier ones, on them. In fact, Late Neolithic burials outnumber remains of other periods on Middle Neolithic sites, suggesting a genuine link between the two. As a third hypothesis, the pottery sequence for Neolithic Southern Italy is quite indeterminate in places. For example, it is clear that Diana wares follow Stentinello wares in Southern Calabria and Sicily, but in spite of many sites excavated, we still lack absolutely-dated contexts. Hence, it is not clear whether this was an abrupt replacement or whether there was a long period of overlap when both were in use. The same is true for the succession of bichrome, trichrome, Serra d'Alto and Diana wares in Northern Calabria and northwards. It is theoretically possible, thus, that the burials are contemporary with the village but, as ceremonial contexts, include "Late Neolithic" finewares (Malone 1985) while "Middle Neolithic" wares were still in use in other contexts on the site. However, in several cases the stratigraphy of the site suggests that burials post-date habitation. This is so at Fontanarosa Uliveto and at Serra d'Alto Village C where they overlie filled-in ditches, and at Corazzo di Soverito where Diana burials are stratigraphically higher than the Stentinello occupation. Absolute dates for both burial and habitation contexts are available only for one site, Serra Cicora (Ingravallo 2001). At this site, the Serra d'Alto burials were dated radiometrically to between 5000 and 4500 BC, while the habitation and several burials associated with it were dated to 5600–5200 BC. The implication (Ingravallo 2001; Robb 2001) is that the association of place, group history, and burials was strong enough that, when settlement patterns changed and extramural cemeteries became normal, abandoned villages were regarded as ancestral places, and people sometimes returned to abandoned villages for up to 500 years to bury their dead.

The Microgeography of Dwelling

Economy and Frequentation

People's use of land extends beyond sites, of course. All activities have spatial extension. As Pred (1990) has argued eloquently, drawing both on Hagerstrand's (1977) time–space geography and Giddens' (1984) structuration theory, space, and time are meaningfully constituted through patterns of activity, and these meanings can be approached by tracing out patterns of movement throughout daily activity.

For the Italian Neolithic, "economic" activities offer the best starting point for land use. As we will discuss in Chapter 4, Neolithic foodways were based principally upon domesticated crops and animals, with additional food from gathered plants and hunted game. In a GIS analysis, Robb and Van Hove (2003) reconstructed land use for a hypothetical village of fifty people subsisting upon a variety of economies. Basic

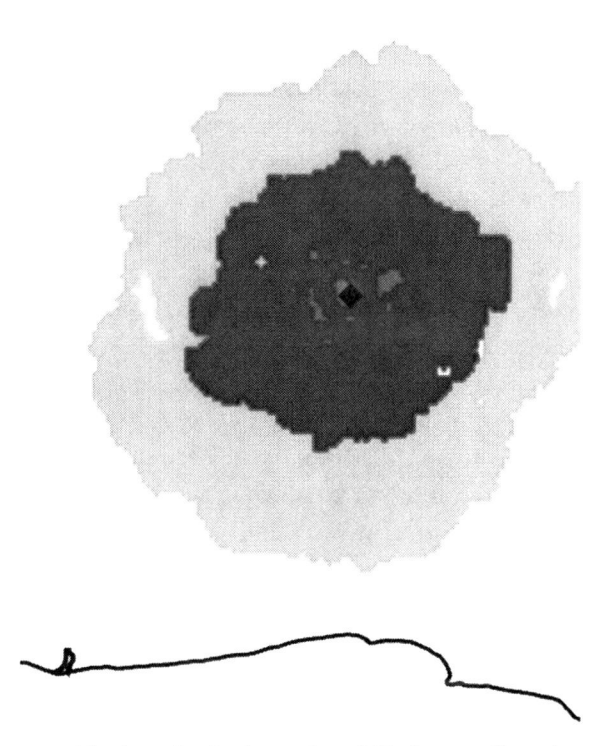

16. Reconstructed land use for Penitenzeria and Umbro; small patches near center represent gardens, intermediate circle represents pastures, outermost circle represents gathered and hunted resources. Land area shown is approximately 8 km n-s (Robb and Van Hove 2003).

parameters of crop yield, herd productivity, game and wild-plant abundance, and nutritional needs per person were taken from Gregg's (1988) reconstruction of LBK economy. We then calculated how much land our model village group would need for different economic uses and used a GIS reconstruction of the topographical and geological landscape surrounding our excavated sites in Bova Marina, Calabria to hypothesise where each activity would have taken place. Figure 16 shows one reconstruction, for a group of fifty people who drew 62 percent of their sustenance from grain and pulses, 23 percent from herds, 3 percent from gathered plants, and 12 percent from game. These results are typical of all but the most specialised economies modeled.

Using such reconstructions, a Neolithic site of fifty people with a mixed, mostly agricultural economy would have needed between 10 and

20 km² of land (Figure 16; Table 8). Surprisingly, even with economies in which the vast majority of calories came from cultivated crops, the limiting factor on Neolithic settlement was not farmland. Because grains and legumes yield much more food per hectare than either herds or wild resources, gardens were much smaller than pastures and foraging areas. Small gardens were scattered on relatively level patches of land surrounding the site. A much larger zone around this was used for less intensive use – pasturage for herds and hunting and gathering. Such extensively rather than intensively used land would have been important for many dispersed or patchy resources – game, nuts, greens, honey, salt, stone, glues and mastics (Campetti, Giachi, and Perrini 2003), and other minerals, and so on. Moreover, space between villages may have been an important social resource, allowing an alternative economy in case of crop failure, areas of privacy and seclusion, and neutral areas for negotiating with other groups. Such villages would have required at least 3–5 km between them to allow for each village's territory, and an intermarrying, stable demographic community would have utilised a minimum of between 80 and 200 km². This is a minimum area based on a static snapshot of the economy; the area used cumulatively over long periods would have been larger (Figure 18).

Economic land uses imply categorization of landscapes and habitual frequentation, both elements in the understanding and experience of space. Production is socially reproductive; work takes place in spaces appropriate for it, and the experience of those spaces helps define work and workers. Here, for example, settlements and gardens are focused spaces people would have known intimately. They were defined by architecture (for gardens, probably fences to protect crops from free-ranging pigs), and people would have spent much time in them, engaging in varied activities, talking and gossiping, and generally being together. They represent small, cleared islands of sociality linked by paths through brush, forests, and rough terrain. Pastures and foraging groups represented dispersed, fragmented activities and isolated groups or individuals. Paths, landmarks such as peaks on the horizon, cliffs, and springs would have been important, especially in a dissected, rugged landscape. In contrast to the familiar and sociable settlements and gardens, such outlying areas were constantly changing, and information

Table 8. Land Use Needs and Possible Population Levels with Selected Neolithic Economies

	Pure Hunter-Gatherer	Pure Herder	Pure Farmer	Equally Mixed	Mixed Forager Farmer	Mixed Farmer-Herder	Intensified Herder	Mostly Farmer
% reliance on crops	0	0	100	33.5	40	48	28	65
% reliance on herds	0	100	0	33.5	10	48	68	25
% reliance on gathered plants	50	0	0	16.5	25	3	3	5
% reliance on hunted game	50	0	0	16.5	25	1	1	5
Total land needs for group of 50 people (km^2)	62.32	21.3	0.41	21.23	32.16	10.22	14.48	6.43
Ideal site spacing for groups of 50 people	9.05	5.21	0.72	5.2	6.4	3.61	4.29	2.86
Maximum possible population density (people/km^2)	0.78	2.35	121.95	2.36	1.55	4.89	3.45	7.77
Maximum possible population Lipari (38 km^2)	30	89	4,634	90	59	186	131	295
Maximum possible population Bova study area (132 km^2)	103	310	16,098	311	205	646	456	1,026
Maximum possible population Malta and Gozo (316 km^2)	246	742	38,537	744	491	1,545	1,091	2,456
Maximum possible population Tavoliere (4500 km^2)	3,498	10,563	548,780	10,600	6,996	22,007	15,534	34,981
Maximum possible population Italy (301225 km^2)	234,161	707,101	36,734,756	709,579	468,322	1,473,127	1,039,854	2,341,612

Note: Estimates consider caloric needs of subsistence only, and treat all land as inhabitable; they should be treated as maxima rather than realistic estimates. Archaeological evidence suggests that typical Neolithic economy is "mostly farmer."

Source: Robb and Van Hove 2003.

gained while moving through them would have been valuable. They held unusual resources, and they required particular knowledge and experience to negotiate (for instance, to find a stone source, to locate game or useful plants at a particular time of year, or to track the movements of strangers) (Figure 17a).

These areas would have had associations with identities. On a personal level, in many tribal societies, for example, individuals gain rights to particular ground by investing labor in it: owned gardens are created by taking collective land and clearing, fencing and planting it. On a larger scale, exploitation territories (Figure 23) would have been regarded as generally belonging to the settlement they surround, even if access was not formally regulated or policed, and interstitial zones may have been considered usable by a number of neighboring communities. Interestingly, in a wooded landscape in which cliffs, hills, and deep valleys provide open vistas, many of the other known Neolithic sites in the Bova Marina landscape are all intervisible. Looking out from the environs of a village, one would have gazed over a variegated social landscape, including the gardens and closer pastures and foraging grounds of one's own village, lands used analogous ways by other settlements and ambiguous, less defined territories in between (Figure 17b).

When we view accumulated land use over a generation, it is interesting that while Penitenzeria's garden areas remain within about a kilometer's radius of the site, the areas cumulatively foraged, hunted and herded upon overlap with the actual habitation and gardening zones of at least six other known Neolithic open-air sites. Because the converse would also have been true, this reinforces that interstitial areas would have had rights of access associated with a collective regional identity (see below) rather than narrowly with specific villages.

The Perception of Time in the Landscape

People moving around in the landscape saw it embedded in time, both rooted in the past and extending into the future with projects yet to finish or to begin. The future-oriented landscape consists of visible prompts for plans and projects, resources potentially usable, and signs of things which could occur: the roof needing patching, the growing crops

a

High mountains beyond crest of plateau 6 km

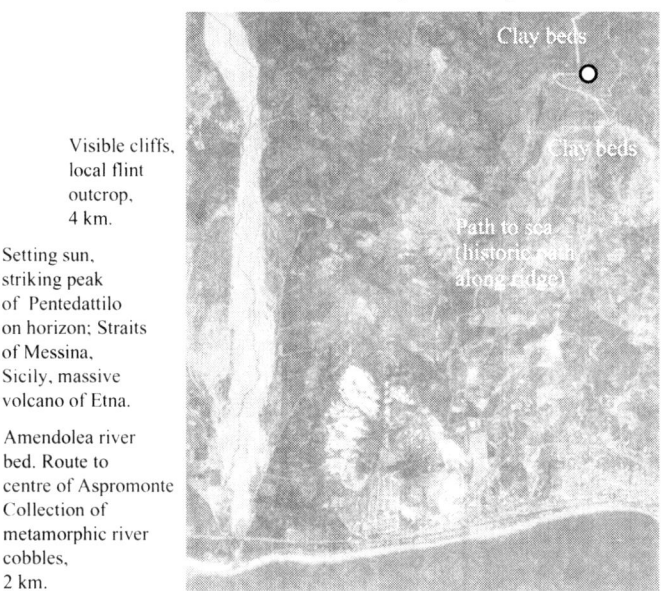

Clay beds

Clay beds

Path to sea (historic path along ridge)

Visible cliffs, local flint outcrop, 4 km.

Setting sun, striking peak of Pentedattilo on horizon; Straits of Messina, Sicily, massive volcano of Etna.

Amendolea river bed. Route to centre of Aspromonte Collection of metamorphic river cobbles, 2 km.

Bova Superiore landmark peak, village, 4 km.

Cliffs, perennial springs, cobbles in conglomerate formation.

Rising sun Landmark peak of Grappidà.

Metamorphic stone, Sandstone, ochre.

San Pasquale village, 5 km.

Sea (shell, obsidian, travelers). Visible from most places 4 km

b

approximate limit of herding/ foraging zone

approximate size and location of gardens

17. The social landscape around Penitenzeria. (a) Possible paths, resources, and landmarks; (b) View southeast from Penitenzeria, showing general size and possible location of gardens and limit of territory exploited for gardening, pasture, and foraging.

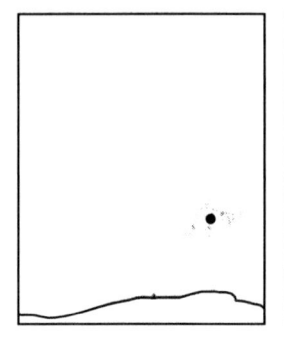

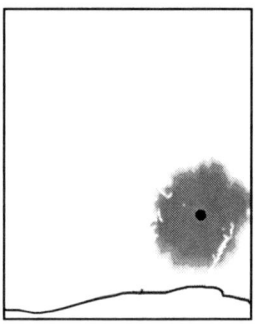

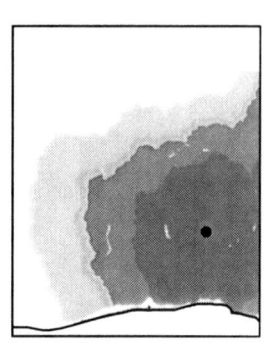

18. Accumulated frequentation areas over 30 years around the site of Penitenzeria, Bova Marina, Calabria, according to GIS reconstruction of land use. Darkness indicates intensity of accumulated use of an area. Left: gardens; center: pastures; right: hunting and gathering (Van Hove 2003, courtesy of D. Van Hove).

to be harvested in a few months if the weather holds, and the hills on the horizon which must be watched for rain clouds, raiders or returning travelers. Except for fossilised interruptions such as the cached axes at Capo Alfiere never re-launched into circulation or the unground grain on the quern in the burnt hut at Serra del Palco, the archaeology of past futures is elusive.

It is easier to identify how the Neolithic landscape embodied history. Figure 18 (Van Hove 2003) shows how human use of their territory would have accumulated as time passed. If we run the static model of land use shown in Figure 16 over a period of time (here, 30 years), we can see that while some areas directly around the site accumulate much more human experience, a much larger area is known and used in shifting patterns. Moreover, this usage remained not exclusively in ephemeral traces – smoke from fires, noises of work or play – nor solely in memories. Rather, it was evident in the physical landscape as well, a present material reality which was inseparable from a specific history and which precluded other histories and presents (Berger and Luckmann 1967; Chapter 1 in this book). Of the accumulated garden patches, some would have been actively planted, while others would have been abandoned clearings in various stages of brushy regeneration. Pollen in the daub from houses at Torre Sabea showed a quite diverse mixture of environments, including fields, salt and freshwater marshes, mature oak woodlands, and scrubby open areas which were

19. Midden, Penitenzeria, Bova Marina, Calabria. Darker, compacter, rockier stratum in lower part of trench is dense, rocky midden deposition from occupation several centuries long. Approximate depth of trench 1.5 m (photo: Robb).

presumably fallow or abandoned fields (Costantini, Biasini, and Lentini 2003). Pastures would show signs of browsing and regeneration, woods of woodcutting and perhaps coppicing or other forms of woodland management (Castelletti et al. 1998). Such material traces provided orientational clues and reinforced the constant presence of known people acting in known ways.

Even the site itself provided an orientational framework. Rubbish is inescapable on Neolithic sites – indeed, it virtually defines them. At Penitenzeria, the site includes a dense, localised midden area of dark, rocky soil full of pottery, stone tools, and other remains (Figure 19). This midden was built up through very rapid deposition, with up to a meter deposited in less than 500 years. Garbage is not meaningless by any means, as our own highly formalised, ritualised garbageways demonstrate. For Neolithic Italy, we do not necessarily need to postulate a spiritual respect for refuse [as in Pueblo Indians' use of discarded ancestral objects as *pahos* or material prayers, (Ortiz 1969)], nor to draw the parallels between the disposal of things and the disposal of bodies in order to understand deposition as a cultural act. Even at the most minimal level, thrown away objects did not permanently vanish, as we prefer our refuse to; rather, they were temporarily released from social relations. People reused discarded items: to take two examples from Umbro, broken sherds served as abraders, and animal bones were made into awls. Given the intensive use of stone tools, which meant that many were used as tiny expedient flakes and cores were completely exhausted (Farr 2001; Chapter 5 in this book), and the casual way in which still usable stone tools were discarded, it seems likely that the midden also served as a reservoir for stone tools, much as among the Wola (Hardy and Sillitoe 2003). Finally, given the general conservatism of most Neolithic pottery styles at timescales far surpassing the human generation (see Chapter 5), it seems likely that the midden served as a long-term library to prompt memory of how to do things such as decorate pottery, much as archaeological sherds have inspired recent Pueblo potters.

But even without these active interactions with the "discarded" past, rubbish presences history (Hodder and Cessford 2004; Lindenlauf 2004; Russell and Martin 2000). There is no reason to suppose that Neolithic people were less observant of material deposition than archaeologists are, and in a world less strewn with garbage than our own such remains would have marked space humans have lived in even more saliently. Approaching a Neolithic village without passing through the accustomed setting of half-regenerated gardens, worn dirt pathways, increasing clearings, smoke from fires, noise from people and animals, and the scatter of discarded broken things and organic debris would have been as artificial and disorienting as a highway with no signs, a university corridor with no notices on the walls, or a train station with no litter, dirt, crowds, or graffiti – like a movie set, complete but sans people, sans history, and sans the unquestionable sense of reality we normally experience in traversing the material world.

As each material trace was the result of a human project or story, the result was a landscape merging temporality and spatiality in activity, a taskscape ["the entire ensemble of tasks, in their mutual interlocking," which "is to labor what the landscape is to land" (Ingold 2000, p. 195)]. However, taskscapes are not objective and impersonal. They are contingent upon invisible knowledge and upon a sense of history. We would expect them to be gendered and aged, as well as stamped with the particular visions and knowledges deriving from different forms of empowerment. Moreover, shared taskscapes are central to the constitution of a community based on local knowledge. This is obvious: where a stranger sees an abandoned garden, a resident sees a garden abandoned when Uncle Joe died 5 years ago and Aunt Sally remarried and moved to the next village. The gulf here is not between archaeologists and generic Neolithic Italians, but between people who have inhabited a particular place and all other people. The latter may read the history of places from material signs to constitute a known place. To the former, the landscape is made up of names and stories which other coresidents, and only them, can be counted upon to also know. Such local knowledge is a component of identity, a collective stock of stories about why the material world is configured as it is which helps constitute a community and distinguish its members as people with a unique understanding of the material world.

Macrogeography: Cultural Landscapes, Regional Identities, and Translocal Action

Sites and their catchments – whether economic, phenomenological, or historical – were set into larger worlds. These encompassing geographies were physical, social, and cosmological.

Cult Sites, Cosmology, and Gender

A number of cult sites relieve the relentlessly habitational landscape of the Italian Neolithic. These have been summarised perceptively by Whitehouse (1992) and can be reviewed briefly here.

Cave sites fall naturally into two groups. The great majority of them involve habitation, short-term visits, or burial. The archaeological remains are found relatively close to the cave mouth, in an area sheltered but still somewhat lit, open, and accessible. Such caves were often occupied for millennia; for example, the spacious Grotta della Madonna at Praia a Mare, Calabria, provided shelter continuously from the Upper Palaeolithic to modern times (Cardini 1970). Human use of them for both shelter and burial often has much in common with use of open air sites. In contrast, about a dozen sites throughout the Italian peninsula and Sicily are found in much deeper, more involuted caves. These caves, typically formed by dissolution of limestone, afford multiple or twisting galleries, often extremely difficult to penetrate, and in several well-known cases sealed by collapse, until reopened in the twentieth century.

The two most famous Neolithic cult sites are the Grotta Scaloria outside Manfredonia in northern Puglia (Quagliati 1936, Tinè and Isetti 1980) and the Grotta di Porto Badisco at the very southernmost tip of Puglia (Graziosi 1980; Whitehouse 1992). Scaloria, sealed during the Copper Age by a rock fall, was rediscovered during aqueduct construction in the 1930s. It typifies both types of cave sites. The relatively accessible Upper Cave provided shelter from the late Upper Palaeolithic through the Neolithic and housed an extensive Neolithic cemetery, dated to the sixth millennium BC (Winn and Shimabuku 1988). The deep and inaccessible Lower Cave was a cult site, dated to the fifth millennium BC (Tinè and Isetti 1980). Although some human remains were found there, the principal aspects of the Lower Cave cult seem to have been the placement of fine painted vessels to catch water dripping from stalactites; some vessels left in place were found cemented into stalagmitic formations (Figure 20).

Porto Badisco is a rock art site. Its date is not entirely certain, as the cave was used from the Palaeolithic through the Copper Age, the excavations of the site have been only partially published, and rock art is notoriously hard to date directly at the best of times. The art has sometimes been attributed to the fifth millennium Serra d'Alto culture, mostly on supposed parallels between abstract motifs and Serra d'Alto pottery motifs, and Whitehouse argues that the paintings were made through much of the Neolithic. Although this may be the case, it is also true that the site has yielded principally pottery in a style transitional between the Final Neolithic and Copper Age. This suggests that the most intense

20. Grotta Scaloria, Manfredonia, Puglia: cult site in lower cave, with fine vessels placed to catch dripping water (Tinè and Isetti 1980, courtesy of S. Tinè).

period of activity at the site was around the end of the Neolithic. In three low, tortuous galleries, hundreds of images were painted using subfossilised bat guano. Most are "nonrepresentational" geometric signs. Among the "representational" signs, some represent males hunting deer with bows (Figure 53c) and women standing in a characteristic posture. In one remote chamber, several dozen child-sized handprints are stamped on the low ceiling. Whitehouse (1992) has demonstrated that clearly representational rock art becomes less common as one penetrates the cave, and that the female figures are found mostly near the entrances. In combination with the juvenile handprints, she interprets the cave as a place where young males were initiated into cults of secret knowledge giving males ritual power.

Beyond Scaloria and Porto Badisco, the Neolithic cult landscape encompasses a few other rock art sites, less florid and poorly dated [e.g., Tuppo dei Sassi (Biancofiore 1965)], a number of caves with odd patterns of burial (e.g., Grotta del Leone, Grotta dei Piccioni, Grotta Patrizi, Grotta Continenza, Grotta delle Felci), which are discussed above, and a few others such as the Pozzi del Piano, which resembles Scaloria in its cult of underground waters (Whitehouse 1992). Perhaps the most remarkable is the unique Ipogeo Manfredi at Santa Barbara (Polignano a Mare, Puglia); (Geniola 1987). Here two fair-sized underground chambers were carved in the limestone, with an entrance ramp for access. At contemporary villages, wild fauna are rare, but here dozens of skulls of deer were piled in these chambers, along with seashells and other fauna (Castelletti, Costantini, and Tozzi 1987; Geniola and Ponzetti 1987). Whitehouse (1992) argues that Neolithic ritual sites provide evidence of cult practices focused upon hidden, secret underground locations, the theme of abnormal water, and hunting. Whether or not one agrees with this bold and stimulating analysis, the recurrent use of deeply buried, inaccessible locations, often with surprising kinds of water, temperature, and humidity, indicates an appreciation of the cosmological potential of natural places as providing a source of difference.

GENDERED SPACES? In *The Domestication of Europe* Hodder (1990) proposed a genderisation of space within a generalised Neolithic European habitus; areas around households formed the locus of female-oriented meanings, and the "wild" areas anchored and generated male-oriented meanings. Hodder's scheme has been criticised as totalising and over-determined, much as Bourdieu's work itself has been, but it does serve as a reminder that it is impossible to imagine a world of gender without a spatial dimension.

Throughout the Italian Neolithic, female imagery in figurines tend to be found on habitation sites; interestingly, figurines found in burial and cult sites tend to be much less clearly gendered (Chapter 2 in this book). The other datum for the entire Neolithic is the skeletal evidence of femur shaft dimorphism, which suggests that males walked or ran much more than females. Although this does not in itself tell where mobility actually took place, it seems reasonable to connect it with travel further afield, perhaps for exchange, political interaction or hunting and foraging. Evidence is more abundant for the period around the end of the Neolithic, when the rock art and cave paintings reviewed above associate males with hunting and with weapon use. As an activity, hunting involves extensive frequentation of remote, peripheral areas between settlements and in uninhabited zones (Figure 21).

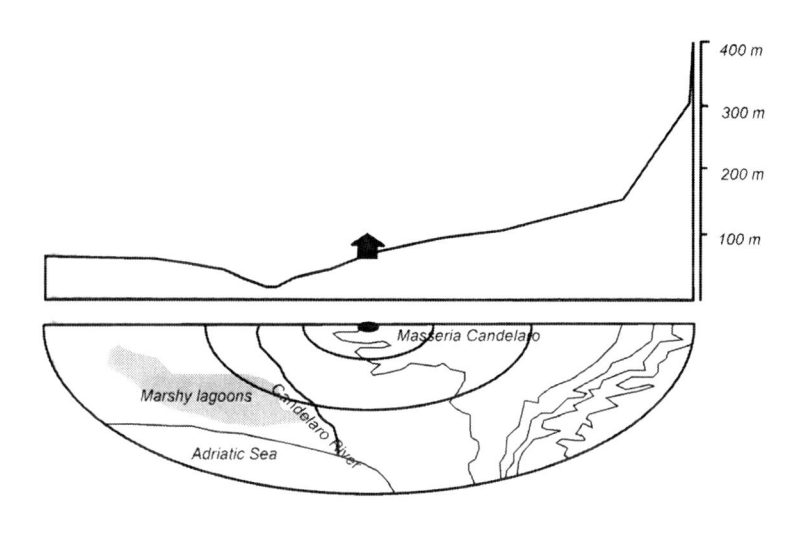

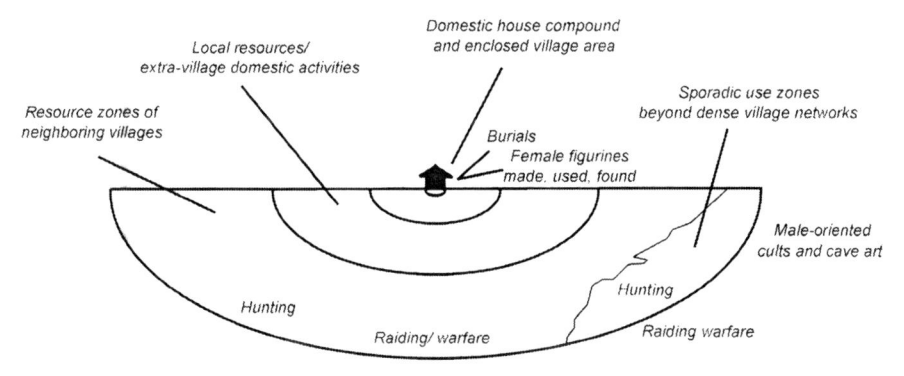

21. Spatiality of gender: Some possible relations (Morter and Robb 1998).

Using the spatial distribution of gendered images, Morter and Robb (1998) argued, tentatively, that space was genderised conceptually, with concentric zones around settlements considered female in some way, while remote, wild or marginal areas were considered male. However, it is important to stress the epistemological underpinnings of this. I do not mean that space was gendered prescriptively, or that these were rigid and uniformly imposed categories. Instead, we wish to draw a link between the lived experience of space as generated in activity (Ingold 2000; Pred 1990). Males and females clearly spent much time together in common contexts; for the experience of gender, spatial contexts when they were apart likely provided diacritical distinctions, and movement through gendered zones may have provided a flexible, context-specific way of generating understandings rather than a rigid and exclusive set of rules.

Natural Places and the Inhabitable World

The "archaeology of natural places" (Bradley 2000) for Neolithic Calabria included other zones both utilised and avoided. Flint from the Monti Iblei near Siracusa, the Gargano peninsula in Puglia, and the Monti Lessini near Verona circulated widely. On the Gargano, the Early Neolithic flint mine of La Defensola is the earliest such mine known in Europe (Di Lernia and Galiberti 1993; Galiberti 1999). Sourcing studies show that particular communities probably visited specific mines; for example the people of Ripa Tetta used flint from mines almost 100 km away on the north side of the Gargano peninsula in preference to some closer to their home (d'Ottavio 2001). Hard metamorphic and igneous stones were collected and perhaps quarried for axes in Northeastern Sicily and Calabria (Leighton 1992), Corsica (Pandolfi and Zamagni 2000) and the Alps. Such stone could have either been quarried or collected as nodules washed down into stream beds. Obsidian was procured on four island sources, on Sardinia and three much smaller islands. Palmarola is close to the Campanian coast, but difficult to access by sea; Lipari lies within sight of Sicily, but Pantelleria lies far south of Sicily.

Most larger inhabitable islands, such as Malta and Gozo, were settled by the sixth and fifth millennia, as were many islands in the Adriatic and in the Tuscan Archipelago (Dawson 2005; Tozzi and Weiss 2000). However, smaller islands in the Adriatic such as Palagruza (Kaiser and Forenbaher 1999) and Tuscan Archipelago were only visited sporadically until the late Neolithic. In spite of the importance of Lipari obsidian, only three islands of the Aeolian archipelago – Lipari, Salina, and Filicudi – were occupied before Late Neolithic Diana times. The Aeolians are small islands with little water and flat land, but Vulcano and Stromboli are as inhabitable as Salina and Filicudi, and there may have been other reasons why they were not settled.

Volcanic places were obviously different and must have posed a challenge to cognition, and they may have been avoided. The island of Vulcano, with a large, bubbling, malodorous sulfurous crater, was never settled in prehistoric times, though Neolithic people frequently sailed close past its shores en route to nearby Lipari. Stromboli, another volcanic island, erupts with plumes of ash regularly many times a day, and the Diana period sites on Stromboli have been interpreted as cult sites (Bernabò Brea and Cavalier 1968). Similarly, there was settlement in the plain of Catania below Etna, but none on Etna itself, a visibly active volcano and a prominent landmark throughout Eastern Sicily and the tip of Calabria. Bubbling hot and cold springs in this area may have attracted Neolithic people to settlements such as San Marco (Maniscalco 1997). Major eruptions took place in Vesuvius in Mesolithic times, and in Copper Age dates, and there may have been activity during the Neolithic as well, to judge from one Campanian site evidencing eruptions between Serra d'Alto and times (Albore Livadie, and Gangemi 1987).

The most surprising road-not-taken leads up into the high mountains. At the present state of research, it appears likely that the high mountains themselves were not occupied for most of the Neolithic, until the Late Neolithic (Diana, late Ripoli and Lagozza periods). The threshold seems to be about 1,000 m. Admittedly, little archaeological research has been carried out in many high mountains, but the argument is not entirely *ex silentio*. In Sicily, survey of the Troina region revealed no Neolithic sites at high altitudes, and even in the steep fastnesses behind Messina, sites such as the Sperlinga di San Basilio still remain below this at around 700 m (Cavalier 1971). Proceeding northwards, in the Aspromonte mountains of Reggio Calabria province, the highest site specifically identifiable as pre-Diana is the Stentinello period occupation at the Castello of Bova Superiore (800 m). Above this, only isolated axe finds and obsidian scatters are known; these may date to anytime in the Neolithic period, and (for the axe finds) indeed up through the earlier Bronze Age, and they need not signify habitation (Robb 2004). In the next massif northwards, the Sila, the first Neolithic occupation above 1000 m seems to have taken place in the Late Neolithic Diana period (Bidditu et al. 2004, Nicoletti 2004). In the Pollino massif on the Calabria–Basilicata border, no highland sites are reported (Bianco and Cipolloni Sampò 1987), and the same is true for Campania (Albore Livadie and Gangemi 1987) where sites in mountainous regions seem to lie along relatively low-lying river valleys. In the well-studied Abruzzo (Radmilli 1997), Neolithic people clearly knew of and used the high mountains; one would need to cross the Apennine watershed to travel from the Adriatic coast to the well-populated Fucino basin (ca. 700 m) – but the only Neolithic sites reported above 1,000 m are the Grotta della Beatrice Cenci at just over 1,000 m and the anomalous and isolated Fonte Chiarano at 1600 m. Further north, in the Apennines between Toscana, Liguria and Reggio Emilia, settlement clustered in piedmonts and valley bottoms, and even mountain sites such as Piano di Cerreto (370 m) (Tozzi and Zamagni 2000) lie in valley bottoms at relatively low altitudes; the high mountains seem to have been abandoned at the end of the Mesolithic (Biagi, Maggi, and Nisbet 1987, Grifoni Cremonesi, Tozzi, and Weiss 2000). Settlement in the high mountains of the Marche seems to have begun in the Late Neolithic (Fugazzola Delpino et al. 2003).

Why avoid the high mountains? One can grow grain above 1,000 m; with traditional farming techniques, historic Calabrian farmers sometimes sowed wheat preferentially above this altitude because it was cooler and wetter. Nor do high-altitude sites lack water, game, or other resources. Neolithic people presumably visited the high mountains at times, if at least some of the sporadic obsidian and stone axe finds date to before the Late Neolithic. However, if this lack of high-altitude sites is not simply a result of lack of research (and this always remains a possibility), it may represent a reaction to a noticeably different kind of setting. The modern concentration of forests and wildlife in high mountains is an artefact of deforestation at lower altitudes, but there are important ecological differences. For instance, in southern Calabria, semitropical and Mediterranean species such as the olive do not grow above about 1,000 m, and there are more Alpine tree and faunal species. There is a sharp and noticeable drop in temperature above this height with much more cloud cover and higher precipitation; when there are clear skies in the lowlands, it is common to see clouds gathering and rain falling up in the high peaks. A few kilometers away and a few hundred meters down, snow rarely falls, but above 1,000 m, it covers the ground for most of the winter. This sense of being in a different world may have been accentuated by accidents of perception. The mountains of Aspromonte, for example, reach almost 2,000 m in their centre, but from outside and below them, one can only see the first ridge at about

22. The shape of land without high mountains: Between sea level and 1,000 m (Calabria, Basilicata, Campania). Highland massifs in western Italy break up territory and channel linkages; Adriatic Italy in contrast presents unbroken expanses.

1,000–1,100 m; the internal world of tumbled, rugged peaks is entirely hidden until one breaches the first crest.

The consequences of shunning high mountains would have been most pronounced in the central Apennines and in the rugged toe of Italy (Calabria, northwestern Basilicata, and southern Campania). In the latter, excluding land above 1,000 m both reduces the habitable area substantially and breaks up its spatial configuration (Figure 22). These effects are even more marked if we also exclude areas of lower height dominated by extremely steep slopes, such as along much of the Tyrrhenian coast of Calabria and Basilicata where mountains fall almost vertically into the sea.

Geography does not dictate social groupings, but it can provide the raw materials for cultural constructions of identity. Cognitively, in such areas, terrain imposes a linearity and set of orientations on visible geography and movement; the basic structure of the land imposes two orthogonal axes of directionality, one coastwise and one extending orthogonally to it from sea to mountains.[2] Socially, rather than the formless space suggested by a map outline, or an unbounded network of communities as in lowland Puglia or Basilicata or the broad Adriatic coastal strip, the inhabitable space in these zones has to be considered as pockets, strips and networks. The plains of Sibari, Crotone, Locri, Gioia Tauro, and Lamezia Terme are like islands linked by narrow coastal strips and river valleys. For other areas of the coastline, such as the south coast of Aspromonte, we have to imagine a narrow grid of communities, three or four settlements deep at most, filling the 5–10 km wide strip between the sea and the high mountains.

People Create Spaces; Spaces Create People

The "sense of place" epitomises the paradoxes this book confronts. On one hand, only the most dedicated solipsist would claim that our act of thinking creates the material world: places, as material configurations, clearly exist outside of the volition of the actor. On the other hand, one person's sacred grove is another person's barbaric wilderness, royal deer park, or future timber revenue: places are defined by the perceptions, activities and institutions of the people inhabiting them as much as they are defined simply by material arrangements. Agency exists in this tension between people and places. The human landscape is created by people acting for proximate goals such as building themselves a house, collecting food, consecrating a place of worship, or doing the right thing with the remains of dead kinfolk. Yet in the instant in which spaces are created by people acting, they also exert power over people. One spatial power is simply the force of existing in the form in which people understand them, an invisible presence which asserts the reality not only of a particular present but also of a past and future as well. Places, as structuring contexts, constitute the agent's ability to act. The

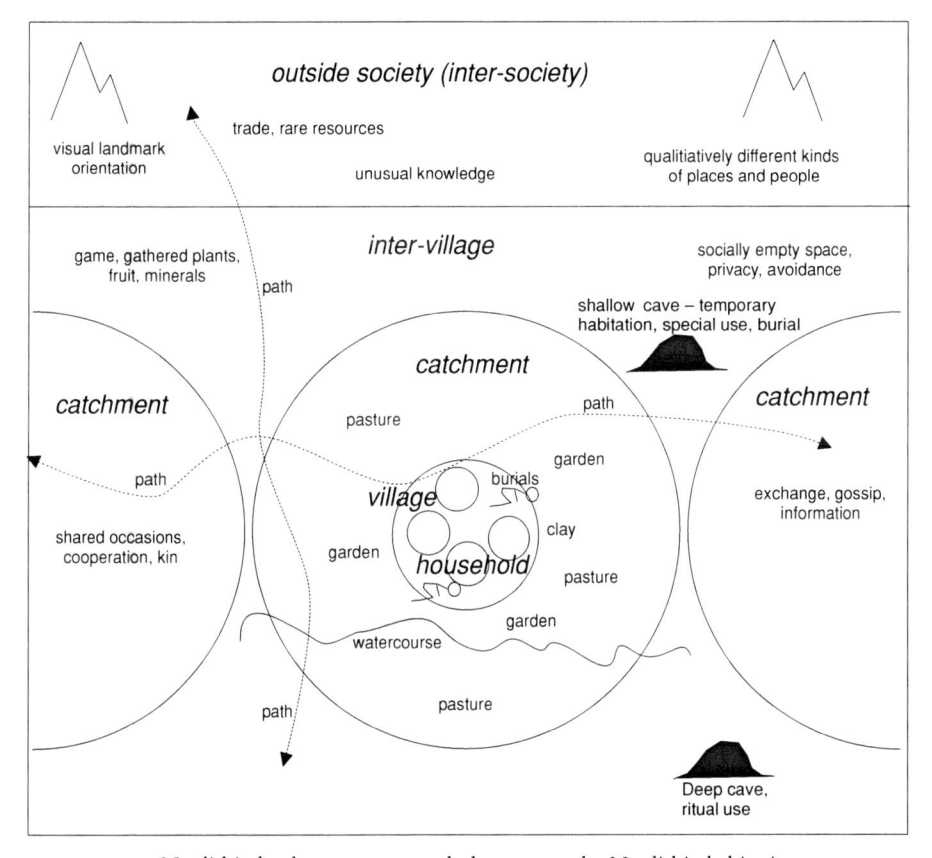

23. Neolithic landscape: zones and places around a Neolithic habitation.

classroom, and the social relations which create it, create teachers and students; villages create villagers, and ancestors present in space and memory create descendents.

In this chapter, we have examined the Neolithic landscape piece by piece. Moving concentrically outwards from the house are (Figure 23).

1. The household, architecturally omnipresent as a basal element of Neolithic society and a collectivity encompassing the complementary capabilities of a minimum set of Neolithic agents sufficient for daily tasks.
2. The village or neighborhood – a web of closely cooperating households which in some areas was concentrated in nucleated

village, in other areas was made up of dispersed households. It would have been distanced from other dwellings by an area of land used for gardens, pastures, foraging and other uses, and the daily frequentation of this zone made up a large part of the Neolithic taskscape.
3. Social space: known areas understood as occupied by people sharing some common way of life and general identity, and encompassing also interstitial zones not closely controlled by any residential group.
4. Areas of social difference, occupied by other peoples: places of trade, warfare, and exploration.
5. Qualitatively different areas, uninhabitable and uninhabited and used only rarely for specific purposes, and likely the focus of cosmological beliefs: the high mountains, volcanos, and the sea.

Synoptic systemizations give the impression of a rigid and prescriptive system, but nothing could be further from the truth: Neolithic spatialities emerged from patterns of movement and action. People occupy unique times and places to the exclusion of others, and difference in location generates different experiences and senses of worldness (Pred 1990). This is most evident in two linkages which have emphasised in this chapter. The first is the bond between landscape and history, forged both by burial practices and time-enduring settings such as villages and by the signs of temporality in the landscape, such that viewing a landscape correctly was akin to reconstructing a history and anticipating its future. The second is the bond between landscape and identity, a community (Canuto and Yaeger 2000) mediated by shared spatial frames of reference, copresence and cooperation, and knowledge of localities. The landscape, thus, embodied a sense of situatedness such that the history of the place was equivalent to the history of the people and the present landscape represented this past and ongoing identity.

FOUR:
DAILY ECONOMY AND SOCIAL REPRODUCTION

"No," he said, "look, it's very, very simple... all I want... is a cup of tea. You are going to make one for me. Keep quiet and listen."

And he sat. He told the Nutri-Matic about India, he told it about China, he told it about Ceylon. He told it about broad leaves drying in the sun. He told it about silver teapots. He told it about summer afternoons on the lawn. He told it about putting in the milk before the tea so it wouldn't get scalded. He even told it (briefly) about the history of the East India Company.

"So that's it, is it?" said the Nutri-Matic when had finished.

"Yes," said Arthur, "that is what I want."

"You want the taste of dried leaves boiled in water?"

"Er, yes. With milk."

"Squirted out of a cow?"

"Well, in a manner of speaking I suppose..."

"I'm going to need some help with this one," said the machine tersely.

Douglas Adams, *The Restaurant at the End of the Universe*. (Adams 1986, p. 161)

The Archaeology of Foodways: From Calories to Cuisine

Social life is generated by the operation of entwined institutions, each of which combines a specific field of economic or practical activity, a set of beliefs and social relations, human experience, and an encounter with material things which provide resistance and form to our agency. Among such institutions, food is one of the most central. In this chapter, I will argue that Neolithic cuisine formed an enduring institution which transformed nutrition into a meaningful experience and reproduced far more than the physical bodies of Neolithic people.

Food has traditionally been investigated archaeologically for what it contributes nutritionally. Thus, food has been an important topic in studies of foraging behavior and a neglected area in studies of agricultural societies who, it is assumed, have mastered coming up with enough calories and got on to more interesting things such as politics. This has been productive in helping to develop sophisticated methodologies for faunal and botanical analyses, though limiting our horizons for social analysis. More recently, in both processual and post-processual traditions the meaning of food has come to the forefront (Twiss 2007). The meaning of food has been explored in an increasing range of theoretical frameworks, including studies of feasting as political behavior (Blitz 1993; Dietler and Hayden 2001), in phenomenology (Hamilakis 1998), and in gender studies (Brumfiel 1991; Hastorf 1991).

Cuisine

In this analysis, the central concept is cuisine, a coherent, institutionalised and meaning-laden set of food practices. Like other fields of action (see Chapter 1 in this book), cooking and eating combine many elements. Beyond a range of "typical" dishes – what we commonly think of as French or Italian or Chinese "cuisine" – foodways involve:

- the senses – the taste of food, of course, but also its smell, texture, appearance, and sound;
- technological and economic systems of food production, preparation, and consumption;

- the symbolic context of food and the moral values placed upon it;
- the social relations involved in producing and consuming food; and
- the time and space embedded in the consumption of food, as a social event whose character marks or defines particular times and places.

These are not separable elements of experience, even analytically: for example, a particular taste – chocolate, curry, salt, wine – can carry moral or emotional connotations, represent a typical social moment or history, and entail unique social relations of production.

Let's take our own food habits as an illustration. Whether we eat Italian or Chinese, it's all capitalist cuisine. The link between food, social organisation, and economy is pervasive, and surprisingly invisible. Obviously, most of us buy virtually all of our food commercially and are conscious of the cost and status of foods, but the nexus goes beyond this. Food exists in time. Capitalist time is crowded, measured, dissected, and endowed with specialised functions. Thus, different meals punctuate and give tone to the working day; functional breakfast and lunch are fuel for work, while dinner is a time segregated for the "private life" of pleasure, family solidarity and social distinction. Then there is how food is made, in rhythms of daily activity. We hear regularly about the subordination of nutrition, human values and local social contexts to the profit-making food industry. But even closer to home, we cook alone or by households, rather than in other groups; we acquire much of our cooking knowledge from disembedded, market driven sources like cookbooks and the media, rather than via personal relationships. Moreover, recipes and packaged foods are gauged for four people, the normative economic unit.

Time is valorised and cooking has an opportunity cost: meals are designed to be assembled in less than half an hour from prefabricated, purchased elements, so that cooking is a highly channeled fraction of a *chaîne opératoire*, most of which is embedded in a seamless supply chain. In our tastes, we have inherited old semantic codes which contrast (for instance) "rich" food versus "plain" food. But these are overlaid with gender, class and moral values – why else would rejecting meat be so often a form of social critique, and why else would we talk so much about fat in moral as well as dietetic terms? Moreover, our tastes reflect finely cultivated consumer behavior. Most people past and present have never expected to eat something different-tasting every day. The fact that modern Western people do so exemplifies the commodification of taste, and the continual invention of new foods brings into the home the shopping mall experience of decontextualised consumption parading as traditions.

So we think *The Joy of Cooking*, but we eat Capitalism, not only economically but culturally and in our bodily experiences. Without prolonging this obvious example, it demonstrates the importance of treating food consumption as a total social fact: the overall ensemble possesses a structure or coherence which can be missed when one analyzes only a particular food or context. This is why the term "cuisine" is useful, as it links an ensemble of foods with an overall way of life. Furthermore, when viewed as a total system, cuisine provides a set of bodily generative practices par excellence which span the gap between the self and the external world and thus help naturalise an arbitrary social order.

This chapter has two goals. The first is simply to bring together evidence for food and eating in Neolithic Italy. This is in itself an important job: the archaeology of food for prehistoric Italy, as in most other places, has been dismembered into component parts reflecting archaeological methodologies rather than seen as an ensemble, and food has never been seen as a social creation rather than a simple economic product. The second is to try to outline the cultural and social significance of food in Neolithic Italy. I am here treating Central and Southern Italy and Sicily for all phases of the Neolithic; later chapters will touch upon some of the important differences between regions and periods within this world.

The Italian Neolithic Food Economy

Not on the Menu

The first point is simply what was *not* eaten. This encompasses several quite disparate categories.

There is no evidence for cannibalism. It must be granted that specialist taphonomic analysis of the kind carried out at the French Neolithic site of Fontbregua (Villa et al. 1986) has never been done and many forms of cannibalism would leave subtle or invisible osteological traces. Nevertheless, at the only site where this practice has been alleged, the Grotta Scaloria (Gimbutas 1991), osteological reexamination found no convincing traces of it (Robb 1991).

More surprisingly, there is little evidence that seafood was eaten consistently. Surprisingly few fish bones are known from archaeological contexts, even from recent excavations with careful recovery techniques; the only well-investigated exception is the Grotta dell'Uzzo, where marine resources, used throughout the Mesolithic–Neolithic transition, continued to be significant in the Neolithic (Tagliacozzo 1993; Tagliacozzo 1997). Shellfish are known from a few coastal sites such as Coppa Nevigata (Cassano et al. 1987), Stentinello and Vulpiglia in Sicily (Villari 1995), Torre Sabea in Puglia (André 2003), and Arene Candide in Liguria (Bernabò Brea 1946), where they formed an important part of the diet, as shown by both shell finds and stable isotope data (Francalacci 1989). On the small, rocky island of Pianosa in the Tuscan Archipelago, mollusks were harvested, opened with stone tools, and eaten (Carnieri and Zamagni 2000), and a specialised form of burin has sometimes been interpreted as a shellfish opener (d'Errico 1987). The best archaeological evidence for mollusk exploitation comes from the Candelaro group of sites, located on a now filled-in lagoon on the edge of the Tavoliere. At Coppa Nevigata, early Neolithic collected mollusks which they opened using specialised pointed microlithic blades. At Masseria Candelaro, Santa Tecchia and Fontanarosa mollusks were also found, this time in conjunction with domesticated animals. Oxygen isotope analysis suggested that at the latter three sites, mollusks were collected year-round from a relatively large area of the shore, possibly as casual collection during other tasks such as herding. In contrast, at Coppa Nevigata, they were collected from a restricted area during the summer only. This was true both in the Neolithic and in the Bronze Age (Deith 1987, Deith 1989). This suggests basically opportunistic use. Shellfish are virtually absent on many other sites, even ones located directly on the waterline. The few marine shells on most sites frequently show working or wear and are likely to have been tools or ornaments rather than food remains. The few stable isotope data available confirm that the amount of marine resources consumed was negligible.[1]

This neglect of fish, which contrasts so strongly with the coastal and riverine Mesolithic throughout Europe, is surprisingly widespread in the Neolithic world. For example, we would expect the Neolithic Maltese, on a small and resource-poor island, to have eaten fish, but stable isotope evidence suggests that this was apparently not the case. Both social and cultural motivations may have been at work. Fishing may not have been especially worthwhile until the development of economic specialisation allowed economies of scale; significantly, Uzzo Cave lies near a major tuna migration route where large prey can be taken with small boats at a specific time of year. If this is so, marine foods may have been gathered and eaten casually or as stopgaps. This seems to have been the case at least for shellfish. Fish in general may have been passed over from a cultural attitude, a pejorative categorisation of marine foods [cf. Thomas (2003) for Europe in general].

Dogs and carnivores, in general, also seem exempt from consumption. Dog bones are known on many sites, but usually in very small numbers, and they do not seem to have been cut up and deposited as other domestic animals were. Although dog-eating has been alleged at Rendina (Bökönyi 1977–1982), the evidence is slender. At most sites, dog remains include disproportionately high numbers of jaws, skulls, and teeth, sometimes apparently placed deliberately [as with a dog skull in a pit at Catignano (Tozzi and Zamagni 2003)]. The famous burial at Ripoli of a woman with a dog at her feet (Rellini 1934) may be read in many ways, but hardly suggests a snack for the afterlife. Remains of other carnivores, such as bear, fox, wolf, badger, and mustelids are found on few sites and in small numbers, and these animals may have been used primarily for furs. For both dogs and foxes, canine teeth are commonly found and were probably used as ornaments; not infrequently they are pierced to be worn suspended (Figure 24). Bear teeth are also occasionally found. For instance, at Grotta all'Onda where one was pierced as a pendant (Amadei and Grifoni Cremonesi 1987).

The picture for undomesticated animals in general is equivocal. Before deforestation and dense human settlement, the principal game species of Italy would have included red deer, the much smaller roe deer, aurochs, and wild boar. Other game available included wolf, fox,

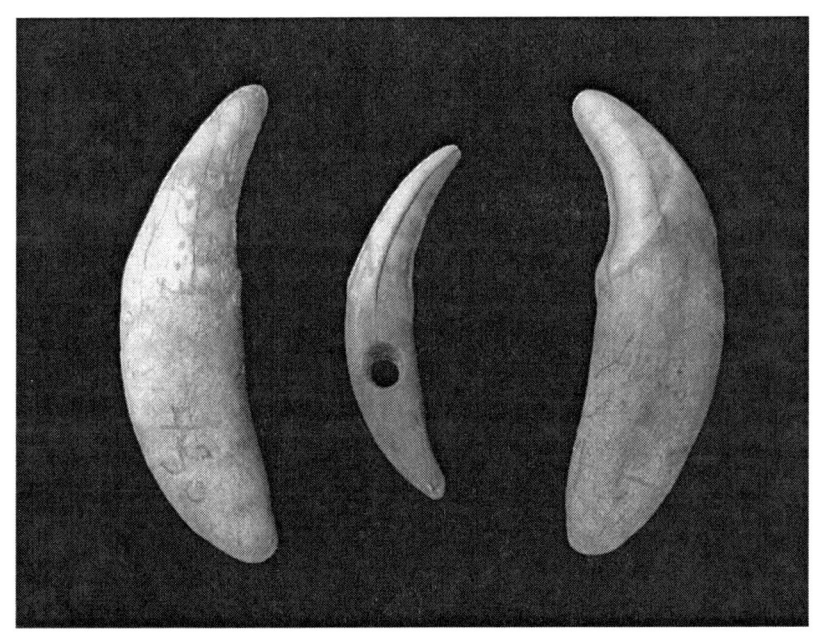

24. Carnivore canines, probably used as ornaments: dog canines (right, left) and pierced fox canine (center). Umbro, Bova Marina, Calabria (photo: Robb).

wild cat, hare, beaver, tortoise, as well as various birds and fishes. Wild fauna would have been sought out not only for their meat but also for useful materials such as antler, boar tusks, furs, feathers, and turtle shells. Faunal data for various periods are available from close to fifty Neolithic sites (Table 9) (Barker 1975; Barker 1981; Bökönyi 1977–1982; Bökönyi 1983; Castelletti, Costantini, and Tozzi 1987; Malone 1994; McVicar et al. 1994; Morter 1992; Sorrentino 1983; Sorrentino 1984; Striccoli 1988). In most cases, however, only percentages of identifiable fragments from various species have been published (the Number of Identifiable Specimens or NISP), not detailed contextual and demographic data which would allow reconstruction of herd management techniques.

As these data show, domestic animals dominate almost all Neolithic samples. While a wide variety of undomesticated fauna is found, it typically comprises less than 5 percent of an overall faunal assemblage and rarely exceeds 10 percent (Wilkens 1989). As Wilkens comments, in the Neolithic game seems generally to have lost almost all its economic

Table 9. *Faunal Data from Neolithic Sites in Central and Southern Italy (percentages of NISP bones in assemblages)*

Site	Period	Date	Ovicap	Bos	Sus	Cervus	Canis	Other
Attiggio, Str. 6	Neo	Lagozza	30	17	47	6	0	0
Berbentina	Neo		60	31	9	0	0	0
Cala Colombo, level 1	Neo	Final Neo	78.6	8.1	0.7	1	10.8	0.7
Cala Colombo, level 7	Neo	Final Neo	76	8.5	6.4	0.3	6.4	2.5
Capo Alfiere	Neo	Stentinello	49.7	33.2	8.1	1.1	0.1	7.8
Capo d'Acqua	Neo	Early Neo	40	13	25	20	0	2
Casatico	Neo		16.8	45.9	34.7	2	0.4	0.2
Catignano	Neo	Middle Neo	35.7	20.6	22	0.5	3.9	17
Fontanarosa	Neo	Middle Neo	64.3	14.3	14.3	0	0	7.1
G. Orso	Neo		34.4	19.7	25.6	0.6	1.9	17.6
G. Pacelli, C.D.	Neo	Middle Neo	40.4	11.34	2.8	1.4	9.21	34.8
G. Pacelli, S. d'A.	Neo	Late Neo	36.8	8.2	5.8	2.7	7.2	39.3
G. Pacelli, S. d'A/Diana	Neo	Final Neo	42.2	13.3	10	0	1.1	33.3
G. Piccioni, Str. 26–18	Neo	Early Neo	52.5	9.8	19.8	5.7	1.7	9
G. Vannaro, Str. 1–5	Neo		12.5	12.5	37.5	37.5	0	0
G. Vannaro, Str. 8–13	Neo		10	8.3	71.7	1.6	0	8.3
Gr. Piccioni, Str. 17–12	Neo	Late Neo	43.6	10.5	22.1	9.8	0.7	12.8
Ipogeo Manfredi	Neo	Late Neo	16.9	13.3	7.5	21.8	1.9	38.5
Lagnano da Piede	Neo	Early Neo	50.6	30.9	10.7	0.6	0.4	0
M. Candelaro	Neo	Middle Neo	47.7	28	22.4	0	1.9	0
M. Valente	Neo	Middle Neo	71.9	11.1	14.9	0	0.4	1.6
Maddalena di Muccia	Neo	Early Neo	15	8	50	25	0	2
Passo di Corvo	Neo	Middle Neo	49.2	36.8	8.8	0.4	4.2	0.63
Pienza, level 1	Neo	Early Neo	62	16	12	1	8.5	0.5
Pienza, level 2	Neo	Early Neo	35	36	18	5.5	5.5	0
Rendina	Neo	Early Neo	60.9	19.6	18.3	0.1	0.8	0.28
Ripa Tetta	Neo	Early Neo	60.5	27.6	9.2	0	2.6	0.1
Ripabianca di Monterado	Neo	Early Neo	64	6	19			
Ripoli, str. 1	Neo	Late Neo	23.1	17.6	49.7	4.5		
Ripoli, str. II	Neo	Late Neo	30.5	25	28.5	8.5	0.2	7.3

Site	Period	Date	Ovicap	Bos	Sus	Cervus	Canis	Other
Ripoli, str. III	Neo	Late Neo	26.9	25.9	26	14.7	0.1	6.4
S. Marco	Neo	Early Neo	38.1	30.6	18.7	39.4	6.5	7.3
S. Maria in Selva	Neo		33	31	20	16		
S. Tecchia	Neo	Middle Neo	48.3	38.1	13.3	0	0	0.3
Tirlecchia	Neo	Middle Neo	47.4	48.0	3.0	0.1	1.3	0.1
Torre Sabea	Neo	Early Neo	64.5	23.5	6.1	2.7	0	3.2
Villaggio Leopardi	Neo	Middle Neo	43.6	12.8	42.3		0.6	0.6

Sources: See text.

purpose — at least as a major food source. Some of this emphasis on domestic animals may result from simple environmental changes due to human presence. Red deer use similar forage to cattle and sheep and pasturing cattle and sheep may destroy their subsistence base, especially near villages where pasturing would have been densest (Gregg 1988). Nonetheless, this dearth of game is probably not entirely due to ecological causes. Neolithic population was thinly spread in many areas (Chapter 7). Italy often affords a mosaic of varied microenvironments and even today adaptable species such as boar are hunted in relatively densely populated rural areas. Even at the woodland marsh-edge site of Neto di Bolasse (Sarti et al. 1985), game still only reached 9 percent of the faunal assemblage.

In spite of the overall trend, a few sites do have a significant proportion of game present. These are due primarily to two causes. In an ecological vein, the earliest Neolithic in Northern and parts of highland Central Italy begins on the average half a millennium later, and appears much less as a neat package, than in Southern Italy. Both early Neolithic sites and later sites in rough, marginal areas continue to include game in their animal economies, particularly in the Alps and Po Valley (Barker 1975, 1985). For example, hunting was important in the Vhò group at sites such as Campo Ceresole (Bagolini et al. 1987). At Fonte San Callisto in the Abruzzo (Radi 1987), red deer reached 29 percent of the collection; in the Gubbio basin, Neolithic projectile points were found at the opposite end of the valley from village sites, suggesting hunting in zones further from habitations (Malone 1994). In Southern Italy, there are a few sites such as the Grotta Pacelli (Striccoli 1988) where small game, such as tortoises, were common. It should also be remembered that some of the pig bones found archaeologically may come from wild animals rather than from domestic pigs; it has been argued that most or all of the pigs eaten at Early Neolithic Arene Candide were wild boar (Rowly-Conwy 1997).

Second, hunted game appears to have been symbolically valued. Throughout Neolithic Italy, atrophic red deer canines were sometimes made into pendants, presumably for necklaces. Indeed, at one site, Vulpiglia (Sicily) imitation deer canine pendants were made from shell. In Puglia, where excavated villages have yielded overwhelmingly domestic faunal assemblages, a Serra d'Alto period artificial rock-cut underground chamber, the Ipogeo Manfredi, contained evidence of ritual occupation and a faunal assemblage with 60.3 percent bones of game, primarily roe deer (*Capreolus* sp.) and red deer (*Cervus elaphas*) (Castelletti, Costantini, and Tozzi 1987). Also in Apulia, the bones of game are occasionally found among grave goods, as at the Grotta Scaloria, where a deer antler was deposited with a young adult male (Winn and Shimabuku 1988). Rock art provides a third source of evidence; both cave paintings at Porto Badisco and the Tuppo dei Sassi and petroglyphs at Val Camonica depict deer with exaggerated antlers and hunting scenes (Biancofiore 1965; Graziosi 1974; Robb 1994).

Thus, for most of lowland Neolithic Italy, hunting was known, but it contributed little to the diet. The low proportion of large game is surprising considering how sparsely populated the Italian peninsula was and how many suitable environments for deer and boar there must have been. There may have been ideological or organisational reasons why game was an overlooked resource. The reliance upon domestic animals may have been based upon economic choices as to the allocation of time and labor. People working in subsistence economies typically do not try to maximise overall production but rather to maximise returns per unit labor (Glass 1991). Once domesticated animals were available, they would have furnished a more predictable, easier to procure source of animal food than game. This is suggested by the earliest Neolithic sites not only in highland Italy but also in Northern Spain and Southern France, which remain Mesolithic in all but the introduction of pottery and domestic sheep and goats (Barker 1985; Davidson 1989;

Guilaine 1993; Lewthwaite 1987). Effectively wild and domestic animals afforded quite different opportunities for meaningful production. Wild game cannot be closely controlled, herded and transacted in the same way as pastoral animals, and domestic animals were the basis of political foodways (see below). But wild animals offer access to a world of extrasocial spaces (see Chapter 2 in this book) and of meanings about gender, otherness, ancestry, and cosmology (Helms 1998). In foraging societies, animals are often considered animate beings and peers to humans, while in herding societies domestic beasts are often considered property or valuables instead (Kent 1989). Hunting itself often provides a drama of identity and gender as much as a source of food (Kensinger 1989; Rosaldo 1986). In Neolithic Italy, the use of wild animals in ritual and ornament suggests that such symbolisations have been their principal social use.

Grains and Legumes: The World of Starches

Neolithic flora from Southern and Central Italy is known from carbonised remains recovered by flotation, from impressions in baked clay daub from house remains, and from water-logged remains in the La Marmotta site at Lake Bracciano near Rome (Rottoli 1993). Floral samples have been published for about twenty Italian Neolithic sites (Table 10). Given small samples and probable biases in seed preservation, it is difficult to quantify relative plant usage, but these figures give an idea of the plants used by Neolithic people.

In virtually all samples wheats and barleys predominate (Table 10, including data from Cassano et al. 1987; Castelletti, Costantini, and Tozzi 1987; Coubray 1997; Hopf 1991; Malone 1994; McVicar et al. 1994; Morter 1992; Sargent 1983; and Zohary and Hopf 1993). These include emmer wheat (*Triticum dicoccum*), einkorn wheat (*T. monococcum*), bread wheat (*T. aestivum*), club wheat (*T. aestivum compacta*), spelt (*T. spelta*), and domesticated barley (*Hordeum* sp.). Each of these has slightly different qualities. Emmer, einkorn, and spelt are bearded wheats, where the seed is enclosed within a tough glume, requiring much more work to thresh than naked wheats such as bread wheat and club wheat (Barker 1981). However, they are more tolerant

Table 10. *Palaeobotanical Samples from Selected Neolithic Sites in Italy*

Site	Emmer	Einkorn	Barley	Other Wheats	Spelt	Millet	Lentils	Peas	Fava Beans	Notes
Capo Alfiere	x	x	xx				x	x	x	
Coppa Nevigata	x		x							
Fontanarosa	x	x	x	x						
M. Covolo	xx	x	x		x					Wild vine, fruits
M. Aquilone	x									
Passo di Corvo	x	x	x	xx						
Pienza	xx	x	x	xx						
Rendina	x	x	x	x	x		x			
S. Marco	x	x	x	x				x	x	Wild vine, fig
S. Tecchia	x	x	x							
Scamuso	x		x							
Torre Canne	x	x	x							
Uzzo	x	x	xx	x			x	x	x	Wild almond, fig, olive, vine

Sources: See text.

of a wide range of climatic conditions than bread wheats. Einkorn and emmer wheats were more commonly used in the Early Neolithic, but with the Middle Neolithic bread and club wheats were used more (Morter 1992). This may be a consequence of taking heavier soils into cultivation. Barley is a traditional staple in Mediterranean subsistence because of its ability to tolerate dry conditions better than wheats. Barley makes up a high proportion of remains from Capo Alfiere and from Skorba on Malta, and Morter raises the possibility that it was used for making beer for communal festivities inside the large structures known at both these sites. However, both sites also lie within the driest and hottest areas of the Central Mediterranean.

The earliest direct evidence of plowing in Italian prehistory comes from the Bronze Age, with rock carvings of oxen yoked to plows at Monte Bego and with an actual wooden ard recovered from the lakeside village of Ledro in Lombardy (Barker 1985). In the Neolithic, it is generally assumed that grain was gardened using digging stick technology.

Early Italian farmers could expect a yield of 500–1,000 kg/ha (Barker 1985, Gregg 1988; Halstead 1981; Jarman and Webley 1975). Wheat contains about 3,300 kcal/kg, and a family of four to six people would have consumed about a metric ton (1,000 kg) of grain per year, providing a diet of about 2,000 kcal/day for adults and 1,000 kcal/day for juveniles. To grow this much, between one and two hectares would have been cultivated. In modern Italy, grain yields with traditional plow agriculture were highly variable, depending on temperature and especially the timing and amount of the spring rains (Jarman and Webley 1975). Cultivating two hectares per family unit would have allowed them to produce a "normal surplus" (Halstead 1989) which would have been stored or used for social consumption in good years and consumed in bad years. Early and Middle Neolithic villages were typically located on ridges of light soils where possible (Barker 1981; Castelletti, Costantini, and Tozzi 1987; Jarman and Webley 1975; Sargent 1983), and fields would probably have been located directly adjacent to the village. A typical small village of thirty to eighty people would thus have required a total of 12–30 ha in grain, with a similar amount in fallow which could have been used as pasture (Robb and Van Hove 2003).

Legumes were also commonly cultivated, including peas, lentils, beans, and vetches. They are highly nutritious, store well, can be used as fodder, and in rotation they replace the nitrogen which grains remove from the soil. They are known from almost all Neolithic floral samples (Table 10). Interestingly, at Capo Alfiere (Morter 1992), pulses were at least as common as grains, and there may have been a trend to increased use of pulses in the later Neolithic (Castelletti, Costantini, and Tozzi 1987).

Domesticated plants are socially interesting for a number of reasons. One is simply that they were the basis of life. What few stable isotope data exist suggest a diet which was close to vegetarian,[2] a diagnosis corroborated by trace element analysis (Salvadei and Santandrea 2003). A correspondingly large amount of time was presumably spent on preparing these foods, to judge from the amount of grain-related paraphernalia found on sites. Crops were harvested with flint-bladed sickles and stored in pits; clay-lined storage pits of $1-2$ m^2 volume are known from a number of sites. They may have also been stored in large pots. Large flat grinding stones and small hand-sized grinders are known from almost all extensively excavated sites and must have been an important trade item in areas where appropriate stone could not be found locally (Figure 25). We do not know how efficiently grinding stones worked, but it is hard to imagine grinding the 2–3 kilos of grain (about 3–4 l) a family would have required daily in less than an hour or two, making it a chronic and time-consuming task. Grinding grain was apparently done in or around houses, though used grinding stones are sometimes found in ritual contexts such as at the Grotta delle Felci on Capri (Rellini 1923).

Hand-grinding grain on querns probably resulted in coarse, gritty whole-grain flour or cracked grains such as bulghur wheat or grits. The most obvious ways to cook the resulting foods would have been to boil them into porridge, pottage, or soup, especially for the legumes, or to make bread – probably flat, unleavened hearth cakes baked on stones or coals. Without additional flavouring, the tastes possible would have ranged from completely bland to mildly nutty; the colours, from tan to murky brown. The tastes would have been experienced at each meal, and the colours have a kind of ubiquitous background, a region of the palette shared by the soil itself, the brown of weathered skins,

25. The household's food source, and hours of labor: grinding stone for preparing grain, Malerba (Altamura Museum; grain is modern; photo: Robb).

the clay used to daub houses, the straw and reeds covering them, and most of the pottery assemblage. Sensorially, grains and pulses shared the earth tones of colour and flavour, an ur-colour and ur-flavour which mirror and represent the availability, spaces and social relations of the starches.

Because of the weight and bulk of grain and legumes, they were probably grown close to settlements, and stored and prepared directly among the houses. Starches were the most *local* of foods. Grain was omnipresent; it was stored in large quantities all year round and prepared as needed. It could be produced and consumed in any quantity, from a small batch for a few people to the trough-like amounts suggested by some of the larger jars. The property relations involved are unknown. However, as an ethnographic generalisation, bulk carbohydrates tend to be produced and consumed by households (Wiessner and Schiefenhövel 1996) rather than communally; gardens tend to be cleared and maintained by individuals or nuclear families, and there is nothing in the technology of digging-stick technology which implies a more centralised production.

Notes of Flavour

In sharp contrast to the bulk starches were the *flavours* – the range of substances which were eaten only in small quantities but which probably made life worth living. These include both spices and the ancestors of our modern fast-food vices: fats, sugars, and salts.

Of two classic Mediterranean products, olive oil and wine, we have no Neolithic evidence. Although Italian Neolithic people used wild grapes and olives, there is no evidence that they had domesticated olives and vines (Barker 1989), and they certainly did not have specialised production of wine and oil in bulk as known from the later Bronze Age at sites such as Broglio di Trebisacce. The prehistory of dairy products is more tendentious. Sherratt's (1981) argument that the first European farmers kept animals only to eat their meat, rather than for wool, milk, and traction, has proved difficult to prove or to disprove. However, there are some hints. Large-scale specialised transhumance is clearly excluded. There is no evidence of the complex political structures which would have been needed to traverse long-distance transhumant routes, nor were there nucleated urban settlements to provide agricultural surpluses and a market to consume specialised pastoral products. Artefactual evidence of plowing, wool production and specialised transhumant sites all post-dates the Neolithic. Faunal kill patterns show that pigs were eaten newborn, before or relatively soon after reaching maturity. For sheep and goats, faunal kill-off patterns are ambiguous, but Neolithic samples typically contain many newborn or juvenile remains and relatively few adults (Tagliacozzo 1992), which seems unexpected both for rational meat maximisation and for specialised wool production. Cattle lived longer, whether to produce secondary products or because they were less expendible for other reasons. There does not seem to have been high kill-off of young males, as we might expect in a intensified dairy regime, or early adult kill-off, as for an intensified meat production (Barker 1981). The proportion of sheep and goats kept seems to rise through the Neolithic, and this may go with a much more intensive occupation of both highlands (see Chapter 3 in this book) and islands, for example, the Aeolians (Bernabò Brea and Cavalier 1991). This suggests more intensive pastoralism with some degree of transhumance, but only towards the end of the period. Lipid analyses of pottery at one site, Favella, show animal fats were used in pots, but could not distinguish between meat lipids and dairy lipids. As far as we can tell, the Italian model conforms well to a model of

Neolithic economy as geared primarily to subsistence rather than specialised production of "secondary products." Before the end of the Neolithic, herding was probably a small-scale affair carried on at mostly agricultural villages, aimed at raising generalised herds for generalised consumption.

Without olive oil, other vegetable oils, or butter, the main fats available would have been animal fats such as lard, tallow, and mutton fat. Fats would have been an important substance not only for cooking, but also for lighting, as a solvent for mixing paint, for lubricating and weather-proofing, and for many other uses. Without our moral strictures about calories and consumption, the fatness of meat would have likely been prized as an element of taste, as in many cultures (Mintz 1994). It is probable that fats would have been saved from butchered animals and stored carefully in leather or pottery vessels.

Without sugar, the main sweetener would have been honey, supplemented by wild fruits. Cherries, apples, and pears are known to have existed at the Early Neolithic waterlogged site of La Marmotta (Rottoli 1993). Although this site has exceptional preservation, fruit remains at other sites where close attention has been paid to palaeobotany, such as Spilamberto, the Grotta Sant'Angelo, and Casale del Dolce (Castelletti 1996; Castelletti et al. 1998; Coubray 1997) suggest that wild fruits and nuts were commonly used. Both fruits and honey are forest products, sporadically available and possibly carefully stored, whose supply would have depended on detailed knowledge of a considerable radius around the habitation.

Probably neither wild fruit nor honey would have been available in large enough quantities to commonly supply fermented beverages. Among other mind-altering substances, beer, poppy sap, and various wild herbs could have been used (Sherratt 1997), though the only concrete evidence for any of these is finds of wild poppy at La Marmotta (Rottoli 2001), and this need not have been for use as an opiate.

Flavouring herbs and gathered plants would have been widely available. Gathered plants such as chestnuts and perhaps acorns may have provided a basic alternative to grain as bulk carbohydrates, particularly in the higher Apennines. Gathered plants may have provided nutritionally important supplements such as greens, fruits, and berries. They may have provided scarcity foods which could be gathered in times of need, particularly by children and people beyond the age for more strenuous labors. They were probably used medicinally as well, as well as for dyes and colourants [e.g., wild saffron and thistle at La Marmotta (Rottoli 2001)]. Finally, gathered plants may have provided important flavourings to add variety and relish to the diet. Even today, one can commonly find native herbs such as rosemary, oregano, mint, and thyme growing wild in the aromatic Mediterranean rocky scrub, and many others would have also been available.

Salt is the most widely traded flavouring in the tribal world and is produced by a surprising range of ingenious techniques, including quarrying from natural deposits (as at Iron Age Hallstatt and in Neolithic Catalonia (Weller 2002), evaporation and boiling from sea water (as in British Iron Age and Roman briquetage), and extraction from ash, as among some New Guinea groups (Lemonnier 1992). Historically, salt was produced in many places around the Italian coastline by evaporating sea water in natural or artificial basins, for example, in lagoons south of Manfredonia in an area of dense Neolithic settlement (Tunzi Sisto 1999). There is no archaeological evidence for the production of salt in the Neolithic. However, the Mediterranean is a highly saline ocean and simple evaporation techniques work extremely well.[3] Small-scale production, probably in coastal locations and involving no tools beyond a few pots or a hollow in a rock, would be almost impossible to identify archaeologically, and it seems very likely that salt was at least collected coastally and traded inland. Beside its use in maintaining domestic animals, its culinary importance in a diet composed largely of grains and pulses seems hard to exaggerate.

This group of foods, the "flavours," is very heterogeneous. However, they share some common characteristics. They were used in small but pungent quantities, in counterpoint to the ever-present quantities of bland porridge, bread, or grits. Like many traditional cuisines worldwide (Mintz 1994), Neolithic Italian cuisine combined large amounts of soft, yellowish-brown, homogeneous cooked starches with smaller amounts of "relishes" (in Mintz's term) which add colour, protein, fat, vitamins, and above all flavour. Temporally, many of the "flavours"

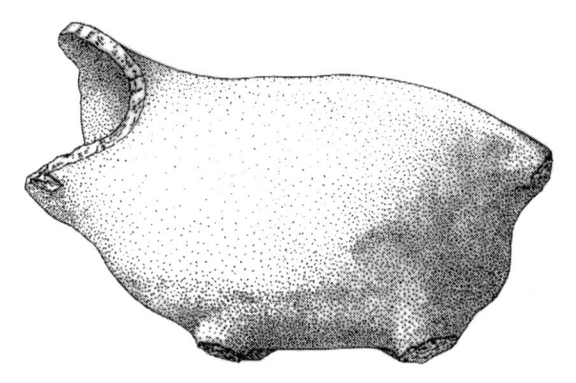

26. Zoomorphic pottery vessel probably representing pig or cow, Colle S. Stefano, Fucino Basin, Abruzzo (Radmilli 1997, courtesy of G. Radi).

would have been available sporadically, in a mosaic of seasonal intervals. Spatially, they were products of the margins and the exotic: from margins and interstices, from wild areas, or from distant places. Socially, while some would have been universally recognised and available to everyone, producing others depended on information about the hinterlands such as when fruit trees were ripening, perhaps infrequently used techniques such as how to extract honey from a swarm of bees, and perhaps social contact. Flavours such as salt and honey especially may often have been obtained through trade, supplied through relations with people elsewhere, outside the realm of family and kin.

Animal Choices

The "fourth food group" for the Neolithic was meat from domesticated animals. This is by far the best studied form of Neolithic food; it is known almost exclusively from bones, though small clay figurines of animals are known from the sites of Stentinello and Contrada Diana, and a unique animal-shaped pottery vessel in the form of a pig or cow was excavated at the Early Neolithic site of Santo Stefano in the Abruzzo (Radi and Wilkens 1989). (See Figure 26.) Although the interpretation of the latter is unclear, it does suggest the social significance of animals.

Until the advent of the horse [attested earliest at the Copper Age site of Maccarese near Rome (Manfredini 2002)] and donkey [attested

Table 11. *Some Characteristics of Domesticated Animals*

	Cattle	Sheep	Goats	Pigs
Preferred browse/forage	Forest browse, grass	Herbs, grasses	Grass, forest browse	Forest pannage
Pasture area/individual	1–1.5 ha/month	0.1–0.15 ha/month	0.1–0.15 ha/month	—
Reproductive potential	Low	High	High	High
Live weight (adult)	300–700 kg	20–40 kg	20–40 kg	30–60 kg
Meat yield (adult)	Ca. 250 kg	Ca. 15 kg	Ca. 15 kg	Ca. 20 kg
Milk yield	Ca. 350 kg	Ca. 45 kg/yr	Ca. 77 kg/yr	—
Other products	Traction, leather, manure	Wool (woolly sheep only), manure, leather	Manure, leather	Manure, leather
Demographically stable herd minimum	30 +/−	30 +/−	30 +/−	?

Source: Based on Barker 1985; Bogucki 1988; Dahl and Hjort 1976; Glass 1991; Gregg 1988; Redding 1981.

earliest at the Bronze Age site of Tufiarello in Campania (Holloway 1975)], Neolithic Italians kept five species of domesticated animals: cattle, sheep, goats, pigs, and dogs. It has traditionally been assumed that dogs were kept for hunting, herding work, guard duty, and companionship rather than for the table; this seems likely (see above). Each of the four major food animals has different food preferences, labor requirements, and returns (Table 11).

Among the most salient differences, cattle require about ten times the pasturing and browse that caprovines do – a key limitation in places subject to harsh summer drought or winters in which cattle must be provided with fodder. A herd of thirty cattle requires roughly 2 km^2 of grazing, pasture, hay meadow, and grain straw a year, while a herd of thirty sheep and goats requires about a quarter of a square kilometre (Gregg 1988). Drinking water is often another important limitation on cattle, as cattle need a minimum of 32 l of water per head every day (Wagstaff and Gamble 1983), and considerable time may be spent moving herds to sources of water. The difference in labor input for herding, milking, and feeding is also significant. At the same time, cattle provide about ten to fifteen times the meat per individual animal, and yield five to ten times the milk per animal per year.

Demography is another significant contrast. While cattle live and reproduce longer than sheep, goats and pigs, they reproduce more slowly. Cows reach adult body size and reproductive maturity in 2–3 years. Sheep and goats reproduce after 1 year and can double their herd size in 8–12 years. Pigs are perhaps the highest in reproductive potential, producing litters of several piglets every year. Both cattle and caprovines are subject to demographic thresholds of scale. Below certain herd sizes, the herd is vulnerable to disease, climatic extremes, and predation which can affect the few breeding females, and herds become extinct easily. Above this threshold, these disasters are unlikely to affect enough breeding females to check herd increase seriously. Although little research has been done on this, Bogucki cites thirty animals as the minimum for a demographically stable cattle herd (Bogucki 1988). No such figure has been published for sheep, goats, and pigs. However, the fact that such a threshold exists is clear from ethnographic accounts such as Black-Michaud's description of sheep economics among the specialist pastoralist Lurs of the Central Zagros mountains in Iran. Poorer Lurs, inspired by the prospective fertility of sheep, typically tried to build up thriving herds from a few animals, only to be wiped out by droughts, cold snaps, disease, or predators which left large herds relatively unscathed and thriving. In this case, the threshold to long-term prosperity seemed to be about 100 breeding ewes (Black-Michaud 1986).

Turning to the actual herding choices made by Neolithic people, the ratio of cattle, sheep/goat, and pig bones on Neolithic sites is typically about 30:60:10 in the Italian peninsula (Table 9) (Barker 1975; Bökönyi 1977–1982; Bökönyi 1983; Cipolloni Sampò 1992; Curci and Tagliacozzo 2003; Grifoni Cremonesi 1992; Mallory 1987; Tagliacozzo 1992). There is much variation around these figures, however. In well-forested Northern Italy and in some Apennine sites, caprovines are less well-represented and pigs are more prominent; variations in central Italy also relate to the mixture of resources locally available. Pigs were commonly eaten at some sites in Central and Southern Italy, too, for example, at Casale del Dolce (Tagliacozzo and Fiore 1997) in southern Lazio and at the Diana period site of S. Mauro in Campania (Albore Livadie et al. 1987). Some sites appear unusually rich in cattle bones, [for instance, Stentinello (Villari 1995) though this may also reflect the grab-sample recovery of large bones in the prescreening era excavations there]. As noted above, there is also a trend to increased use of sheep and goats as the Neolithic proceeds. As an overall generalisation, however, between half and three-quarters of the animal bones on most sites are from sheep or goats.[4]

The picture changes completely, however, if we look at the total amount of meat eaten. It is often noted that percentages of bone fragments are a misleading gauge of how much a species contributes to the diet, but it is difficult to appreciate just how great a difference calculating other kinds of figures makes without an example. Detailed faunal data have been published for three Apulian sites, Early Neolithic Lagnano da Piede (Mallory 1987), Middle Neolithic Passo di Corvo (Sorrentino 1983) and Middle/Late Neolithic Grotta Pacelli (Striccoli 1988) (Table 12). Meat yield per animal is estimated at approximately 15 kg for sheep and goats, 20 kg for pigs, and 250 kg for cattle (Barker 1981; Dahl and Hjort 1976; Gregg 1988; Redding 1981). At both sites, between half and two-thirds of the domestic animals were sheep and goats, but over 75 percent of the meat consumed would have come from cattle.

Table 12. *Neolithic Sheep, Goats, Cattle, and Pigs at Lagnano da Piede, Passo di Corvo and the Grotta Pacelli*

Site	Animal	NISP	% NISP	MNI	% Total MNI	Meat wt. (kg)	% Total Meat Wt.
Lagnano da Piede	Sheep/goat	90	54.9	10	52.6	150	10.1
	Cattle	55	33.5	5	26.3	1,250	84.4
	Pig	19	11.6	4	21.1	80	5.5
	Total	164	100	19	100	1,480	100
Passo di Corvo	Sheep/goat	1,494	51.9	104	63.0	1,560	15.7
	Cattle	1,119	38.8	31	18.8	7,750	78.2
	Pig	268	9.3	30	18.2	600	6.1
	Total	2,881	100	165	100	9,910	100
Grotta Pacelli (Ceramica Dipinta)	Sheep/goat	57	74.0	4	57.1	60	10.3
	Cattle	16	20.8	2	28.5	500	86.2
	Pig	4	6.0	1	14.3	20	3.5
	Total	77	100	7	100	580	100
Grotta Pacelli (Serra d'Alto)	Sheep/goat	274	72.5	13	65	195	15.5
	Cattle	61	16.1	4	20	1,000	79.7
	Pig	43	11.4	3	15	60	4.8
	Total	378	100	20	100	1,255	100
Grotta Pacelli (Serra d'Alto/Diana)	Sheep/goat	269	64.4	10	50	150	10.0
	Cattle	85	20.3	5	25	1,250	83.3
	Pig	64	15.3	5	25	100	6.7
	Total	418	100	20	100	1,500	100

Note: Meat weights calculated based on 15 kg sheep or goat, 250 kg cattle, and 20 kg pig.
Sources: Lagnano da Piede, Mallory 1987; Passo di Corvo, Sorrentino 1983; Grotta Pacelli, Striccoli 1988.

Although data are rarely published systematically, this point is corroborated by occasional figures from other sites such as Santo Stefano di Ortucchio in the Fucino, where cattle accounted for 6.4 percent of the bone specimens but 50.7 percent of the meat (Radi and Wilkens 1989). As a general rule, in order for cattle and sheep/goats to contribute equal amounts of meat to the diet, using the meat yield estimates above, we would need 16.7 caprovines for each cow. Assuming this translated into a roughly similar NISP, we would get bone fragment percentages with a maximum of about 10 percent cattle – even less if pigs, dogs, or wild fauna were present at all. This is the case at only a handful of sites. It seems safe to conclude that throughout Neolithic Italy, cattle provided the bulk of the animal contribution to the diet.

The Sociality of The Food Economy

The Sociality of Herds

At this point, let us turn to the sociality of herds. Though herding choices are often related to local environments (Barker 1975; Halstead 1981), animal herding was not a purely economic or ecological activity but was deeply embedded in social relations.

Herd demography provides an interesting point of departure. Although it is impossible to estimate the subsistence needs of a basic household, if we maintain the ratio of animals cited above, 0.25 cows, 1.5 caprovines, and 0.5 pig per person per year would have supplied 90 kg of meat a year, or about 250 grams of meat a day – the equivalent of two hamburgers or a medium-sized steak. If a third of the herd was eaten each year, this means a household of five to ten people might have held four to eight cows, twenty-three to forty-five caprovines, and seven to fifteen pigs [calculations are modeled upon (Bogucki 1988)]. These are made-up figures, and we cannot be sure how large a herd families or villages maintained. Nor can we be sure exactly how animals were herded, and different kinds of practices would clearly pose different labor requirements. Cattle and sheep require containment and protection if they are not simply to escape; pigs can be kept semi-ferally to roam with periodic round-ups, though if they are crops and gardens require protection from them. But these estimates seem very generous. Stable isotope evidence does not suggest a heavily meat or milk-based diet (see discussions of human bone stable isotopes in Chapter 2 and grain in this chapter). Even keeping this many animals would have involved much labor and extensive pastures – between 0.5 and 1 km² for our hypothetical family and up to 2.5 km² for a village of fifty people. Furthermore, given the amount of labor needed to care for stock, it is reasonable to assume that people would not have kept several times more animals than they needed simply to achieve herd security.

The real point of this is that people probably kept far fewer animals than would have been needed for their herd to be demographically secure. Although a family herd of seven to fifteen pigs might have been demographically stable, neither twenty-three to forty-five caprovines nor four to eight cattle are likely to be viable long-term herd sizes. As discussed above, herds of at least thirty to fifty animals, and preferably more, are needed to ensure long-term demographic stability. The only way to achieve long-term herd stability with fewer animals is to participate in networks circulating animals. In effect, a large, biologically stable herd is fragmented into many smaller family herds, with animals changing hands as necessary to even out demographic shortfalls or surpluses among both animals and humans, and to weather the hazards of weather, disease, and fluctuations in fertility. If we suppose that primitive communism did not prevail and animals were owned by groups like families, animals would have been constantly changing hands among them. Moreover, a family's herd would have grown and shrunk as the family itself included more or fewer productive adult members (Black-Michaud 1986; Dahl and Hjort 1976). At any given point, thus, many herds would be small, unstable herds beginning or finishing their growth cycles.

Given ethnographic accounts of how people use animals, it would have been highly unusual if the circulation of animals were *not* embedded in complex and meaning-laden social transactions. Among many pastoral peoples, herds are the basic form of wealth, and their basic use is for successfully fulfilling cultural obligations and achieving prestige, even when grain forms the actual bulk of the diet (Galaty 1989). Among the Maasai, for instance, cattle are even named according to their social use (e.g., as the return of a debt, as an exchanged animal, as a blood-wealth or bridewealth payment, as a friendship gift, as booty from a raid), the name of their original donor, or the name of the recipient they are destined for (Robertshaw 1989; Russell 1998; Russell 1999). Their aesthetic qualities furnish a never-ending topic of discourse (Coote 1992). As an ethnographic generalisation, cattle in tribal societies almost always serve as social valuables (Russell 1998; Russell 1999). They may have individual names and identities, they may be destined from birth for a particular purpose or transaction; they furnish a yardstick of family prosperity (Dahl and Hjort 1976).

Animal production was embedded in time and space. Even without long-range transhumance, animals would have moved around between pastures, especially as the open mosaic forest probably prevalent in the ancient Mediterranean (Horden and Purcell 2000) would have offered a variety of habitats. Caring for herds would have involved a greater radius of movement than gardening, and with it more chances to learn what was new in the area, to see people outside the local group, and so on. It may have involved movement through different kinds of spaces. Except for the largest villages, many transactions must have required moving animals between settlements. Temporally, herding would have involved both seasonal and annual rhythms of moving herds, slaughtering, and long-term planning. If so, producing animals in Neolithic Italy was not simply a matter of putting meat on the table; building and maintaining a family herd was a long-term social project which involved continual transactions among animal-holders and which may have required years of strategic planning.

Eating: Rhythms and Tastes

Just as animals were produced socially, they were eaten socially. In this chapter, we concluded that about two-thirds of animals eaten were sheep or goats, but the vast bulk of the meat eaten was from cattle. This has two important implications. First, the social rhythm of meat eating involved a counterpoint between relatively common events where smaller animals were eaten, punctuated at intervals by less frequent events at which large amounts of meat were eaten. Second, each kind of animal was probably circulated and eaten in a specific way.

Consider slaughtering a cow. What does a family of five to ten people, half of whom are children, do with 250 kg of beef in the land before refrigerators? There are two strategies: peasant storage and tribal feast. The storage strategy, familiar to modern peasants from the Mediterranean to Appalachia, involves converting an animal into a staggering variety of hams, sausages, scraps, chitterlings, hocks, ears, tails, rendered fat, and so forth. Techniques include drying meat (making jerky), salting, pickling, and curing or smoking meat. All of these were certainly possible in the Neolithic, except possibly for pickling in the absence of vinegar, and there is no evidence for or against their use. It seems likely that specific and valuable parts of animals such as hides and fat would have been saved, processed, and stored. But this picture is based on societies encapsulated in market economies, with an ethic of limited reciprocity and family self-sufficiency. Significantly, for the pre-market world, the famous examples of meat storage come from full-time hunters (such as North American prairie bison hunters) and fishers (such as Northwest Coast salmon harvesters), for whom meat is a real daily staple analogous to grain in farming groups. In many tribal societies with an ethic of reciprocity, in which it is difficult to refuse requests to share food, an individual family's surplus of foods which other people may not have available at the moment is often quickly consumed by friends and relations. Thus, while there is little concrete evidence, peasant storage seems unlikely for the Italian Neolithic.

In tribal communities, sharing meat is often one of the prime foci for norms of redistribution (Dietler and Hayden 2001), and slaughtering even imminently moribund cows usually occurs in the context of a feast, ceremony, or sacrifice (Dahl and Hjort 1976). The solution to meat glut is to hold a large feast. Ethnographies of pig feasts in New Guinea make clear that people often look forward to such feasts as a change from an almost vegetarian daily diet and may consume staggering amounts of meat at them. With the feasting strategy, the meat flows through the community in punctuated, festive bursts of roasted gluttony rather than in a continual dribble of thin prosciutto slices. Sponsored collective eating, or "commensal politics" (Dietler 1996), is a ubiquitous feature of politics in societies in which social relations are dominated by collective action, persuasion, and reciprocity rather than accumulation and coercion. From the owner's point of view, feasting upon animals successfully converts an excess of rapidly perishing meat into obligations, prestige, control over the scheduling, scale and performance of rituals (and the life events they accomplish), and rights to share in others' meat in the future.

Animals, and particularly cattle, were thus not only biologically produced and consumed for nutritional purposes, but were also socially produced and consumed. From the animal's point of view, it was not just calories on the hoof, but a valued being with its own biography of social transactions beginning with the specific plans for an animal and ending in its festive demise. From the human point of view, the normal context for eating beef would have been in a large social gathering, possibly dedicated to a specific event, purpose or transaction. Indeed, it seems quite possible that the typical Italian Neolithic person only ate beef at or in the aftermath of a large social gathering.

Returning to our idea of cuisine, like the "flavours," meat would have involved movement and sociality on a larger scale than starches, through different kinds of areas, and in more punctuated, irregular rhythms. Sensorially, the comparatively richer, fat and protein laden taste of meat, mirrored in its ochre-like reddish-brown colours, may have combined with these rhythms and occasions to form the taste of sociality.

Is there any evidence from the Italian Neolithic for this scenario? Needless to say, there are only suggestive scraps. Faunal data sometimes show cattle killed at quite advanced ages, in contrast to sheep, goats and pigs. At Torre Sabea, for example, 40 percent of the cattle survived to 5 years of age or more (Vigne 2003), and at Casale del Dolce pigs and sheep/goats were generally eaten young, while cattle were kept to older ages (Tagliacozzo and Fiore 1997). As noted above, stable isotope evidence suggests that meat and dairy products did not form the bulk of the diet; we may perhaps infer that meat was eaten in small quantities and/or irregularly. Rather than pure subsistence, the prestige of possessing cattle and the ability to fulfill social obligations such as feasts or marriage payments may have been one of the primary motives for building up a cattle herd. As for ownership and use of animals, the only evidence for the form of ownership comes from the Tavoliere, where ditched villages are commonly subdivided by smaller internal enclosures. These subenclosures have been interpreted as cattle *kraals* (Jones 1987), implying that individual family groups controlled their own small herds. It is also suggestive that sites with the highest proportion of cattle tend to be larger, aggregated villages such as in the Siracusa area. In areas such as

Table 13. *Spatial Differences in Sheep/Goat and Cattle Bones at Passo di Corvo*

	MNI Bos	MNI Ovis/Capra	NISP Bos	NISP Ovis/Capra
Inside c-ditches/ ditch fill	52	68	878	1,255
Outside c-ditches	18	15	480	578
Chi-squared	Chi-squared 3.13, p = 0.077		Chi-squared 5.12, p = 0.024	

Source: Data summarised from Sorrentino 1983.

Southern Calabria, cattle appear to have been eaten less often. Though cattle were kept, population may have been too dispersed to regularly get up a quorum to eat one.

Some further evidence comes from the Tavoliere. At Passo di Corvo [Table 13; data summarised from Sorrentino (1983)], within Tinè's excavations two areas were enclosed by small "c-ditches" thought to mark family compounds. When the faunal assemblages are summed by location, fauna from inside the c-ditches, and from their ditch fill has relatively more sheep and goat bones. Fauna from outside of the c-ditches, in what was presumably communal space, has a slightly higher proportion of cattle bones. Although cattle bones are more robust than sheep, and there may have been more destruction by trampling outside family compounds than in ditch fill, this would not seem to account for the difference, as caprovine bones from ditch fill and external areas show about the same proportions of robust and fragile body parts. The preferential cleaning of larger bones inside family compounds would not be a factor because the bones would likely simply have been dumped in the ditch fill. Instead, the difference may reflect social factors and may suggest that cattle and sheep were consumed in slightly different contexts: sheep/goats in family compounds, and cattle in areas shared by many families.

At this point we must ask: why bother to keep sheep and goats at all? Choices in domestic animals are often explained through reference to the mixture of resources locally available (Barker 1981; Halstead 1981), with pigs and cattle as woodland foragers and browsers, and caprovines as pasture grazers. But most of Italy had not yet been deforested in the Neolithic period (Delano Smith 1979; Delano Smith

1983; Malone 1994), and, before intensive pastoralism, herds may never have outgrown the pasture available nearby. Instead, studies of modern subsistence herders suggest that there are two basic motives behind the mixture of animals we see in Neolithic Italy. The first concerns herd security. Typically pastoralists who specialise in one animal get larger returns of a few products and have herds with higher growth potential, but they sacrifice the security that comes from a diversified resource base (Glass 1991). Sheep and goat herders in the Middle East historically gauged their mixture of sheep and goats to achieve long-term herd security rather than the maximum possible return in a given year (Redding 1981). African pastoralists as well almost always combine several animals in their herds (Dahl and Hjort 1976). Even where cattle are the main focus of herding, sheep and goats are kept for their ability to survive droughts, to hedge against cattle disease, to provide milk in the dry season when cattle are dry, and for their ability to build up a herd quickly after a disaster or for young herders just getting started. In temperate zones, pigs serve a similar purpose. They require minimal supervision, use different resources from herbivores, cost little to raise compared to cattle, and grow quickly. In the Neolithic, mixed herds probably provided ecological insurance. The second concern is that if cattle served primarily as valuables for storing labor and converting it to prestige and social control, sheep and goats would have formed the "small change." Providing less meat and reproducing rapidly, sheep and goats are often sacrificed at minor or private rituals, or are used for serving honored guests within the home or for daily family consumption rather than general distribution.

Cooking

How did Italian Neolithic people cook? Grain and legumes were presumably either boiled in pottery vessels or in other kinds of vessel such as leather bags or baskets, or baked as bread or hearth cakes. It is not surprising that there is little actual evidence for such food preparation, which involved simple technology and would leave little trace beyond utilitarian pottery, grinding stones and hearths. Significantly, given a fire and prepared ingredients, these techniques involve little labor and could be done equally easily for small or large quantities of food.

In contrast, earth-pit cooking provided a quite distinct way of preparing food which involved more labor and was used for greater quantities of food. The key evidence here comes from the so-called *strutture di combustione* ["burning structures"] found on many Neolithic sites and known from the beginning of the Neolithic (Guilaine and Cremonesi 2003) through its end. These are shallow pits filled with charcoal and burned rocks. For example, at the Contrada Diana site on Lipari, Bernabò Brea and Cavalier (1960, p. 12, Tav. 3, 5) found many hearths in an area apparently free of houses and other structures. These were all a meter or more in diameter – larger than one would need for cooking hearth cakes or pots of liquid food – sometimes dug into the ground surface by up to 30 cm, and filled with a thick layer of charcoal at the base of the hearth, with a dense heap of small stones on top of it. At Mileto near Firenze, three such structures were excavated, this time rectangular and with clay-lined bases reddened through exposure to heat (Sarti et al. 1991). They were filled with cobbles and charred remains of large branches still remained in situ at their base (Figure 27a). The smallest was 120 × 90 cm, the second was 210 × 90 cm, and the largest 410 × 120 cm. Similar structures have been found at many other sites throughout the Italian peninsula (Cremonesi 1988; Sarti et al. 1991); a notable example is Catignano, where the largest pit was 8.5 m long (Tozzi and Zamagni 2003). *Strutture di combustione* often seem to have been used only once or over a short span (Bernabò Brea, Castagna, and Occhi 2003) and this may suggest that they were not features of daily or permanent use but created for special occasions.

These stone-filled hearths are clearly to be distinguished from "normal" hearths, which are usually smaller, less substantial, and not filled with stones. They have been interpreted as open pits for firing pottery, in which stones helped to conserve heat and reduce the thermal shock to the pots being fired (Sarti et al. 1991) However, this view seems doubtful for a number of reasons. In the first place, they are too large. Estimates for the Greek Neolithic (Perlès and Vitelli 1999; Vitelli 1995) suggest that each potter would have made only a handful of pots a year, requiring a smallish kiln or pit. Bonfires larger than about a meter in diameter are found when specialist potters are producing large numbers of vessels for market economies (Rice 1987). A kiln, or firing pit no larger than necessary would have allowed better control of firing as well as concentrating heat rather than allowing it to dissipate. Second, although stones do conserve heat, they also cool rapidly from very high temperatures; although they maintain relatively low heat for a long period, they would rapidly fall below the 600°C needed to fire pottery. Finally, rocks tend to explode when moisture trapped along fracture lines expands; this is especially true for shales, cherts, flints, and similar stones. A fire on a bed of cobbles is almost always accompanied by the crack of rocks exploding. At Mileto the excavators note "the fractures and alterations of the rocks caused by the fire's action were very evident" (Sarti et al. 1991, p. 119). It is difficult to imagine this being anything but a severe liability inside a small enclosed space full of fragile unfired pottery vessels. Probable ceramic kilns are known from several sites, including Trasano and Ripa Tetta (Cassano, Muntoni, and Conati Barbaro 1995) in the south and Casa Gazza in the Po Valley (Bernabò Brea 1987). These are smaller (usually not exceeding a meter in diameter), circular, and have raised clay walls which may be related to the need to control the air and temperature during firing. We may also discount the possibility of heating rocks to be dropped in pots for heating food or for creating steam for saunas or sweat lodges. Both would probably result in rocks removed from hearths rather than remaining in them; neither would require such large structures.

Instead, it is likely that these large stone-and-charcoal filled pits are in fact the remains of earth ovens (Figure 27b) (Dering 1999). Earth ovens are a widely-known tool for slow-cooking a wide variety of foods (Sillitoe 1997; Steensberg 1980). One digs a shallow pit, lines it with stones, and builds a large fire in it. More stones are put in the fire to heat up. After several hours, the fire has burned down to embers and the rocks are very hot. At this point, most of the hot stones and embers are removed, and the food is placed in the pit, wrapped up in bundles inside leaves or greens. The food is covered with a layer of grass or leaves, or, in the case of North American clambakes, seaweed; this covering serves to hold heat and moisture in. The hot rocks and embers are replaced on top and the whole thing is buried under a layer of soil typically 10–20 cm thick. The soil seals and insulates the capsule of food and hot rocks inside, which steam away for a time interval ranging from several hours through several days. Earth ovens are a very versatile way

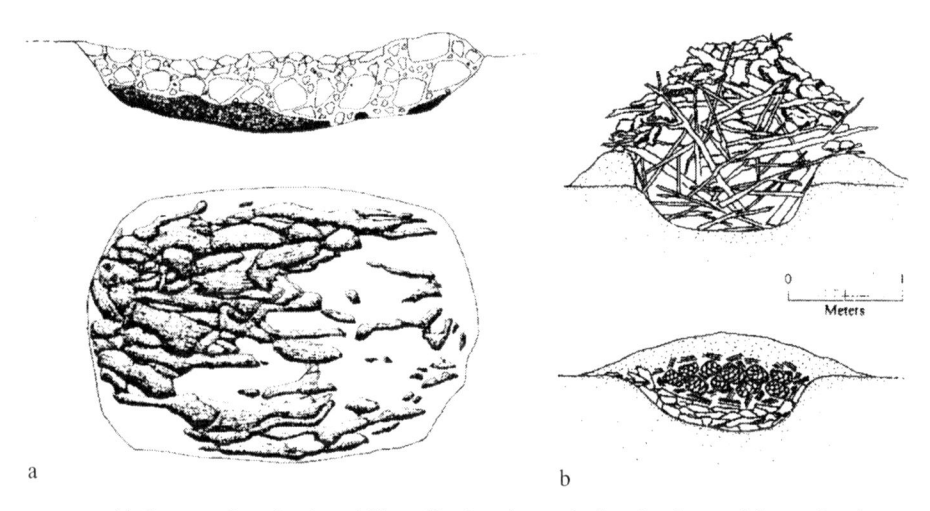

27. (a) *Struttura di combustione*, Mileto (Sarti et al. 1991), showing layer of charcoal and ash underlying burnt rocks; (b) Earth oven from ethnoarchaeological reconstruction, showing rocks, coals, and food buried under earth during cooking (Dering 1999).

of cooking. In Native North America, for instance, hunter–gatherers used them to roast fibrous roots and tubers which required very long cooking (Dering 1999). In New Guinea, they were the standard way of cooking pig meat for feasts, as well as other kinds of food on other occasions (Sillitoe 1997; Steensberg 1980). In Polynesia, they were used for large pig roasts in which many kinds of food were cooked, including occasionally humans.[5]

Archaeologically, earth ovens would consist of broad, shallow pits filled with a mixture of charcoal and burnt stones. This closely matches the pits with filled with rocks above beds of charcoal known from Italian Neolithic sites. It is true that the *strutture di combustione* rarely contain animal bone or food remains (Sarti et al. 1991). However, one would hardly expect food to be left in cooking pits after cooking, especially if it consisted of large, easily collected pieces rather than small, easily dispersed items such as grain. Moreover, as the fires increased in size, they would tend to become long and rectangular; for 10 m^2 of cooking area, it would be much easier to maintain and control a linear fire 10 m by 1 m than a circular conflagration 3 m in diameter. This is probably the reason for the elongated *strutture di combustione* at Mileto and Catignano.

What was cooked in earth ovens? Among the foods we know were eaten, grains and legumes would have needed either prolonged boiling in liquid or relatively short baking, as in making breads, though one cannot discount the possibility of covered pots full of grains and legumes being buried in earth ovens to steam or boil. Whether or not this was the case, it seems highly likely that earth ovens were used to cook large cuts of meat, as in Melanesia and Polynesia. We cannot document the association of earth ovens with particular species of animal, and they could have been used to cook all the animals, but they do suggest meat consumption on a relatively large scale, either when found in substantial numbers as at the Contrada Diana or when found in particularly large examples as at Catignano.

Special modes of cooking in themselves are an important part of a cuisine, an element often paired with particular foods, occasions and assemblages of people (Lupton 1996; Wiessner, and Schiefenhövel 1996). Combined with evidence that the daily diet involved predominantly vegetable foods cooked in varying quantities around household hearths, we begin to have a picture of large numbers of people aggregating infrequently to feast on large amounts of specially-cooked meat and other foods.

Culinary Prehistory: Neolithic Cuisine as Habitus and Taskscape

Let us now draw together the basic argument. I have argued that there were four basic "food groups" in the Neolithic diet (Table 14).

1. The first is potential food resources which were in fact never or seldom eaten, including other people, dogs, and probably other carnivores, fish, and often game. Probably each of these had its own rationale for exclusion from the diet or low consumption; the economic organizsation of task activities seems a possible reason for both game and fish.

2. The bulk of the diet came from grain and legumes. These were produced locally, probably by households, prepared in any quantity needed, and eaten in large daily doses – probably close to a kilo of

Table 14. *Summary of Possible Neolithic Food Resources*

	Archaeologically Attested	Possible/Probable but Not Usually Archaeologically Attested	Available but Apparently Not Used or Little Used
Bulk starches	Wheat, barley, peas, lentils, vetch	Chestnuts, acorns, wild nuts	
Protein	Cows, sheep, goats, pigs; shellfish; game (deer, turtles, etc.) in some regions	Snails; (milk and cheese?)	Fish; game (in many regions); (milk and cheese?); dogs; other people
Vegetables		Wild greens, roots, tubers, etc.	
Fats		Domestic animal fats	Wild animal fats?
Sweeteners		Honey, wild fruits	
Flavourings		Salt, wild herbs	
Food additives		Wild yeasts (fermentation, bread rising); smoke (preserving); sun (preserving)	
Alcoholic beverages		Beer, fermented honey or wild fruits	
Narcotics		Poppy	

bread, porridge or pottage per person every day. They created a basic brownish-yellow, bland canvas for the cuisine.

3. Supplementing these were the "flavours" – salt, fats, honey, wild fruit, herbs, and so forth. These were pungent and flavourful, used in small quantities, gathered seasonally or opportunistically, and involved moving in peripheral or strange lands and trading. They added nutrients, variety, flavour, and colour, and references to other qualities and places.

4. Finally, meat was produced socially through transactions circulating animals and consumed socially in punctuated episodes of feasting; these may have been marked by special modes of cooking in earth ovens. Sheep and goats were eaten most frequently, but cattle provided most

of the meat. Cows would have been social valuables appreciated and circulated during their lifetimes; when they were eaten, large numbers of people got together for a social occasion.

We can now return rapidly to our idea of cuisine and the anthropology of food. If this reconstruction of Neolithic diet is correct, at least in broad outlines, food would have been a fundamental way of constituting social meanings. Coherences and contrasts among kinds of foods furnish a vocabulary for experiencing and understanding social distinctions. There are several possible theoretical platforms for understanding the experience of food. One is the poststructuralism of Bourdieu. In discussing the Kabyle habitus, Bourdieu (1977) integrates cuisine with elements such as architecture, sensory qualities, directional orientation, and time. An alternative approach is the strain of phenomenology proposed by Ingold (2000). Although Ingold's work is not immune from criticism, his emphasis on the temporality and spatiality of everyday activity is invaluable here. Ingold's concept of taskscape (Chapters 1 and 3 in this book) expresses very well the sense of temporal rhythms, spatial embeddedness and social occasion which make food so important.

As we noted in Chapter 1, structuralist analysis, though a bad master, can be a good servant; as a tactic of analysis it can afford an entrée into systems of meaning. Neolithic cuisine was centered in a series of contrastive relations between categories of food. But these contrastive relations were latent and experienced, not synoptically static. I do not claim that Neolithic people would necessarily have verbalised the structure of their cuisine in the way I do above. We do not need to suppose all of these meanings were discursive and explicit. As with many meanings, the meanings of culinary experience may have been taken for granted, and uttered primarily on festive occasions when eating was heavily ritualised, or when the basic principles of cuisine were violated.

Here the contrast between elements of cuisine gave them a potential for signification which each would not have possessed upon its own. Each kind of food had its own concordance of technology, taste, times and places, and social interaction (summarised in Table 15). Contrasts in these categories allowed foods to be experienced meaningfully. Thus, the starches, the familiar and unaccented canvas of culinary experience, contrasted with both the flavours, as notes of distinction in many

Table 15. *Neolithic Cuisine as a Generative Map*

Not Eaten: Fish, Shellfish, Game (Variable), Dog, Carnivores, Other People		
Starches	Flavours	Meat
Yellow-brown, homogeneous colours	Sometimes bright, highly varied colours	Reddish-brown colours
Bland flavours	Sharp, highly varied flavours	Rich flavours (fat and protein)
Produced in any amount desired	Possibly limited supply dependent on production/trade	Produced in animal-sized packages
Continuously consumed in large amounts	Consumed in small amounts, possibly irregularly	Eaten sporadically in large amounts by groups
Locally produced, circulated and consumed; household sociality	Produced via extended social relations/ knowledge of surrounding area	Produced in wide social range of pasturage and transactions

ways – taste, temporality, spatiality, sociality, and with meat, whose spatiality, temporality, and sociality was redolent of extra-household sociality and heightened interaction. Foods such as meat are not "natural symbols" with universal meanings, nor are they completely arbitrary signifiers whose meanings were governed simply by contrastive opposition. Rather, the experience of consumption would have in part derived from the social organisation, the rhythm and sense of occasion created by eating events. Taste is an integral part of memory and remembered sensations of taste and smell form much of the substance of a sense of occasion; they provide compelling mnemonics (Hamilakis 1998; Hamilakis 1999). Thus, for example, if meat was consumed primarily in large quantities on sporadic, convivial occasions, its taste would have come to form the sensory representation of these occasions, in contrast to daily foods; cattle would have stood to sheep and pigs as meat in general did towards other foods, as a signifier of larger scale gathering and festivity. Conversely, while archaeological discussions of food have tended to emphasise meat, drink, and feasting and, hence, to implicitly devalue plain starches, they may have been experienced precisely as a signifier of social relations which were dependable, intimate, and safe, part of a stable core of being – the daily bread, the taste of home, the dependability of the household, or the social recognition inherent in the common tribal practices of expectable hospitality.

Hence, food served up meanings as part of a habitus, as a way in which basic structuring principles of social life were reproduced and experienced daily. Nutrition was a social process: ultimately it was by acting out social strategies and experiencing cultural meanings that the environment was transformed into people's bodies. Neolithic cuisine formed a generative map for social life. In effect, we have the opposite of our experience of a decontextualised "ethnic" recipe concocted of supermarket ingredients in a 30-minute slot after the evening commute. Eating and drinking as a social activity require commitment to a way of life. To eat a cow in the correct Neolithic way (or even to devise a new way of eating it which would make sense as a statement within a Neolithic context) one would have to live and act as a Neolithic person over many years.

The practices of cuisine must have interlocked inextricably with other fields of action. For example, I have said little of the skill and experience needed to procure, prepare, and serve Neolithic food, but an individual's knowledge and capacity at gardening, herding, butchery, baking, and cooking may have been a recognised and cultivated part of their social identity. On a material level, there were chains of provision linking cuisine with other tasks such as making pots, stone tools, and fire-making. Organisationally, the strategic logic of procuring and choosing an animal or other food for a feast would have involved careful consideration of things such as where people lived and the potential for aggregation and customs and rules for transactions. Politically, highly structured eating may have been an essential part of Neolithic politics, as in most premodern societies (Dietler 1996; Dietler and Hayden 2001). Experientially, the sensory and organisational contrast between starches and flavours may have mirrored colours, the contrast between the basic mud-brown of a Neolithic village and the small bright notes of ochres, fur and feathers and so on. Both cuisine and the colours and materials of daily life would have helped sustain more general concepts of kinds of spaces established through travel.

To conclude, Neolithic cuisine formed a fundamental part of the Italian Neolithic taskscape, the temporally and socially embedded accumulation of tasks and activities. Food as an institutionalised set of practices merges beliefs, social relations, economic and technological systems, space and temporal rhythms, and sensory experience. By discussing the total food practices, or cuisine, of a society as a coherent entity, we can understand how food consumption was central to social reproduction. Eating Neolithic porridge, or bread, or beef, with Neolithic tastes in a Neolithic setting may have combined a particular sensory experience, a sense of sociality, the rhythm and periodicity of Neolithic life, and a wide range of social relations and obligations. Cooking the Neolithic way meant reproducing Neolithic society. Hence, Neolithic foods provided symbolic resources for social agents, and Neolithic cuisine as an institution provided a generative map for different kinds of meanings about the social world, meanings which were continuously generated in the practices of eating and which provided a symbolic resource for actors planning and carrying them out. The result of this is a kind of thick description of Neolithic life, and it goes some way to explaining both why people are committed to an arbitrary social order and how their active, intentional endeavors reproduced this social order with great stability over long periods, and then changed it rapidly.

Finally, normality and change are inextricable. Even if we are not fundamentally interested in paleocuisine, we must understand the meaning of food if we are to make sense of long-term economic change. This point has been made for discussions of why Mesolithic foragers may have adopted cultigens at the beginning of the Neolithic (Price 2003; Robb and Miracle 2007; Thomas 2003). However, we have not considered the Late Neolithic and the Copper Age economic change in this light. We will return to this question at length in Chapter 8. Here, it provides an example of the value of the approach taken here.

Late Neolithic Italians turned took up herding much more extensively, a trend which probably continued into the Copper and Bronze Age with innovations such as transhumance in high mountains. Why? There is no real evidence for pressure on resources, and if they simply needed to come up with more calories to cope with population increase, the most effective tactic would have been simply to grow more grain, and there were certainly land and labor available for this. I would argue, instead, that the limiting factor on Neolithic political formations was simply one's ability to recruit labor and convince people to cooperate in more extended formations rather than being self-sufficient. If we are correct in linking animals and inter-household sociality and starches with household solidarity, meat was the principal food entailing cooperative production and reciprocal obligations in consumption. It is no surprise that people manipulating inter-household social obligations made use of foods associated, in their experience, with the taste of sociality.

FIVE:
MATERIAL CULTURE AND PROJECTS OF THE SELF

I used sometimes to despair that I never discussed anything with the young men but livestock and girls, and even the subject of girls led inevitably to that of cattle.
> E. E. Evans-Pritchard, *The Nuer.* (Evans-Pritchard 1940, p. 19)

Listen again. One evening at the Close
Of Ramanán, ere the better Moon arose,
In that old Potter's Shop I stood alone
With the clay Population round in Rows.
And strange to tell, among the Earthen Lot
Some could articulate, while others not:
And suddenly one more impatient cried –
"Who *is* the Potter, pray, and who the Pot?"
> Edward FitzGerald, *The Rubaiyat of Omar Khayyam,* first edition: LIX–LX (FitzGerald 1859/1957, p. 48)

Archaeological Classics

Evans-Pritchard went to the Sudan hoping to study Nuer social structure. Instead, he found himself becoming an expert on Nuer cattle because that is what the Nuer wanted to talk about. This neatly captures the relationship between the archaeologist and her materials. We want to learn about people, but what we have is broken pottery and thrown-away stone tools. The redeeming aspect of the situation is that things were important to ancient people, probably in a much more intimate way than in our world, where systems of production distance people from material things and disposability and substitution are rife. The challenge is to walk a fine line, learning enough about cattle or pottery or axes to understand the material conversations they formed part of without succumbing to the specialists' myopia that the artefacts themselves are the most important thing.

In this chapter, we turn to the heart of traditional archaeology: durable artefacts of clay and stone. Although there is an enormous theoretical and methodological literature on each of these, my goal is not to discuss them encyclopedically, or even comprehensively. Instead, I try to situate each within a set of material practices. Every field of material production involves specific meaning-laden forms of agency. As natives, we negotiate the material discourses of life without thinking. But as archaeologists, we often try to relate pottery design and grand social patterns, or axes and ancestors, or exotic goods and prestige competition, without first asking how people actually made and used these things. We need to tack back and forth between emerging patterns of variation and our choice of methods – in effect, the archaeological equivalent of listening sensitively to our informants and talking about cattle if that is what interests them.

Thus, for each genre of artefact, after reviewing some basic background, I try to bring out the salient points of the data in a thick description which inevitably finishes by slipping into the archeology of the subjunctive mood – as all ambitious interpretation should; if we are not pushing the limits of the data we are not asking enough questions.

At the outset I would like to make a plea for the reader's informed sympathy. An exposition of what pottery and lithics meant has to thread a delicate path between two perils, not unlike Odysseus' twin whirlpools Scylla and Charybdis.[1] On one hand, much of the meanings involved are subtle and tacit at best. Hence, a reader interested solely in the "big story" of economic survival or political process might well conclude that the finer points of pottery decoration are basically trivial – something like analyzing the structural contrasts of red and blue in the campaign posters of a presidential election; it certainly can be done but it may not bear upon what we really want to know about politics. I believe this is ultimately not the case, but only by reviewing a huge amount of what looks like minutiae can this be argued persuasively. On the other hand, implicit meanings, expounded explicitly, almost always sound overblown and forced, as if we claim portentously to read the meaning of the universe in a single grain of sand. This is the fallacy of symbolic explication.

Pottery and stone tools can never be skeleton keys to unlock all of Neolithic secrets. But they do tell us something, and perhaps something important. If nothing else, they can tell us about the ordinary order of things, the diffuse power of the quotidian to create a sense of inevitable normality in the constructed caprices of social life and an inescapable backdrop for other stories we might wish to tell.

Pottery and Meaning

Italian Neolithic Pottery: A Social History

A BIT OF HISTORIOGRAPHY: As a graduate student at the University of Michigan, I often wondered why the required archaeological theory course there was known as "Archaeological Systematics." Behind this austere tribute to ancestral days when debates on Midwestern pottery taxonomy filled the corridors of Ann Arbor, there lurked a serious issue, one I only understood years later when I tried in earnest to understand Italian Neolithic pottery. Before we can sort out our potsherds archaeologically, we need to have an idea of how people used and thought about pottery, and this is an issue which goes to the heart of social theory.

The traditional pottery typology of the Southern Italian Neolithic was constructed by systematically applying concepts only partially suited to the material. Like culture historians throughout Europe, pioneering synthesisers assumed that the archaeological record was formed by a succession of styles, each following the last and each typical of a particular area (Radmilli 1974; Rellini 1934). This approach was the principal one taught in mid-century European archaeology, and in Italy as elsewhere it grounded an enormous advance in systematizing pottery sequences to the point where sherds could often provide a reliable means of dating a site. The cultural sequences constructed this way still form the backbone of Italian prehistory.

However, this method had several limitations for social analysis. Each assemblage was assigned to a typological "culture" based on a small fraction of "typical" sherds, usually decorated finewares, wasting much potential information. Rather than a neat succession of styles, it frequently turned out that several pottery styles were used together, not merely for a brief interval of transition, but for generations or centuries. Finally, some styles, particularly trichrome and Serra d'Alto wares, were used in many regions together with other wares, rather than representing something "typical" to a particular region or period. Italian prehistorians have generally reacted to these difficulties with empirical commonsense, by adjusting the relevant culture histories and by increasingly using pottery only for dating sites rather than for any social inference. Theoretical revision came from Anglo-American archaeologists. These criticised the typological concepts along the lines outlined above (Whitehouse 1969) and tried to make social inferences. Malone (1985) argued that some wares, especially painted and Serra d'Alto wares, were used primarily in ritual contexts and were traded over long distances. Although thin-section studies (Muntoni 2003; Skeates 1992; Spataro 2002) have generally suggested local production for almost all vessels of all types, and painted wares are often found in nonritual sites, Malone is undoubtedly correct that vessels of different styles within an assemblage probably had different social uses. More recently, Skeates (1998) and Pluciennik (1997) have made persuasive arguments that Italian Neolithic pottery must be contextualised within local social relations.

This stratigraphy of reasoning exemplifies wonderfully the principal ways in which archaeologists have contemplated material culture around the world – as tradition-bound traits, as New Archaeology–style social tokens whose prestige-value derives from an exotic origin or special use and as symbolically-laden creations whose significance is related to use in particular contexts. Each method is supported by its methodological armature. In the culture historical tradition, one focuses on the typical rather than upon variability and assigns artefacts to typological categories, in the processual version one tackles contextual variation with statistical analysis, and in the post-processual version the focus is upon contextual variation and symbolic exegesis. All three approaches have made significant contributions to our understanding of Neolithic Italian pottery.

THE GENEALOGY OF POTTERY TRADITIONS: Pottery came to Italy with the earliest Neolithic, almost certainly from the Ionian Islands of northwestern Greece where coarse Impressed Wares are known (Papathanassopoulos 1996). At this point, the pottery repertory consisted of coarse vessels in a narrow range of bowls and jars, either undecorated or sprinkled all over with casually made impressions. Firing was at relatively low temperatures even by Neolithic standards, resulting in coarse, crumbly reddish-brown fabrics. In this early, evanescent interval, known from very few sites (such as Prato Don Michele on the Tremiti Islands), these Impressed Wares seem to have spread to enclaves all around the Italian and Sicilian coasts to Liguria, where a particular version known as Cardial Ware provided the progenitor of the next long-range coastal expansion westward into Southern France and Spain. A simultaneous spread of pottery up the east coast of the Adriatic resulted in very similar early Impressed Wares along the Dalmatian coast and in Istria (Forenbaher and Miracle 2005).

Very shortly after the initial spread of Impressed Wares – probably within a few generations at most – the internal dynamics of pottery assemblages changed dramatically.[2] This was with the development of finewares (Figure 28). Within each assemblage, we find distinct kinds of vessel, each with specific forms, surface treatments, and decorative patterns. Such wares would have been recognised by natives as distinct categories of vessel in production and use. A typical assemblage (Figure 29) contains several wares:

- large storage and processing vessels, undecorated or decorated with imprecise, rapidly executed all-over impressions made with sticks or fingers;
- moderate-sized vessels with rough or smoothed surfaces, undecorated or decorated with geometric arrays of impressions, in forms suggesting cooking and utilitarian uses; and

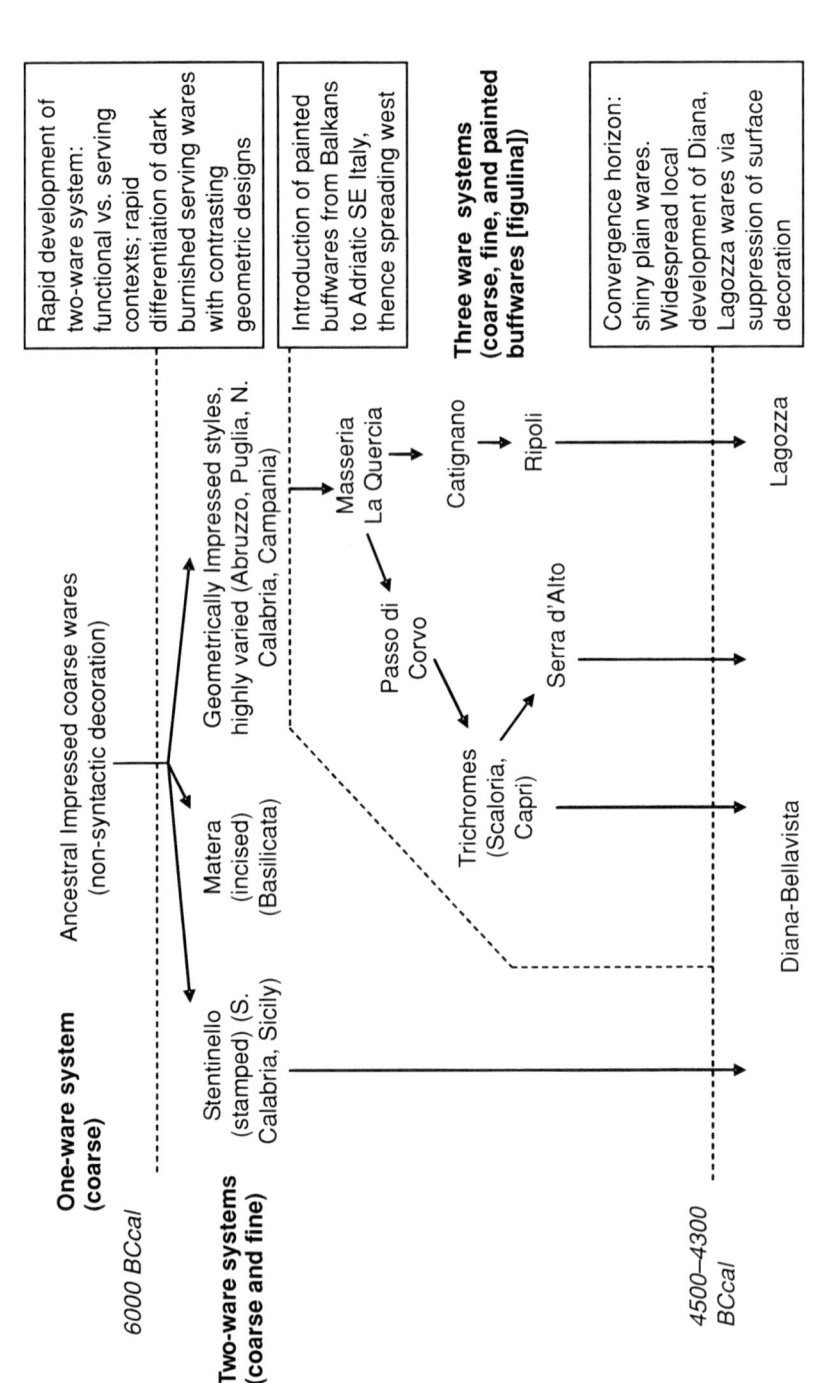

28. Genealogy of Neolithic pottery traditions.

29. Typical Neolithic vessel forms (drawing: J. Robb and J. Skinner).

- small and medium sized vessels in forms suggesting serving, eating and drinking (cups, small bowls, large bowls, flasks), with smoothed or carefully burnished surfaces, often decorated elaborately

Finewares probably developed as pottery use spread to new social contexts of eating and drinking. Their elaborate decoration suggests a concern with presentation of the potter, if not of the consumer, in moments of sociability. Fineware decoration varies regionally. For this reason, finewares have normally provided the "type fossils" used in culture histories; coarser wares, especially large plain or impressed vessels, are fairly interchangeable throughout peninsular Italy and Sicily for most of the sixth and earlier fifth millennia. Among local styles (Figures 30 and 31; Table 16), in Puglia people adapted the technique of impressed decoration to make elaborate geometric designs. In eastern Basilicata, similar patterns were creating by scratching designs on the pots after firing (Matera Scratched Wares). In southern Calabria and eastern Sicily, impressing was combined with motifs made with fired clay stamps in dense geometric designs (Stentinello wares). In western Sicily and Malta, the designs resembled Stentinello designs, though usually with a looser, less regular geometry and without stamped designs. The high point of ceramic diversity was the early to mid-sixth millennium, when there

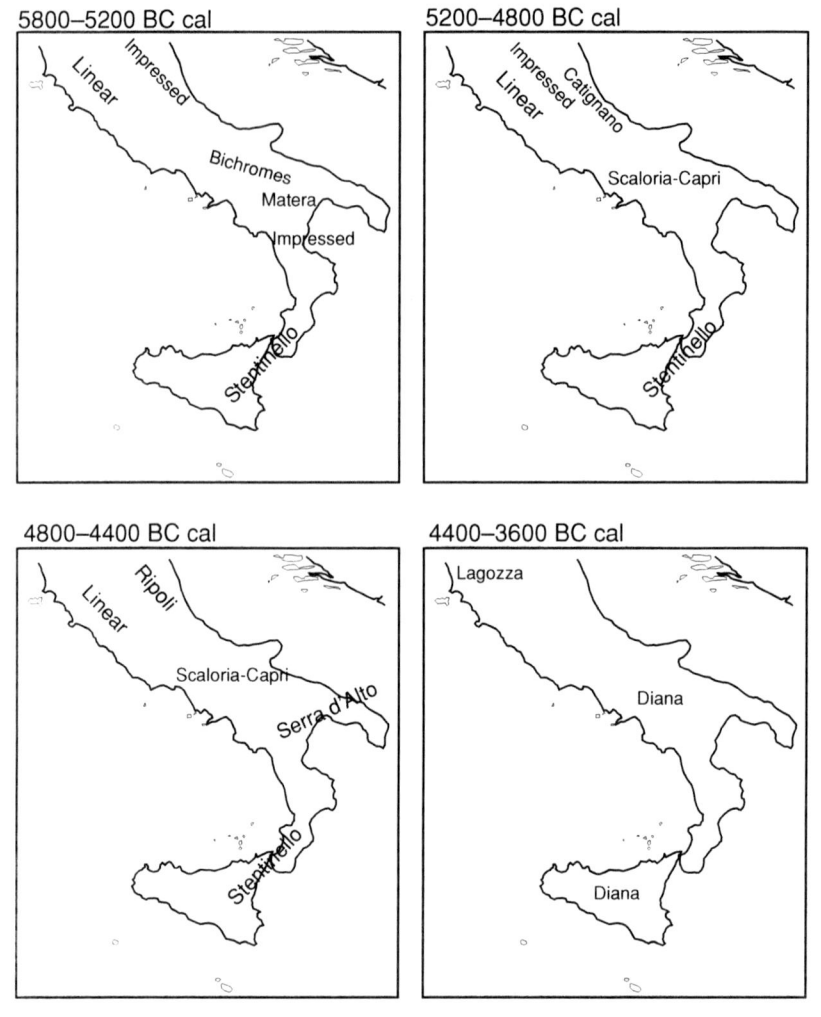

30. Approximate distribution of pottery styles through the Neolithic; note that this synoptic view masks much detailed variation both within regions and within assemblages.

were at least half a dozen distinct styles of serving vessels in use across peninsular Italy and Sicily (Figure 30).

To complicate matters, along the southern Adriatic coast, the technique of painting red, yellow, and black designs on a buff-firing fabric was learned or invented early in the sixth millennium BC (Figures 28 and 31). As a technique, painting shows clear technical links

Table 16. Ceramic Chronology

	Malta	W. Sicily	E. Sicily/ S. Calabria	Lipari	N. Calabria/ Campania	Matera	Puglia	Central Adriatic	Highland Abruzzo	Toscana/ Lazio/ Umbria	Emilia-Romagna
6500											
6250							Impressed			Impressed/ Linear	Impressed/ Linear
6000		Impressed/ Stentinello	Stentinello		Impressed/	Impressed/ Matera	Impressed/ MLQ	Impressed			
5700											
5500	Ghar Dalam			Stentinello			PdC	Catignano	Impressed		VBQ
5250			Stentinello		Trichrome						
5000	Skorba			Trichrome			Trichrome	Ripoli	Ripoli		
4750				SdA	SdA	SdA	SdA				
4500								Lagozza			Lagozza
4250		Diana		Diana	Diana	Diana	Diana		Ripoli/ Lagozza/	Ripoli/ Lagozza/	
4000	Mgarr		Diana						Diana	Diana	
3750											
3500								V			

Note: This table follows traditional conventions in including only one "typical" ware per time and region. Also note that absolute dates are lacking for many regions and in such cases dates are based on extrapolation from neighboring areas. PdC = Passo di Corvo, MLQ = Masseria la Querica, SdA = Serra d'Alto, VBQ = Vaso a Bocca Quadrata.

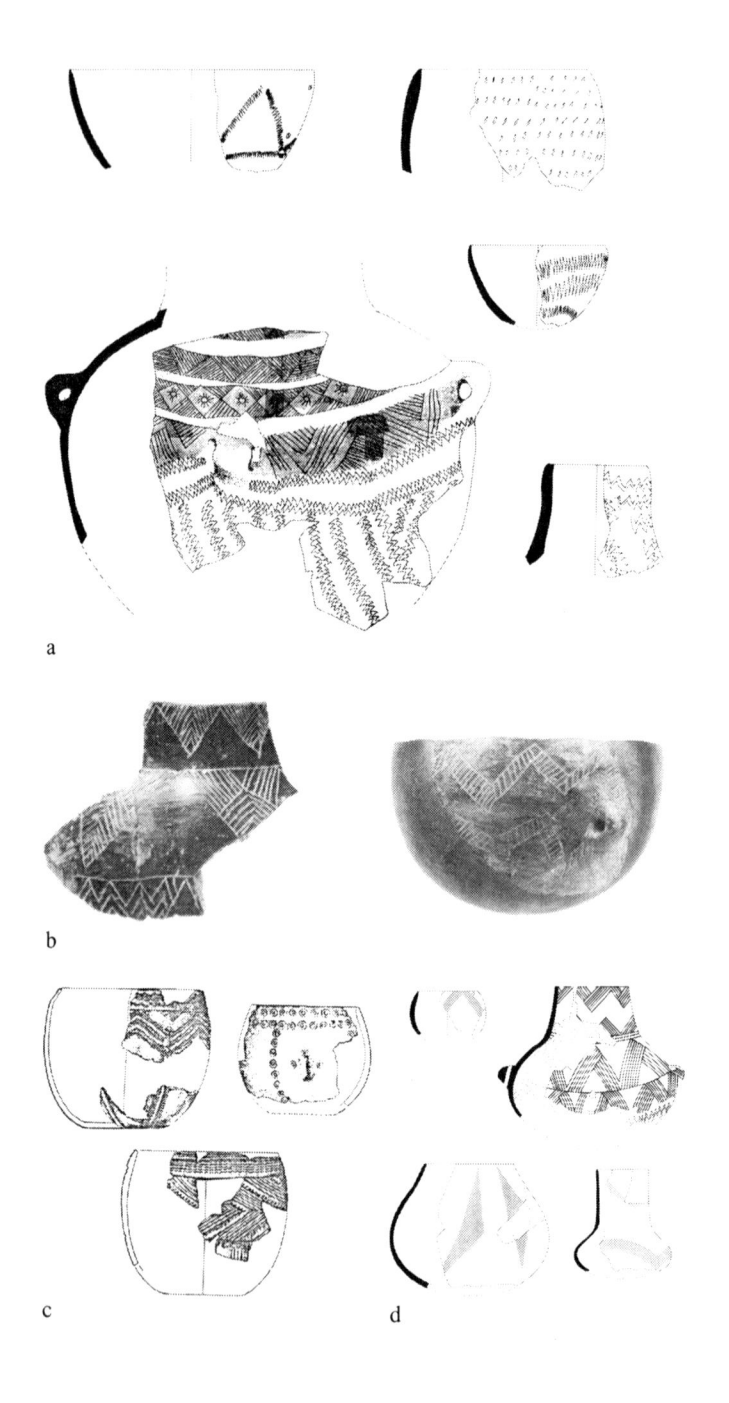

a

b

c   d

31. Examples of regional pottery styles. (a) Impressed wares from Lagnano da Piede (Mallory 1987, courtesy of J. Mallory); (b) Matera scratched wares from Grotta dei Pipistrelli (left) and Tirlecchia (right) [Soprintendenza Archeologica della Basilicata (1976), courtesy of *Soprintendenza Archeologica della Basilicata*]; (c) Stentinello wares from Capo Alfiere (Morter 1992); (d) Bichrome painted wares from Passo di Corvo (Tinè 1983, courtesy of S. Tinè); (e) Trichrome painted wares from Grotta delle Felci, Capri (National Museum, Naples; photo Robb); (f) Serra d'Alto wares from Serra d'Alto (Soprintendenza Archeologica della Basilicata (1976), courtesy of Soprintendenza Archeologica della Basilicata); and (g) Diana wares from Contrada Diana, Lipari (Bernabò Brea and Cavalier 1960, courtesy of M. Cavalier and Museo Archeologico Eoliano).

to contemporary Greek ceramics, and it is not by chance that it is first found in southeastern Adriatic Italy. What is fascinating is that, after an initial interval when people experimented by using the new technique on the same fabrics and with the same grammars as in impressed finewares (producing La Quercia wares [see discussion of "hybrid sherds" later in the pottery section of this chapter]), a convention was quickly established which would endure throughout the Neolithic. In this convention, impressed and *figulina* painted wares were made as quite distinct genres with little technological or stylistic overlap, even when they occur within the same assemblage. Throughout the Adriatic region, throughout the sixth millennium, painted wares supplied one fineware component of assemblages, normally complemented by dark burnished undecorated wares. For eastern Italy, thus, various styles of painted ware provide the basic framework of type fossils for taxonomy (e.g., Passo di Corvo wares, Catignano wares, Ripoli wares, and Serra d'Alto wares). They spread gradually westwards to Campania and northern Calabria as an important part of the fineware element. They are commonly found elsewhere throughout peninsular Italy and Sicily as a small but consistent minority of most assemblages, probably for use in special contexts. The social role of painted buff wares is contentious, and it may have varied from place to place. On the one hand, they are clearly highly valued vessels produced with great skill, they usually form only a small fraction even of assemblages they are supposed to typify, and they are often found preferentially in ritual sites. On the other hand, they are present on most if not all settlement sites in contexts which suggest everyday usage as well. Hence it seems likely that painted wares formed a distinct and highly valued ware which was used in daily social occasions but which was also felt particularly appropriate for use on special occasions or deposition in favored contexts.[3]

Is there a social reason why Italian Neolithic finewares were so highly decorated? The proliferation of local styles, particularly on the Tavoliere may perhaps have been related to the concentration of population in dense networks of villages, but the functional linkages between style and social identification and the negotiation of social relations are poorly specified. We also find equally elaborate pots in parts of Italy where people lived in dispersed clusters of houses, as in Calabria.

The final act in the Neolithic pottery drama was the monochrome horizon. By the later fifth millennium, all of the elaborate, locally idiosyncratic decorated wares were replaced by uniform, much plainer pots. "Diana" or Diana-Bellavista wares (known after the Contrada Diana site on Lipari) (Bernabò Brea and Cavalier 1960) and the Masseria Bellavista site in Taranto (Quagliati 1906) have plain, often shiny surfaces ranging from orange to black. The range of forms is primarily shallow bowls and jars. Diana wares replace earlier styles everywhere from Malta, (in variants known as Grey Skorba and Red Skorba wares) (Trump 1966) to Central Italy. Without going into details, Diana wares probably did not originate in any one place but rather converged from local undecorated antecedents in many places. Though evidence is not clear, they seem to have been used for special purposes within assemblages dominated by other styles in the early to mid-fifth millennium before becoming dominant themselves near its end.

Diana wares vary regionally; for example, the so-called Bellavista style found in Puglia principally includes dark grayish wares. Some of this variation is no doubt due to regional differences in their antecedents. Moreover, a Diana assemblage includes a range of wares. The stereotypical fine bowls are a minority in most assemblages, and as a pottery style, Diana really replaces not just finewares such as painted vessels but the entire range of pottery in use in earlier styles. What unites Diana wares throughout their range are three elements, all visually extremely salient: the uniform shiny reddish look of many finewares, the rejection of elaborate surface decoration, and the stereotypical "spool" handles (*anse a rocchetta*) which are as instantly identifiable as an army uniform.

The monochrome horizon extended far beyond the Diana zone of Italy. A contemporary, parallel shift to plain, glossy vessels is evident across much of Southern Europe. In Adriatic and highland Central Italy the Ripoli tradition had always contained both dark burnished wares and elaborately painted trichromes, but as the fifth millennium proceeded dark burnished wares came to dominate almost exclusively (Cremonesi and Tozzi 1987). In Northern Italy and Southern France, a similar dark burnished ware horizon is evident with Chassey-Lagozza wares. This shift took place as far afield as in the Balkans (for example, with the replacement of Sesklo by Dimini wares) and in Spain with various post-Epicardial traditions. Sweeping away a long tradition of ornate pottery,

Diana wares represent an aesthetic revolution whose social significance is discussed in Chapter 8.

Skill, Orientation, and the Layering of Local Knowledge

The operational sequence or *chaîne opératoire* concept of potting gives an entrance into the social world of the potters, particularly to see the constraints on action and to locate points where social choices were important (Dobres 2001; Lemonnier 1992). As Dobres notes, technological creation is a process of self-realization as well (cf. Chapter 1 in this book). Table 17 reconstructs the approximate operational sequence for making a pottery vessel at Penitenzeria and Umbro, based on contextual evidence for pottery-making at these sites, availability of local raw materials, informal replication experiments, and ethnographic accounts (Rice 1987; Rye 1981; Shepard 1956).[4]

From start to finish, potting took at least a week or two, probably in the dry summertime, and the work required composing a range of materials, places, and tools. The scale was probably small, with a few pots produced at a time (Vitelli 1995). Although there is no concrete evidence, it would be unusual if potters did not work in small groups, at least for operations such as preparing pastes and firing where work could be effectively pooled and experience was important. If so, the work would involve a rhythm of alternation between collective and individual activity. Patient tasks, such as smoothing and burnishing, can also be done sociably. Other rhythms involved alternation between freely variable tasks such as stockpiling fuel and drying pots, and more enchained tasks where a timing and regime was closely imposed by the task. The latter include building large or composite pots, where periods of forming and joining parts alternate with periods of drying, and decorating rapidly-drying greenware and firing.

The culmination of the potting *chaîne opératoire* was firing (Rice 1987, Rye 1981, Shepard 1956). Pots can be fired even in relatively small fires; virtually anything that burns can be used as fuel, with wood and dried animal dung as common choices. Although it is common to heat the unfired pots by the edge of the fire first to drive out any remaining moisture, the process is highly variable. Firing pottery requires raising it to above 500°C for at least a short interval (ethnographic firings

Table 17. *Operational Sequence for Producing Pottery at Umbro and Penitenzeria*

Step	Materials and Facilities	Time	Space
Collecting raw materials	Clay, temper (sand, schist), water	About half a day	Trips to clay outcrops, springs, sources of sand, schist for temper (2–3 km radius)
Raw material preparation: grinding clay, crushing temper	Grinding stones, collecting basins or pits?	2–4 days per batch of pots, depending on size of batch and number of participants	Around settlement
Mixing paste	Clay and temper; water; pits or basins?	Brief (an hour or less)	Around settlement
Molding vessel body	Clay paste, water	Variable but less than 2–3 hours (15 minutes for simple bowl, longer for larger vessels or composite forms)	Around settlement
Surface preparation and decoration	Small tools (sticks, pebbles, shells, etc.)	Intermittent throughout day: half hour to two hours for bowl, plus waiting time for surface to dry enough for burnishing, impressing, etc. Variable according to interest, skill	Around settlement
Drying	Shaded place	Minimum 2–3 days in hot, dry weather, but can be longer as firing batch accumulates	Around settlements, in shaded out-of-the-way place
Preparation for firing: collecting fuel, preparing location	Fuel (about a cubic meter of wood, dry animal dung, or other fuel); possibly a constructed hearth, kiln, or clay fire ring	One half of a day?	Around fields and woods; hearth probably away from houses or just outside settlement
Firing	Fuel, pots	Actual firing minimum 1 hour; total process minimum 3–4 hours	Probably away from houses or just outside settlement

maintain peak temperatures for between a quarter of an hour to several hours). This temperature can be achieved in open fires. Kilns are useful for raising the maximum temperature achievable, for minimizing temperature fluctuations, and for controlling the air supply, particularly to achieve specific colour effects, for example, in firing painted buff finewares. Few kilns are known in the Italian Neolithic, though probable kilns are known at Trasano, near Matera, at Ripa Tetta near Lucera (Cassano, Muntoni, and Conati Barbaro 1995), and at Casa Gazza in the Po Valley (Bernabò Brea 1987). A circular daub ring which enclosed a fire in the Late Neolithic levels at Umbro may have also been used for pottery firing. Many vessels were apparently fired in open fires, however, to judge from variations in colour on their surfaces and from the fact that larger vessels tend to show less control of colour and a more oxidizing atmosphere than small vessels. Firing pots in open fires has a highly variable rate of success and even expert potters frequently find pots emerging from the ashes broken. As a part of a technical drama, firing pots involves considerable uncertainty, it places a premium upon expertise and experience, and it is highly structured temporally, with careful tending, close observation and quick adjustment. The culmination was a moment of drama: raking aside the ashes from the fire to see which vessels have survived the firing and whether the desired effects have been achieved.

Pot-making materials were freely available locally; the critical resource was knowledge, skill, and experience. Acquiring skill in potting was a project of the self which may have required years to complete. Even the maladept can quickly learn to hand-form a bowl through pinching and coiling clay; it takes prolonged experience to create a thin-walled vessel with a smooth surface of uniform thickness and curvature. The potter's knowledge base would have included not only the basics of technique and tradition but quite detailed understanding as well. For example, apparently identical clay sources around Umbro and Penitenzeria vary greatly in workability and require different recipes. Experience would have been needed in aspects such as the careful judgement of timing. Hand-building large or composite vessel forms and impressing surface decoration on green pots to achieve a specific effect involves frequent halts, resumptions and tactics to hasten or delay the clay's drying. The same is true for the skills involved in firing, particularly when a

MATERIAL CULTURE AND PROJECTS OF THE SELF

32. Penitenzeria, Bova Marina, Calabria. Stentinello style decorated bowl probably made by a learner (photo: Robb).

particular homogeneous surface colour was aimed at. Uniform dark surfaces were sometimes achieved, for example, by tactics such as carefully smudging or smothering an oxidizing fire at the last minute.

Neolithic Italian potters took their agency seriously. We know from the care and time expended to make smooth, symmetrically formed, well-finished, and often quite thin-walled vessels that potting was a seriously regarded craft. Moreover, in the surviving vessels, which presumably represent only the successful subset of all those attempted, different levels of skill are sometimes evident; skilled potters may have been informal but recognised specialists (Michelaki 2006; Vitelli 1995). Skill is a matter of forming the bodily reflexes of the self in response to experience, in effect bridging the internal-external dichotomy (Ingold 2000); skill with wheel-throwing pots, for example, does not automatically translate into skill in hand-building. Display of such technical abilities may be considered iconic of valued personality characteristics such as patience, strength, or a sense of timing (Rosaldo 1986; Sinclair 1995). In this sense, some of the more technically difficult pieces may have been attempted in part *because* of the ostentatious difficulty involved; one certainly suspects this may have been the case for the painted finewares of Adriatic Italy at least. All of these suggest the materiality of agency (Dobres 2001): working the material world as a creative drama or expression of the self.

One of the best insights into the agency of potting comes from the learning process. Figure 32 shows a fragment of the so-called Stentinello style of Early-Middle Neolithic pottery excavated at Penitenzeria. It is of a bowl about the size to fit into an adult hand, a typical vessel used to eat and drink. This vessel was probably made by someone learning to be a potter. The clues are known from ethnoarchaeological studies (Crown 2001; Kamp 2001). The most obvious is the inner surface (not shown in the photograph), which is thick and lumpy, rather like a sherd with a clay tumor. It is relatively thick-walled for a vessel of its kind. Potters learning to make coil-built vessels typically start by making uneven, thick vessels: thin, even walls take skill and practice. Moreover, the design is anomalous. The design is credible – the potter has learned the local trick of making diamonds by combining V-shaped stamps and stringing them in long rows. But compared to the rest of the assemblage, it is both imprecise and slightly blurred (in details such as the alignment of stamps to form the corners of diamonds), and ungrammatical. For example, in almost all our other vessels, the basic orientation of the design is horizontal, in bands parallel to the rim. This vessel has something like a basic Penitenzeria design but rotated at right angles. Learners often grasp the basic principles of design before they are able to execute them precisely; for example, in a canonical vessel, the nested diamonds on the left would be connected rather than floating in space. On their own, such details might well mean simply that the potter intended to make a different design, but combined with the irregular vessel walls it suggests a learner at work.

A learner at work, but not alone. Our apprentice is working with a paste identical to that found in many other pots, and one which took considerable experience and local knowledge to create from local clays. The surface is carefully smoothed. To make the design, he or she used at least four different V-shaped stamps and one linear stamp – a wide repertory of tools for these designs and a bit unexpected for a beginner. Firing vessels in an open fire is a delicate business and experience is important. It would be surprising for someone still learning to form a bowl to carry out a successful firing. All of these give the impression of someone working alongside experienced potters who gave him or her a lump of clay, passed tools around, and included the bowl in their firing. And why fire the bowl at all? A potter expert enough to produce the regular, well-smoothed, finely decorated bowls normal at Penitenzeria presumably would either have corrected the lumpy interior or consigned the pot to the midden unfired. Firing this vessel seems an act of tolerated imperfection, of tutelage.

So what? New potters have to come from somewhere; moments of learning can be taken for granted, can't they? Perhaps; but before we dismiss them, we need to consider what is taught and how. Here we are learning a way of doing, which is far more complex than a recipe or set of computer instructions. On the one hand, there is skill, the training of motor reflexes to learn movements and to understand and react to the constantly varying resistances of the clay in the hand. Training takes time and commitment, a willingness to form the self. On the other hand, the potter becomes a member of a field of action through the same process as mastering it. This is a contingent act of inclusion. There may already have been restrictions (for instance, as to the gender of potters), and there will be limits to the space of experimentation (for instance, how divergent a design one can make without being corrected). Some of the rules of the genre will be enforced by range of tools at hand, such as the V-shaped stamps, and others by the examples available for imitation, all of which follow principles of geometric designs on a rectilinear grid. The social relationship between experienced and learner potters resulted from the intersection of multiple agencies and the nature of this relationship may have been part of the field of action itself ("this is how one learns to be a potter..."). Then there is the context (proper times, places, assembly of materials, relations between people such as elders and juniors, and so on), which formed part of the order of daily life. As suggested above, the most important things we learn may be those taught nondiscursively as part of the educational process. The potter here struck out boldly by reorienting the design vertically, but did so only through conforming himself or herself to the taken-for-granted context and structures of pottery-making as an activity.

Pottery is paradoxically momentary and eternal; the act of firing closes the process and fixes the product as everlasting in comparison to the short lives of humans. Effectively, this sherd inscribes a moment in a process of social mastery and inclusion, fixing it as a point of reference and memory for both the potter and others. This sherd, for instance, attests a moment of play in design, an area in which potters had latitude to experiment and to express themselves, but the new design created remained a one-off, consigned to juvenilia rather than imitated and reproduced.

The Social Geography of Italian Neolithic Pottery

"What did it mean?" is probably the wrong question to ask about Italian Neolithic pottery. We need to understand the creative process in its own terms prior to attempting to burden it with external significances. Pottery designs referenced each other through their shared principles of composition at the same time as every one was unique. Through making pots, potters participated in material conversations. Potters were, in de Certeau's (2002, p. 34) phrase "unrecognised producers, poets of their own affairs." Like many fields of social action, pottery decoration functioned to maintain open and available a space within which people could exercise their agency as potters.

FRACTAL STYLES AND IMPRESSIONIST MAPS: How did pottery-making, as a social process, create the large scale patterning we see archaeologically? By way of illustration, we will take the Stentinello culture bowls excavated at Penitenzeria and dating to sometime between 5400 and 5000 BC (Figure 33). Theoretically, this discussion uses Barth's (1987, 2002) concept of the reproduction of knowledge. As Barth argues, a historical tradition is continually reinvented in moments of cultural production. In his example, the salient features of Mountain Ok ritual practice, particularly its florid variety and fervent, dogmatic local difference, derived from the fact that it was recreated in rituals held at long intervals by secret conclaves of old men with unreliable memories. The point of this suggestive example is that we can read large-scale historical patterns of culture by relating them to the moment of practices in which actors reproduced a particular field of action.

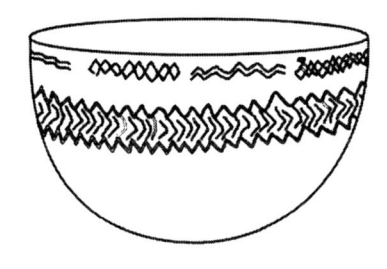

33. Penitenzeria Stentinello bowls. (a) Basic design pattern summarizing principles found in most decorated bowls (drawing: Robb); (b) Variation in actual vessel designs (photo: Robb).

When potters created a pot, they came to it armed with a repertory of techniques and ideas found throughout peninsular Italy and Sicily. The common language of pots found throughout the peninsula comprised many elements:

- technological methods and processes for collecting clay, forming pastes, shaping, and firing pots;
- a widely shared repertory of vessel forms, including bowls and jars of all sizes, tall-necked flasks and large footed cups;
- surface treatment techniques, such as smoothing and burnishing;
- decoration techniques, such as impressing, incising, scratching, and (in many regions) slipping and painting;
- decorative elements, such as dots, triangles, checkerboards, cross-hatching, diagonal slanting lines, chevrons, and other motifs; and
- principles of syntax and grammar, such as the band of motifs below the rim, the common division of a pot into horizontal zones, and the "hanging" point-down triangle.

This common repertory of resources gives Italian Neolithic pottery a distinctive feel of family resemblance. When comparing pots from different regions or styles, one still almost always finds something in common, some basis for relationship.

To create a pot, potters recombined these elements and techniques freely. The most technically unconstrained moment in the operational sequence was decorating the surface, and hence this provides the greatest scope for free self-expression. But creativity and recombination were the norm and, with a practiced eye, we can read their texture at even the finest scales. For example, the Stentinello cups from Penitenzeria, Calabria (Figure 33), are dominated by a particular design template which not only specifies a particular arrangement of elements, but also involves violating grammatical principles found in some other Stentinello pottery assemblages (e.g., the rule that all motifs must be connected in horizontal bands rather than free-floating). Yet among Penitenzeria cups laid out according to this highly rule-bound template, no two are alike; some vary the number of grammatical zones involved, the grammatical slots are filled with different motifs, and there is even variation in how a specific motif is produced (e.g., a grid motif may be made with diamond- or V- shaped stamps, linear impressions or a combination of both). While it is here shown as a schematic design, it is perhaps better understood as a set of generative reflexes for producing designs within a certain bounded possibility space. This is variation on the most local scale possible; at Umbro, 200 m away and some few centuries earlier or later, Stentinello pottery designs are found which are unknown at Penitenzeria. In Barth's terms, the recreation of knowledge at this point was the generation of difference – difference comprehensible in terms of received elements and rules but visibly novel. Creativity and innovation was the standard, but within narrow limits.

The generation of difference occurs at other scales as well, giving ceramic variability a distinctly fractal quality. Very fine-grained local variability contributes to regional sub-styles. Among Stentinello wares, for example, there are recognised sub-styles in Central Calabria, Southern Calabria, Catania, Siracusa, and Malta (Leighton 1999). These in turn are nested within the recognised regional styles such as Stentinello wares, Matera Scratched Wares, Impressed Wares, and the various styles of painted wares.

CREATIVE PROCESS AND ARCHAEOLOGICAL PATTERNING: The key point, however, is not subordinating ceramic variability to an classificatory taxonomy. Rather, the real crux is how the process of generating difference created archaeological patterns. In this, the ways in which Italian Neolithic pottery resists simple classification tell us the most about how it was made.

In this sense, the fact that styles are geographically blurry is more informative than frustrating. There is almost never uniformity within assemblages and clear difference from one's neighbors. Rather, difference ranges along a scale from the uniqueness of each vessel to the family resemblance of widely separated assemblages. Geographically, the map shows blurring, a rather Impressionistic quality. Geographic variation would have often taken the form of a cline rather than clearly bounded stylistic areas, a fertile source of taxonomic controversy. For example, in eastern Sicily, Stentinello pots share the rigid geometry and use of stamped V and diamond motifs found in southern Calabria. In western Sicily and in Malta, these features are absent and looser impressed designs prevail. Yet, there is no clear border which might demarcate these into clearly distinct typological "styles" and there is much overlap in techniques, motifs, and designs. Similarly, the distinctive feature of the Matera region was the use of designs scratched on the surface after firing. But most other features such as vessel form, surface treatment, motifs and designs are shared with neighboring regions in Puglia, scratching in known sporadically in Puglian assemblages, and other techniques such as impressing and painting turn up consistently in Materan assemblages. Only in highly unusual social circumstances can we spot archaeologically a clear, long-standing stylistic boundary. One example, the Stentinello-painted ware boundary in northern Calabria, is discussed in Chapter 7.

The analogue in time to geographic blurring is stylistic creep. Because potters recycled similar elements from similar canons, innovations tended to have limited effect on changing an overall canon, and they tended not to spread far. One result is a general conservatism; the average stylistic tradition had a lifespan of at least half a millennium, with some, such as Ripoli and Stentinello wares, persisting for over a millennium. Without abrupt breaks, long standing, recognizable traditions nevertheless shifted gradually. As one generation drew on the productions of the previous ones for its raw materials, the cumulative effect of minor shifts in choices mounted into archaeologically visible changes. At Capo Alfiere, Stentinello wares evolved over a period of centuries from predominantly dark, geometric surfaces to reddish, less rigidly structured decoration (Morter 1992). Over a millennium, the balance of Ripoli wares gradually tilted from painted wares to dark burnished wares, though both were always present (Cremonesi and Tozzi 1987).

A third formal effect of the creative process is to create what can be called "90 percent rules." Neolithic potters made pots by creative recombination, not by photocopying "typical" designs. Hence, although we can define statistical tendencies, there are virtually no unbreakable rules. Just as one swears that painting and impressing are never combined on the same vessel, that motifs near the rim always form a continuous horizontal band, that decoration is densest at the rim and decreases towards the belly of a pot, or that triangles are always placed point downwards, base upwards – examples to the contrary turn up.

Finally, pottery fixes moments of action, and we can sometimes spot actual acts of creative recombination. These are most evident either at the finest scale, as in the close reading of Penitenzeria finewares above, or at the grossest scale, when elements from completely distinct traditions are recombined. For example:

- As noted above, painting is virtually never combined with impressing; the exception is the La Quercia style, an early- to mid-sixth millennium enclave in northern Puglia with some extension to Matera, where painting was added to the preexisting technique of impressed surface decoration (Figure 34a).
- Throughout Southern Italy and Sicily, "rocker" decoration was used almost exclusively to spread over the surface of large, coarse vessels in a more or less random way. However, in the Bari-Brindisi region, the rocker motif was slotted into the role of other impressed motifs in geometric fineware (Figure 34b) (Todisco and Coppola 1980). Similarly, elsewhere, rocker was used on finewares in highly specific and restricted ways. For example, in Matera and northern Puglia, rocker decoration on finewares is found almost exclusively on the base of broad bowls which also bear painting, impressing or incising in a much more usual location around the rim.

34. Examples of recombinant pots. (a) Mixing of painting and impressing in Lagnano da Piede style, Fonteviva (Ashmolean Museum; photo: Robb); (b) Use of microrocker decorative technique in Impressed Ware assemblage, Masseria Mastrodonato, Bisceglie (Todisco and Coppola 1980, courtesy of L. Todisco); (c) Scratched rendition of "impressed" c-motif, Serra d'Alto [Soprintendenza Archeologica della Basilicata (1976), courtesy of Soprintendenza Archeologica della Basilicata]; (d) Impressed rendition of trichrome-style motif, Passo di Corvo (Tinè 1983, courtesy of S. Tinè).

- Figure 34c represents another recombination of motifs and techniques from distinct traditions. A band of c-impressions under the rim is a widespread motif within Impressed Ware traditions, well-suited to being created rapidly with a punch or stick jabbed into wet clay. Here, however, at Serra d'Alto in

Matera, an area where scratching predominated as a technique, this motif it has been recreated in Matera Scratched Ware by laboriously etching each "impression" into the fired surface (Soprintendenza Archeologica della Basilicata 1976).

- Figure 34d comes from Passo di Corvo, where painted wares were known as well as dark-surfaced impressed wares. Here, however, our potter has experimented by using impressing to recreate a jagged, free-form design typical of Scaloria trichromes and quite distinct from the rigidly bounded geometries of impressed decoration (Tinè 1983) (Tav. 118).

Again, the key point about such "mutant" sherds is that, while the results are atypical and easily identified, the process generating them was identical with that generating the thousands of "typical" sherds: potters recombining locally available elements to create make tolerable differences.

DIFFERENCE, SITUATED PERCEPTION, AND LOCAL KNOWLEDGE: How was difference perceived and understood? We do not have to posit that ceramic decorations were understood identically by all within a group, for instance by makers and users of pots. However, we are on firmer ground when we consider geographic perceptions.

All the evidence suggests that the practices of pottery-making and using were socially situated; they were agency within a very specific frame of reference shared by a particular group. On a technical level, potting is a highly local activity; clay sources differ in how they need to be worked; one is not a good potter in the abstract, one is a good potter of a specific place.[5] The localness of potting is confirmed by thin-section studies which generally show that pots were not transported any great distance (Muntoni 2003; Skeates 1992; Spataro 2002). Moreover, interpreting pottery designs involves socially contextualised knowledge. Among possible ways of viewing our Penitenzeria assemblage, someone from Northern Italy would see bowls decorated with plastic impressions, unlike the curvilinear grooved decorations back home. A visitor from Adriatic Southern Italy would probably be struck by the lack of painted wares. Someone from Basilicata or southern Puglia might well recognise familiar geometric principles – a dark surface marked with a band of geometric decoration around the rim – but the design would be carried out in unfamiliar stamping instead of being impressed or scratched on after firing. Someone from elsewhere in the Stentinello world – say, from the east coast of Sicily, visible across the Straits of Messina from Penitenzeria – would probably see the sherd as belonging to a regional style noticeably different from their own. Someone from 10 or 20 km along the coast might well identify the minor differences of composition and style, and someone from the village might well peg the sherd to an individual potter or group of potters.

The point here is that the multiplication of small differences effectively created layers of understanding whose penetration depended on local knowledge. In that sense, vision of a pot was similar to vision of a landscape. Just as in a landscape, local people would have a shared knowledge of the burials lying unmarked beneath the village, of a recently-abandoned garden's owner and history, of a village's historical relations to other villages, local people would read the fine distinctions in a pot in ways inaccessible to strangers. If shared knowledge is part of the experience of co-identity, then sharing an understanding of a complexly decorated pot – or being able to create an appropriate vessel in an appropriate way – was situated agency, agency qualified by identity and circumstance.

FORESHADOWING PATTERNS OF SOCIAL ACTION: Looking ahead to Chapter 6, it is useful to look ahead here briefly from specific media to general reflexes of social action. Elaborate Neolithic pot decoration was not functional; instead, it resulted from a general cultural pattern of creating small differences along many axes of evaluation. Southern Italian Neolithic pottery has a heterarchical quality of design. Because of the complexity of designs and their polythetic structure, there is no clear single axis of evaluation possible. Rather, in any comparison of two sherds, whether from the same site or from 1,000 km distant, there are common elements and differences; there is always the basis for some relationship, but never for complete identity or for simple ranking. Without generalizing too much from the meaning of only one kind of material production, which was used specifically for food consumption and was probably almost always used by people who knew each other personally and often well, this suggests a relatively fragmented and complex approach to evaluating social relationships or distance between people.

Lest this seem obvious, consider the following period, the Late Neolithic Diana period. Late Neolithic "Diana" style finewares appear basically identical from Sicily up to Rome. All surface decoration has been abolished, replaced by a completely different aesthetic. The goal is to produce a glossy, uniform surface, typically red, decorated with a stereotypical handle which is instantly recognizable even by the novice archaeologist. The goal is not to produce fine-grained difference, but to produce similarity. The potters are no less skilled, but the target involves a much simplified scale of evaluation – gloss and colour are the principal attributes – which allows unlayered identification and interchangeability. There is a single standard of comparison, with potters competing for an egalitarian sufficiency.

Obsidian and Flint

The Lithic Economy in Neolithic Italy

We now turn to the second classic genre of Neolithic artefacts, chipped stone. As with axes and pottery, there is a huge amount of data, but it has been collected in several quite distinct scholarly traditions which can be difficult to break out of. Culture historical archaeologists typically considered lithic choices simply as a typical culture trait, and lithic analyses were rarely quantified until the 1960s. From the 1960s, Italian lithic analysis has been dominated by the statistical typology of G. Laplace. Laplace's methodology, analogous to the better-known Bordes method, involves tabulating the prevalence of different formal types of stone tools. As with pottery typologies, it has often been used to create esoteric technical descriptions of assemblages detached from any social inference (Mussi 2001). Only recently has an alternative, based upon the concept of the reduction sequence rather than the form of the final product, been applied (Ammerman and Polglase 1993; Kuhn 1995).

Cryptic, and normally rendered more obscure rather than less by archaeological discussion, stone tools are still worth bothering with. They were an essential component of ordinary life, providing the basic

35. Neolithic use of obsidian and flint. (a) Obsidian core for producing small blades, Castellaro Vecchio, Lipari; (b) Core for producing long blades from honey-coloured Gargano flint, Passo di Corvo (Ashmolean Museum); (c) Waste flakes from reducing obsidian nodules, Gabellotto Gorge obsidian source, Lipari; (d) Obsidian and flint bladelets and expedient flakes, Umbro, Calabria; (e) Formal tools of local flint, Gargano flint and obsidian, Arpi, Puglia (Ashmolean Museum). All photos: Robb. Not to scale.

Table 18. *Lithic Raw Material Use in Selected Areas*

	Expedient Cutting Edges (any local material; direct percussion or bipolar crushing)	Formal Tools (high-quality flint, direct or indirect percussion on specialised blade cores)	Special Social Functions (obsidian, direct or indirect percussion on specialised blade cores)
Lipari, Northeastern Sicily and Southern Calabria	Obsidian	Flint (Sicily?)	Obsidian
Crotone	Local chert, obsidian	Flint and obsidian	Obsidian
Tavoliere	Local chert	Gargano flint	Obsidian
Po Valley	Local chert	Monti Lessini flint	Obsidian

cutting edge for most tasks, and they provide concrete witness of an extensive and intriguing trade system.

Throughout Italy, flakeable stone came from three basic sources (Figure 35; Table 18). Local cobbles of poor quality chert are widely available in stream beds, redeposited from sedimentary formations. They also often occur in beds within clay or conglomerate formations; this is a typical, immediately local source at many Tavoliere villages. High-quality flint is available in a few locations in beds in limestone bedrock. Of these the most notable sources are the Monti Lessini near Verona [whence the Tyrolean Ice-Man's grey flint knife came (Spindler 1994)], the Monte Iblei near Siracusa in Sicily, and the Gargano peninsula in Puglia. Indeed, in the Gargano, flint was mined in shaft and gallery mines from early in the sixth millennium BCcal, as shown at the sites of La Defensola and Valle Sbernia (Di Lernia and Galiberti 1993; Galiberti 1999; Palma di Cesnola and Vigliardi 1984; Tunzi Sisto 1999). Finally, obsidian is found in four locations, all of them on islands (Lipari, Palmarola in the Pontine islands off Campania, at Monte Arci on Sardinia, and Pantelleria between Sicily and Tunisia). Sourcing studies (Ammerman et al. 1990; Bigazzi et al. 1991; Bigazzi and Radi 1981; Cann and Renfrew 1964; Hallam, Warren, and Renfrew 1976; Mello 1983; Phillips 1992; Randle, Barfield, and Bagolini 1993; Tykot 1997; Tykot 1998 Tykot and Ammerman 1997; Warren and Crummett 1985) have shown that virtually all of the obsidian used in Italy came from these four sources.

Neolithic Italians used a generalised tool kit. To make a formal tool such as a scraper or burin, one began by carefully preparing a conical or cylindrical core to produce a long blade, which was then broken and retouched to the right length and form. Among formal tools, the only ones commonly ascribed a particular function are blades probably hafted as sickle blades, which sometimes display so-called sickle gloss.[6] Although bows were used, formal arrowheads or spear points are almost unknown until late in the Neolithic in peninsular Italy, though somewhat earlier in Northern Italy. Instead, small trapezes or similar tools were probably mounted to form compound arrowheads. However, the presence of some formal tools should not mislead us. All assemblages contain many unmodified flakes and relatively few specialised or formal tools; it was an "economy of debitage" (Conati Barbaro et al. 2003). As suggested by use-wear studies at Masseria Candelaro, which found that many tools lacked use-wear traces (Conati Barbaro et al. 2003), this suggests perhaps a rather sparing use of lithics, which may have been used mostly as generalised tools to produce tools in other materials rather than to carry out intensive, repetitive tasks. Stone tools were not the functional equivalent of a modern knife; they were probably used for a narrower range of functions which could not be done in some other way.

In making sense of raw material use, there were three basic patterns of manufacture, based upon distinct niches in the lithic economy (Table 18; Figure 35). First, unretouched flakes which needed only an expedient cutting edge were often made from local cobbles of poor quality chert, though on Lipari and around the Straits of Messina, obsidian was commonly used. Second, tools which required a particular form or a retouched cutting edge were usually made on good quality flint, which was imported from some distance away if necessary. For instance, at Tavoliere villages these are usually made from Gargano flint (Giampietri and Tozzi 1989; Mallory 1987; Ronchitelli 1983). Some Tavoliere flint was quarried at deep mines on the Gargano peninsula; as abundant high-quality flint was available in surface outcrops, the reason for digging deep mines is not immediately evident. The most striking instance, however, is from Lipari and southern Calabria, where virtually entire assemblages are of obsidian. Here small pieces of multicoloured flint were imported, possibly from the Monte Iblei. The reason is clear; obsidian is sharp but very brittle, and formal tools such as scrapers were probably made for repetitive tasks requiring some tougher material. Finally, most assemblages contain a third category of tool, small, thin blades of obsidian and the debris from working them. These are discussed further below.

A given stone such as obsidian, thus, shifted in use throughout its geographical range. In Southern Calabria, closest to Lipari, obsidian makes up almost all of the lithic assemblage on many sites, and was used for all three uses, with flint relegated to tools with particular functions such as sickle blades and scrapers (Ammerman 1985; Farr 2001). In Central Calabria, obsidian still makes up over half the assemblage at Capo Alfiere and in the Stilo region, and is used for all types of tools (Hodder and Malone 1984; Morter 1992). Here it still clearly occupies the "prestigious exotic material" role and the "expedient flake" role, though the latter are increasingly made up from local chert. Further northeast, in Basilicata, Puglia, and Central Italy, obsidian is found in very small quantities and is used almost exclusively for very thin bladelets of questionable function.

How important were stone tools? The salutary lesson here for archaeologists is provided by Sillitoe and Hardy's ethnographic work of the Wola of highland New Guinea (Hardy and Sillitoe 2003; Sillitoe 1988). In this stone tool-using group, lithics were remarkably unimportant. When someone needed a sharp flake to cut with, they hunted around a settlement until they found one somebody had discarded previously; they picked it up, used it briefly, and dropped it again. The total time of interaction between humans and lithics was on the order of a couple of minutes, and there was little attempt to shape flakes to any preconceived form. Such a casual usage certainly is in accordance with the simple unmodified flakes which form the bulk of Italian Neolithic assemblages, and with the casual, unstructured way in which most lithics were deposited at the end of their lifespan. One suspects our archaeological fascination with lithics derives mostly from their durability, from the tradition of classifying them formally, and from our *a priori* assumption that cutting edges are important, technical, male-oriented things (Gero 1991). In contrast, the Wola spent far more time, energy and conscious attention upon string, normally dismissed in our society as mundane, uninteresting and, if anything, a female preoccupation.

Although it is a tempting moral, we should not conclude merely that lithics were far more trivial than our elaborate typologies would suggest. Lithics were used in structured practices. There was not a random use of any cutting edge for any purpose. Rather, lithic usages show an interesting concordance between raw material and reduction technique. Expedient flakes could be, and ordinarily were, produced either through direct percussion or through bipolar reduction. The former required hitting the core with a hammerstone or antler billet at the correct angle with some force; the latter is an unsophisticated technique involving smashing a core or nodule between two rocks and using sharp flakes from the resulting shatter. In contrast, the other two niches in the lithic economy – blades and formal tools – required much more sophisticated skills. One prepared a dedicated blade core – a matter of considerable foresight, strategy and dexterity, as it meant shaping a rough nodule into a cylindrical or conical shape whose top edge sloped away at a precise angle. One then used either very carefully controlled direct percussion or indirect percussion with a punch of some sort to knap off blades around the edge of the core.

The blade-based tools require skill and practice a quantum level higher than the simple flakes, and they used materials from different social contexts. Local chert would have typically been collectable casually from outcrops and stream beds within a group's home territory. In contrast, high-quality flint and obsidian would normally have required venturing beyond it. In many cases, procuring flint or obsidian must have happened through inter-group exchange. Even on Tavoliere villages, where Gargano flint was commonly used and from which the Gargano peninsula is almost always visible less than 30 km away, collecting flint directly would have meant moving through territories occupied by other people into a different kind of landscape, with encounters and negotiations with other people an important part of the process.

I am not arguing for "specialists" in lithic production and trade in any commercial sense. At the same time, it is important to realise that although some kinds of lithics could have been procured and produced by anyone within a society, others required skill, practice and social networks and there is no reason to think these were distributed equally throughout the society (Perlès and Vitelli 1999). As with pottery, one's ability to manage the group's lithic needs may have been an important part of some people's social capacity. This was probably formalised in what is the most glaring departure from the undifferentiated baseline of expedient flakes, the obsidian "trade."

The Obsidian "Trade"

The Central Mediterranean obsidian trade is the largest and best known trade system in all of the European Neolithic.[7] Obsidian is a black volcanic glass which was used around the world as a source of tools. In the Central Mediterranean, obsidian use began around 6000 BC in the Early Neolithic, though there may be a few Mesolithic precursors [e.g., Perriere Sottano, Sicily (Aranguren and Revedin 1998)]. Obsidian was used throughout the Neolithic, increasing greatly in the Late Neolithic. In the Copper Age, the obsidian trade crashed, possibly because metals, or the idea of metals, substituted for some of its social roles. Obsidian has been exhaustively studied from one point of view, chemical sourcing. Yet this has been balanced by a surprising neglect of the social mechanisms and meanings underlying obsidian circulation (Tykot 1998; Tykot and Ammerman 1997). The obsidian "trade" was not a simple phenomenon, and understanding it poses all sorts of problems: reconciling widespread usages and local meanings, integrating technological function with cultural understandings of technology, and overcoming our own preconceptions about what things mean.

Four sources of obsidian in the Central Mediterranean were used in prehistory (Figure 36). Samples from each source can be clearly identified by distinctive chemical impurities (Ammerman et al. 1990; Bigazzi et al. 1991; Bigazzi and Radi 1981; Cann and Renfrew 1964; Hallam, Warren, and Renfrew 1976; Mello 1983, Phillips 1992; Tykot 1997; Tykot 1998; Tykot and Ammerman 1997; Warren and Crummett 1985; Zarattini and Petrassi 1997). The two major sources were Lipari and Monte Arci on Sardinia. A line joining Rome and Venice provides an approximate watershed. North and west of this line, obsidian from both sources is found, though Lipari obsidian becomes increasingly sporadic in the French Riviera and northeastern Spain. South and east of this line, Sardinian obsidian is virtually absent and Lipari is the dominant source. Of the two minor sources, Palmarola obsidian is more extensively distributed than original studies had indicated, with an extensive distribution in Campania and Lazio and fragments known from Puglia, northern Italy and even the coast of Croatia. Pantelleria, a tiny island in the channel between Sicily and North Africa, supplied obsidian primarily to Sicily, Malta, and Tunisia.

Contextual evidence for obsidian use comes mostly from its distribution. Near outcrops on Lipari and Monte Arci scatters of waste flakes indicate quarrying and roughing out sites (Bernabò Brea and Cavalier 1991). Obsidian dominates assemblages close to sources. As noted above, in Calabria, for example, up to 100 km from Lipari assemblages are still more that 90 percent obsidian. The percentage drops steadily but even in central Calabria, several hundred km from the source, assemblages still hover at 50 percent obsidian. Beyond this, and in other directions such as westwards into Sicily and northwards into Campania, the proportion drops steadily. In most of the Central Mediterranean region, the typical Neolithic site has very little obsidian, rarely more than 1 percent of the assemblage.

In spite of this, obsidian still made its way astonishing distances; the most distant pieces of Lipari obsidian known are found in coastal Southern France and in Dalmatia, both more than 1,000 km away as the crow flies and considerably more by coastal routes. Obsidian was transported coastally by sea whenever possible. The evidence for this comes from matching GIS models against sourcing data (Robb and Tykot 2003). For example, if travel over land and travel over sea are modeled as equally easy or preferred, we would expect to find obsidian throughout the Adriatic coming from Sardinia and Palmarola, as these sources are closest in a straight line. Instead, except for a few pieces from Palmarola, Adriatic obsidian comes exclusively from Lipari; Lipari is the closest major source by coastal routes.

Two further factors beside distance complicate obsidian's occurrence on sites. First, obsidian circulation increased throughout the Neolithic, from very low levels in the Early Neolithic to much higher ones in the Late Neolithic Diana period (late fifth and earlier fourth millennia BCcal). Secondly, some sites relatively far from sources have anomalously high amounts of obsidian. At Palinuro in southern Campania, for example, more than 90 percent of the Serra d'Alto period

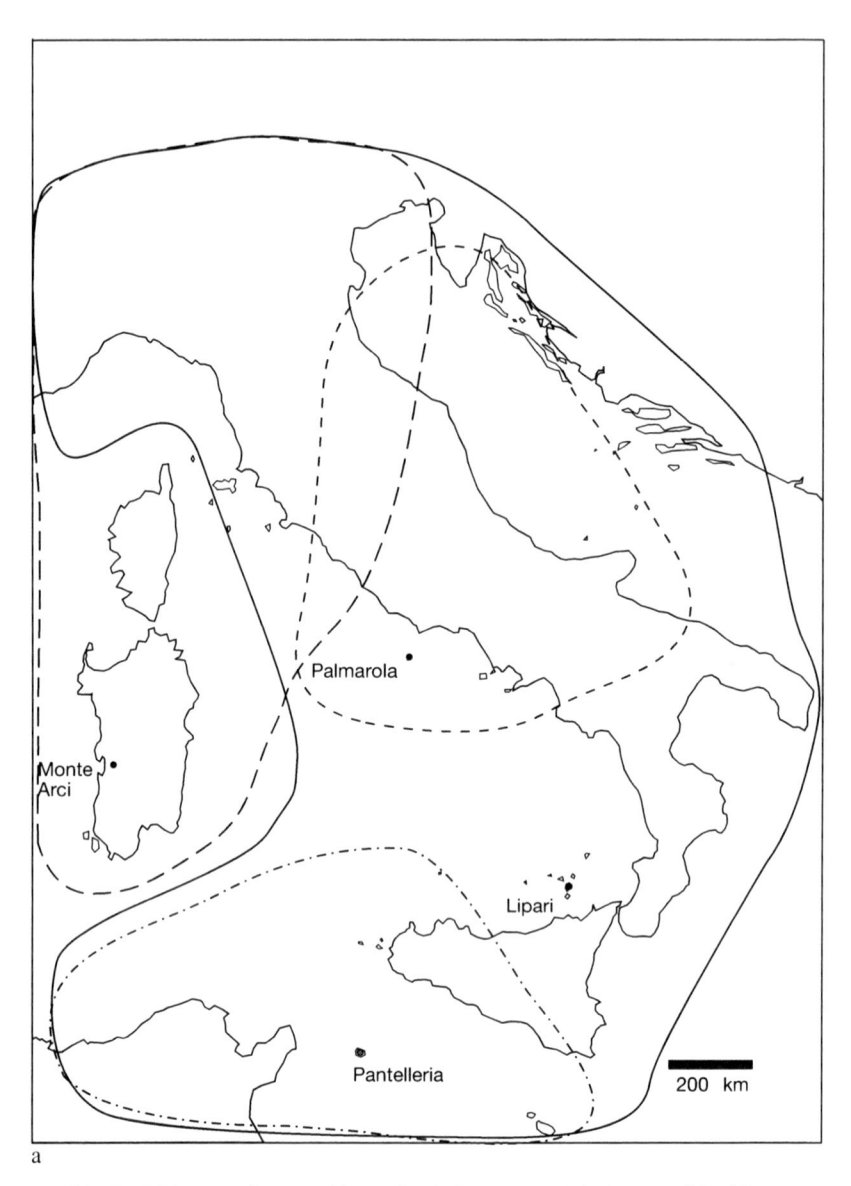

36. (a) Neolithic use of sourceable geological raw materials (Farr and Robb 2005). Right: circulation of some stone materials; left: circulation of obsidian from the four Central Mediterranean sources [Monte Arci (Sardinia), Lipari, Palmarola, and Pantelleria], all of which are upon islands.

b

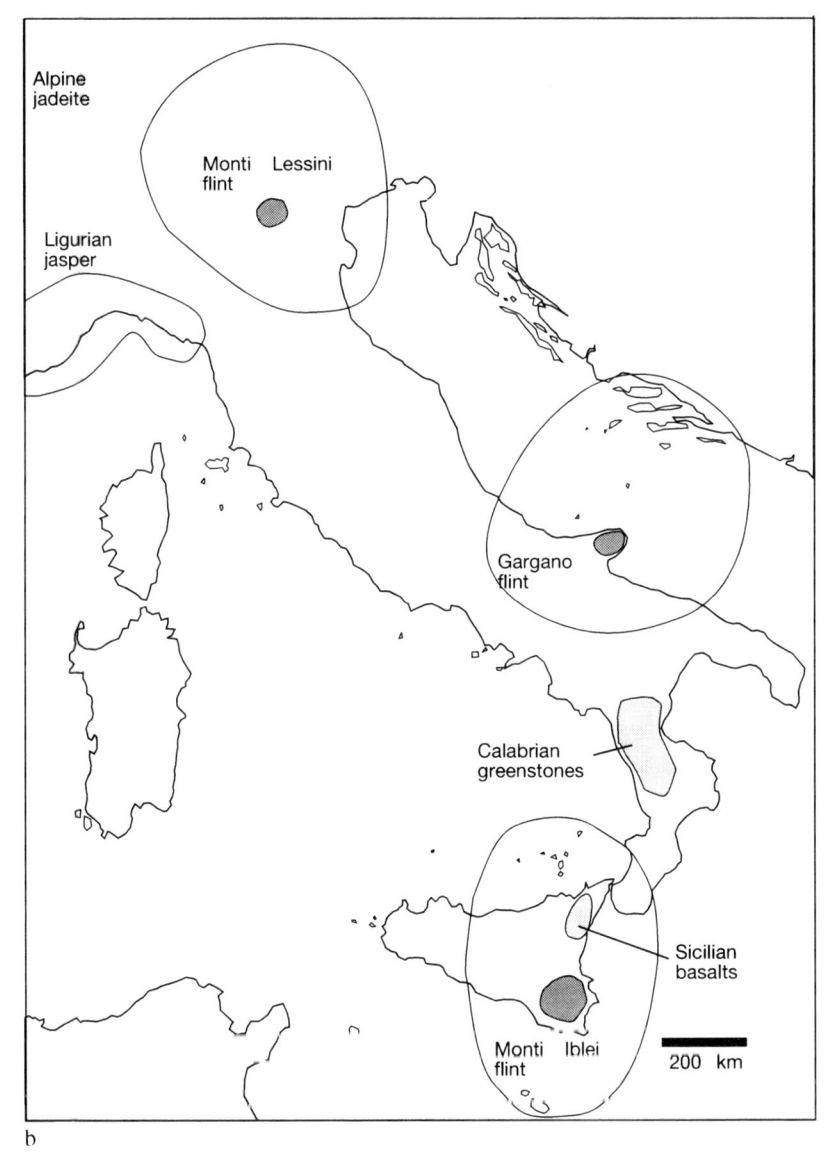

36 (*continued*)

lithics were obsidian (Romito 1987). Other examples include Mulino Sant'Antonio in Campania (Albore Livadie et al. 1987), Passo di Corvo in Puglia (Ronchitelli 1983), Gaione in Reggio Emilia (Ammerman and Polglase 1993), and other sites in Toscana (Radi 2000). It is not clear how to interpret such "broker" sites, but they imply, at the very least, that not every group was equally active in trading obsidian. Rather, there may have been a network of long-distance links between larger or more active sites, from which it was redistributed locally.

When obsidian was traded, it appears to have been in the form of cores and blades. Cores were roughed out on Lipari (Bernabò Brea and Cavalier 1957; Bernabò Brea and Cavalier 1960; Bernabò Brea and Cavalier 1980) and on coastal sites in Calabria (Ammerman 1985) and obsidian appears to have arrived at villages as cores, judging from the general lack of core preparation flakes at such sites (Farr 2001). These cores were dedicated particularly for the production of small, thin bladelets (Figure 35). When they became too small to produce bladelets, they were smashed between two stones, in bipolar technique reduction, to provide usable flakes (Farr 2001). Throughout obsidian's range, aside from irregular flakes, it is typically found as bladelets less than 3 cm long and 1 cm wide, only a millimeter or two thick, and often translucent.

In trying to put flesh on the minimal outline of the obsidian trade, even rough figures, whose every term is guesswork, may still be thought-provoking. Obsidian does not decay; with appropriate recovery techniques, what was deposited is what you find. Penitenzeria is a small site, inhabited at most by ten to twenty people for an interval of 100 to 400 years. At Penitenzeria, we have excavated about 10 percent of the total midden area. Naturally, some obsidian used may have been used up off-site or shipped elsewhere (though Penitenzeria, as an inland site, may have been an end-node rather than participating extensively in the flow of obsidian to the Adriatic which passed coastwise only a few kilometers away). Even so, the 1,299 pieces of obsidian recovered at Penitenzeria weigh a total of 935 g – an average weight of 0.72 g per lithic (Helen Farr, personal communication). As an approximate guess, therefore, the entire site might contain perhaps 10 kilos of obsidian – ten lumps about the size of a grapefruit or a softball. One can calculate the number of person-years the site represents in various ways. But at the most generous, on-site deposition, in a region where obsidian provided over 90 percent of all cutting edges, would have come to about 10 g per person per year, or perhaps one or two flakes per person per month.

This remarkably low figure makes several points. First, it gives us an idea of the scale or magnitude of the lithics "trade." For their annual cutting needs, or at least those represented by on-site deposition, the two to four families living at Penitenzeria needed to procure somewhere between 25 and 100 g of obsidian – a core between the size of one's thumb and a golf ball (for comparison, the core in Figure 35a weighs about 25 g). Compared with the much larger amount of grain, animals, clay, water, herbs, ochre, fat, fur, feathers, and other materials which would have constantly been entering and leaving sites, this seems quite a small amount. It certainly gives perspective to the commonly posed question of "what was traded the other way?"

Second, it reinforces what was said above about the generally low use of stone tools in the Italian Neolithic. Although we might expect somewhat higher usage at sites where local chert was used, lithics seem sparingly used. It also explains perhaps why lithics tend to be small and worked until exhausted (e.g., whole cores of obsidian and good quality flint are rare). Interestingly, this intensive use does not necessarily relate to scarcity; surely people procuring one small core a year in an area where obsidian circulated freely could have imported two if they wanted. People seem to have been content importing small amounts of stone and then using them exhaustively; this suggests a casual, Wola-style view of lithics.

Finally, it poses the problem of organizing skill and knowledge. As with pots, only a few blades may have been produced annually in a family or small group. Yet, as opposed to expedient flakes, producing blades, and even more, blade cores, is a highly skilled business: producing blade cores in particular requires a much more sophisticated level of planning and skill than producing the blades themselves once a dedicated core is achieved (Hirth 2003).[8] On one hand, it seems unlikely that such a skill, practiced infrequently, would be shared equally within a group; on the other hand, such skills must have been practiced regularly enough to guarantee their maintenance and transmission.

Obsidian and Cultural Practices: The Alternative View

With this background, the time has come to tackle the biggest unanswered question about obsidian, one we have almost completely

Table 19. *Some Possible Motives for the Obsidian Trade*

1. Obsidian was valued because it was technologically superior to other cutting materials
2. Obsidian was valued because it was an exotic and hence prestigious alternative to other cutting materials
3. Obsidian was used as a functionally identical alternative to other cutting materials, without any particular associations, uses, or symbolisms
4. Obsidian was used for special technological functions, with or without any particularly strong symbolic associations
5. Obsidian was an important cultural symbol, perhaps due to its physical characteristics such as colour or translucency
6. Obsidian was used in a symbolically elaborated social role

overlooked. Why did people want obsidian in the first place? Why did they bother with a tiny chip of broken glass?

There are two standard answers to this: because obsidian was technologically superior, and because obsidian was prestigious. To these we might add four other potential explanations, which have however never been systematically argued (Table 19). It goes without saying that no one model need apply to all societies throughout the obsidian-using world; it is demonstrably the case that obsidian was used in different ways in different areas. Obsidian may also have had several roles within a single society.

Not surprisingly how one interprets the social mechanism of the obsidian trade is closely linked to what obsidian was valued for. The traditional view, that obsidian was valued because it provided a superior cutting edge, assumes that prehistoric trade functioned much as historic trade within market economies did, simply to provide a desired substance, in this case a sharper blade. In this view, Lipari was the commercial center of Neolithic Italy, whose prosperity was founded upon a thriving trade in this superior material. The second view, that obsidian was prestigious because it was exotic, is set firmly in New Archaeological studies of tribal exchange (Earle and Ericsson 1977). In this view, the major issue raised was whether obsidian was passed from hand to hand "down the line" or whether it was circulated by long-range direct procurement (Renfrew and Dixon 1976; Torrence 1986). The social value of obsidian as an exotic material has also been proposed within Italian archaeology (Cazzella and Moscoloni 1992). Theoretically, both models rely on a modern idea of trade as a rational enterprise involving a value ranking of cost and benefits of competing products, with commodities traveling essentially according to market conditions.

To begin with the first hypothesis, obsidian has often been assumed to be technologically superior to flint. It is indeed sharper than flint, a consequence of its much finer crystalline structure; a freshly knapped flake supposedly has an edge one molecule wide. It slices soft materials wonderfully. However, sharpness can be a liability; a thin glassy edge is very brittle, dulling and breaking readily. This is especially so when the edge angle is very thin, as in small bladelets, and especially on hard materials such as stone, bone, wood, or antler. Moreover, a thin, brittle edge is useful principally for slicing knife-wise, not for transverse motions such as scraping or whittling. Neolithic people were well aware of these characteristics; in Calabria and on Lipari, where the basic cutting edge was of obsidian, when people wanted a scraper with a steep, retouched edge, they normally imported flint to make it. Macroscopically, most obsidian tools recovered archaeologically show little or no edge damage. Although one cannot judge what a tool was used for without microscopic analysis, it is difficult to imagine harsh use on hard materials leaving fragile bladelets whose thin edges look pristine. Microscopically, there has been little use-wear analysis of Central Mediterranean obsidian, but what research has been done suggests that obsidian was principally used for slicing soft materials (Hurcombe 1992); obsidian was also used to work hard materials at Vulpiglia in Sicily, but this is in an obsidian-rich zone and obsidian (32 percent of this sample) may have been used for a wider range of functions than was generally the case (Guzzardi, Iovino, and Rivoli 2003). Hartmann's use-wear analysis at Acconia demonstrated that only minority of blades were heavily used, which may perhaps relate to blade production for exchange at this site (Ammerman, Shaffer, and Hartmann 1988). There is one intriguing case of residue evidence: in the Early Neolithic flint mine of La Defensola, an obsidian blade found in the mine had trades of red ochre on its edges (Galiberti 1987).

Obsidian, thus, was distinctly inferior to flint for many uses. Indeed, for slicing soft materials, we do not know whether it was so much superior as to make a salient difference (as opposed, say, to the manual dexterity, strength, or experience of the person using the stone tool). In flint-dominated assemblages, where it could have been substituted as a superior functional equivalent, it does not appear to have been used exhaustively; we do not find obsidian artefacts heavily damaged or reduced through wear, as we might expect if it were appreciated principally for its functional characteristics. If it was valued for its sharpness, it would have been so for particular tasks in particular contexts.

The prestige-good hypothesis for obsidian makes the essential point that material goods do not have an a priori meaningful existence but are created and valued within particular social institutions. However, its limitations in interpreting obsidian derive from treating prestige as a self-evident quantity without a symbolic context. If exotic goods were procured because they were prestigious, but they were prestigious because they were exotic, the argument furnishes us with a minimal, perhaps tautological, description; it requires further specification. For instance, equating exoticness with prestige does not explain what was *not* traded. Exotic flint did not travel as widely as obsidian, even when it was highly coloured (as with Ligurian red jasper). Nor did other types of stone. Some steatite and marble were traded in the Alps (Barfield 1981) and some Campanian and Sicilian lavas were traded as grinding stones, both at distances comparable to good-quality flint. But elsewhere all sorts of colourful, attractive, and useful rocks and minerals remained where they were. The same is true for marine shell and fish bone; the famous Central European Neolithic *spondylus* trade is not mirrored in Italy. The point is that exoticness alone does not suffice to make something an eminent trade good; some context of belief or practice is called for. Similarly, in considering the social value of exotic goods, equating distance with prestige relies on an empty, absolutely quantifiable view of space (Shanks and Tilley 1987). To us it may seem obvious that the further away an object comes from, the more valued it will be. However, Neolithic people would have had much more localised geographic knowledge (see Chapter 3); presumably any item coming from over the horizon, whether from 100 or 1,000 km distance, would have been equally mysterious, and all enmeshed in cultural geographies about alien lands, peoples and qualities.

Logically, the concept of prestige good relies on a system of distinction between alternatives, and this system of distinction must be maintained practically. If too many of the "prestigious" alternative are in circulation, they become devalued. We can hardly expect that obsidian would have been a restricted status good in Calabria, where it made up over 90 percent of many assemblages. On the other hand, at the other end of the range, the prestigious alternative must be available enough to supply a recognised category and a pursuable option – for a status car, one buys a Mercedes, not a moon buggy. Throughout Italy north of Calabria, obsidian makes up less than 1 percent of most assemblages; at such low frequencies, it is difficult to imagine it anchoring a social game of the kind implied by the "prestige competition" concept.

Empirically, there is little contextual evidence that obsidian was actively used in prestige competition. We have a good idea of what prestige competition in lithics might look like from phenomena such as chipped stone daggers in Italy and throughout Europe later on in the third millennium. In particular, we would expect an emphasis on particularly large and fine pieces, production of elaborate and difficult forms with ostentatious skill (such as pressure-flaked bifaces), and use and deposition in ways visible during social display (as weapons, articles of costume, etc.; as were *spondylus* ornaments in Central Europe) or at key ritual moments such as burials. None of these is the case for Neolithic obsidian. Obsidian was used in very small pieces which took standard forms such as bladelets. As far as we can tell, it was not worn or displayed in any particularly ostentatious or even visible way. It was not deposited in burials, hoards, or other special contexts; it is usually found on sites mixed with ordinary refuse.

The point is not that prestige did not exist in Neolithic societies, or to rail against a straw-man view of prestige as a decontextualised, symbolically empty token. The point is that if obsidian was regarded as prestigious, it was for a specific, symbolically elaborated view of prestige relevant to a particular context. The context of obsidian use would have specified particular characteristics which excluded other exotic materials, which may have related it to cosmological geographies of alien places, identities and peoples, and which specified particular usages different from those archaeologists usually consider typical of competitive display.

The third and fourth hypotheses seem to apply respectively to the obsidian-rich zones of Sardinia, northeastern Sicily and Calabria and the obsidian-poor zone elsewhere. In the obsidian-rich zones, obsidian was used lavishly as a general purpose functional alternative to other cutting materials. In obsidian-poor zones, it seems likely that obsidian was not used as a general purpose cutting edge but for some special functional use. Without microwear studies, we have to rely on lithic form and characteristics. The blade form was commonly used for flint and obsidian, but flint blades were often either truncated or retouched or both. Both truncation and retouch are uncommon on obsidian blades in most of Italy. The use of a particular form, unmodified bladelets, for circulating obsidian suggests a specific use or uses. As we discussed, as thin bladelets, obsidian is primarily useful for slicing soft materials. Some possible candidates for such materials are discussed later. What of obsidian as a cultural symbol? For lithics, the classic ethnographic example deals with Aboriginal stone use in Australia (Jones 1989; Morphy 1992; Taçon 1991). These studies note that some stones, particularly translucent quartzite, were thought to have active supernatural powers. Somewhat like radioactive materials, they were valuable, but also dangerous, particularly when too much of them were concentrated in one place. One reason for long-distance trade in quartzite, thus, was to disperse these dangerous materials widely. This is not to say that Neolithic people necessarily held similar beliefs about obsidian, but it does illustrate that stone tools can be the focus of cosmological belief and that such beliefs are likely to involve their physical attributes. One reason behind the wide circulation of Lipari obsidian may have been its exceptionally glassy, translucent black colour and texture, finer than the greenish material from Pantelleria and the often grainy Palmarola material. At Gaione in Emilia Romagna (Ammerman et al. 1990) obsidian from Lipari and from Source A on Monte Arci was used preferentially for bladelets, perhaps because they had a finer, less grainy texture and more translucent black colour than obsidian from other sources.

Adding up these arguments, we arrive at a scenario where our final hypothesis, a special social role, seems quite possible (and a particular social role, in fact, would supply what is missing from both the technological-superiority argument and the prestige-goods argument: a context specifying uses and meanings). For much of the Central Mediterranean, obsidian arrived in very small quantities as small cores or a few bladelets, and presumably much of it left the area in the same form. It was not conspicuously displayed or deposited in ritual contexts, but probably used for a particular function related to its form which left little legible wear or damage on the bladelets. It may have been considered particularly fitting for this function due to its colour and translucency, although these did not make it unusable for other uses when available in enough quantities. I would, in fact, argue that obsidian was an "extended artefact" in the sense outlined in Chapter 1 – an artefact at the heart of a specific set of practices imbued with particular values and beliefs.

For slicing relatively soft materials in socially important ways, we could imagine many possible uses, but I would suggest two prime candidates. One is butchery. As discussed in Chapter 4, animals were important social valuables in Neolithic Italy, and it was probably a significant occasion every time one was killed and eaten. Butchery would have been a dramatic public moment, and may have involved an element of sacrifice. A sharp flake or bladelet would work quite effectively to kill an animal by cutting an important vein. If so, the rise in obsidian in the Late Neolithic may be related to an increased emphasis on pastoralism, though other materials must have also been used in obsidian-poor zones. The second possibility may have been modifying the human body. Among the myriad ways humans change their bodies are many which require some cutting tool. Cutting hair, shaving, performing scarification and tattooing, piercings (ears, lips, and noses), cosmetic surgery, and circumcision are found in many cultures, including our own; there are few people who have not come under the knife at some point. In Neolithic Italy, there are documented cases of trepanation and of intentional tooth removal (see Chapter 2 in this book); for soft tissue modification, the Tyrolese "Ice Man" mummy, although not shaven and apparently not circumcised, had had his hair cut and bore several tattoos (Spindler 1994). Bodily modifications may have been carried out in special contexts or by people in particular social relationships, they may have been symbolically loaded in ways making certain colours appropriate, they would have required a constant but very low-level supply of tools, and they certainly exemplify a context in which surgical sharpness may have been appreciated!

We do not know exactly in what practices obsidian was used; in a sense this entire section is a research agenda for formal analyses, contextual analyses, microwear studies and residue studies to find out. Nevertheless, some aspects of its social organization are clear enough.

Obsidian is a reductive technology with a short use-life; cores and blades were small, and caches are unknown. We have to imagine a constant sparingly-used, low-level trickle of obsidian sleeting horizontally through Neolithic societies, rather than curated heirlooms descending in time. Within groups, not everybody may have possessed the social contacts needed to procure obsidian or the skills needed to produce blades. Among groups, it is intriguing that obsidian spread throughout the Central Mediterranean not just as a raw material but also as a technological *koine*. Producing bladelets from dedicated cores is a highly channeled operational sequence, and this constrained *chaîne opératoire* was spread across many societies. This implies a continuous chain of not only technical knowledge and skills but also of goals and purposes in how obsidian was appropriately used. It is this above all which suggests that, even if (as seems possible) every society had its own symbolic exegesis, there was a core of shared beliefs and practices throughout the obsidian-using range. It has been suggested that obsidian may have been used as an ethnic marker (Tykot 1998). I would argue precisely the opposite: the types of identities and relations created through the use of obsidian were translocal, diametrically opposed to those local meanings created through pottery. In this sense, the system of practices surrounding obsidian use may have been a vector of transgroup "distributed personhood" (Gell 1998).

Axes and Their Life-Paths

Axe Basics

With axes, we have much better explored archaeological pathways to travel than for pottery, but much worse data to actually work with. Prehistoric axes were almost always traded over long distances, they can be sourced to geological areas, and they are often deposited in unusual contexts. They have inspired many creative analyses, including the use of sourcing data to outline the social mechanisms of axe trade (Bradley and Edmonds 1993) and artefact biography studies (Lillios 1999a; Lillios 1999b). For Neolithic Italy, however, axe studies are bedeviled by lack of research and by contextual problems. Throughout Italy, nineteenth and early twentieth century antiquarians accumulated large collections of axes, often by purchasing them from the peasants who found them and who often held superstitious beliefs about them (Douglas 1938).[9] This means, for example, that only items which looked recognizably like whole and saleable axes were collected, and that almost all are surface finds without context. Relatively few axes have been excavated from known contexts, and little sourcing work, or indeed analysis of any kind, has been done (Leighton 1989; Leighton 1992; Leighton and Dixon 1991; Leighton and Dixon 1992). Evett (1975) attempted to correlate axe form and size with distance from the raw material source, and O'Hare (1990) charted geographic variability in size and form. Skeates (1995) has discussed the biographies and ritual deposition of small axes.

Polished stone axes were widely used as functional tools throughout Neolithic Italy. In fact, the archaeological rubric "axe" covers at least three distinct kinds of tool made of different materials and probably used for different purposes. The stereotypical "axe" is 10–15 cm long, weighs between a quarter and a half of a kilo and has a pointed butt and a sharp cutting edge. Such axes were made usually from hard metamorphic stones such as amphibolite or serpentinite, ranging from dark green to black in colour. Interestingly, they were not made from all usable materials; even where other fine-grained hard stones such as diorite were available, these "greenstones" were the first choice. There may have been aesthetic preferences for rock of a certain colour or for rock which could be polished to a high glossiness. A block was first flaked to a rough-out form, then it was pecked with a hammerstone to the shape required. Finally, the roughed-out axe was polished laboriously with abrasives to a fine gloss. Although axe workshops are unknown in southern source areas, some are known in the Alps, interestingly, a workshop at Rivanazzano was located not at the rock sources but over 100 km away from them in the piedmont along a route to Po Valley trade destinations (D'Amico et al. 2003). Although a finely polished edge may have increased an axe's cutting performance, axes were polished even on surfaces presumably covered by hafting. This suggests both that the aesthetics of axe appearance were vital to its social role, and that axes may have been handled and circulated unhafted.[10]

If unused, axes were basically indestructible, and they traveled over long distances; these facts are undoubtedly responsible for the great homogeneity in form they display throughout Italy over the long Neolithic.

Woodworking would have been an important use, but in many axe-using groups axes are also general-purpose tools (Burton 1984; Sillitoe 1988). They may well have been used as weapons (as later, Copper Age stelae suggest) (cf. Fornaciari and Germanà 1979 for a case study of axe-related skeletal trauma from Copper Age Toscana). Because they were not deposited in graves or depicted iconographically, we have no idea of how they are associated with the kinds of people who would use them. However, it is worth noting that both in archaeological situations such as the Central European LBK and in ethnographic situations in Melanesia (Lillios 1999; Sillitoe 1988; Steensberg 1980) axes are strongly associated with males, and this seems to be the case at the earliest point for which we have iconographic evidence, the Copper and Bronze Age of Northern Italy (cf. Chapter 8 in this book). If we suppose that all or most adults, or at least adult males, had access to axes, we must suppose that axes were far more common in daily life than their scarce presence in the archaeological record would suggest.

Besides such axes, we also find larger and smaller categories of polished stone tools. The larger ones are blunt, unwieldy heavy tools made from pebbles of whatever hard stone was locally available, including granite, diorite, basalt, and even sometimes limestone. These often show minimal shaping, were presumably used as mauls or hammers as well as axes, and one suspects they frequently pass unrecognised archaeologically. The third genre of tool which archaeologists lump under the category of "ground or polished stone" includes smaller tools, usually finely polished of greenish metamorphic stones. The commonest are thin trapezoidal or triangular blades, often less than 3 cm on a side and 5–10 mm thick. These "axettes" or "axe-amulets" (Skeates 1995) are made from similar hard metamorphic stones as larger axes, but often seem to include more distinctly green coloured stones as well. These are usually thought to be hafted woodworking tools, though some are also pierced, presumably for suspension on a cord, possibly for wearing. Other forms include thin chisels or "scalpels."

The best-understood issue is raw material source. Most of peninsular Italy and Sicily consist of sedimentary rocks such as limestones, shales, and clays. The Po, Arno, and other broad valleys are in-filled alluvial plains. Hard metamorphic and igneous rocks can be found only in the Alps, in volcanic regions of Campania, and in the mountains of Calabria and north-eastern Sicily. These areas, presumably, were the sources of axes. Sourcing studies (Leighton 1992; Leighton and Dixon 1992) have delineated distinct spheres of circulation of basalt axes from the Etna region within Sicily, and of greenstone axes from northern Calabria throughout Calabria and Sicily. Although O'Hare (1990) did not carry out petrographic studies, he identified macroscopically axes of Calabrian greenstones and Campanian volcanic rocks throughout Southern Italy. Very few axes of identifiable Alpine material are known from peninsular Italy.

The distribution of raw material has a noticeable effect upon axe use. Although detailed quantitative comparison has not been carried out fully, in Southern Italy, for example, axes seem fewer and smaller in Puglia than in Calabria. One of the most interesting consequences is the development, in the Central Adriatic where no suitable stone for axes was available locally, of the specialised Campignano industry. The typical Campignano artefact is a bifacially flaked flint axe, and they are found throughout the Neolithic from Puglia to the Marche. Although the Campignano was first considered a chronologically bounded Late Neolithic "culture," it is now understood as a strategy for providing flint axes in the area of the Italian peninsula equally far from Calabrian and Alpine sources of polished stone (Leighton 1992, p. 28).

Although we know approximately where axes came from, we know virtually nothing about the circumstances in which they were actually produced. Quarry and production sites are unknown south of the Alps, and essentially all we know about axes is what we can deduce from the axes themselves and their scanty archaeological context. There are basically two possible lines of inquiry: geographical distribution and depositional context.

Like chipped stone, axes are a reductive technology; they grow smaller with use-wear and resharpening. As axes were transported from hand to hand over long ranges, we might expect axes to diminish in size with remoteness from their source. However, this is not the case; greenstone axes from Adriatic Italy, for example, are not significantly smaller than those from Calabria, or do they show a greater degree of use-damage (O'Hare 1990). The implications of this interesting point are discussed below.

Contexts of Axe Deposition

The most interesting point to emerge from the scanty axe data is a clear correlation between where axes were deposited and their condition. Axes are found in three common contexts: habitations, ritual sites, and surface depositions. There is also one clear case of an axe cache on a habitation site at Capo Alfiere.

Axes found in habitation debris are normally well into their useful life-span, if not actually at the end of it (Figure 37). In our excavations of midden contexts at Umbro and Penitenzeria, 10 of 11 axe finds were fragmentary; the only whole example is a very small axette. Besides this, only one near-complete axe was found, and this had been broken, partially reworked, and re-utilised as a hammerstone before being discarded (Figure 37a). The remainder of the corpus consists of small fragments of axes, spalls, and several rough stone fragments which attest either working new axe blanks or reworking axes drastically. This contrasts with the four complete or near-complete axes we have found as surface finds nearby, and with many complete surface finds of axes by local amateurs.

This general destruction of axes seems the rule for habitation sites. The much more extensive excavations at Catignano provide comparable data (Tozzi and Zamagni 2003). Only one whole axe was found, and that was made of limestone. Fragments of two further axes in sandstone and calcarenite were also found. In greenstone, there was one axe fragment from Alpine sources, one whole "scalpel" (chisel) and one fragmentary "scalpel." Catignano demonstrates the general tendency for habitation sites to yield mostly broken axes, as well as the limited use of greenstone in the Adriatic side of Italy and its substitution with tools of softer sedimentary stones and with flaked Campignano bifaces (Figure 38) (Tozzi and Zamagni 2003). To take a few other examples, at Capo Alfiere, among the settlement debris, six axe fragments were found, some of which had been reused as hammerstones (Morter 1992). At Skorba, the count was one complete and one fragmentary axe (Trump 1966). At Passo di Corvo (Tinè 1983), the corpus includes three complete axes,

37. Working axes from habitation sites; note breakage and edge damage. (a) Umbro, Calabria; note partial refashioning and re-use as a hammerstone; (b) Penitenzeria, Calabria; (c) Pizzica Pantanello, Basilicata (courtesy of University of Texas Metaponto project); (d) Passo di Corvo (Ashmolean Museum). Not to scale. All photos: Robb.

four broken axes, and four axes not illustrated in the publication and hence probably broken. At Rendina (Cipolloni Sampò 1982), both axe finds were broken. The Marcianese corpus (Geniola 1992) included four fragmentary axes and only one complete example. On Pianosa (Bonato et al. 2000) no complete axes were found, just seven fragments and about twenty spalls from axe-working. The same is true for many other sites throughout Italy.

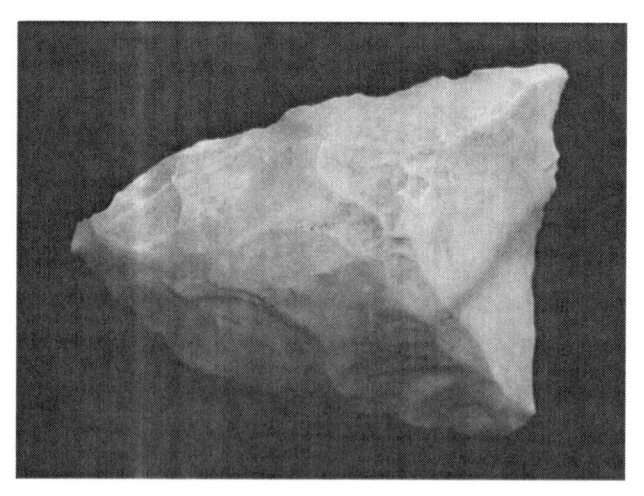

38. "Campignano" style flaked bifacial axe from Masseria Schifata, Puglia (Ashmolean Museum; photo: Robb).

The habitation site evidence suggests that axes were common enough to be used in tasks harsh enough to chip and break them, to require them to be resharpened and reshaped, and ultimately to destroy them. Such activities consumed axes, leaving broken fragments and working debris on sites. Where whole axes in good condition are found on excavated sites, they tend to be in unusual contexts. For example, at Capo Alfiere near Crotone (Morter 1992), five unusually large greenstone axes were found carefully cached below a living floor in a room possibly used for ritual (Figure 39). Capo Alfiere is on the coast below the Sila massif where the raw material for many axes came from, and Morter suggests that these may have been cached while waiting to trade them.

The second context in which axes are found is ritual sites (Figure 40). In one famous example, the monumental underground burial chamber of the Hypogeum of Hal Saflieni on Malta yielded several hundred small greenstone axettes (Evans 1971). In Italy, axes from ritual sites tend to be small, complete axes or axettes, as at the Grotta Patrizi (Grifoni Cremonesi and Radmilli 2001), the Grotta Pacelli Serra d'Alto-Diana levels (Striccoli 1988), and the Grotta dei Piccioni (Cremonesi 1976). At Grotta Scaloria, axes from living debris showed battered edges, while axes from the cemetery area were in pristine condition (Winn and

39. Cache of axes beneath house floor at Capo Alfiere, Crotone, Calabria (photo: Morter).

Shimabuku 1988). Similarly, at the Grotta all'Onda in Toscana, deposits included two virtually complete axettes, a chisel-shaped implement, and a polished stone mace-head (Amadei and Grifoni Cremonesi 1987). At the Villa Badessa, a small greenstone axe was found with a female burial (Germanà et al. 1990), and at Quinzano, small axes were found with burials of both sexes. In general contrast to axes found on living sites, axes in ritual contexts tend to be smaller (often axettes), and complete or nearly so. They may also be made of slightly different ranges of stone; while they tend to be of dark or greenish metamorphic stone everywhere, in some regions such as the central Adriatic this stands in contrast to axes on habitation sites, which may be made from relatively poor stone such as limestone, even sandstone or quartzite, or of flaked flint.

The most common axe context – represented in large antiquarian collections in most museums (Figure 41) – is surface finds. These present severe evidence problems. Very few axes finds have any detailed information on context, and because of the way these collections were formed, there may be a strong sample bias against broken or severely damaged axes and against forms which do not look like a stereotypical axe. This is a problem because axes found on the surface are generally

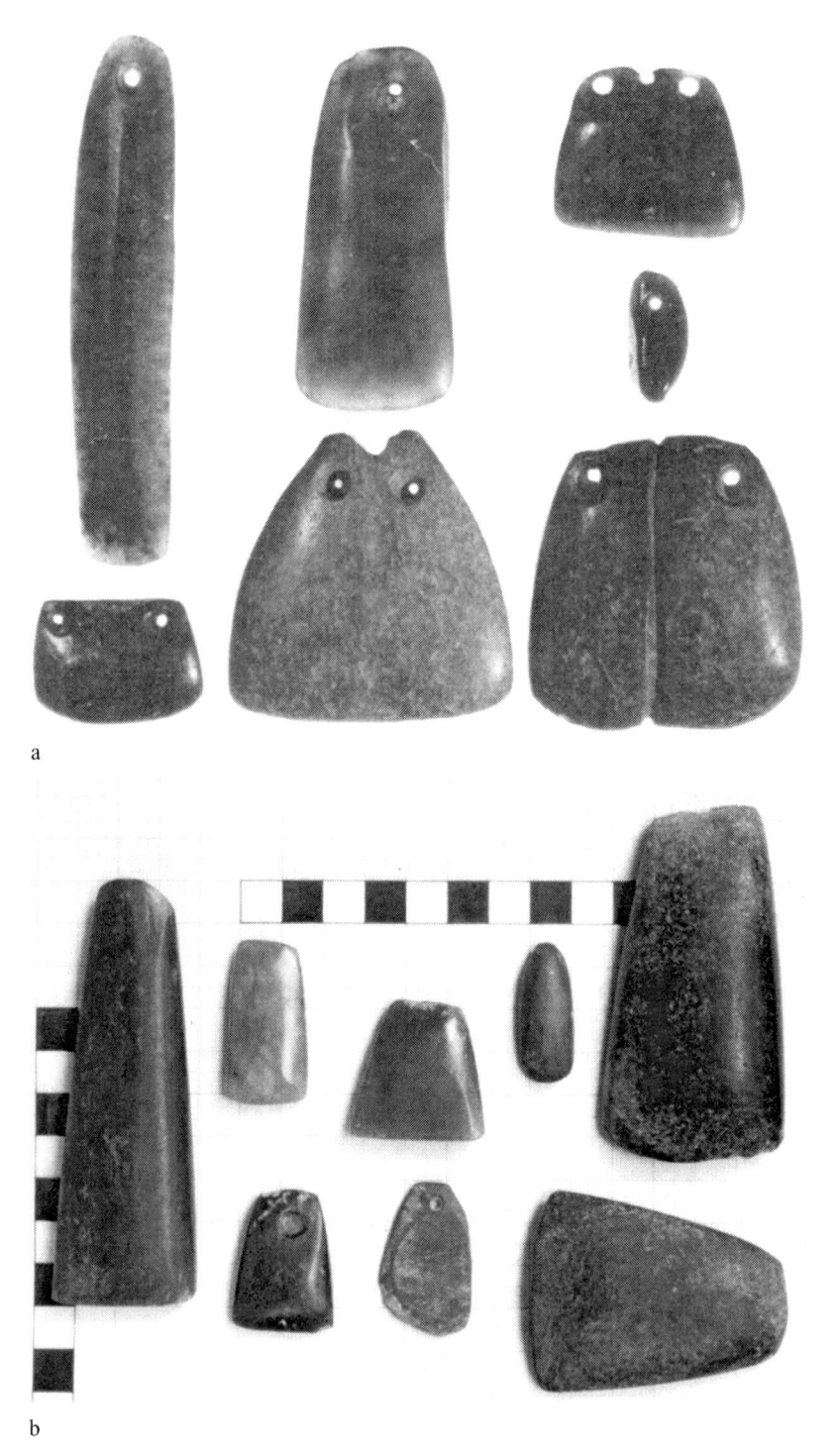

40. Axes from ritual sites. (a) Hal Saflieni Hypogeum, Malta (Evans 1971); (b) Grotta Scaloria, Taranto (photo courtesy of G. O'Hare).

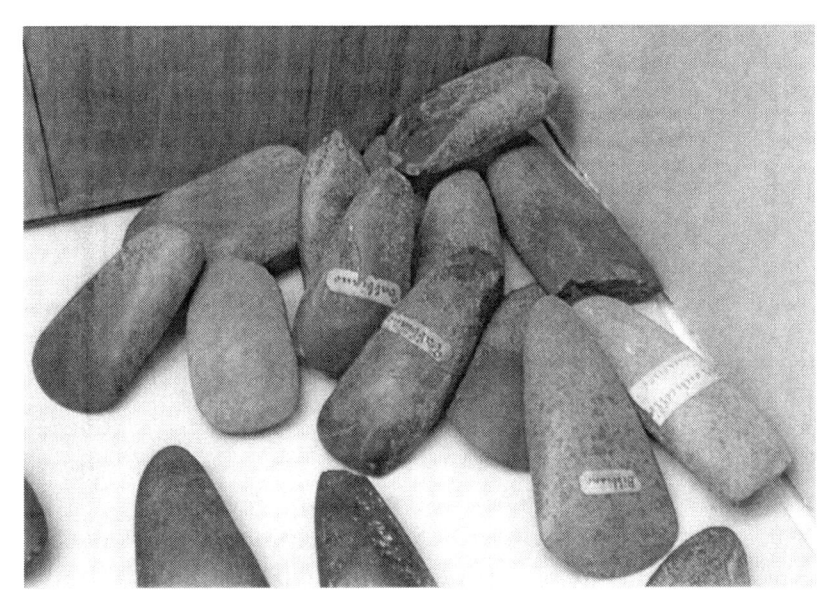

41. Surface finds of axes, as represented in antiquarian collections (Parma, Museo Archeologico Nazionale, photo: Robb).

larger and in less damaged condition than axes coming from excavations; while this could indicate deposition of different kinds of axes in different places, it could equally well simply reflect the kinds of axes antiquarians and their sources recognised and collected. Detailed statistical analysis of collections may be able to resolve this question, but such research has yet to be done.

Nevertheless, we should question why so many axes are found as surface finds. It is commonly assumed that sporadic axe finds represent either plunder from unrecorded sites or axes lost casually by prehistoric people traveling or working away from home. Although the former assumption is no doubt sometimes true, it is sometimes demonstrably not the case. In some cases, we have been able to ground-check areas of sporadic axe finds during the Bova Marina field survey; in no case has this led to discovery of a site. Similarly, sporadic axe finds sometimes come from areas apparently uninhabited before the Late Neolithic, such as the high mountains of Aspromonte and the Sila (see Chapter 3 in this book). This suggests that at least some axes may have indeed been deposited off sites. Equally suggestively, we need to account for the size and condition of many sporadic finds. Axes were valued items, essential for many

Table 20. *Axes from Different Contexts*

Context	Size	Form	Material	Condition
Habitation	All sizes	All forms	All materials	Damaged, reworked, fragmented
Ritual	Medium–small	Often axettes	Greenish and black metamorphics	Pristine or with very little damage
Surface finds	Medium–large	Axes	Greenish and black metamorphics	Pristine or with little damage

social tasks, procured by exchange from far away, worked painstakingly to impressive appearance with careful labor, probably associated with the individuals who owned and used them, and apparently either curated carefully or used until exhausted. They were probably among an individual's most valued possessions. This does not suggest something which would frequently be lost carelessly. An alternative possibility is that some axes were intentionally discarded away from sites.

To summarise, there are demonstrable differences between axes found on habitation and axes found in ritual sites and other intentional depositions such as caches. Furthermore, pending further research, we must at least entertain the possibility that some of the numerous surface finds of axes represent intentional off-site depositions (Table 20).

Axe Biographies and Agency

Drawing together these strands, we can now make a stab at reconstructing the social biography of axes. An axe entered a group through exchange, presumably with a neighboring group. Exchange presumably involved a context of critical comparison and discussion, judging from the relatively standard form and narrow range of stones and colours of most of the axes that have been found.

Once procured, an axe faced the big choice: use or curation? If used, it would be damaged, require resharpening and reworking, and eventually break or grow too small to be used. When it reached the end of its functional lifespan, however, it may have been given a new lease on life as an axette (Figure 42). Although axettes could have been used

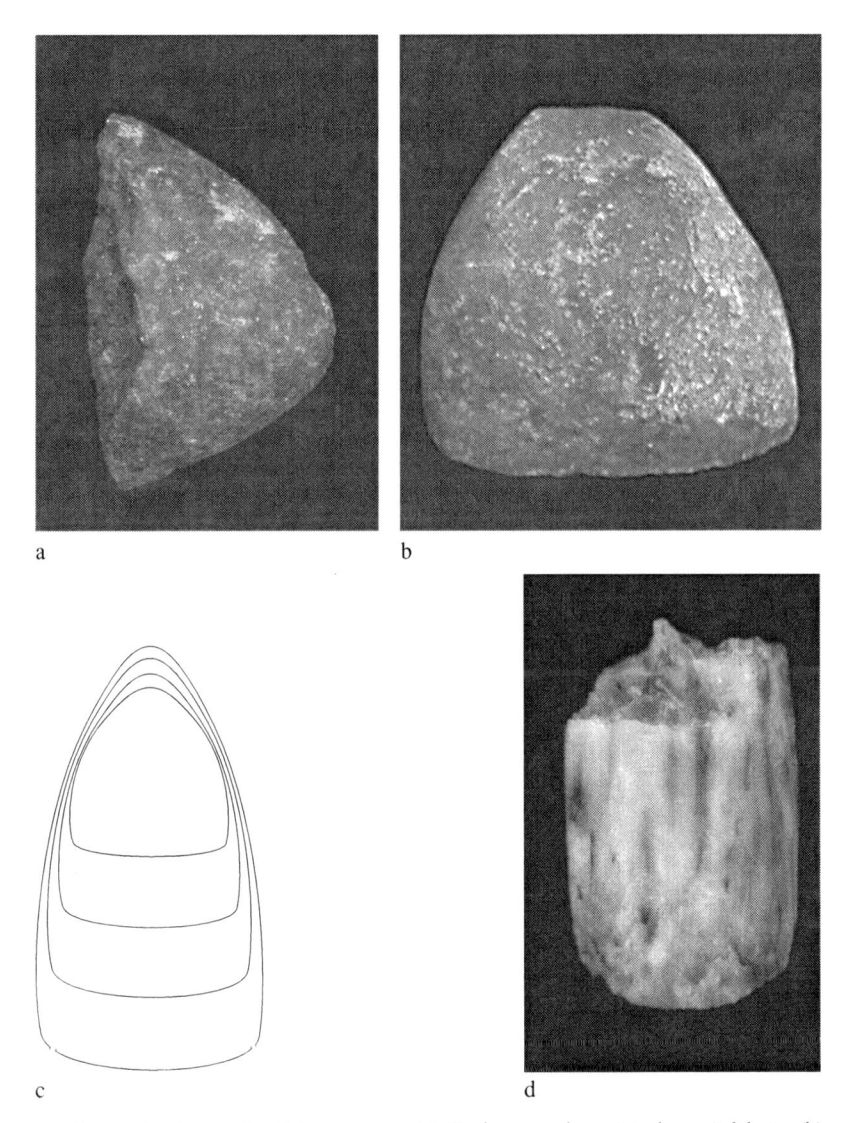

42. Axe reduction and miniature axes. (a) Broken axe butt, Umbro, Calabria; (b) Axette, Umbro, Calabria; (c) Hypothetical sequence of reduction of axe to "axe-amulet" or axette; (d) Miniature axe replica of phyllite, Umbro, Calabria (all photos: Robb).

for woodworking, some are pierced for suspension, suggesting use as ornaments. Skeates (1995) has suggested that the small, thin, trapezoidal axettes represent the end point of reduction for normal axes. This is entirely plausible: an axe with linear cutting edge and pointed butt, repeatedly damaged and reworked on the cutting edge, would become progressively more triangular or trapezoidal as well as thinner. Similarly, some of the smaller, thinner and less regular forms of polished stone such as chisels may have resulted from the fragmentation of axes, whether simply as a way of prolonging the social lifespan of a fragmented axe or as a way of creating many artefacts which shared a common substance. However, some axettes may have been made in that form directly from the raw material; if all were derived from axes, we should find axes or axe fragments in the entire range of raw materials axettes are composed of, and many axettes specifically of highly greenish stone appear to have no antecedents as axes. Moreover, we lack many examples of the transitional forms axes should have passed through en route to becoming finished axettes.

If an axe was curated, it was given a quite different destiny. There are several attested destinations for undamaged axes. First, curated axes could be cached indefinitely, as at Capo Alfiere. Secondly, they could be traded. The fact that axes found far from raw material sources are sometimes as large and undamaged as axes close to sources (O'Hare 1990) suggests that unused axes, in particular, were exchanged. Finally, they could be deposited intentionally off-site, a permanent and irreclaimable end to their social lifespan. As a transaction, the meaning of this deposition intentionally outside of human reach may have paralleled that of exchange with humans.

Effectively, then, we have outlined two distinct modes within which axes were given social existence (Figure 43). They entered one's ownership as curated social valuables; even when marking time in caches, they were held as curated valuables. Curated tools went through time lightly; they could be years or centuries old without visible signs of age, and we do not know if they were retained or kept in motion through many hands. During their history as curated valuables, axes may have acquired particular histories or statuses (Lillios 1999). Curated axes left a group in a similar status, either via exchange or deposition in unoccupied areas. The other pathway, a much more rapid route to oblivion, was

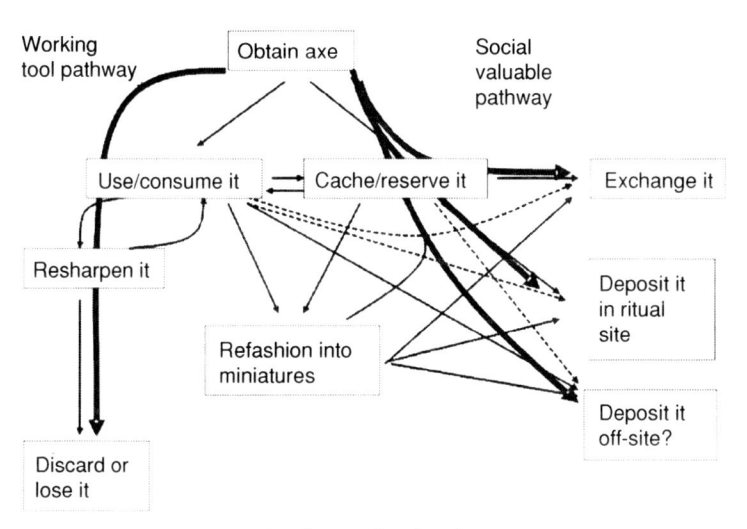

43. Axe biographical pathways.

to be used as working tools. This would have led to damage, reworking and resharpening, reduction in size, and eventually fragmentation, presumably within a few years.

The idea that axes were social valuables is not new; Evett in 1975 already proposed a correlation between material, distance from source and social use (Evett 1975). What is interesting here, however, is that we do not seem to have distinct categories of axe defined by their raw materials. Rather, the same kind of axe could be channelled into quite distinct biographical pathways. This bifurcated artefact biography allowed space for important social decisions. The actual life course of an axe could be quite complicated (Figure 43), with different destinations having different connotations: an discarded off-site might be both a social and functional termination, but refashioning an axe into an axette or multiple smaller polished stone tools might allow the axe to continue as a social presence while terminating its functional usefulness, perhaps to preserve its historical associations, reconstitute them as a social valuable, or memorialise its social priorities. In any case, the most important, and irreversible, was the decision to consume a curated axe through use. As a strategic decision, this would have meant a decision to convert potential social capital to immediate use, rather like the decision to kill a valuable animal. Yet, if the axe was an essential tool for many tasks which responsible adults had to perform, caching, or trading an axe would have been a secondary act, possible only once immediate needs had been met.

A Methodological Note on Artefact Analysis

In Chapter 6, we combine the disparate arguments worked through here to provide the real conclusions about economy and social reproduction. However, it is worth pausing here to reflect briefly on artefact analysis as an archaeological preoccupation.

Artefacts are defined through their relations with people in fields of practice (Chapter 1). Hence, in all three cases – pottery, lithics, axes – we have to start by placing the archaeological medium in its immediate context of usages and practices. In some cases, this has meant cavalierly disregarding entire fields of arcane archaeological lore, with apologies to the specialists, while fixating on the kinds of naive questions which schoolchildren ask and professionals are taught to be blind to ("How did they make them? Where did they get the materials? What did they look like?").

In all three cases, it is clear that our archaeological materials are the detritus of meaningful action, and even allowing for the usual discourses meant to allow us to calibrate our vision for the effects of millennia of entropy, we can approximate some understanding of what meanings may have been involved. But we cannot short-circuit the reconstruction of specific fields of material practice in the quest for general meaning; it is through very specific material conversations that artefacts can be induced to speak to us, and, although there is no guarantee they will discourse on the themes nearest our hearts, we can be confident they will reveal something important to themselves.

SIX:
NEOLITHIC ECONOMY AS SOCIAL REPRODUCTION

But all the story of the night told over,
And all their minds transfigur'd so together,
More witnesseth than fancy's images,
And grows to something of great constancy;
But, howsoever, strange and admirable.
          William Shakespeare, *A Midsummer*
Night's Dream. V, i, pp. 23–27.

People at the Center of a Decentered Narrative

Bottom the weaver and his rude mechanicals have struggled back from a night of confusion and chase in the fairy-haunted wood and are trying, incoherently and inarticulately, to report what has happened to the ducal court. The duke dismisses their tales as the rambling of idiots. His duchess points out that, however tangential and fragmentary their accounts, they add up to something consistent and substantial – and strange and admirable.

The archaeologist cannot help but sympathise with Bottom. We began with the deceptively simple goal of understanding the Italian Neolithic in terms of people rather than artefacts. This stated, we plunged almost immediately into serial discussions of topics as disparate as how to eat a cow, how to decorate a pot, and how to dispose of an axe. Even worse, each section demonstrated that each activity had to be taken on its own terms, without reducing it to a totalizing schema of social life. Social life, thus far, is fragmented, and leaving a vacancy at the heart of our story: we have seen people only in passing, sighted in fleeting glimpses. Now we have to tie these vignettes of human presence together, to find the common ground and sift out the constancy; to give up blundering around in thickets and return to the craft of weaver.

This is not an easy challenge, and only the reckless would claim the result is a complete or balanced portrait of an entire social world. There are near-universal archaeological laments such as the absence of perishable organic materials (Where is the clothing? Where are the wooden tools? Where are the posts, roofs, statues, masks, and drums?). But the greatest single difficulty afforded by the Italian Neolithic archaeological record is the forcible averaging of values and distinctions. Activity, so central to the notion of agency used here, exemplifies this problem. It would be ethnographically unique if the Italian Neolithic were a society without a division of labor, in which all people did all activities without distinction. But without iconographic depictions of activities, burial associations between bodies and tools, or similar evidence, we are at a loss as to what this division of labor actually was. This limitation goes beyond debates such as whether we are content to assume traditionally that men hunted, women made pottery, and so forth. I argue below that there was an inherent tension between fields of action in which the value produced had reference to local contexts (as in potting, ritual, village maintenance and burial) and those in which it had reference to translocal contexts (such as exchange and travel). But was this tension worked out within the lives of individuals practising these activities simultaneously or between categories of individuals whose labor was divided and complementary? The project poses theoretical challenges as well. It is difficult to reconstitute a world of social reproduction based on the accumulation of small meanings, inherently intangible and elusive. It is even more difficult to describe it in words without reducing action to the workings of static structural arrangements, effacing contingency and agency.

By resolving these problems, the analysis below does not claim to be remarkably original. Problematising daily life and tracing human subjectivity to material relations has been a challenge addressed by many, perhaps most social theorists. The work of Foucault (1977) on power,

Gell (1998) on material culture, Strathern (1988) on personhood, Latour (2005) on social technologies, and Ingold (2000) on landscape all in some way decenter the commanding actor and recenter our vision on relationalities between people and between people and things. Many archaeologists have followed these thinkers. But archaeological attempts to pursue this strategy have almost always been fragmented, privileging one medium (such as stone tools, monuments, or landscapes) which stands for the whole of materiality or one dimension of relations (such as hierarchy or gender) which stands for the whole of sociality. Very few analyses (Thomas 1999; Tilley 1996) have attempted the holistic discussion necessary to understand the narrative density of normal social life. Whittle's (2003) admirable *Archaeology of People* is perhaps closest to the spirit of this work, but it pursues these themes through the most striking examples culled from all of Neolithic Europe rather than with the inevitably more patchy materials found by restricting analysis to a single area: the archaeologist as mobile observer rather than resident.

A Quick Recapitulation

As a baseline for synthesis, it is useful to recapitulate the individual analyses briefly.

BODIES: Neolithic people were smaller than either Palaeolithic or Copper Age people and gracile, and their skeletons commonly show the traces of hard physical labor and childhood stress. Childhood mortality was high, as was death in early adulthood. Long bone architecture suggests that males were significantly more mobile than females. Their physical bodies also were the objects of social acts: besides the tattooing attested from the very end of the Neolithic, many women had teeth knocked out in life and some individuals – perhaps one in every few communities – were trepanned. Bodies were social operators through acts of violence as well, which were relatively common and which affected men and women both.

Burials and representations show the transformation of the body. The principal archaeologically visible medium for representing the body is figurines of female or ambiguously gendered bodies. Figurines were probably used in a narrowly specified ritual context, and they display an astonishing variety of ways in which the human body can be abstracted and reconfigured – a variety which can only be ascribed to highly decentralised communities of ritual practice. One semantic which links burials, figurines, and trepanations seems to have been a head-body distinction through which the head represented particular or special beings, the body a kind of generic physicality [cf. Talalay (2004) for a similar discussion of the Greek and Anatolian Neolithic, also based upon both figurines and skeletal depositions]. Burials display a paradoxical situation: the normative burial (for archaeologists as well as Neolithic people) was individual inhumation, but the actual majority of the Neolithic dead are known as fragmented, disarticulated remains, and much of this disturbance apparently occurred during Neolithic times. This tension between an ideal and an actual fate for mortal remains can be resolved by considering timescale. The period of burial was the closing phase in a biography unfolding in social time; the onset of disturbance marks the lapse of social memory, a transition to a different kind of time. This longer timescale was important via a generic association of ancestry and place, an association attested by the practice of depositing later Neolithic burials at remembered earlier Neolithic villages.

Burial provided a flexible template for closing a biography, and alternative rites allowed the process to be abbreviated (for children, whose burials are more commonly disturbed), lengthened via skull curation and manipulation, elaborated for important ritual leaders, or rerouted to accommodate mass deaths (epidemics? massacres?) and the disposal of stigmatised individuals. Although age was clearly an important social category, what burials do *not* do is provide a clear map of adult identities. Gender differentiation was limited to a correlation between sex and side of burial, and neither grave goods nor burial treatment give any clear indication of a standard, commonly applied status hierarchy.

PLACES: The simple Neolithic Italian wattle and daub hut was an embedded technology whose construction involved assembling several tonnes of raw material, environmental modifications such as the systematic harvesting of large amounts of tree shoots, and a *chaîne opératoire* spanning months at least. It used materials and techniques familiar from other technologies. The division of space which huts created, through divisions of sensory space, knowledge, and co-presence, emphasised the segmentation of the group into small nuclear family groups, a segmentation echoed in the process itself; unlike many Neolithic constructions elsewhere in Europe, raising a hut involved no tasks which would have required more than two or three able-bodied adults. Many, perhaps most, houses were intentionally burnt at the end of their lifespan, probably to close their social existence.

Settlements were important. Many daily activities happened in the open, collective areas of villages between houses. Villages were places of burial and historic presence. One important variation was whether people lived in scattered houses or clusters of houses, as in much of peninsular Italy and Sicily, or in nucleated villages, as in lowland eastern Sicily, southeastern Basilicata, and all along the Adriatic lowland coast up into southern slopes of the Po valley. In some of these areas, this clustering was further emphasised by village ditches, which imposed a symbolic boundary dividing space into contained areas and outside context. Interestingly, ditches were often used as burial places, interposing the dead between the living and the outside world.

Beyond living sites, the landscape was constructed through human presence (including zones of daily frequentation), sporadically used ritual sites, social spaces occupied by known people in other settlements, and increasingly distant and generic places experienced during trade, warfare, and travel and populated by people with incomprehensible languages, alien customs, and unknown or different histories.

Overall population was sparse, and there may have been real differences in settlement density, for instance between lowland Adriatic Italy and mountainous Calabria, western Basilicata, and Campania. The social landscape also included natural features, for instance qualitatively different kinds of places such as islands, the ocean, and volcanoes. Rather unexpectedly, after the end of the Mesolithic, mountains about 1,000 m may have been abandoned until the Late Neolithic. This may reflect both economic production and cultural beliefs, and it certainly breaks up the inhabitable space of many regions into fragmented, highly channeled strips and enclaves.

FOOD: Neolithic people spent considerable time and work producing food, and a detailed examination suggests that they did so not in generic or optimally efficient ways but in their own culturally specific way. Foodways afforded categories and idioms for social relatedness.

Some potentially edible resources were shunned or infrequently exploited, including other people, carnivores and sometimes game generally, and, rather surprisingly, marine foods: shellfish were sometimes eaten opportunistically, but never intensively collected, and both faunal remains and stable isotopes show little use of fish. Hunting was probably valued more for furs, feathers, ornaments, and other wild substances, and, from the Late Neolithic, as a prestigious activity. The bulk of the diet appears to have come from grains, to judge from stable isotope evidence. Grains were bulky, time-consuming, and probably produced and consumed on the household level. A third category of foodstuffs, the "flavours," includes fats, salt, honeys, and gathered herbs and spices – originating from socially and spatially varied sources, traded and stored carefully, consumed in small amounts but adding disproportionate amounts of colour, taste, and variety.

Animal foods were deeply social. With relatively low levels of meat consumption and no apparent intensive pastoralism, households probably kept relatively few animals. The demographically stable collective herd would thus have been broken up into smaller family herds, with a continual circulation of animals among them. Ethnographically, animals in tribal societies are important valuables, particularly cattle, and the fact that cattle were sometimes killed relatively old may imply a long social lifespan of transaction before an animal was finally eaten. When animals were eaten, meat would have been redistributed among many people. Particularly for cattle, the animal's biography as a social valuable probably culminated in a large social gathering, possibly dedicated to a specific event, purpose, or transaction. Indeed, it seems quite possible that the typical Neolithic person only ate beef during or after such an event. Archaeologically, the *strutturi di combustione*, the remains of earth ovens often found on Neolithic sites, may have been used for preparing food for such gatherings.

Cuisine as meaningful practices emerges from the interplay of all foods, not from a single element such as meat or grain. Neolithic cuisine was centered on contrastive relations between the experiences of different kinds of food. Grains, flavours, and meats had characteristic ways of production, rhythms of consumption, colours, and tastes. In the habituated senses, grains and legumes afforded the taste of household life, meats the taste of a broader sociality.

ARTEFACTS: Material things are both meaningful and genre-bound; we as discussed in Chapter 1, they originate in specific fields of practice and their creation and use is an important part of the agency specific to their context. Neolithic pottery, stone tools and axes have to be interpreted contextually as qualitatively different kinds of things. We need to think about them with different concepts.

Potting was a valued skill, carefully learnt and exercised. The *chaîne opératoire* spanned a minimum of several weeks and required knowledge of many materials and processes. Much of this knowledge was location-specific, either of technicalities such as how to mix up pastes from different local clays or of parochial conventions such as the correct way to ornament. Much effort was spent on decorating surfaces ornately, particularly for food serving vessels. When a potter decorated a vessel, he or she did so by recombining techniques and motifs from a local repertory to create a novel design. Archaeologically, this creative process can be tied directly to the "systematics" of Italian Neolithic pottery, for instance the great variety of decoration at all scales, the existence of long-lived but gradually evolving regional decorative traditions, the fuzzy boundaries between style areas, the existence of general decorative tendencies rather than unbreakable rules, and the occurrence of "mutant" sherds recombining techniques and motifs from distinct traditions. Experientially, how one experienced the ceramic landscape would have been highly situated: how one read a given vessel would have depended on the social distance between viewer and potter, and the experience of co-knowledge would have been an important component of common identity.

Flaked stone tools were divided into three distinct niches. The most common cutting edge everywhere was an unmodified flake from poor-quality local material; the only exception is in some parts of southern Calabria and Sicily, where such expedient edges were made of Lipari obsidian. Secondly, high-quality flint was circulated regionally up to 100 km and used for blades and blade-based formal tools. Finally, people everywhere used small, thin, obsidian bladelets obtained from remote sources by long-distance trade. This final category is the only one for which there is much evidence of an elaborated social role for lithics. Evidence is scanty and inferential, but the most plausible hypothesis is that obsidian was an important cultural symbol and/or used in a very specific social role – something involving the social slicing of soft materials, perhaps animal or human bodies. In terms of time–space embeddedness and the social distribution of knowledge, obsidian use invoked and created trans-local identities in counterbalance to the locally based ones created through pottery.

Axes had a strange dual life, as tools used in many everyday tasks and quite possibly as weapons, and as valuables which were curated, cached, traded over long distances, and ritually deposited in caves and cult sites (an additional, completely uninvestigated possibility is that the numerous open-air surface finds of axes represent intentional off-site ritual deposition). Each of these two pathways consigned axes to a particular biography and mode of deposition. Using an axe as an everyday tool consumed it through breakage and reworking, resulting in the highly fragmented specimens typically found on habitation sites. Curating, trading, or ritually depositing it resulted in potentially much longer social biographies and the deposition of whole objects. To a variable extent, these two pathways involved axes made of different materials and forms, but often the same objects could pass through either biography. Axe biographies, therefore, show moments of action, of decisions to dedicate an object to a specific social end, to commit it to specific fields of action or to disengage it as social capital.

The Social Senses

The elements of habitus extend across fields of practice. These cross-domain terms of experience give coherence to daily normality and provide resources for innovation; indeed, they do both these goals at the same time, so that daily life is less playing out a predestined script than a process of continually resolving expected challenges with conventional tools to achieve an accepted outcome. Sensory regimes are not completely inaccessible archaeologically (Hamilakis 1998, 1999). Nor are sensory experiences normally experienced as divided senses. Rather, they tend to be understood synesthetically, with sight, sound, touch,

44. The colour red. (a) Red ochre stain on grinding stone from ritual site, Grotta delle Felci, Capri (Naples, Museo Archeologico Nazionale; photo: Robb); and (b) Red ochre fragment (Umbro, Calabria; photo: Robb).

taste and smell comprehended through inter-sensory dimensions which reference each other and cosmological and social qualities (Houston and Taube 2000).

Vision and particularly colour are the best investigated dimensions (Jones and MacGregor 2002). This is true also for Neolithic Italy. The most commonly used pigment was ochre, a variety of iron-bearing minerals which form in many geological settings (Figure 44). Ochre is often found on Neolithic sites, though often poorly published. Bright red seems to have been the preferred colour. Although ochre's natural colour varies from yellow through orange to bright red, it can be transformed from yellow to red by heating. This technique was known in Italy at least since the Bronze Age (La Rocca 2005) and it may have been practiced at least from the Neolithic as well; at Umbro and Penitenzeria, for example, over 90 percent of the ochre fragments found on site were red, though red ochre is rare in the area and yellow-orange ochre can be readily collected. Ochre was ground on grinding stones, which occasionally still bear reddish stains. Whether red ochre was locally produced or traded for, red was clearly a valued colour. For most of the Neolithic, what ochre was actually used for remains mysterious. Pottery vessels with red surfaces, for instance, seem to generally have used red-firing clay, though ochre was probably used sometimes as a pigment in red-painted wares. There is no evidence that house walls were painted; rock paintings are sometimes executed in ochre but as often in dark brown or black pigments instead (Graziosi 1974). Ochre pastes were sometimes used to fill impressions or incisions on pottery, and pebbles painted with ochre are known from a number of sites, predominantly along the Adriatic (Cassano et al. 2003). Ochre had a clear ritual use, and is found on ritual and burial sites increasingly as the Neolithic progresses, sometimes on ritually deposited grinding stones (Figure 44) or sprinkled on skeletons as at Masseria Bellavista (a use which continues and even increases in the Copper Age). Among archaeologically undetectable uses, ochre pigments may well have been applied to human bodies. Without context, the meanings of redness remain unknown, though it seems reasonable to postulate a semantic connection with blood, and, hence, with life.

There is less evidence for the use of other colours. Shells afforded white beads and pendants, and white chalky pastes were used to fill impressions on dark pottery. Blacks and browns were produced on pottery surfaces by careful choice of clays combined with reduction firing, and manganese-containing minerals were used to produce dark brown paint for painted figulina ware. Flints were used in all colours from grey and brown through whitish yellow and dull pink. Polished stone axes varied in colour from greyish to black, though the most commonly used part of the spectrum lay between dark green and black. Colour was clearly important for axes: distinctly greenish stone such as serpentinite is much less common naturally than greenish-black stones such as amphibolites and diorites, and these rarer greenstones seem to have been preferentially used for axes and axettes deposited in ritual contexts.

Table 21. *The Possible Neolithic Colour World*

	Surroundings	Archaeologically Attested	Food
Blue	Sky, sea; some copper ores; feathers; flowers		
Purple	Flowers, feathers		Fruits?
Red	Flowers, feathers, ochre; clays; furs (fox); light (sunrise, sunset); blood	Ochre; painted and oxidation-fired pots	Raw and cooked meat; fruits?
Orange	Ochre; flowers; light (sunrise, sunset)	Ochre	
Yellow	Flowers, ochre; light	Ochre	
Green	Vegetation; malachite; greenstones	Axes	Herbs? gathered greens; fruits
Black	Sea, night, obsidian; stone	Axes, obsidian	
Brown	Wood, soil, mud, dry vegetation; manganese ores; furs (dog, bear, wolf, etc.).	Pottery, daub; house roofs; most wild animals; domestic animals?	Cooked meat; grains (soup, bread, porridge)
Grey	Sea; clays; limestones	Pottery; sheep?	
White	Chalk; gypsum; shell; salt	Chalky concretions; shell	Salt?

A much purer black was provided by obsidian, whose translucency may have also been visually appealing (see Chapter 5 in this book).

Our view of colour is biased by archaeological preservation, but it is probably not completely unreliable. Earth tones of reds, yellows, browns, and black are relatively common in nature. Chlorophyll is common but fades, and the sky changes; natural, lasting and controllable sources of clear greens, blues, purples, and whites are much rarer: What we are probably missing most are small bright notes of colour afforded by rare minerals, furs, feathers, flowers, and shells. This usefully also suggests why qualities such as shine and sparkle, known naturally from obsidian, mother of pearl, rare crystals, mica and quartzite, creatable through the use of fats and oils, and created through burnishing pottery, may have had a great visual impact. If we were to roam the Neolithic world with a colour meter, counting hues, beyond vegetation and light, much of the ordinary scenery of life, and the great bulk of humanly created things, would fall into the range of relatively muted grey-brown-reddish tones (Table 21).

As the vast research into colour terminology has demonstrated (Chapman 2002), colours are defined culturally and the existence of coloured things does not mean colours were recognised according to our colour taxonomy, though the colour contrasts on trichrome pottery suggest minimally a red–black–white colour system. Leaving aside the question of how colours were categorised, what is interesting here are the possibilities for social synaesthesia (Houston and Taube 2000). It was argued above that cuisine embodied a three-fold contrast between omnipresent, bulk grains and pulses with relatively bland flavors and muted brownish-yellow colours, smaller amounts of richer, reddish-brown, meats carefully deployed for social eating, and specially obtained, stored and used substances with very distinct and particular flavors. This three-fold contrast is echoed in the division of colours in the natural and humanly created world, for example, in the predominant hues of villages, the limited but well-known use of ochre as a social colourant, and small notes of white, black, green, and other colours created through bringing together substances such as obsidian, shell, and special stones in a way possible only through a combination of exchange and detailed knowledge of extraordinary spaces. The coincidence between the colour phenomenology of the Neolithic environment and the colour-flavour world of Neolithic cuisine suggests that both formed part of a synaesthetic set of reflexes for generating and understanding social experience. If so, this may explain why both the reddish pottery and the use of ochre are extended, significantly, in the Late Neolithic in both Italy and Malta (see Chapter 8 in this book).

Unfinished Business: Space, Time, Projects

Moving beyond the senses to social involvement, our first impression is of the sheer busyness of Neolithic life. One way of expressing this complexity is through space–time diagrams. The ones used here are not identical to those pioneered by Hagerstrand (1977), as they track material flows rather than human movement, but they express some similar senses. Settlements, as relatively fixed places, span several human generations at least. They provide the settings for action. Within settings, houses (Figure 45a) similarly provide a structuring context for action, making plain coresident households, though they have a determinate lifespan delimited by acts of construction and destruction, probably on the scale of a generation or less.

Human projects involve composing and directing channeling material flows of varying directionality and duration, within networks of related settlements. Flaked stone tools, for instance, are a reductive technology which has a short lifespan; they do not seem to have been curated and the overall human-tool interaction is unidirectional and relatively brief. Transported and traded lithics – obsidian, specifically – must be considered as a flat, horizontal flow with a specific directionality based on a settlement's place in trade networks extending outwards from obsidian sources (Figure 45f). In contrast, pots have a longer duration, though the lifespan of serving and eating vessels tends to be on the order of a few years (Rice 1987) and, except for infrequent examples of repair, their lifespan is unidirectional, though once broken they remained on site as a witness to tradition. They appear to have moved little (Figure 45e). Axes (Figure 45d) originated outside settlements and had much more varied lifespans, moving, breakage, and refashioning, traded away, ritually deposited.

Food harvests were a string of annual movements in from short ranges away, though clearing new gardens may have been multi-year projects (Figure 45b). Herds, in contrast, were a long-term project with a strong temporal structure. It would have taken a number of years to build up a family herd, particularly of relatively slowly-reproducing cattle, and herds would have risen and fallen in parallel with family cycles. Spatially, herds would have moved within short ranges of villages. Relations between herds would have been mediated by periodic transfers of animals (Figure 45c). Both crops and herds involved daily labor and short-range movement within annual rhythms. The heterogeneous flavours and use of game and forest products involved a different structuring of space, time, and knowledge: irregular journeys to less-frequented areas for gathering particular resources, perhaps trade or unplanned social encounters, the dilation of time through storage within villages.

It is difficult to know the cumulative structure of time and space – here one would ideally want genuine Hagerstrand time–space geographies of individual movement. However, time and space are both elastic

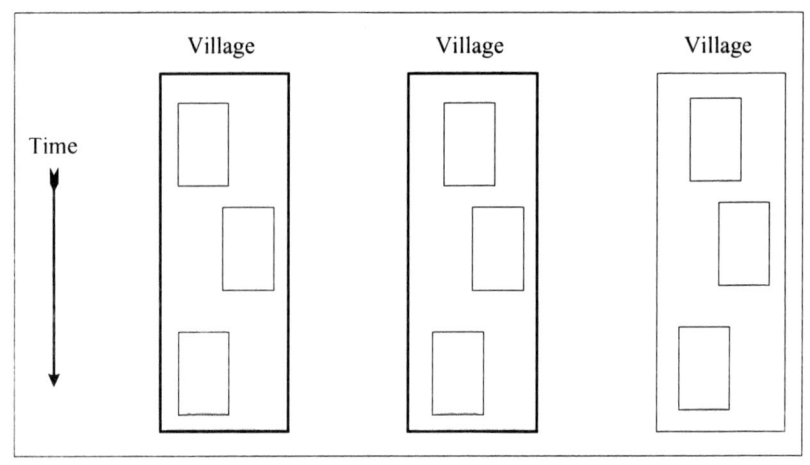

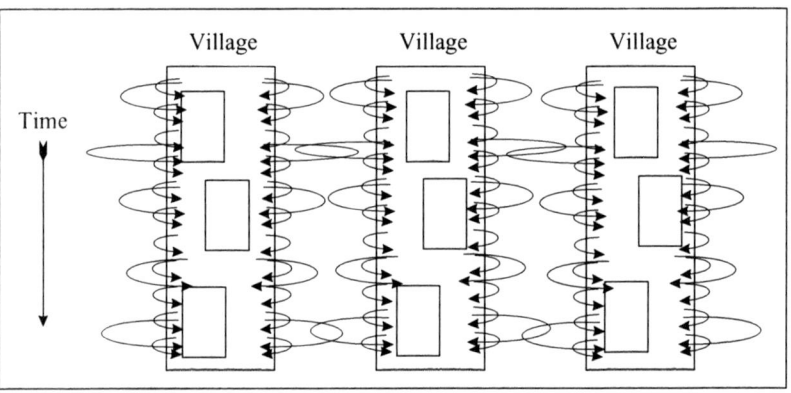

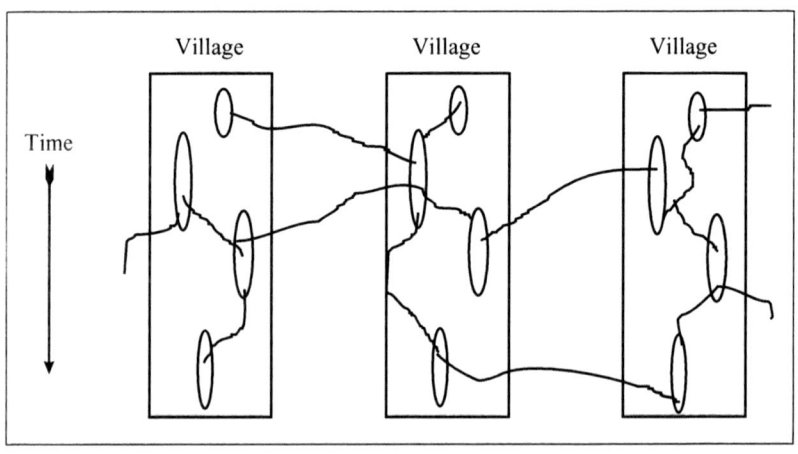

45. Material flows in space and time. (a) Houses and villages; (b) Food; (c) Animals and herds; (d) Axes; (e) Pottery; and (f) Obsidian.

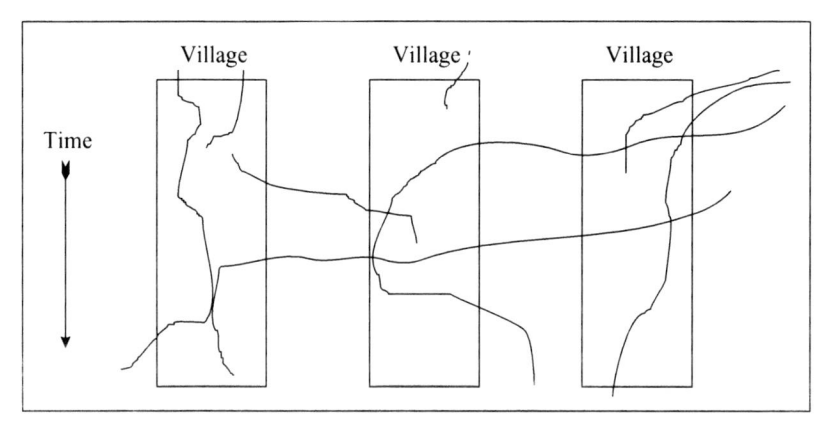

d

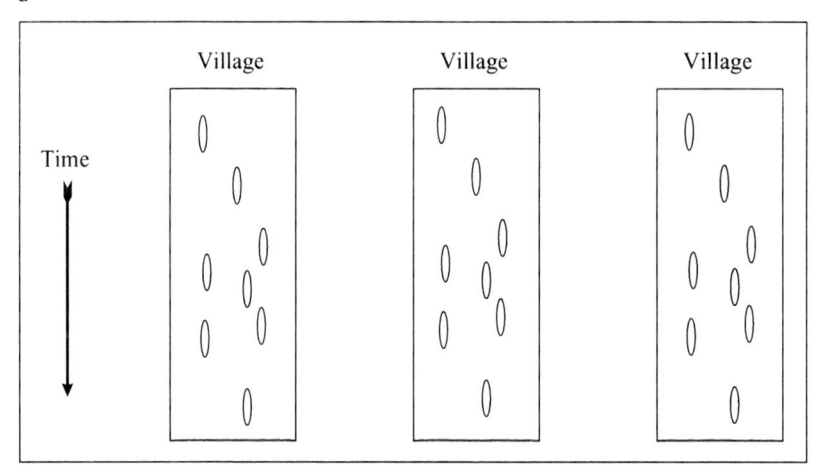

e

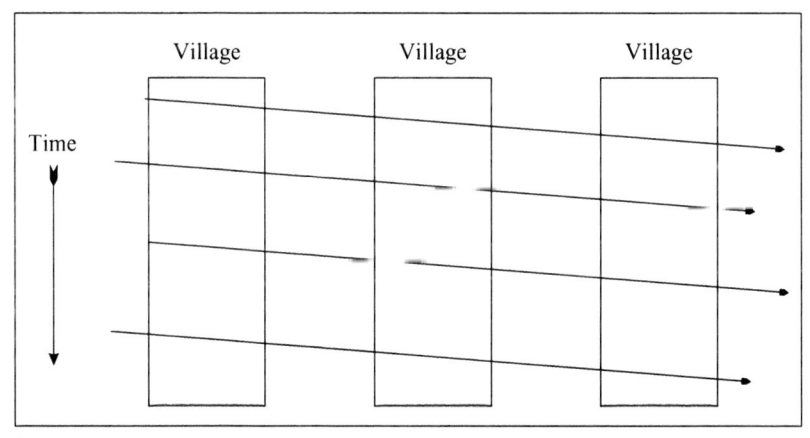

f

45. (continued)

Table 22. *Archaeological Approaches to Material Agency*

Dimension	Human–Material Interaction	Transformed Thing	Transformed People	Narrative of Relationship
Bodies	Embodiment	Defined bodies, habituated senses	Identities	Biography
Landscapes	Inhabitation	Place	Inhabitants	History
Things	Materiality	Extended (social) artefact	Makers/users/ owners	Artefact biography

and hybrid dimensions or, rather, senses. At one end, they are generated during the busyness of ordinary activities; our orientational senses of time and space emerge from the rhythms of daily life, which, moreover, impose a unique perspective on each person's orientation due to the unique place for participation and observation which each body occupies. We become our routines. On the other end, time and space dilate, become abstract, and articulate with the cosmological planes of pure definition. The sense of locatedness thus links specific bodies with the world around them.

The Neolithic scale of frequentation would show both a drop-off in inhabitation and encounter and qualitative shifts in the nature of space as one moved outward from the village (Figure 23; Chapter 3). Similarly, the composite structure of time would reflect periodicities and recurrencies on many scales, from daily events to lifetimes. Many processes and events would presumably be organised around an annual alternation of seasons and activities, but some would be more sporadic – the building of a new house occurs every 5–10 years, the digging of a new village ditch occurs once a generation, the abandonment of a site and founding of a new one as a historic event. It is the cumulative temporal landscape resulting from the accumulation of activities which represents a taskscape (Ingold 2000), the generation of knowledge through situated activity rather than static discourse.

Archaeologically, we can see Neolithic time structured in many ways. One is the rhythms of the daily activities discussed above, the metronome of social life. Beyond these, we can also observe intentional time markings which are interventions in the existence of specific objects in order to bring them into line with an appropriate master narrative (Table 22). Bodies would have been given biographical form through their own culturally understood processes of maturation and change, but moments such as tooth ablation for women and trepanation for selected older adults may have marked defining points in the history of an individual body. Time marking is also evident in burial practices. Death was a transforming point in the social history of a specific body: burial seems not to have been intended to provide a permanent and undisturbable repository so much as to provide an interval of memorialisation. The social lifespan of bodies would thus cycle from living person to a remembered specific person to, on a longer scale of time, a generic ancestral presence through awareness of the burials disturbed periodically on the site, and this cycle could be extended, abbreviated, or circumvented in appropriate circumstances. Landscape time marking is evident in many practices, such as occasional foundation deposits below houses, building houses and digging ditches, and the gradual accumulation of settlement detritus and visible landscape change around sites. Its most dramatic instance is the intentional destruction of houses as an act of closure. Artefact biographies are much more varied, but all genres of material activity discussed show acts of creations, acts of prolongation (caching axes, repairing pots), and acts of closure such as killing an animal, permanently depositing an axe, or intentional fragmentation or destruction (Chapman 2000). Acts of initiation and of closure may have been used to render human lives, the history of social groups, the lives of houses, and the lives of artefacts, parallel with each other.

There are two hints that these varied narratives may have been linked in larger narrative (perhaps as occasionally realised potential interpretations rather than explicit or liturgical stories). One is the common context of recovery in unstructured site debris for most finds, which suggests which suggests that, after being released from wholeness, social relations, functionalities and specific memories, artefacts, architecture, and even human bodies were consigned to a role as generic evidence of the past. The second is the Late Neolithic practice of sometimes burying the dead at abandoned Early or Middle Neolithic villages, which suggests that such general, mixed and fragmented debris, embedded in historical tradition, was sufficient to act as a signifier of ancestral presence. The result is a temporally-bound "aesthetics of depositional practice" (Pollard 2001), but with unstructured, not structured depositions.

This is useful, but "material flows" and taskscapes are still somewhat too abstract terms. They mask the sense that each action or transaction was something which specific people did carefully and knowledgably for a proximate goal. Perhaps the best way to put it is to say that social transactions themselves have *chaîne opératoires*: even things which are entirely programmed and expectable must be made to happen through active interventions. The quotidian practices we observe in the Neolithic archaeological record provide witness of dense and immediate social actions.

Beyond this, as we noted in Chapter 1, things are material commitments. They commit their users to plans of action, to creation, correct usage, maintenance and disposal. Axes were necessary and universal tools, but in most areas could only obtained through regular participation in exchange networks. Heavy reliance upon crops precluded too great a degree of settlement mobility, required constructed weatherproof storage places, and committed households to frequent if not daily bouts of probably quite tedious grinding. Herds require continual care and tending. However, juxtaposed, autonomous fields of action were also linked by enchainment and commitment. As life projects, no field of activity was free-standing. Procuring obsidian, axes, and grinding stones required travel and social occasions; travel required boats; boats required axes; social occasions required settlements and pots; settlements required axes; pots required clay and ochre; ochre required grinding stones – and this only scratches the surface of the most generic and functional relationships. Hence, one project implied many others. In this sense, artefacts are really not static things so much as ongoing programmes of action, and to the extent that these programmes can be executed well or badly, they are dramas, narratives of projects with a rooted history in particular circumstances and an anticipated extension well into the future.

This is Neolithic economy as social reproduction. As practices of everyday life, the superimposed density of material flows (Figure 46) really portrays the density of narrative experience of daily life. This is important in understanding the compelling quality of action. One of the sociological problems of normality is the question of why arbitrary social worlds are so encompassing: what is it about today which makes tomorrow inevitable? In the above discussion, the answer lies in the

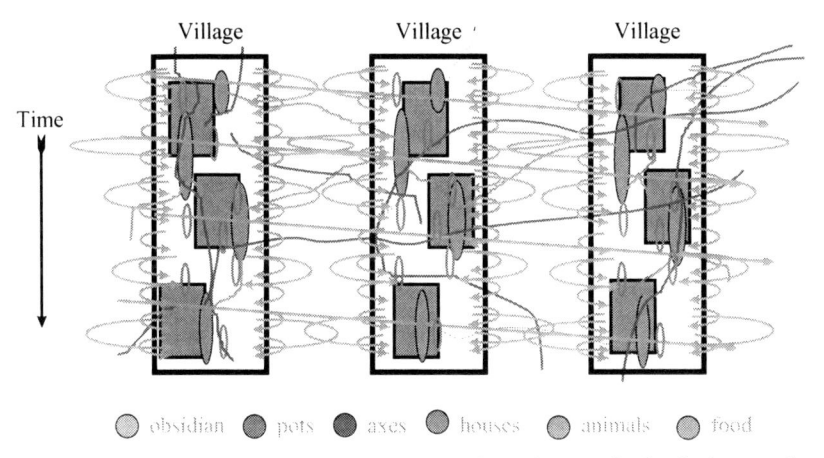

46. Cumulative material flows in space and time (for pathways of individual materials, see preceding diagrams).

materiality of Gulliver's dilemma, the web of social reproduction implied by action (Chapter 1). The millennia of the Neolithic were not merely duration but time with a human structure. The long stability of the Neolithic way of life results from an engagement with time through interwoven, overlapping, and successful projects, an active negotiation of the future, inevitability born not of passivity or grim determinism but of human agency.

Projects of the Self

The exercise of agency creates agents, and material projects can also be considered projects of the self. The busyness of daily life cannot be carried out by undifferentiated, generic bodies or persons; it requires specific dexterities and habituations. Forming and exercising these capabilities, and being known to do so, is an essential product of daily activity. This theme has been traced out most clearly for pottery, as of our analyses it affords the highest resolution picture of agents at work. Potters supplied vessels for storage, cooking, eating, and drinking. The elaborate designs they often created on the surface of these vessels were not intended to convey information about their identity to strangers, as in some theories of style, nor probably to convey specific iconographic representations. Instead – as a minimal definition of stylistic behavior – they were probably meant simply to elicit senses of pleasure, recognition of pattern, and familiarity or appropriateness. But in order to do so, they depended upon a past discourse about the nature of appropriate designs – a material conversation in which decorative style itself was an active element.

Hence, we may draw three relations between pottery decoration and identity:

1. Making pottery appropriately required not only technical experience learned within a community of potters, but also participation over time in the decorative discourse.
2. Seeing pottery appropriately meant placing it within a particular frame of reference defined by a decorative discourse. This may or may not have been the same frame of reference as the potters, both for people from other communities and for people within the same community (e.g., nonpotters may have seen surface designs differently than potters did, perhaps as generic ornamentation rather than as sharply distinct statements of difference and conformity).
3. How one viewed a vessel was an act of positioning; it established and reinforced a spatially, temporally and socially situated frame of reference. Cultivating and exercising a form of activity established one's ability to do so, and the coincidence between frames of reference through which different people understood a field of action formed a way of gauging their relative social positions.

People are defined by their knowledge, and one measure of relationship is through shared or different knowledges. For our Neolithic studies, pottery bears a particular parallel (and not a coincidental one) with landscape. It is a truism that there is no absolutely defined landscape; what the landscape is depends upon one's relationship to it and to other people within it. Monet's haystack paintings are the work of a disengaged urban dweller interested in the haystack's essential haystackness as an exemplification of vision in general; it does not matter whether the haystack is abundant or scanty, who owns it, or whether it will be sold for cash or used to see the cows through the winter. People from anywhere within the Neolithic Italian world would have understood the components of landscape elsewhere – huts, gardens, traces of past activity – but only those inhabiting a particular place intimately would know them as individual places associated with people, stories and involvements. Such knowledge is social capital to be accumulated by elders, and sharing common lifeways and historical knowledge is a criterion for belonging to a community (Canuto and Yaeger 2000). Houses, too, are structuring devices relating shared experience and knowledge associated with identities at a smaller, nested scale. Thus, as Pred (1990) notes, inhabiting particular social spaces is essential to biography formation.

Difference and the Organization of Value

Politically, Italian Neolithic societies were "tribes." However, as Anglo-American archaeologists generally use such terms, this is an unhelpfully negative definition: it characterises these societies principally by their lack of formal social hierarchies, and actually tells us very little about them (see Chapter 2 in this book). Recent British prehistoric theorists offer little more help, generally preferring to speak of social process, symbolism and experience and maintaining a determined postmodern taciturnity on shopworn but important issues such as social and political organization. Here, however, we may usefully bring together these two opposed lines of thought through concepts of the organization of value.

In the processual tradition, the defining feature of a society was the presence of social hierarchies, understood as clear and permanent principles of organization. It was generally assumed that hierarchical structures were singular, and that leaders were propped up by, and rewarded with, an equally singular prestige and power. In other words, the leader's prestige summarised a single, generalised kind of value (prestige or power), and his (the gender is not coincidental) power spanned many or all domains of social action. This basic assumption about value, hierarchy, and identity underwrites methodologies such as burial analysis.

Unfortunately, the ethnographic world is rarely so tidy. Critical development of this model has come from at least three directions. Within processual archaeology, deconstruction of chiefdoms as a hopelessly heterogeneous category was rapid (Feinman and Neitzel 1984), leaving "segmentary societies" more of a residual catch-all category than ever. In Britain, and in Europe generally, this view foundered upon the Neolithic–Bronze Age transition, in which one ambiguously hierarchical society was replaced by an equally ambiguous but utterly different one; Renfrew (1976) made sense of this as a transition from "group-oriented" to "individualising" chiefdoms, a perceptive interpretation strangely prescient of the attempt several decades later to divide prehistoric societies not according to their level of social organization but according to whether their leaders pursued "corporate" and "network" strategies respectively (Blanton et al. 1996; Feinman 2001). A further critique was developed through the concept of heterarchy. Heterarchy has already been introduced as a way of looking at political structure in Chapter 2. The term provides a way of describing the organizational qualities of systems in which elements cannot be ranked because they are defined in qualitatively different ways (Ehrenreich, Crumley, and Levy 1995). The concept of heterarchy is principally a description or definition (Saitta and McGuire 1998), but it is a useful one which unearths much buried in conventional views. For example, the concept demonstrates how limited the concept of hierarchy is in capturing important elements of social process when used in isolation; even prestige itself, so central to hierarchical models, always combines a qualitative definition of value with a comparative scale of attainment (Hatch 1989).

Meanwhile, in Melanesian ethnography, Godelier (1986) argued that, besides the Big Men and Chiefs so poetically described by Sahlins (1963), traditional Melanesian leaders included "Great Men" who were renowned in a particular field of endeavor such as hunting, warfare, gardening, ritual or oratory, but who did not wield a generalised leadership. Godelier's own ideal type of "Great Men" and his structuralist model based upon the contrast with Big Men have been critiqued, and it has also been claimed that Big Men were in fact created by colonial contact (Godelier and Strathern 1991; Knauft 1993; Roscoe 2000). But the point remains that there are multiple forms of leadership, and that they are distinguished not so much by formal organizational structures as by the way in which value is created and understood. This general conclusion coincides well with post-processual handling of the problem in which a Neolithic regime of social reproduction based upon ancestry and ritual authority evolved into a qualitatively different Bronze Age regime based upon specific genealogical claims and competition for prestige.

How does this illuminate the politics of Neolithic Italy? It has already been argued above (Chapter 2) that the burial evidence suggests a heterarchical situation. With few exceptions, burial was not used to proclaim the social importance or identity of the dead. Moreover, exceptional burials are all unique, emphasizing ritual difference, rather than representing greater or lesser actualization of a common standard of prestige or identity. This fragmentation of prestige symbolizations seems generally to have been the case. For example, hunting was practiced throughout Italy, and, given its economic unimportance, it was probably important for symbolic or prestige reasons. However, it is only near the end of the Neolithic that symbolizations of hunting (in rock art and specially crafted bifacial points) appear which might suggest that prestige from hunting was relevant to other contexts. The same is true for warfare and exchange.

In other words, Neolithic people engaged in many distinct activities involving effort, skill, and social recognition, the conduct of which recreated social relationships within and among households, settlements and wider communities, and probably genders and age groups as well. What they did *not* have, inasmuch as the archaeological record provides a guide to Neolithic people's interests and priorities, was a system of a few static, central political identities around which the different kinds of value created in these projects were organised. The resulting political organization was heterarchical, based principally upon participation and enactment rather than role or status.

Formal structures are always reifications of social process, sometimes helpful and sometimes not. Rather than pursuing typological resemblances, it is more useful to look at how Neolithic Italians actually used difference. This theme has already arisen in several fields of action.

In pottery, the agency of the potter involved free play of decoration within set parameters to create similar differences. The pots they created thus share in complexly heterarchical patterns of relationship rather than simple categorical difference, a fact which has bedeviled traditional attempts at typology; in comparing any two vessels, there are always commonalities to unite them and differences to separate them. In other plastic media, the amazing variety of figurines suggests small communities of ritual practice reinterpreting a common idiom to create local differences. Distinct communities of ritual practice are also responsible for the increasingly varied range of burial practices in the later Neolithic, and for the patchy adherence to generalizations (rather than rules) about sex and side of burial. Beyond this pattern of creating difference within genres of action, there is also a pattern of lack of transferability between spheres. With the exception of a few painted fine wares deposited at ritual sites in Puglia, no matter how skillfully produced a pot is, it rarely winds up in a burial or a special context of any sort.

I am suggesting, thus, that as a cultural reflex, Neolithic people tended to create difference, both in maintaining separate spheres of value and in playing with difference within a given field of action such as pottery-making, ritual, and so forth. This does not necessarily imply a tension-free, harmonious society. Social difference always carried the possibility of contradiction. In hierarchical societies, contradiction and conflict are organised around stratified statuses and the criteria of access to value or resources which define them. In nonhierarchical societies, contradiction rooted in differing definitions of social value may take different forms. In such situations, access to value and prestige is likely to be regulated by the situational patterning of life chances rather than by formal exclusionary criteria; in one typical example (Kelly 1993), only about half the older men in a group achieved the recognition, theoretically open to all, of respected village elder. Different forms of social action afford alternative strategies to recognition for people of different ages and genders, or among which people can choose according to their specific situation. There may be gender and age inequality based upon unequal access to cosmological value and prestige (Kelly 1993); Whitehouse (1992) draws upon Godelier's work for an interpretation of gender inequality in Neolithic Italy. Youth wants to raid for glory while age wants to make peace and exchange (Trigger 1969). Elders may dominate their juniors through control of ritual or marriage (Meillassoux 1981), and spirit mediums draw on different spiritual authority than elders (Kelly 1993). Men's work and women's work and exchange carry different and sometimes conflicting values. One can draw upon the support of agnatic kin or of trading partners, but these may make conflicting demands (Wiessner and Tumu 1998).

Neolithic Italian societies must surely have been characterised by different access to fields of action and by structural tensions between these fields, but evidence is sparse; paradoxically, a society in which activities are not assimilated to a few formal statuses is much less likely to supply clear archaeological evidence for divisions of labor and value. Nevertheless, not all projects afforded the same potential meanings. Indeed, while agents maintained a common lifelong habitus, construing all activities as repeating the same basic themes seems both reductionist and unlikely. Indeed, spheres of activity both opposed and depended upon each other. If we trust the slender skeletal evidence for greater male mobility and, assuming continuity, retroject the Late Neolithic rock art evidence for male hunting and warfare (see Chapter 2 in this book), one axis of difference may have been the spatialisation of gender-defining activities in different zones. As a second axis of difference, household and village participations delimited parts whose separateness was essential to their coming together through transactions of people, animals and things and which came together in solidarity at feasts.

More generally, there is a contrast between local and trans-local activities. Potting, gardening, burial, and the curation of group history and tradition relied upon intensely local patterns of frequentation, frames of reference and knowledge bases. Travel, exchange, warfare, and hunting were translocal, relying upon sharing frames of reference with like individuals in other groups and on extensive rather than intensive information. With obsidian, we find identical products made with identical techniques in widely different cultures (indeed, as both dedicated cores and bladelets themselves seem to have been traded, the *chaîne opératoire* itself spans many communities). However, the skill involved in producing blades and cores, the social relations of trade involved in getting obsidian, and the restricted amount in circulation suggest obsidian use may have been restricted to a subset of the local community, even if it was one defined only by age, gender and experience rather than by formal specialization. Hunting and herding required detailed knowledge of a broad, continually changing area, and perhaps negotiation with members of neighboring groups. Raiding and defense would have required similar diplomacy and monitoring of a social landscape, and obtaining or exchanging valuable things such as axes would have required long-term relationships with people outside one's normal social network.

Local and translocal activities were surely not rigidly defined or restricted, but they did require distinct ongoing commitments in terms of knowledges and relationships to maintain. To the extent that different kinds of relationships require different persons (e.g., between those able to understand highly specific meanings buried in layers of local knowledge and those who have had the appropriate background to discuss exchanging with other exchangers), they afforded distinct and opposed avenues for self-definition, a recurrent tension which was probably genderised and aged in some contexts but not in all. Yet both were essential for social reproduction, and, like other fields of discourse cited above, local and trans-local activities were also bound together in antonymic and mutually defining relations. Hence some of the most commonly found kinds of Neolithic action, for example feasting, may have been long-lived because of their ability to incorporate contradictory elements by integrating the external and the internal.

To summarise, participation in contrasting activities was a means of negotiating and using difference in the composition of lives. It is in this context that we need to understand moments of decision, such as routing an axe towards daily use and consumption or curation and circulation: as points of fluidity between alternative relations between people and things. To the extent that participation in or exclusion from fields of activity was formally prescribed, gender and age probably the key ordering principles. Effectively, the individual body of a particular age and gender contained the potential to be all social bodies except those formally defined as complementary. In this sense, the malleability of the body shown in the extreme choices of schematism in figurines (Figures 5 and 6) really gives a sense of the many social potentials within the Neolithic body.

The Commonwealth of People and Things

Here we can return to the epigraph of Chapter 2. A group of Torajan woodcarvers from Sarawak spent several months living in a standard London house (Barley 1989). Among the numerous things which perplexed them was the way in which Londoners worked long hours in order to afford houses in which they consequently were able to spend very little time (Barley 1990, p. 51). This unusual moment of cultural critique – unusual in that it features a critique of ourselves by others rather than the converse – instanciates some of the key themes of this chapter.

Lives, from inside, always appear inevitable and necessary. Agents participate in goal-oriented, necessary projects which, furthermore, interlock functionally. It is obvious that one goes to work to pay the mortgage and the car payments, just as without a place to live and a way of getting to work one cannot hold down a job. It is also obvious that, given these projects, one might dedicate effort to do them in a particular way – to strive for a particularly good house, or a personally satisfying or well-paid job. What is often beyond the margins of the native's field of vision is why these conventional projects are defined they way they are: for instance, why one needs a house in which most spaces are unused most of the time because it is assumed that distinct functions need different spaces or that people will prefer to spend most of their time in separate rooms, apart from each other – another English custom which seemed paradoxical and fundamentally antisocial to the Torajans (Barley 1989, p. 184).

Human consciousness proceeds from activity; in acting to carry out their life-projects, people reproduce the social and symbolic conditions of activity, from the most abstract cultural structures to the most particular details of how a particular task should be accomplished. Projects require considerable social and material entanglement: resources, contexts, and relationships. Moreover, a time slice through the life of a community at any point reveals a multitude of overlapping, entangled projects whose progress and conclusion gives meaning to the past and whose planning propels individuals into projected time of the future. Furtherance of these immediate works is the shuttle on the loom of experience. The material conversations they involve form the basis of the collective reproduction of the arbitrary social reality they are grounded in. And each activity changes the self; there are things one only knows or does after becoming a girl, an initiated adult, a parent, a homeowner, a hunter, an executive. In the largest sense, the human biography is created through undertaking myriads of nested projects whose undertaking marks one, through knowledge and commitment, as a certain kind of person. Material activity, thus, forms also projects of the self.

Neolithic things are "the lost thread of a thousand stories" (Ingravallo 1999, p. 19, translation Robb). In some ways, the basic argument of this chapter is best expressed in metaphors. In our common sense, and in traditional archaeology, people are seen as independent and integral things, as free-standing bodies and protagonists. When they pass through the fragmentary lens of the archaeological record, it is as if a person is wandering through a many-roomed house, only some rooms of which contain windows or mirrors through which we can see them. Assuming the continuous and whole being; we have then to reconstruct it from discontinuous and partial reflections. If, however, we take seriously the idea that human subjectivity is constructed, and that this happens through social and material relations, the ground of metaphor shifts abruptly. What appears to be a solid figure is more like a hologram, the intersection of light from many sources; people are not reflected in their social and material relations so much as constructed by them. If so, then it is in the intersection of their programs of action that we should locate the construction of this too solid flesh.

Olsen (2003) argues persuasively that archaeologists need to consider things and people as entities of equal potency in constructing society, and there is an increasing weight of argument for a social theory which takes a more sophisticated view of the role of material things in structuring human life. Yet it is equally mistaken to make material culture "active" at the cost of making people passive. Arguing about whether guns kill people or people with guns kill people (as in the U.S. National Rifle Association's slogan) is a moral polemic which misses the point theoretically. Agency is relational: what kills is the relationship between people and guns. And this is determined not by the individual human hand alone, nor by the gun, nor even by the history guiding and shaping them, but by the conjunction of all three in particular circumstances.

This book has intentionally chosen a challenging ground to work out these ideas: rather than selectively choosing traditionally fruitful terrain or promising, narrowly-defined topics, it attempts a broad review of an ordinary, patchy and quotidian archaeological record, hopefully without spending too much time in the subjunctive mood. Through investigation of an entirety, one can think about the ordinary frame of reference within which people lived. The drawback of refusing to cherry-pick the archaeological record is that one inevitably finds oneself citing the lack of data over and over, like a broken record.

Is a comprehensive archaeology of the typical possible? No, but nor is it not worth trying. It has demonstrated four general points. As comparison with the quite different societies described in Chapter 8 shows, these conclusions are not generic, one-size-fits-all reconstructions but address the Italian Neolithic with some specificity:

1. Through the tactic of systematically extrapolating programmes of activity from archaeological finds, it has illustrated the density of routines and projects involved in generating ordinary life. For Neolithic Italy, one implication of this, which is particularly important for deep prehistory and for bridging the gap between ethnographic time and archaeological time, is that long-term stability can result from people actively pursuing projects important to them, rather than simply reflecting a lack of agency due to environmental constraints, the grip of tradition or the lack of hierarchical politicians.
2. In line with the concept of relational agency, these routinised projects created people as well as things (Berger and Luckmann 1967; Giddens 1984). Projects required commitment to a shared reality and to the internal and external conditions of action. In Yeats' words (see Chapter 1 in this book), they provided the dances which defined the dancers. It is due to this that the material remains of the Italian Neolithic are not simply a disparate collection of archaeological facts but an interpretable human record. Material remains are highly structured

in a way which is contingent prospectively and determinate retrospectively: things interacting to make people.

This relationship is evident in three dimensions which have often been discussed separately in archaeological literature but with strikingly parallel theoretical controversies: landscapes, bodies, and material culture. Each has its own form of human-material interaction, which creates new people as much as it creates a world for them to work. Each has its master narrative which guides how it unfolds. Bodies (see Chapter 2 in this book) are defined and experienced through processes of embodiment which define the relationship of people to their bodies, provide the basis for the definition of genders, ages, and biographical pathways and produce identities for these bodies; the result is biography as a master narrative of an appropriate human life. Landscapes (see Chapter 3 in this book) are inhabited through acts of definition, frequentation, and abandonment, which create both places and inhabitants; the result is history. Things (see Chapters 4 and 5 in this book) relate to humans via processes of materiality. One result of this process is the transformation of a thing into an extended social artefact defined by meanings as well as by material, effectively part of an extended, decentered cognition system (Gell 1998; Malafouris 2005). The converse result is a person whose identity is defined or modified through this relationship and the knowledge, capacity, or social relations it creates. The narrative of the human–artefact relationship is the artefact biography, shaped by cumulative appropriate decisions and transformations.

3. Although social reproduction happens through the medium of many genres of activity, it cannot be reduced simply to the analytical level of specific fields of discourse. Rather, generalised principles of understanding and reaction, or habitus, give coherence to the ensemble of social life. The body and landscape (in the sense of all spatial environments) are essential to this, but material practices are as well. In Neolithic Italy, these binding threads of social life are visible in such elements as synesthetic connections between cuisines, colours, spaces, and occasions, in spatial and temporal rhythms, and in temporal

practices of deposition and burial which coordinated human lives and histories of communities.

4. Identity and political process are encompassed within, and emerge from, processes of social reproduction, and the form they take will depend on cultural patterns. In Neolithic Italy, for example, an important element of habitus was the creation of difference in many scales and contexts. One reflex of this is that Italian Neolithic politics is not best characterised as a static system of formally defined roles, but rather as a process of the individuation and capacitation of specific aged and gendered bodies in a heterarchical range of activities.

Like Bottom's dream, the Italian Neolithic world which emerges from our investigation is indeed strange, admirable, and of great constancy. There is one further test to which a reconstruction of Neolithic social life can be put. Our goal in archaeology is clearly to get beyond the synchronic and generalised discussion and to address variation and change. Can the generalised Neolithic social world be transformed into the great range of specific and situated Neolithics we actually track archaeologically? And can it be seen to develop and change, not superficially as a chronicle of events, but organically, as something whose reflexes and responses contain the seeds of millennial development? This is the challenge of the next two chapters.

SEVEN:
NEOLITHIC ITALY AS AN ETHNOGRAPHIC LANDSCAPE

It is almost axiomatic that large-scale types will be modified if not refuted as the complexities of local-level processes and variations are taken into account.
    Bruce Knauft, *South Coast New Guinea Cultures: History, Comparison, Dialectic.* (Knauft 1993, p. 118)

The Mandans are certainly a very interesting and pleasing people in their personal appearance and manners; differing in many respects, both in looks and customs, from all other tribes which I have seen. They are not a warlike people; for they seldom, if ever, carry war into their enemies' country; but when invaded, shew their valour and courage to be equal to that of any people on earth. Being a small tribe, and unable to contend on the wide prairies with the Sioux and other roaming tribes, who are ten times more numerous, they have very judiciously located themselves in a permanent village, which is strongly fortified, and ensures their preservation. By this means they have advanced further in the arts of manufacture; have supplied their lodges more abundantly with the comforts, and even luxuries of life, than any Indian nation I know of.
    George Catlin, *Letters and Notes on the Manners, Customs, and Conditions of North American Indians, Volume 1.* (Catlin 1973, p. 93)

One of the hardest things for archaeologists to do is to get off site, to see the larger world not only as an archaeological landscape but as an ethnographic landscape, full of defined places, relations of causation, and peoples situated in difference. As Knauft points out, regional analysis always involves a dialectic between scale-dependent heuristics, or useful analytical fictions, such as regional cultures and the data themselves. Yet we must imagine each Neolithic Italian community as existing in relation to its close and distant neighbours, much like the groups in the ethnographic landscape traversed by travelers such as Catlin. Rather than insisting either upon the absolute uniqueness of each group or upon a common culture to which each group must have conformed rigidly, it is the complex relations between the local and the regional which pose important interpretive challenges.

Neolithic Italy has been presented thus far as a generalised synchrony, in terms of the commonalities which bound it together as a cultural world. Here, however, we approach the same materials with an eye towards how Neolithic Italian societies varied from place to place and changed over time. There are compelling reasons why even local histories cannot be understood without a regional and historical dimension, but understanding how human agency interacts with time and space has proven a surprisingly recalcitrant topic. Most "regional" analyses in archaeology, for instance, either iron out regional variations as superficial disguises of an underlying unity or trace them as parallel but unrelated traditions; there are few analyses of cultural areas as networks of related, interacting, independent cultures.

The finest variation is simply small-scale historical process. Except where dendrochronology, microstratigraphy, or an abundance of radiocarbon dates calibrated with Bayesian technoques allow very fine-grained chronological resolution, action at this scale is normally inaccessible. Even when we can follow high-resolution sequences of events, interpretation can be ambiguous: does a moment of abandonment represent a normal moment in the life cycle of a site or a secular change in ways of life? For the Italian Neolithic, temporal resolution is coarse. Because few sites are absolutely dated, even those absolutely dated sites are nonetheless free-floating, as it is unclear how they relate to the undated archaeological context around them. Spatial resolution is equally coarse, mostly because research has been patchy: are more sites known on the Adriatic side of the peninsula because it was more densely populated, because land surfaces are better preserved, or simply because more research has been done there?

Without access to the finest-grained level, we can nevertheless address questions of regionality at a more general scale. This chapter considers Neolithic Italy as an ethnographic landscape through consideration of spatial demographic models, regional variations in settlement, and travel, trade and warfare. Finally, it turns to case studies of two issues of particular interest: communities and regional networks, and the local history of unique places.

Spatial Demography

How did people fill up the inhabitable world? Spatial structure may be discerned at three basic levels: the household, the locality, and the region. At what level groups were self-sufficient or recognised a common identity clearly depended both upon factors such as group size and population density and upon the purpose at hand.

Households are well-defined architecturally (see Chapter 3), and were, presumably, the basis for many tasks, such as the daily production of food. They presumably encompassed any complementarities of personal capacity needed to carry on daily life. Yet, we have noted, the household, and, often, the settlement itself, would have been insufficient for many collective tasks where a quorum of people with specific capabilities was needed. Moreover, many activities may have required people in specific relation to each other. Marrying without incest is the most obvious case, but other prescribed relationships based on kinship or agnatic relationships may have existed. Thus, residential communities such as hamlets and villages would have been grouped into larger units, local networks of cooperation with some shared sense of community. Although archaeological consideration of such self-recognised groups above the local network level has been seriously neglected, they must have been central to how people understood their social identity and structured relations of cooperation, marriage, alliance, trade, hospitality and ritual, and conflict.

The size – in population and in territory – of these communities is entirely conjectural, but it is worth sketching out some possible parameters. The demographic models reviewed in Chapter 2 suggest 175–475 people for a stable mating network. Ethnographically, typical group sizes for self-recognised tribes in New Guinea and North America typically range between about 1,000 and 5,000 people, with most towards the lower end of this range and a few larger examples. In terms of size, using the GIS land use modeling above (Robb and Van Hove 2003), a network of 1,000 people would have required at least 200–400 km² of territory, depending on their economy and the terrain. Boundaries between such groups need not have coincided with geographic, ecological or economic differences, but major landmarks such the coasts and islands would have both structured the possibilities of communication and provided focal points for construction of difference. Several geographically well-bounded regions of appropriate size supply obvious candidates for ancient social territories: mountain valleys such as the Fucino or Gubbio basins, small coastal plains such as the plain of Catania or the various enclaves along the Calabrian coastline and sufficiently large island groups such as Malta and Gozo. The south coast of Aspromonte, a ribbon of land 8–10 km wide, may have supported one or two such groups. In more open landscapes, the Tavoliere would have been capable of supporting 5,000 or more people, whether as a single overarching group or as several. In contrast, with any economy not 100 percent reliant upon crops, the Aeolian Islands never would have supported more than a few hundred individuals, and even the estimates presented in Table 8 must be scaled down when one takes into account the fact that much of the islands' area consist of very steep volcanic slopes. This suggests that the archipelago may never in fact have supported a stable, self-sufficient population, particularly before the Diana period when only Lipari, Salina, and Filicudi were inhabited.

Although every region of peninsular Italy was populated by farmers by 5500 BC, they may not have been occupied with equal density. Population density in tribes varies immensely. Sometimes settlement variation is ecological: the Enga of highland Papua New Guinea encompass both dense, valley-bottom gardening groups and the more scattered, high-altitude groups who mostly forage (Wiessner and Tumu 1998). In other cases, it seems to be political in origin. In ethnohistoric eastern North America, some areas (such as the Mohawk Valley and Huronia) held dense agglomerations, while other, equally productive areas held only thin populations or were empty, maintained as buffer zones and tribal hunting grounds (Trigger 1978). Even if major features of the Native American landscape were restructured by colonial encounters (Wolf 1982), the example usefully reminds us of some likely characteristics of Italian Neolithic social geography: At any given time, some areas may have been densely populated and others sparsely populated or abandoned. One obvious gradation is between lowland and highland zones, but there may have been significant differences in density among lowland zones as well.

It is the very elusiveness of such regional differences and identities which makes it worth reminding ourselves ethnographically that they must have existed. Social boundaries need not have been, and probably were not, expressed in any archaeologically visible media, particularly pottery (Stark 1998). However, at any given time, the Italian peninsula and Sicily would have been occupied by a finite number – 20? 50? 100? – of fluid, regional groups sharing an identity and, potentially, bounded from each other. Travel more than a few dozen kilometers from one's home probably meant contact with strange peoples, with both the attraction of the exotic and different and the danger of the alien.

These discussions suggest that Neolithic Italians participated in multiple kinds of networks: residential groups such as hamlets or villages, local networks of cooperation and common identity, and larger regional groups which spanned several or many such groups for social and demographic purposes. Moreover, in the precolonial world, such multiple identities would have been shifting and situationally invoked rather than permanently fixed into a rigid taxonomy of tribal nomenclature.

Travel, Trade, Warfare

Nothing is known of land travel beyond the fact that many sites in mountainous zones lie astride passes and river valleys (for example, Ariano Irpino on a pass across the Apennines between Campania and Puglia). It can be assumed that a principal issue with long-distance travel on foot would have been negotiating social relations with each group occupying territory along the route.

Maritime travel is somewhat better understood. One Neolithic boat is known from Italy, a canoe found at the submerged site of La Marmotta in Lake Bracciano north of Rome (Fugazzola Delpino and Mineo 1995) (Figure 47). This canoe, about 10 m long from prow to stern and about a meter across, was hollowed from a single massive oak trunk with expert carpentry; it presumably would have taken at least three to four paddlers to power and steer it, and could have accommodated a crew perhaps twice that size. The La Marmotta canoe lacks a keel, and vessels of this kind would probably have been unstable in choppy ocean waters; but similar vessels built for ocean voyages rather than lake travel may have been given keels, outriggers, or other stabilizing devices. In any case, the La Marmotta canoe, a unique find at a waterlogged site, gives us a striking example of one way in which Neolithic people navigated, and attests both the commitment of labor and the skill devoted to travel.

It is generally assumed that Neolithic navigators paddled or rowed small boats or canoes rather than using sails, which are first attested in the third millennium BC. It is also generally assumed that navigation generally followed coastlines, avoiding open water crossings out of sight of land (Farr 2006). For the island-dotted Central Mediterranean, the only unavoidable long open-water crossing appears to have been between Sicily and Pantelleria; Corsica and Sardinia were reached via the Tuscan Archipelago rather than directly over open water. This inference supported both by the circulation of obsidian – Sardinian obsidian is not found in the Southern Tyrrhenian – and by the fact that until the first millennium BC these islands either develop along their own trajectory or show linkages to Upper Tyrrhennian Italy, rather than, say, with Sicily which is not far away in a straight line from Sardinia but requires a deep-water open crossing. The Adriatic both can be seen across on a clear day and affords an island bridge across its centre via the Tremiti Islands, Palagruza and the Dalmatian islands.

Neolithic navigation is a remarkable example of skilled action (Castignino Berlinghieri 2003; Farr 2006). Transported materials such as obsidian demonstrate regular coastal sailing and crossings. Boating was probably embedded in seasonal rhythms, both to take advantage of calm summer weather and avoid stormy winter seas and to fit a crew's prolonged absence into other work programs. One needs detailed knowledge and experience of variable conditions to successfully negotiate passages such as the Adriatic or the Straits of Messina (Farr 2006). Currents are complex (in many places coastal and off-shore currents circulate in opposite directions), locally variable, and changeable. Moreover, in many places, currents and winds can move a boat faster than the speed of paddled reed boats or dugouts. The task of navigation, thus, is less like driving a straight line from origin to destination than like jumping among unstable conveyer belts running in different directions. Even when the destination is clearly visible upon the horizon, getting to it would have involved carefully calculated curving routes to cope with transverse currents. Tricky passages, such as getting through the Straits of Messina to Lipari, required waiting for a precise window of wind, current and tidal conditions; it is estimated that the jump from Sicily to Lipari would take only 3–4 hours with a strong following wind, but it could be much longer or even impossible in other conditions (Pennacchioni 2003). Luck was needed: on longer crossings such as legs of the trans-Adriatic journey or the passage from Sicily to Malta, boats would spend extended periods too far offshore to outrun a storm back to land (Farr 2006). Such conditions would place a premium upon skill, local knowledge and experience, with ritual (Malinowski 1922) perhaps filling the gaps.

Trade is the most evident form of "action at a distance," to use Renfrew's (1975) phrase. Exchange relations in Neolithic Italy are best understood at nested levels of spatial structure (Figure 47). The longest-distance trade systems are the obsidian trade and the circulation of polished stone axes. Both materials routinely reached more than 500 km from their source; the maximum circulation is represented by Lipari obsidian in Southern France and in Croatia (Tykot and Ammerman 1997) and by Alpine jadeite axes in Sicily and Malta (Leighton 1992). At a middle level of circulation, most groups participated in regional exchanges of good-quality flint from sources such as the Monte Iblei, Monte Lessini, Ligurian jasper sources, and the Gargano peninsula; these may have had a radius of over a hundred km. Other geological raw materials circulated at over similar ranges, with ochre traveling from Sicily to Malta and marble circulating throughout the Alpine area. Similarly,

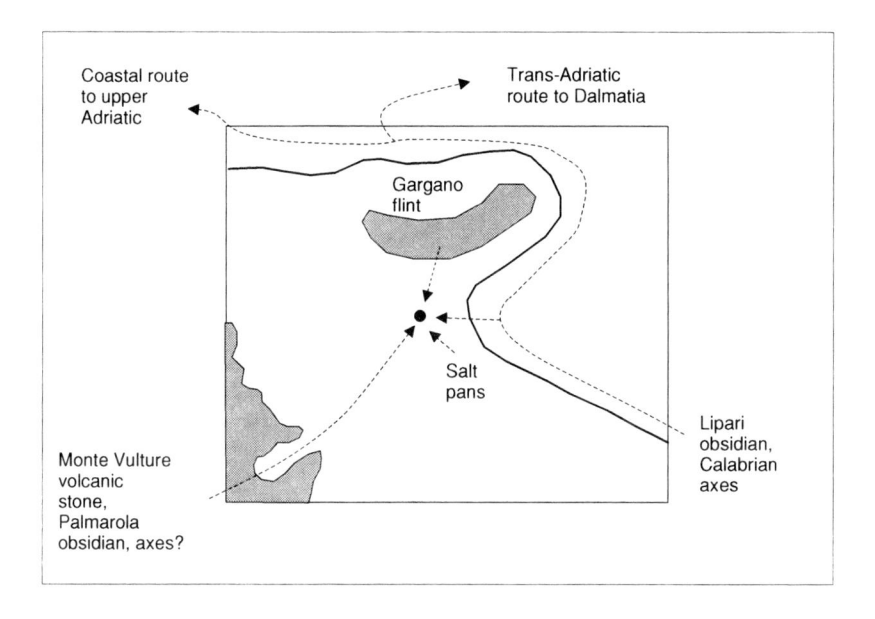

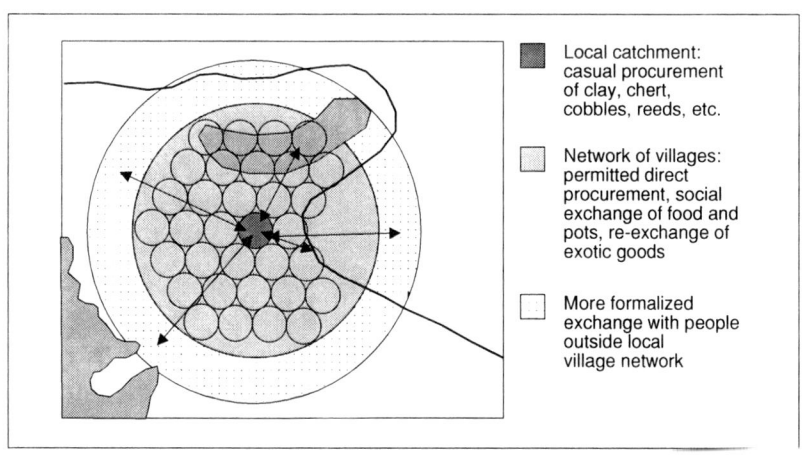

47. Spatiality of exchange: A Tavoliere example (Farr and Robb 2005).

steatite was worked in specialised workshops such as La Puzzolente where beads and pendants were made (Sammartino 1990) and circulated to sites in Liguria and Toscana [e.g., Casa Querciola, where steatite rings were presumably used as ornaments (Iacopini 2000)]. More local exchange is hard to trace; repeated petrographic studies have shown that pottery was only infrequently transported far from where it was manufactured (Muntoni 2003; Spataro 2002). Communities may not have participated equally in exchange, judging from the quite variable amounts of obsidian at sites far from obsidian sources; some groups may have been regional brokers of specific commodities.

The obsidian and axe trades were discussed in detail in Chapter 5. Here a few general points suffice. First, "trade" should not be construed in a narrow economic sense; in many cases, transported goods were probably prestations whose value did not derive from their function, but would have been to establish or maintain a relationship, and they presupposed a shared context of practices, techniques, and understandings. Obsidian, it was argued, cannot be understood simply as a way of circulating a functionally useful or prestigious substance; the small quantities involved and the consistent and widely shared practices involved may imply some sort of prestation associated with a particular social or symbolic role. Moreover, although material culture can be redefined as it changes context, both obsidian and axes seem to have been used technologically and socially in similar ways throughout their range, implying shared regional practices as well as local meanings. Additional evidence for regional communication and sharing of practices comes from highly similar artefacts, probably made locally, at widely separated sites. For example, very similar figurines of an idiosyncratic pattern have been found at Baselice in Campania (Langella et al. 2003) and at the Grotta Pacelli (Striccoli 1988) and Cala Scizzo (Geniola and Tunzi Sisto 1980) in Puglia. Similarly, a specific form of small, closed-necked globular pot with paired ridge handles has been found in Late Neolithic burial contexts from Girifalco in Calabria to Serra Cicora in the Salentino and Gaione in Reggio Emilia. Particularly the obsidian trade, which makes little sense in functional terms, suggests that the purpose of trade was to exploit the value of distance, converting social difference as relationships outside the group into social capital. "Spheres of exchange," to invoke classic archaeological jargon, thus represent a convergence in which social relations and spatiality give meaning to each other.

Warfare is the negative side of intergroup relations. Evidence is sparse. There is no iconography or elaboration of material culture related to weaponry until the Late Neolithic; if they were not made entirely of wood, weapons must have been the stone axe and transversely headed arrows. However, nucleation into settlements is a common response to the threat of raiding (Feil 1987; Knauft 1993) and larger, nucleated, ditched or palisaded villages probably bespeak at least a concern for defense. If so, this would suggest a higher level of conflict in more crowded lowlands. Moreover, skeletal remains give evidence of a level of healed traumas as high as that in later periods when warfare appears to have been much more celebrated (Robb 1997). Interestingly, both males and females appear to have been the victims (see Chapter 2).[1] Although no skeletal analysis has been published, two mass burials, at the Grotta Pavolella in Calabria (Carancini and Guerzani 1987) and the Diga di Occhito in Puglia (Tunzi Sisto 1999), may represent massacre events as known elsewhere in Neolithic Europe. The former contains the partially burnt remains of at least twenty individuals, the latter the jumbled bodies of about a dozen (Figure 8c). It is possible that some of the isolated skulls found in settlements (see Chapters 2 and 3 in this book) may be trophies rather than ancestors. In any case, the skeletal and architectural evidence suggests at least some warfare, perhaps carried out as lethal raids by small groups.

Travel, exchange, and warfare form similar kinds of extended projects. Journeys take the dramatic form of stories (de Certeau 2002); they are often ways of testing, establishing or demonstrating their identity and status; they require knowledge and experience, and these may be the most important things one brings back from them (Broodbank 1993; Helms 1983). Exchange is often not merely the means of procuring things not available locally, which may be technologically superfluous in any case. Rather, it provides a venue for forming social relations outside of the normal range of interaction and for exercising agency in different contexts; the traded goods may be as much signifier of this as cause of it. Warfare is spatialised in that it is almost always organised territorially in terms of geographic identities. Although lethal, it is no less a drama of abilities, loyalties, and standings, as well as a corporeal practice bound up with ideas of the constitution and value of the body. All three genres of practice go far beyond the functional needs of getting somewhere, getting something or getting even; they have to be understood as fields of action which treat distance and cultural difference as a resource agents can use in carrying out meaningful life projects.

Culture Areas and Differing Lifeways

What would a traveler see walking across Italy at some point in the Neolithic? How would it differ from one place to the next?

It is an exasperating project to wrench a knowledge rooted in archaeological taxonomies into a different form. We almost always know more than we think we do, but it requires continually battling one's reflexes (for instance, it is difficult to liberate oneself from referring to sites according to the type of pottery found there). In later European prehistory, the most illuminating attempt to tackle this simple and obvious question is Whittle's synthesis of the European Neolithic. Whittle's understated maps (Whittle 1996, figures 10.1–10.4) present a series of time-slices characterizing Europe in areas defined by their way of life – a feat whose rarity is surprising and, indeed, embarrassing. Whittle paints prehistoric Europe in culture areas defined by features which are both basic to defining a way of life and archaeologically visible: forms of settlement, economy, mobility, and general cultural patterns. It is easy to dismiss the resulting map as old-fashioned descriptive ethnology, but only at the cost of giving up any ambition of social analysis at the regional scale rather than through free-floating case studies: a reflexive postmodern ethnography of the traditional Hopi presupposes rather than negates knowledge of their basic Puebloan terms of living.

On the continental scale, Neolithic groups throughout peninsular Italy, Sicily, and indeed adjacent areas such as Malta and Dalmatia, shared a common way of life as relatively sedentary farmers whose social relations were reproduced through a densely textured daily life, accompanied by a rather muted ritual life (Chapter 6). As a regional culture, this contrasts strongly with contemporary ways of life in the Balkans, Alps, Central Europe, and indeed along the Atlantic façade of Britain and Scandinavia, whose Neolithic, when it occurred some time later, took quite a different form.

Moving to a finer scale, finer differences emerge. The most obvious spatial variations are related to geographically restricted materials. Beyond obsidian-rich and obsidian-scarce zones, areas such as northern and southwestern Italy were relatively well-supplied with polished stone axes, while in areas such as the central Adriatic they may have been less

Table 23. *Spectrum of Settlement Definition*

Neighborhoods of isolated houses	<<>>	Unditched villages	<<>>	Ditched villages	<<>>	Ditched villages with formal internal divisions

so, to judge from the fact that flaked flint or even limestone or sandstone were used. Settlement and economy are probably the most important regional variations visible archaeologically. As we noted in Chapter 3, the household was a basal unit everywhere, but there were important regional variations in how many households were aggregated into living sites and how rigidly sites were bounded. This created multiple ways of inhabiting the landscape, which form a continuum of intensity and formalization of settlement (Table 23).

Economy shows important variations as well, and there are smaller, unique areas archaeologically known. Hence, there were at least four ways of being Neolithic during the Early and Middle Neolithic (the sixth and earlier fifth millennia).

Village Farmers

The stereotypical "site" is a nucleated agglomeration of houses in close proximity to each other and with a perceptible edge. These are known throughout Adriatic Italy and down the Ionian Coast at least as far as Northern Calabria, with substantial villages also known in Sicily, eastern Basilicata, and north of the Apennines in Emilia-Romagna.

The best-known village landscape is undoubtedly the Tavoliere, a large plain which occupies most of Foggia province in northern Puglia (Cassano et al. 1987; Cassano and Manfredini 1983; Jones 1987; Mallory 1987; Simone 1982; Skeates 2002; Tinè 1983; Tozzi and Verola 1990; Tunzi Sisto 1999). By a happy combination of circumstances, Neolithic sites were ditched, and the local bedrock renders such features highly visible on aerial photographs (Bradford 1949). At last counting, over 500 sites have been counted (Brown 2003), and there have been at least a dozen excavations of Neolithic villages. From these, it is clear that Puglia was the first area of Italy to become Neolithic, at least two or three centuries before 6000 BC. From the very outset, there was a virtually stereotypical Neolithic way of life, with heavy reliance upon domesticates, ditched villages, and the entire suite of new technologies such as polished stone axes, grinding stones, and pottery. Although some are very large, with Passo di Corvo, the largest, exceeding 800 m in ditch diameter, this is untypical. Most are less than 200 m in diameter, and there is some suggestion that they become larger over the course of the Early and Middle Neolithic. Many have several ditches, and many have small c-ditches surrounding individual house compounds within the major ditch. The Tavoliere *villaggi trincerati* lasted for about a millennium, vanishing around or shortly after 5000 BC, when settlement moved to the margins of the plain. The causes of this abandonment are unknown, but a dessication of Tavoliere has been blamed (Boenzi et al. 2001).

The second famous concentration of ditched villages in the south is at Matera, where Ridola and Patroni excavated a series of sites almost a hundred years ago, particularly the famous three villages at Serra d'Alto (Lo Porto 1978; Lo Porto 1989; Patroni 1902; Ridola 1924; Ridola 1925; Ridola 1926). Survey (Geniola, Camerini, and Lionetti 1995), reanalysis, and a modern excavation at Trasano (Guilaine and Cremonesi 1987) have greatly augmented our knowledge. Of the Materano sites, only Trasano has been dated absolutely, but, like the Tavoliere sites, they seem to date to the sixth millennium. A bit confusingly, the Serra d'Alto pottery style actually seems to date to the phases after the ditches were at least partially filled in at its type site. Like the Tavoliere sites, the Materano sites show an early and consistent establishment of a thoroughly Neolithic way of life.

Ditched villages are known elsewhere, particularly around Siracusa in southeastern Sicily [Stentinello, Megara Hyblaea, Matrensa, Vulpiglia and others (Guzzardi, Iovino, and Rivoli 2003; Orsi 1890, 1921)], sporadically in the hinterlands of Bari in Apulia, in the Adriatic [Ripoli, (Cremonesi 1965)] and even in Reggio-Emilia at sites such as Quinzano and Fornace Cappuccini (Antoniazzi et al. 1987). Surrounding these pockets, there is a much broader area which contains basically similar villages, but apparently without ditches. This extends the full length of the Adriatic coast and in the slopes on the margins of the Po Valley, and in the lowlands of Southern Italy, and in parts of Sicily. Moreover, villages elsewhere may have been bounded in less archaeologically visible ways; at Lugo di Ravenna the village was enclosed with a wooden palisade 3 m high (Von Eles Masi and Steffè 1987).

Other people can be both a social resource and a potential source of problems: we can devise both "push" and "pull" models for why Neolithic Italians chose to live in villages. People everywhere must have belonged to networks of a certain size, whether this network was organised into many dispersed small sites or a cluster of larger ones. Nucleation may have been a way of coping with conflict, by allowing mutual defense. Larger villages would have been much less vulnerable to small demographic fluctuations, and greater group size allowed larger cohorts for age and sex specific activities, as well as a more stable and deeper historical memory (Tables 1 and 2). Sociality, in rites and gatherings, may have been positively valued; as noted above, there may be a correlation between villages and the relative proportion of cattle (see Chapter 4 in this book). Dense networks of villages may have also been more dynamic stylistically, with smaller microstyle regions and a quicker tempo of stylistic turnover; the paradigm case here is Puglia. But, as they incorporated more and less closely related groups, conflicts within communities were probably more common and serious. With larger villages, relations with other villages may have been less for daily cooperation and more for periodic ceremonies or collective expeditions. Moreover, communities at the larger end of the Italian Neolithic scale probably verged on being capable of endogamy.

Village life as a collective project was basically ambiguous, balancing practical advantages, such as defense and the attractions of sociality, with possible internal tensions and the constraint on household relations caused by limited mobility and commitment to coresidence. This ambiguity must have lain at the heart of the rather peculiar history of villages. On one hand, rather counter intuitively, the original Neolithic settlement of Italy was village-based; dispersed settlement was not a precursor but a follower which developed rapidly in some regions of Italy. Villages lasted stably for about a millennium. On the other hand, the rapid disappearance of villages around the end of the Middle Neolithic makes sense when we consider them as an equivocal institution, finely balanced between solving and creating problems, between centripetal attractions and centrifugal tensions.

Dispersed Farmers

To an archaeological imagination nourished on images of Jericho, Çatal Hüyük, Balkan tells, LBK sites, and Alpine lake towns, Neolithic means villages. Italy obligingly responds to the stereotype with unmistakable village landscapes across the peninsula and islands. The realization that nucleated villages were only one form of Early–Middle Neolithic dwelling is relatively recent, though Late Neolithic people have long been seen as living in dispersed settlements. It is difficult to assess the true extent of non-village settlement due to archaeological biases. Not counting cave sites, almost all of the largest and best published excavations are at village sites in lowland areas. Moreover, when a site is known from surface finds or when only a small area has been explored, it is generally assumed that it is an imperfectly-known village site.

Dispersed settlement was first defined explicitly at Acconia in southern Calabria (Ammerman 1985); survey and excavation established that people here inhabited scattered houses some distance apart. For other sites, the maximum possible extent of the site can sometimes be estimated from local topography. Penitenzeria, for example, lies on a terrace about 50 m to a side, bounded by cliffs, and the area of the site with dense archaeological deposition is smaller still. Elsewhere in Calabria, Capo Alfiere, though a long-lived site with an unusual, substantial stone house, is nevertheless of limited extent, and this is typical of other sites in the Crotone area such as Corazzo – Casa Soverito (Marino 1993). Similarly, except for along the eastern coastline, few large sites are known in much of Sicily, particularly in the northern half of the island. For the Tyrrhenian side of the peninsula from Calabria up through Toscana and Liguria, and for the Apennine mountain spine of the peninsula, data are patchy (particularly for Campania), but if we take the sample of excavated and published sites at face value, the overall impression is that people rarely lived in sites of any great extent.

At first impression, there appears a clear correlation between denser, nucleated settlement in lowlands and dispersed settlement in mountains. While this is probably the case on a coarse scale, this is not a simple case of topological determinism. There are fair-sized lowlands such as the plains of Catania, Locri and Gioia Tauro, and much of Etruria consists of low and gentle hills which are not more rugged than those on the eastern slopes of the peninsula. Even in relatively steep localities, there are normally pockets of level or moderately sloping land sufficient for sites much larger than are actually found, and Neolithic economies were feasible in broken terrain. Environmental limitations probably did not affect the location or economies of individual, carefully situated habitations, but rather the overall density of population possible in a region. Hence, although there may well have been a link between natural terrain and mode of settlement, it cannot have been a simple response to lack of open landscapes. Rather, it appears to have been a genuine regional tradition – perhaps a Mesolithic continuity. The same is true of economic choices. Although sites throughout this region were small and scattered, in hills which must have abounded with game such as deer and boar, within the resolution of archaeological data (see Chapter 4 in this book), the economy was overwhelmingly based upon domesticated grains, legumes, and livestock, with relatively little variation.

Living scattered across the landscape may reflect a lack of need for defense, which may be related to a lower overall population density, with more distance between unrelated groups. The social context of projects such as coordinated rites, mate exchanges, and animal exchanges would frequently have been the neighborhood or region rather than the settlement. It also suggests a greater flexibility in social relationships, with less constraint or commitment imposed by coresidence, and this may have meant fewer stresses or conflicts. However, the drawback would have been the limits of small scale, for instance the difficulty of assembling cohorts or task groups of a critical size (Table 1).

Mixed Mountaineers and Lake Villages

Although the great majority of Neolithic groups fell into the categories above, several other ways of life are known. In several regions, mountaineers living in dispersed settlements practiced a mixed wild-domesticated economy. One such area was the central Apennines, where faunal collections from zones such as the highland Marche, the Gubbio basin, and the Fucino basin yield a relatively high percentage of wild game (Barker 1975; Barker 1981; Castelletti, Costantini, and Tozzi 1987; Tagliacozzo 1992). The same is true for the Alpine valleys north of the

Po Valley such as in the Trento region. A third area is northern and north-western Sicily, where Uzzo Cave in particular shows a frequent use of wild animals in the initial phases of the Neolithic (Tagliacozzo 1993, 1997), an economic choice also found at the Sperlinga di San Basilio where red deer made up almost a third of the sample (Cavalier 1971). In these areas, wild resources appear to have made a genuine contribution to subsistence economy. The most straightforward interpretation is simply that this was an effective ecological adaptation in high mountains. Yet there must have been an element of cultural choice; equally mountainous areas elsewhere were exploited through predominantly domesticate-based strategies. Reproducing social relations through the consumption of game cannot have been without social consequences, but the dearth of social archaeology in these regions leaves us at a loss to address this in any detail.

Lake villages gained fame as a Neolithic way of life in the nineteenth century, due to discoveries of sites with remarkable preservation of waterlogged organic material around Swiss and French lakes. Discoveries of lakes villages around lakes in Lombardia soon followed, both for the Bronze Age and for the Neolithic (one example is the Late Neolithic site of Lagozza di Besnate on the lake of Varese west of Milan). The most important recent advance has been the remarkable excavations of the underwater site of La Marmotta in Lake Bracciano in Lazio north of Rome (Fugazzola Delpino, D'Eugenio, and Pessina 1993; Fugazzola Delpino and Mineo 1995). The La Marmotta excavations have established that Neolithic lake dwellings not only extend to Central Italy but also date back to the Early Neolithic, with radiocarbon dates in the early sixth millennium BC, making La Marmotta at present the earliest Neolithic lake dwelling in Europe. The most puzzling question with La Marmotta is resolving how many of the site's unique features are preservational, reflecting the extraordinary waterlogged preservation of plants and wood, and how many represent features genuinely unique to lakeside villages. At La Marmotta, people lived in substantial rectangular wooden houses raised above the lake on oak piles. The abundant use of large oak timbers bespeaks a heavily forested environment. The economy appears to have been based principally upon domesticates, but there is also represented a remarkable range of wild plants, including wild fruits such as apple and cherry, nuts such as acorns, and possible

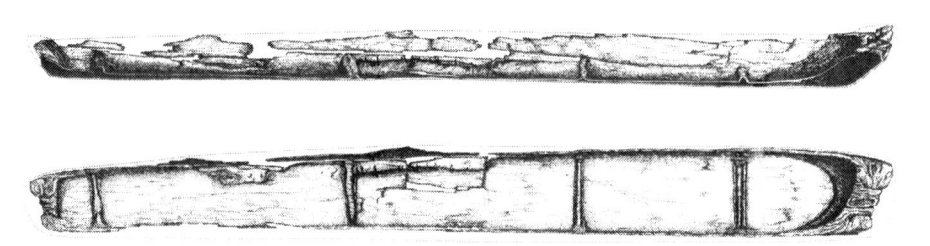

48. Early Neolithic canoe from "La Marmotta," Lake Bracciano (Fugazzola Delpino and Mineo 1995, courtesy of M. A. Fuggazola Delpino. Image copyright Museo Nazionale Preistorico/Etnografico L Pigorini, Roma EUR – by concession of the Ministero per i Beni e le Attività Culturali).

dyes or flavorings such as wild saffron. In addition to the usual range of Neolithic material culture, axes and a relatively high percentage of obsidian were found, attesting participation in long-distance trade, a small steatite female figurine may represent a Palaeolithic find reused by Neolithic people, and pottery replicas of boats were found (Figure 6c). Remarkably, the site also yielded a boat, a dugout canoe made of oak some 10 m long and about a meter wide (Figure 48). This represents a substantial craft for simply traversing and fishing in the lake, and it probably gives us a good idea of ocean-going craft at this time as well. Intriguingly, pottery models of boats were also found at the site.

Interpreting Regional Differences

The overall impression from the above is that there were more Neolithic people living in bigger groups, closer together, in eastern Italy, and particularly in lowland areas. What do regional differences in population and way of life mean? Archaeologists have long been accustomed to regard the regional differences either as taphonomic artefacts which simply signify that one area has been better researched or has more visible sites than another, or as political manifestations of a core-periphery dynamic. For Neolithic Italy, the effects of metropolitan cores can be discounted; there were none. Varying intensity of research and site visibility is certainly important, particularly with Puglia especially among the best-understood regions. Yet there is now a fair density of research in well-studied patches throughout Italy, and there are probably also real trends as well.

Geographically, within the Central Mediterranean, the most important topographic and climatic differences are not latitudinal so much as these are vertical; a similar economy and way of life was possible in lowland areas throughout the region. To the extent that there was a geographical reason behind regional variations, it probably relied upon topography rather than climate. In mountainous regions, land of comparable potential was broken up into small areas by steep slopes and valleys, with more dispersed populations and an overall lower population density. Yet, geography alone is not the sole factor; in some lowland coastal plains of southern Calabria, for example, people still preferred to live in dispersed settlements. Rather, underlying the choice of how to settle was a combination of the possibilities offered by the landscape, regional cultural traditions, and undoubtedly pragmatic factors such as the need for defense, which may have been greater in densely settled areas.

The east–west divide is remarkably reminiscent of the differences noted between northern Greece (particularly Thessaly) and southern Greece (particularly the Peleponnese), a "North-South Divide" which, it has been argued, connotes a real difference in both settlement and culture (Cavanagh 2004; Halstead 1994). As Cavanagh perceptively notes,

> The more crowded landscape of Thessaly implies an authority with less room for maneuver (for example, land for distribution, while sufficient, was not as plentiful as in southern Greece) but also greater frequency of everyday association with the next village (say 20 rather than 40 minutes walk away). The physical spacing of the villages was quite as much an expression of cultural distancing as of ecological constraint. The Peloponnesian villages, will, therefore, have exercised greater autarky, but at the cost of a less dense network of support. Different social systems and different values lay behind the different patterns of occupying the landscape. (Cavanagh 2004, p. 182)

As in Greece, the resulting distance would have affected the intensity with which people pursued interactions such as visiting, intermarrying, and exchange of goods and animals. Cavanagh concludes that people throughout Greece shared much the same way of life, but that they chose to pursue different intensities of processes such as exchange.

And so it is in Italy as well. Why this pattern emerged and persisted for at least a millennium is difficult to say, and may reflect not only terrain but imponderables such as autonomous cultural values or the persistence of Mesolithic values in some areas. However, it is a great leap forward even to consider simply that the differences we see archaeologically may actually connote real ethnographic variations in how people lived.

Social Networks: The Calabrian Stentinello World

It was suggested above that, during the Neolithic, the Italian peninsula, Sicily and Malta would have been occupied by perhaps twenty to fifty tribal groups, with each group occupying an area perhaps half the size of a modern province, and with at least this much linguistic diversity. Furthermore, it was also suggested that such groups were not rigid, static and tightly bounded, as tribal societies often become under colonial contact or administration. Rather, social groupings provided situationally relevant, shifting and oppositional identities of the kind first made famous by Evans-Pritchard's (1940) description of the Nuer.

Archaeologically, social boundaries are often virtually indetectable (Shennan 1989; Stark 1998), and this is particularly difficult for non-state societies in which a cultural sense of common identity may be regional but political organization is strictly local. Traditional enemies share very closely related ways of life (as with the Nuer and the Dinka, the Crow and the Sioux, or the Huron and the Iroquois) as often as they live in different ways (as with the Hopi and Navaho). People with different economies may be part of a single tribal grouping (as with the Ojibway and the Enga, who displayed an altitudunal cline in economy), close allies (as with the Huron and Algonkins) or have varied and complex relations (as with the Bantu and the San). Diacritical markers of identity may be archaeological evanescent things such as dress and language.

Given this, what likely signs of geographic identities might be expected to be visible in Neolithic Italy? This is unclear. While we can list many items under the general rubrics of daily practices and frames of reference, historical traditions and a sense of common origin (Canuto and Yaeger 2000), not only are many of these things archaeologically inaccessible, but which ones are actually mobilised as signs of identity in any particular situation varies immensely. A minimal set, which specifies the conditions within which a regional identity may have existed rather than demonstrating that one in fact did, might include evidence for

1. Common practices of everyday life;
2. Common ritual practices focusing upon group origins, history and identity;
3. Spatially discrete areas, separated by ecological differences, uninhabited zones, or geographical discontinuities;
4. Bounded or asymmetrical networks, with sustained and regular contact within them and more regular communication in some directions than others.

The third of these, *geography*, does not determine identity, but it can both channel communication between areas, affect economic possibilities, and provide a ready symbol of identity differences. Italian prehistory affords many examples of the structuring effects of geography [as in the different trajectories of the Adriatic and the Tyrrhenian sides of the peninsula in many periods, as well as between the peninsula and areas north of the Apennines in Northern Italy; cf. also Robb (2001) for a Maltese example]. It also affords examples of periods in which cultural boundaries did not coincide with apparent natural frontiers, for example the Apennine Bronze Age.

Within the resolution of the archaeological record, the common practices of everyday life were shared throughout Italy and Sicily (Chapter 6), but evidence for bodily practices, foodways, and ritual is too patchy and poorly dated too pick up fine variations in these things beyond the coarse differences in lifeways discussed above. Similarly, ritual sites which might be interpreted in terms of common origins beliefs are so sparse – particularly before the Late Neolithic, only a handful are known – that each one is unique not only among regions but within them. Burial traditions plausibly relate to group history and origins, but they vary little before the later Neolithic and when they do so, it tends to be upon a site-by-site rather than regional basis. Effectively, then, definition of Neolithic social networks has to rely upon material evidence for communication networks, supplemented by geography.

Rather than giving up on this important aspect of social life, it is worth attempting inevitably incomplete interpretations, if only to spur further research. Pottery provides the most sensitive indicator available of communication networks. Note that this derives from an explicit social model of how Neolithic people made and used pottery (Chapter 5); I am not assuming either that pottery style forms part of a normative way of life which necessarily corresponds to ethnic identity, as in traditional approaches equating pottery styles with peoples (Shennan 1989), nor that pottery was intentionally used to signal group identity, as in early processual models of style as information exchange. Given the "creative recombination" model of how Neolithic pottery was created socially, it makes sense to think that sharp stylistic discontinuities may indicate changes in the density of communication. For an indication that this is specific to Neolithic social contexts, see below, where it is clear that a similar approach would not work in the Late Neolithic as the meaning of pottery as a communicative medium changed.

Pottery boundaries in Neolithic Italy are often fuzzy and unstable. In the Puglia-Matera area, for example, several distinct finewares were used in the later sixth and early fifth millennium BC, and we can define regional centers of gravity for each, but many co-occur at the same sites and it is difficult to draw clear boundaries between them. Similarly, Stentinello wares in Sicily change throughout their range, but in a gradual way; while stereotypical Stentinello wares are found in eastern Sicily (where the type site itself is found), both in Western Sicily and in contemporary Maltese Ghar Dalam pottery, the wares are noticeably Stentinellian in tradition but tend to have a less rigid geometrical grammar and to make much less use of ceramic stamps. Where we do observe clear discontinuities, they tend to coincide with major geographic boundaries (for instance, Linear pottery traditions north of the Apennines and in Toscana and northern Lazio, or, later, VBQ pottery north of the Apennines). In the absence of such major barriers, it is thus quite anomalous to see a sharp, long-standing pottery boundary.

One such boundary occurs between central and southern Calabria and northern Calabria (Figure 49). From Crotone south to the Straits of Messina, on both the Tyrrhenian and Ionian coasts, it is still unknown whether the Neolithic began with a transient Impressed Ware phase. However, for most of the Neolithic, pottery assemblages are dominated by Stentinello wares (Ammerman 1985; Ammerman, Shaffer, and Hartmann 1988; Cardosa 1996; Costabile 1972; Cuda and Murgano 2004; Marino 1993; Morter 1992; Robb 2004; S. Tinè 1988; S. Tinè 1992; V. Tinè 2004). Many sites yield a few sherds of painted *figulina* wares, but this is never more than a tiny percentage of the assemblage.

North of Crotone, the steep and rocky Sila massif virtually spans the peninsula between the two coasts. North of the Sila, the pottery sequence follows that of the lowland areas to the east in Basilicata and Puglia. In the next major pocket of lowlands, on the plain of Sibari, Archaic and then Evolved Impressed Wares are followed by assemblages containing figulina wares painted with broad red bands, then trichromes and Serra d'Alto wares (S. Tinè 1962; S. Tinè 1964; V. Tinè 2004). Although few open-air sites later than Impressed Ware have been excavated, this seems to be the case in caves both used for ritual (e.g., Grotta Sant'Angelo) and for other purposes (e.g., Grotta San Michele). Although some Stentinello wares have recently been reported from the latter site,[2] they are infrequent and generally absent. This pattern is also found in the mountainous areas of northern Calabria. For example, at the classic excavations at the Grotta della Madonna at Praia a Mare, a site overlooking the Tyrrhennian sea at the foot of steep mountains, painted figulina was well-represented and almost no Stentinello wares were found (Cardini 1970). Pottery styles thus suggest a clear discontinuity in communication running across the peninsula from somewhere between Crotone and Sibari, on the east coast, to somewhere between Nicastro and Praia a Mare on the west coast – a stable boundary which endured for at least a millennium.

This boundary coincides with several other differences. The Calabrian Stentinello world was principally a world of dispersed settlement in hills, and the painted-ware world includes the main areas of lowland-villages in Southern Italy. More telling is lithic usage. The edge of the Stentinello world coincides with a marked change in lithic economy. Within the Stentinello zone, obsidian is common. In Bova Marina (Farr 2001) and in Acconia (Ammerman and Andrefsky 1982), over 90 percent of assemblages are composed of obsidian. The most extensively excavated Neolithic site in central Calabria is Capo Alfiere,

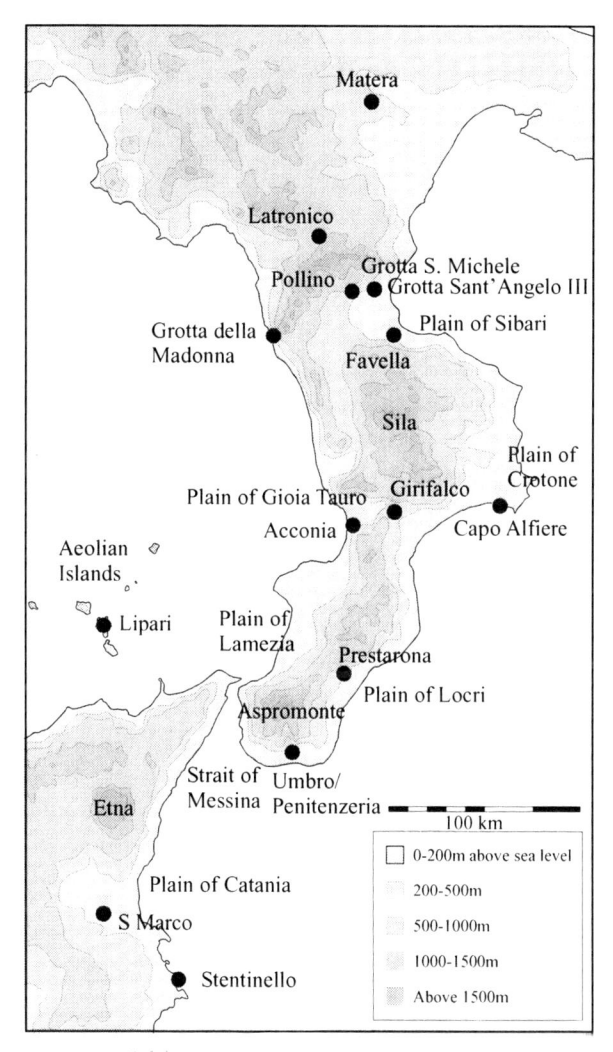

49. Calabria, Eastern Sicily, and adjacent areas.

near Crotone, where obsidian totals reached 20 percent in the earlier Stentinello levels and more than 60 percent in the later Stentinello assemblage (Morter 1992). Results from elsewhere in the Crotone area corroborate the high frequency of obsidian on Stentinello sites (Hodder and Malone 1984, Marino 1993). Obsidian is found both as bladelets and blade cores, as core preparation flakes, and commonly as flakes used for expedient cutting edges. In contrast, in Northern Calabria and beyond, although some sites even far afield have noticeable concentrations of obsidian, it almost never exceeds 10 percent of an assemblage, and normally is far less [the principal exception is the Grotta San Michele where over half the assemblage is of obsidian, but this is for the Late Neolithic Diana levels rather than for the Early-Middle Neolithic levels (Tinè and Natali 2005)]. Obsidian is used differently, in a narrower and more specialised range of tools (principally bladelets and blade cores). In both obsidian frequency and usage, there was not a gradual but a qualitative change between central and northern Calabria.

The Calabrian peninsula is broken up by a series of high and steep mountain massifs (see Chapter 3 in this book). Excluding land above 1,000 m, people lived in pockets of coastal plain linked by narrow corridors of low coastal hills, rather like beads on a ribbon. Although travel across the peninsula was certainly possible, particularly through saddles linking Locri and Gioia Tauro, Catanzaro and the Golfo di Sant'Eufemia, and the Crati river valley extending inland from Sibari to Cosenza, much communication between groups must have run coastally, and the Stentinello-using population along the Ionian and Tyrrhenian coasts would probably have been a stretched-out series of low-density, related groups in frequent contact with each other.

Procuring obsidian, a principal lithic raw material, must have involved regular travel up and down the coastlines, and annual cycles of travel may have performed an important role in integrating communities strung out along these long, narrow coasts. If so, this would explain the clear directionality of contact, with communities in central Calabria having more contact to the southwards than to the northwards. Although we have no reliable way of reconstructing such variables as rates of travel, it seems quite possible that groups up to several hundred kilometers away may have procured their obsidian directly from Lipari or from nearby points in southern Calabria such as Acconia (Ammerman and Polglase 1993). If so, this would imply that the drop-off in obsidian visible in northern Calabria marks a shift from direct procurement to down-the-line mechanisms of trade.

Patterns of obsidian distribution represent social networks (Nicoletti 1997), and changes in distribution mechanisms may mark social boundaries. Radi has perceptively noted a correlation between sourced obsidian, social networks, and ceramic styles in Early Neolithic

Toscana: Palmarola and Lipari obsidian tend to be found at sites with southern-style Impressed Wares, while Sardinian obsidian tends to be found at sites with Northern Tyrrhenian-style Cardial Wares (Radi 2000). In Calabria, virtually all the obsidian probably came from Lipari, but the coincidence of a sharp stylistic boundary (suggesting a drop in communication) and changes in how much obsidian was used and how it was used suggests a similar bounded network. We may perhaps also postulate that, within the Calabria Stentinello world, travel related to obsidian may have been a distinct institution involving specific kinds of travel and sociality integrating groups strung out along the long coastlines like beads – a now-shadowy system on the scale of the kula.

The plain of Sibari is the last bead in the chain – the last pocket of land sandwiched between mountains and sea. On the other side of the large Pollino massif to its north the hills give way to the much more open lowlands of eastern Basilicata. The Pollino massif is precipitous and reaches virtually to the sea on both coasts; routes northwards from the Sibari plain are not obviously easier than those southwards. It may have been a historical accident why the principal communicative traditions of this locality linked it to the painted-ware-using communities to the north rather than the Stentinello-using communities to the south, or it may have represented the breaking point, where distance took its toll and travel southwards to obsidian was too protracted.

The Social History of Unique Places: Lipari

London or Cambridge can teach us about modern or medieval European cities, but they also have unique histories. A history of Cambridge which made no mention of the university could not explain why its development differed so much from that of Huntingdon, Wisbech, or other undistinguished fen-edge towns. This is equally true for prehistory, where there is no reason to expect that all places either are typical or vary simply according to their place in a hierarchy of size or political centrality. Indeed, many of the places prehistorians commonly use to sum up entire cultures and epochs – Stonehenge, Lascaux, Harappa and

Mohenjo-Daro, Macchu Picchu – are demonstrably aberrant, unrepresentative of the typical if not entirely unique.

The Lipari (or Aeolian) Islands, about 20 km north of the northeastern corner of Sicily (Figure 50), do not seem a promising place for Neolithic settlement. The seven islands contain only 115.9 km^2 of land, with 37.6 km^2 on Lipari itself, the largest island. All seven are made principally of steep volcanic cones with little level land except on Lipari itself and few reliable water sources. Two islands (Stromboli and Vulcano) are very active volcanoes (indeed, the entire population of Stromboli was evacuated because of volcanic threats in 2004) and Lipari was also active in historical times. But the great attraction for Neolithic settlement was obsidian. Volcanic flows at Monte Pelato on the northeastern coast of Lipari were the most important source of this natural glass for an obsidian trade which lasted at least 2,500 years and spanned the entire Central Mediterranean (see Chapter 5 in this book).

Lipari's archaeology is well-known, thanks to the monumental research of L. Bernabò Brea and M. Cavalier over five decades between the 1950s and the 1990s (Bernabò Brea 1987, 1947, 1947, 1954, 1957; Bernabò Brea and Cavalier 1956, 1957, 1960, 1968, 1980, 1991, 1995; Castignino Berlinghieri 2003; Cavalier 1985; Tusa 1993, 1997). At a moment when the prehistory of the entire region was embryonic at best, Bernabò Brea and Cavalier excavated sites of all periods from the Early Neolithic through Classical times, and they carbon-dated a deeply stratified prehistoric sequence from the Acropolis (Castello) of Lipari, directly beneath the Classical, medieval and modern town of Lipari. Much as Bernabò Brea's excavations at Arene Candide provided the first reliable stratigraphy for northern Tyrrhenian, the Lipari sequence thus provided the essential cornerstone for the prehistory of the southern Tyrrhenian and Sicily. In interpreting the sequence, Bernabò Brea and Cavalier perceptively linked Lipari's Neolithic fortunes to the obsidian trade, particularly for the Late Neolithic Diana culture, when the Contrada Diana site on Lipari was the largest known anywhere in the region and the obsidian trade was at its height.

This interpretation supplies the essential foundation of any view of Lipari. Yet since the principal Lipari excavations, we have accumulated considerable new knowledge on regions which were an archaeological void at the time, and this may lead us to nuance it somewhat differently.

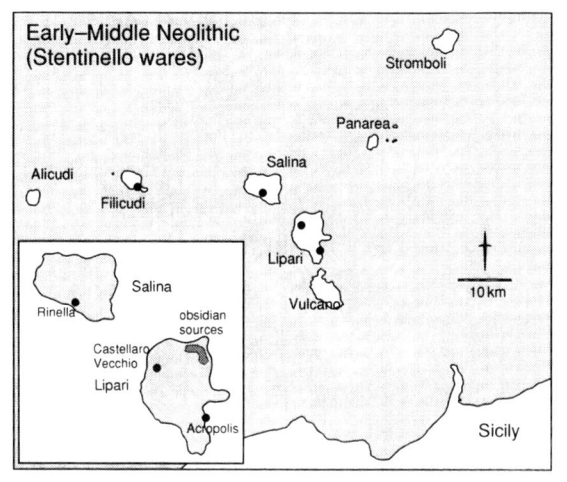

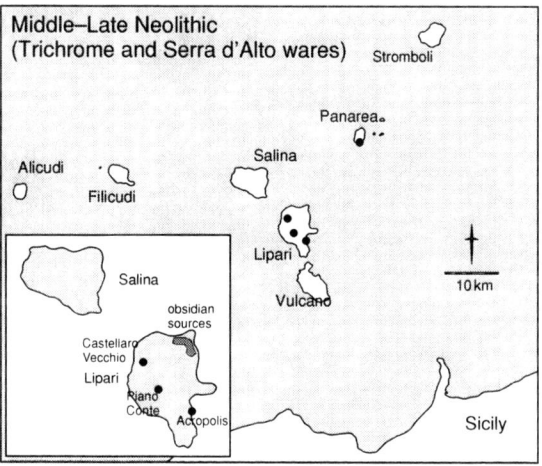

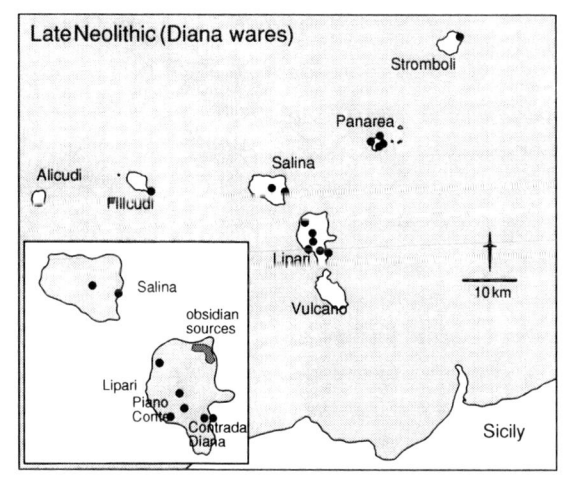

50. The Lipari archipelago during the Neolithic.

The idea of Lipari as a prosperous obsidian emporium, in its *floruit* rather like a medieval Tuscan hilltop town at the height of the wool trade, rests on three assumptions: that the trade was principally commercial or functional in nature, with residents trading a prized local product for other commodities, that the Lipari sequence is typical of the surrounding region, and that Lipari sites were normal habitation sites like sites elsewhere.

Whatever the social or material function of the obsidian trade (see Chapter 5 in this book), we cannot assume that locally it happened through a quasi-commercial exchange. It is an ethnographic cliché that trade in tribal societies is often conducted for the sake of the social relationships created rather than for a profit-oriented exchange of necessary commodities. On Lipari, there is no evidence that the island's residents tried to, or would even have been able to, control access to obsidian sources. This is especially so during the Early Neolithic when the few sites known are located inland and well out of site of navigation routes along the east coast of the island. The Middle Neolithic move to the Lipari town area might be seen as an attempt to monitor travel along the most probable sea route to the obsidian mountain, from Milazzo past Vulcano and Lipari town. But there are no clearly habitational sites known around the obsidian flows themselves, in spite of many scatters of worked obsidian found around the sources and in spite of the availability of a good harbor with some level ground directly adjacent to them at Canneto. Moreover, the population of the islands must have been very low. Only three Early Neolithic sites are known (Castellaro Vecchio on Lipari, Rinicedda (Rinella) on Salina and Casa Lopez on Filicudi). The economic estimates presented in Chapter 3 suggest a maximum population for Lipari of some hundreds if all available land were exploited (see Table 8), and the sparseness of sites known suggests that actual land use was much less than this. A very low population for Lipari would imply little ability to control obsidian sources. It would also highlight how much residents of the islands depended upon neighboring societies in Sicily and/or Calabria not only for imports of flint, polished stone, grinding stones and even clay to make pots from (Williams 1980), but for human relationships as well. A completely isolated population of a few hundreds at most would never have been demographically stable, and the Liparese must have maintained close kin relationships with

Sicilian and/or mainland groups. Beyond meeting demographic needs, such cooperative ties must have been essential in weathering ecological variations such as extended droughts on small, dry, resource-poor islands. Hence, rather than a quasi-commercial trade on the beach, we should probably imagine a visiting season with more open, perhaps cooperative procurement among people who often knew each other well or were related. As Castagnino Berlinghieri (2003) perceptively points out, a substantivist rather than formalist model is more appropriate for what must have been closely linked kin networks.

This baseline model works well for the Early Neolithic, when settlement in the archipelago consists of a scant handful of sites on inland areas favorable for farming but not noticeably convenient for trade and travel. Early Neolithic pottery at the sites of Castellaro Vecchio on Lipari and Rinicedda on Sicily is in fact highly similar to that found in the surrounding Stentinello world of eastern Sicily and southern Calabria. Interestingly, petrographic analysis shows that at Rinicedda, fine decorated bowls were more likely than coarsewares to have originated outside the islands (Williams and Levi 1995); if these vessels were used principally in eating and drinking, this suggests a certain sociality to the circulation of people.

However, things become more puzzling in the Middle Neolithic, and here the question of Lipari's pottery sequence becomes critical. Dated sequences in Southern Calabria and Sicily have shown clearly that the Lipari sequence, far from being typical of the region, is unique or hybrid (Table 24). As noted above, Early Neolithic pottery closely resembles Stentinello wares from the regions of the Straits of Messina. But later in the sequence, Stentinello wares are superseded first by trichrome painted wares similar to those known in northern Calabria, which are then supplemented by a rather idiosyncratic local ware termed "meandro-spiraliç" which resembles nothing so much as Serra d'Alto designs executed in a dark burnished fabric. During these periods, Stentinello wares continued to be used in Southern Calabria and Sicily. Finally, Diana wares take over, superseding all local styles throughout Sicily and Southern Italy.

In the Middle Neolithic, thus, the Liparese adopted pottery styles which affiliated them with more distant regions in Northern Calabria rather than with their immediate neighbors who continued to use

Table 24. *Neolithic Sequences from Lipari, Southern Calabria/Sicily, and Northern Calabria/Campania*

	Northern Calabria/ Basilicata/Puglia/ Campania	Lipari	Southern Calabria/ Eastern Sicily
6000 BC	Impressed Bichrome Trichrome	Stentinello	(Impressed?) Stentinello
5000 BC	Serra d'Alto	Trichrome "Meandro-spiralic"	
	Diana	Diana	Diana
4000 BC			

Note: Dates are approximate.

Stentinello wares, and they reworked these styles into idiosyncratic local wares. A range of wares, including elaborate painted vessels, were made locally, sometimes using imported clays (Williams and Levi 2001). Accompanying this, many residents of the islands moved to the area of present-day Lipari town, where they found level land to work, water sources, the best harbor in the archipelago directly astride the principal sea route, and a defensible acropolis – a combination so attractive that it has been the archipelago's principal center in all subsequent periods.

This period of Lipari's Neolithic which is poorly dated but probably spanned the first half of the fifth millennium BC, becomes only more puzzling the more we consider it. On the one hand, contact between Lipari and the Stentinello world did not cease, but increased, if anything: regardless of its ultimate destination, most or all of the obsidian coming out of the island passed first through the Middle Neolithic Stentinello world. Moreover, Lipari continued to depend upon demographic, ecological, and economic contacts with mainland societies, just as before. Even clay was imported to the island from Sicily to be made into pots (Williams 1980; Williams and Levi 1995, 2001). On the other hand, the presence of painted wares implies closer relations with Northern Calabrian groups, and the almost-complete lack of Stentinello wares at the principal site, the Lipari Acropolis (Bernabò Brea and Cavalier 1980), suggests that contact with the world of the Straits, while regular, was less intimate in nature than previously. Moreover, Middle Neolithic sites elsewhere in the region are not typically fortified (with the possible exception of the cluster of ditched villages around Siracusa) nor located on defensible peaks. In its positioning, the Lipari Acropolis site suggests a quite unusual concern for defense which hardly suggests entirely cordial relationships with nearby Stentinello groups.

These pieces, which suggest that not just pottery styles but also relations with the nearby mainland had changed, can be put together in several ways. One working hypothesis might be that, for some reason of unreconstructable tribal politics – and in such a small setting quite idiosyncratic events might have had important and visible effects – the residents of Lipari threw in their lot socially with groups from Northern Calabria or from sporadic areas in Central and Western Sicily who were experimenting with painted wares at the time [e.g., Stretto di Partanna (Tusa and Valente 1994)]. They distanced themselves from their former kin and neighbors in the Stentinello network discussed above. Yet, the Liparese continued to obtain flint, clay, axes, and probably other materials from places within the Stentinello world, and people from the Straits area continued to come from Lipari to procure obsidian. With the balance of population in the region living in Stentinello-network groups, preventing access by force to obsidian sources was not a possibility: hence the nucleation of the Lipari population in a single defensible settlement.

The settlement of the archipelago exploded during the Late Neolithic Diana period. All of the islands except Vulcano and Alicudi were occupied (Stromboli for the first time, Panarea probably as well; the only evidence of earlier settlement on the latter is a single Serra d'Alto sherd found at Punto del Milazzese). This mirrors the colonization of small islands throughout the Central Mediterranean at this time (Dawson 2005). Why they were occupied is not clear; some sites, such as the Fossa delle Felci in the inaccessible crater on one of the twin peaks on Salina, must have been used for some purpose such as herding or shooting birds rather than habitation and farming, and small, predator-free islands would have made useful places to keep an occasionally visited herd of hardy sheep or goats. More extensive use of local resources is also shown by the use of local clays in potting (Williams and Levi 2001). On Lipari itself, many more sites are known, in all zones of the island, including both coastal places and central plateaus such as Piano Conte.

Perhaps the oddest site is the Contrada Diana itself, the name given to the settlement in Lipari town in this period and the type site for Diana pottery (Bernabò Brea and Cavalier 1960). In the Late Neolithic, the main focus of settlement moved from the acropolis to the coastal plain just below it, which may perhaps suggest a less belligerent political atmosphere with less need for defense. Surface remains are reported from throughout modern Lipari town, suggesting a site of at least 10 ha, by far the largest known for this period in Italy. Bernabò Brea and Cavalier excavated 23 trenches in various locations throughout Contrada Diana, though in most of them prehistoric deposits were disturbed by a Classical Greek necropolis or later works. Nevertheless, their major undisturbed trench was approximately 250 m^2 in extension, making this one of the most extensive Neolithic excavations in Southern Italy.

Aside from the site's size, the most striking feature of Contrada Diana was the hundreds of kilos of obsidian found — almost as much obsidian as pottery was recovered. Much of it was roughing-out flakes from reducing nodules to cores or blades. In some places, small heaps of obsidian were found, as if from single knapping episodes. The large size of the site and its specialised production of obsidian cores led Bernabò Brea and Cavalier to interpret it as a specialist producer town at the height of its prosperity during the Late Neolithic zenith of the obsidian trade.

Yet, there are several puzzling features at odds with this view. The principal one is architecture. Based on sketchy notes from Orsi, who originally found the site, Bernabò Brea and Cavalier expected to find huts; they had found a clear and well-made Bronze Age structure here, as well as daub from Neolithic structures at Castellaro Vecchio, which confirms that Aeolian populations shared the common techniques of building. Although they found one scrap of an insubstantial wall, they specifically note that no houses were to be found. Nor do they note postholes, daub or potential building stones from destroyed houses. This anomalous use of space is reinforced by the absence of other features. Virtually no Neolithic villages had been excavated in great extension in 1960, and so it was difficult to appreciate the absence of the ubiquitous cobbled pavements, clay pavements, and small ditches and pits which give most Neolithic sites their distinctive Swiss cheese-like appearance.

Instead of houses, the predominant feature was hearths, found virtually everywhere, which must have been in open areas:

> Mentre l'Orsi accenna vagamente a resti di capanne che sarebbero state viste nelle trincee da lui scavate, ma sulle quali non dà alcuna indicazione, nel nostro scavo non si trovò traccia di capanne. Si incontrarano invece resti di numerosi focolari che dobbiamo immaginare all'aperto. [Although Orsi vaguely mentions the remains of huts that would have been seen in the trenches he excavated, but which he gives no information about, in our excavation no trace of huts was found. Instead, we found the remains of numerous hearths which we must imagine in the open.] (Bernabò Brea and Cavalier 1960, pp. 10–12, translation Robb)

Although Bernabò Brea and Cavalier do not note the exact number of hearths, there were a great many. Moreover, the hearths generally seem to be the type known as *strutture di combustione* (see Chapter 4 in this book): wide, shallow pits, sometimes lined with stones (somewhat mysteriously, grinding stones were sometimes used), and filled with a mixture of burnt wood and burnt stones. Moreover, there are several other anomalies with the site. While quantification is impossible, the repertory of material culture seems to include many more grinding stones and polished stone axes than one would find at a "normal" domestic site. Grinding stones were not uncommonly deposited in nondomestic contexts in Neolithic Italy; some of the grinding stones here bore traces of red and yellow ochre. A second anomaly is the well-preserved nature of features such as accumulations of obsidian and *strutture di combustione*, which argues for a relatively extensive rather than intensive use of space. Finally, the site, more than 10 ha in area and comparable in size to the modern town of Lipari, probably could not have been occupied all at once; it is not clear how many people Lipari could support, even with expanded pastoralism and perhaps even periodic imports of foodstuffs.

Table 25. *Overview and Possible Interpretation of the Lipari Sequence*

Period	Ceramic Connections	Settlement	Obsidian Trade	Nature of Settlement
Early Neolithic	Stentinello wares – S. Calabria and E. Sicily	Few sites on Lipari, Salina, Filicudi; inland	Low-level; some specialised core-making at Castellaro Vecchio	Normal Stentinello villages with obsidian trade added
Middle Neolithic	Northern Calabria/local re-interpretations (trichromes, meandro-spiralic wares)	Few sites; principal site is defensible Acropolis of Lipari town above good harbor	Increasing; some specialised core-making	Trade-oriented community, with continuing strong contact with Straits region but use of pottery to define identity
Late Neolithic	Diana – in common with entire region	Occupation of all islands in archipelago; very large undefended site with little architecture, lots of hearths at Contrada Diana	Intense; great quantity of core reduction at Contrada Diana	Seasonal aggregation at Contrada Diana, with or without permanently resident community

The Contrada Diana site may represent a change in Lipari's role. Hearths, not houses: rather than simple habitation, the Contrada Diana may have been some form of aggregation site, where a small local, permanent population was supplemented by people coming together in large but temporary numbers to procure obsidian and to eat together. This is consonant with the changing meaning of pottery decoration and the increasing prominence of trade in the Late Neolithic (see below). Presumably the trade was seasonal; it is often assumed that navigation took place primarily during the summer or autumn when the sea was calmer (Castignino Berlinghieri 2003). I would thus suggest (cf. Castignino Berlinghieri 2003) that Lipari may have been a focal point where people from diverse areas met during a visiting season to exchange quite diverse things found in their respective areas. If so, the attraction of periodic sociality may have been as important as the obsidian, which may have served as a pretext, ancillary, or souvenir of the encounter rather than the driving motive behind it.

As a reinterpretation of this classic sequence (Table 25), the "Lipari kula" version (using the term in a general sense to suggest an extensive trade system, not as a specific parallel) clearly pushes the evidence, and is perhaps most valuable in suggesting new research directions to pursue. Yet, regardless of the specifics, it seems clear that the unique nature of settlement in the archipelago, the social context of the obsidian trade, and Lipari's relations with neighbouring societies changed qualitatively several times over the long course of the Neolithic.

EIGHT:
THE GREAT SIMPLIFICATION: LARGE-SCALE CHANGE AT THE END OF THE NEOLITHIC

> There was no agreement among the scholars of Chelm on how the town came into existence. The pious believed that God said, "Let there be Chelm." And there was Chelm. But many scholars insisted that the town happened as the result of an eruption.
> Isaac Bashevis Singer, *The Fools of Chelm and Their History*. (Singer 1973, p. 3)

> If we want things to stay as they are, things will have to change. Do you understand?
> Giuseppe di Lampedusa, *The Leopard* (1960, p. 40).

The Leopard is a story of change – of the passing of a faded feudal aristocracy swept away by the unification of Italy in 1860. Di Lampedusa's words above are spoken by a young Sicilian aristocrat who rides the storm to take away his ancestral estates and privileges by joining Garibaldi's militia and marrying into the up-and-coming bourgeoisie. His words underline the paradox of explaining social change in human terms.

Explanations of change are always teleological and retrospective; as in I. B. Singer's mythical village of Chelm, origin stories are closely tied to the identity and nature of the phenomenon. They are defined by the problem to be solved, the change to be accomplished. "Origins" research, thus, is inherently suspect due to its ability to provide a powerful tool in objectifying and legitimating the present (Conkey and Williams 1991; Gathercole and Lowenthal 1990). But this unavoidable relativity, and its often flagrant abuse, does not mean that all explanations of change per se are inherently suspect: the fact that we compose a photograph by choosing a wide angle or close-up lens does not break entirely our relationship with the object photographed. Depending upon the goal of our interpretation, we may legitimately interpret a site as an exemplar of decades of stability or centuries of change, of continent-wide patterns or local idiosyncrasies.

In long-term studies, we have remained blocked at the temporal threshold of ethnographic vision [the "tyranny of the ethnographic record" (Wobst 1978)]. Although the rhythms of cultural time have been well-explored (Gosden 1994; Lucas 2004), and the interaction of cultural action and environment has sometimes been approached through simulation studies (particularly in the American Southwest), we still lack theoretical concepts to bridge ethnographic time and archaeological time. Moreover, our theorizations of change have been influenced by the concept and timescale of modernity; for example, ethnographers have never conceptualised long-term cultural stability, on the scale of centuries, as other than the passive reproduction of tradition. These gaps are all the more crippling for periods in which we are faced with widespread cultural changes happening across decentralised small-scale communities, as with the spread of agriculture or the social changes marking the end of the Neolithic.

For a theory of historical practice to be useful, it must be able to help us interpret large-scale change as well as smaller histories and variations. Explaining long-term change has been a striking lacuna in recent archaeological theory.

European societies display a general transformation between about 4000 BC and 2000 BC, a transformation visible from Russia to Ireland and acknowledged by theorists of every school. In general terms, landscapes marked by tells, villages, or large ritual monuments give way to dispersed settlements and more evident cemeteries of individual graves, small barrows, mounds, or small collective tombs. Settlement consolidates in highland and marginal areas, probably indicating an intensification of pastoralism. Technological innovations include metals and perhaps wheeled vehicles and the plow. The domestic horse is introduced, and in many areas hunting increases. Socially, adults, especially males, are often buried with relatively standardised "status kits" of gender-marked goods, particularly weapons, ornaments, and drinking vessels. This general suite of changes begins earlier in southeastern Europe and latest in northwestern areas such as Britain, and encompasses a range of well-known archaeological cultures such as the Corded Ware and the Bell Beakers.

To traditional culture historical archaeologists, the explanation for these widespread, radical changes was obvious: they were borne along by migrating peoples. The favored candidates were "Indo-Europeans," supposed to be warlike, patriarchical, metal-using pastoralists moving in waves from east to west (Gimbutas 1991; Mallory 1989). Such accounts, however, rely upon nineteenth-century Romantic and nationalistic notions of "peoples" (Díaz-Andreu and Champion 1996), they do not explain why such movements should have occurred, and they do not cope well with evidence for continuity in many places and with the complexity of the transition. Among economic models, Childe (1957) regarded the introduction of metals as the trigger for change, although change in Italy and other regions began well before metals came into use, and the relationship may well have been the converse. Sherratt's (1981) secondary products model has drawn attention to the common denominator of economic intensification evident in plowing, dairying, and the use of wool. However, it makes economy and technology into autonomous prime movers diffusing from the Near East to catalyze stagnant native cultures, and recent work has complicated the history of techniques such as dairying rather than confirming his scenario.

Economic, technological and population replacement models also hide rather than highlight the fundamentally social nature of changes. A range of Marxist models have been used to address fourth and third millennia transformations (Chapman 2003). Gilman (1991), for example, draws a straightforwardly materialist linkage between the control of necessary economic resources and the rise of hierarchies in southeastern Spain. However, the question of whether access to material resources should have analytical priority in non-class societies is not straightforward, particularly when the form of property ownership is completely unknown. In a rather different formulation, Cazzella and Moscoloni (1985) interpret the Italian Copper Age as an age-stratified society in which elders controlled juniors by controlling their access to goods needed to marry. Other, more general syntheses of this period (Cardarelli 1992; Guidi 1992) emphasise that the circulation of prestige goods was extensive but took place within a society that remained essentially unranked. Anthropological discussions of the Great Man-Big Man transition and the prominence of trade are not particularly helpful, often ultimately blaming various effects of colonial contact (Godelier and Strathern 1991; Whitehead 1992), or particular marriage patterns or customs such as homicide and injury compensation (Godelier 1991; Lemonnier 1991), though the link between the introduction of the sweet potato and competitive exchange of pigs (Feil 1987; Modjeska 1991) may parallel the role of herds below.

Shennan (1982), Thorpe and Richards (1984) and Braithwaite (1984) all perceptively noted that the end of the Neolithic in Western Europe involved changes in the basic nature of social relations, with the replacement of large-scale ritual by the competitive consumption and display of valuables. Corded Ware and Bell Beaker burials were seen as evidence of the rise of a new category of political individuals. This insightful approach rendered trade, burial, and politics as fields of action through which authority was reproduced rather than as autonomous, separate "spheres," and it linked well with ideas of gender and habitus. A more recent formulation emphasises the reproduction of social relations among the living as mediated by changing relations with the dead, from generic ancestors continually present in society to specific individuals through which political genealogies were constructed (Barrett 1994; Thomas 1999).

These current social interpretations of the great changes sweeping across Europe in the fourth and third millennia are the most illuminating approaches available, but they really leave two questions unanswered. First, they tend ultimately to describe relations among the phenomena which changed without specifying any causal mechanism, which rather implies that new systems of social reproduction arise because they do. Second, they do not address the question of why changes arising in one place should have spread to other groups across Europe, and why this spread should have been so rapid, and, apparently, unidirectional.

With the rejection of extralocal factors such as grand migrations or the diffusion of new technologies, we are left with the paradox of continent-wide, directional effects with local, undirected causes.

Practice and History

Historical Practice: Life without a Primum Mobile

In principle, placing human agency at the heart of historical process is simple (see Chapter 1 in this volume and Pauketat 2001). Human agency is ever-present: every historical moment is the present for the agents creating it. Social reproduction is an ongoing process; people act creatively in contexts and tools of action inherited from the past and their actions create the next moment's contexts and tools of action. Historical process thus involves the continual encounter of inherited structures of thought and behaviour with new circumstances (Sahlins 1985), the working out of habitus in changing objective conditions of existence (Bourdieu 1977). Except in circumstances of traumatically abrupt change, change, and continuity are therefore inextricable.

Unfortunately, this is one of those ideas which is simple to explain, and with which few would disagree, but which actually specifies little about how one goes about archaeology. The devil is in how one actually works it out in a given interpretation. Does one emphasise "external" circumstances such as environment or foreign contact, "social" ones such as economic structure or political leadership strategies, or "cultural" ones such as symbolic traditions? All of these positions have been argued by well-developed archaeological traditions.

As a starting point, dividing the past into separate conceptual boxes such as "politics," "symbols and ritual," and "environment" represents a false dismemberment. For example, whether an environmental change potentially impacts a group's way of life depends upon how they understand, exploit, and indeed shape their environment: culture is inescapable. Even an outcome apparently overwhelmingly determined by environment, such as the abandonment of the Viking settlement of Greenland in the Little Ice Age, is mediated by cultural perceptions and choices: Greenland was uninhabitable to people choosing to be Norse farmers, but why not simply adopt an Inuit way of life and stay there? Such considerations muddle any clear division between nature and culture (Ingold 2000).

But this point of view does not mean that culture can be regarded, equally monocausally, as an ultimate cause of change. History involves an intimate and reciprocal interaction between how people choose to live and their "existential conditions" (Knauft 1993). The introduction of the sweet potato to highland New Guinea between 200 and 400 years ago transformed native economies, but not in what we might consider the most obvious or efficient way; rather than human consumption, the sweet potato was used for pig fodder and allowed an enormous expansion of ceremonial exchange systems (Wiessner and Tumu 1998). But one effect of this was a dramatic rise in population, a filling-up of the landscape which in turn changed patterns of warfare, ritual and trade. Knauft's inspiring work tracks related societies on the South Coast of New Guinea who shared common cosmological beliefs about the renewal and circulation of life through rituals, headhunting and sexuality, but who implemented them through very different practices. Different practices gave each group a quite distinct historical trajectory. For example, among the Marind, intense ritualised sexuality was related to high rates of infertility and a very low birth rate; this was compensated for by the adoption of children captured in frequent and large-scale headhunting raids. Because they only directed headhunting raids against other groups, in the ethnohistoric present they were expanding rapidly by absorbing, annihilating, or driving away neighbouring groups whose cosmological practices were less warlike. As these examples suggest, theorizing long-term social change means tracing a continual dialectic between human choices and their real-world consequences.

Temporal Scale, Regional Analysis, and Patterns of History

Life without a prime mover can be unnerving. But the greatest problem in theorizing prehistoric change is probably not causation but scale. Theories such of historical practice have typically been generated in "ethnographic time" – a few years, a generation perhaps. History is limited to literate societies, of course. There are many studies of how nonliterate societies changed during moments of colonial contact, some prolonged over several generations and some viewing indigenous culture as an active structuring element (Clendinnen 2003; Sahlins 1985). But it takes determined ethnohistorical reconstruction to try to track change in nonliterate societies over longer spans of time and in situations where colonial contact may not be the dominant element structuring the situation; Weissner and Tumu's (1998) study of the highland New Guinea Enga, using oral history to achieve a time depth of ten generations, is a virtually unique effort. What this means is simple: ethnographic and historic models provide pictures of nonstate societies which either exclude change, in the stop-action vision of the ethnographic present, or which are changing rapidly, and often traumatically, in conditions of colonial contact and modernity. For any way of seeing traditional societies over more than a generation or two and without states as bullying neighbours, we are on our own.

Why does this make any difference? The reason is that time scale itself may be an important structuring factor in historical trajectories.

Deep time may pose two several specific challenges to explanation. One is that, over long enough time spans, infrequent moments of catastrophic change become inevitable and even common. For example, Southern Calabria experiences a major, catastrophic earthquake every century or two, with the last ones in 1908 and 1783. Although these earthquakes raze cities, empty lakes, and level forests disastrously, they are infrequent enough that earthquakes always come as a surprise, an interruption to normality rather than a calculable factor in settlement, land use, or cultural awareness. Yet, over the course of the Neolithic, at today's rates, there would have been perhaps twenty major earthquakes. The other challenge is gradualism, or the "compound interest" problem: changes so small as to be invisible over any observational interval may cumulate to dramatic changes over deep time. For example, in a small village 1 percent per annum population increase would show up as the birth of a new baby or two over the course of an ethnographer's fieldwork, indistinguishable from the annual irregular flux of births and deaths; yet, over the next 70 years, the population would double. Some processes such as erosion, environmental depletion and demographic transitions may involve such long-term gradualism. Although these two factors suggest that we need to include a broader range of factors in explanations of long durations than is customary for ethnographic accounts, they do not imply that the nature of causation itself changes over millennia. In particular, it is a non sequitur to assume that, although decades-long processes are social, millennial processes are environmentally or economically determined:

At the short end of the spectrum, there may be a limit to how quickly basic conditions of life can change without a feeling of traumatic dislocation. If the basic conditions of habitus change over less than a generation, subjects who are already oriented adults must re-experience the process of acquiring orientation in the world. In the absence of the rapid or traumatic change typical of the last several centuries, or of the disorienting experience of difference caused by colonial encounters, traditional societies may be marked by fundamental conservatism of basic values on a scale difficult to imagine.

Yet this does not mean they are frozen in time. On the timescale of centuries, Weissner and Tumu's ethnohistory demonstrates clearly that dramatic changes in the nature and scope of major social institutions – a ten-fold increase in population, a change in the purpose and organization of warfare, the hyper-development of the *tee* system of ceremonial exchange – can occur within a couple of centuries. This is corroborated by ethnohistoric accounts from elsewhere in the world (Kelly 1985; Knauft 1993). This is also suggested by historical demographers who argue that apparently minor changes such as a shift in age of marriage can catapult a demographic regime from stasis to fast growth within a few decades (Livi-Bacci 1999). Recent fine-grained climatic change curves suggest that climatic change can be sharp and happen over a few decades or a century. Interestingly, this "historical time" may also be a common span for the construction of group memory focused around remembered major events. Usefully, and not coincidentally, for many parts of the world, the scale of a few centuries approaches the limit of how finely prehistorians can date major changes.

In bridging the gap from ethnographic time to historical time, a model of social reproduction implies that not all elements of a cultural world are equally changeable. As Rappaport observed (Rappaport 1979), abstract propositions which underwrite many branches of behaviour refer to immaterial values; they supply the basic tools of thought, and must be interpreted situationally in order to be applied to a given genre of behaviour. Hence, while they are drawn upon in creative action, they are rarely questioned directly, and their truth value is buffered from the vagaries of change. For example, disciplined control of the body conveys authority in modern Western society (Foucault 1977); this semantic recurs in genres of action from military comportment to speech, dress and music; it can be drawn upon freely to formulate new kinds of behaviour (e.g., rock music and associated dress and hair styles in the 1960s); but even such inversions and rejections do not question the underlying relevance of bodily discipline to authority. As di Lampedusa's nobles point out, change simultaneously maintains continuity, in the terms of argument if in nothing else.

Implementing this point of view analytically means considering space as well as time. It has long been recognised that regional "cultures" are useful fictions, masking complex patterns of variation: to what extent can one really speak of "Native American" culture, "Pueblo" culture, or "Hopi" culture? Such frames of reference never provide a unique way of understanding a particular situation, but instead are relative to the analytical problem they are intended to address (Knauft 1993). It is not necessarily the case that the most detailed description of a particular society will be the most useful representation of it; such a description may, for example, sacrifice our ability to see its historical derivation as a local transformation of inherited general principles. Moreover, if ethnographic landscapes are produced by people in common or parallel traditions following independent historical trajectories, we would expect variation between societies at any given point to follow the same pattern noted above for development within one tradition: shared sets of basic principles of habitus, worked out, applied and understood different in many ways: a counterpoint of deeply entrenched reflexes and terms of discourse and uniquely local ways of doing things. Knauft's survey of indigenous groups on the South Coast of New Guinea discussed above provides one convincing account of such a situation, as does Barth's work on how cosmological beliefs are invented in highland New Guinea (Barth 1987).

To summarise, the timescale of most interest for observing the historical workings of practice is likely to be neither the span of decades nor of millennia, but on the order of a few centuries. Change within this span, moreover, is likely to be characterised by an inseparability of innovation and tradition, a somewhat paradoxical combination of great stability in fundamental abstract values and the continual development and disappearance of new forms of practice. The ethnographic landscapes produced by history will show a similar patterning at any given time. Because of the nature of historical practice, causation is not easily assignable to "internal" or "external" causes (or any similar simplifications): humans act within inherited conditions and their acts reproduce and change these conditions. Moreover, the pace of change is likely to be highly variable, with great stability and slow, gradual change punctuated by episodes of rapid change.

The Late Neolithic and Copper Age in Peninsular Italy and Sicily[1]

Most of the changes found throughout Europe occur in Italy as well, though the picture is quite complicated in detail. The principal traditions of the Late Neolithic period are the Diana culture in Southern Italy and Sicily, and the Lagozza culture in most of Central and Northern Italy. Following this, throughout Southern Italy, there are a range of transitional Copper Age regional descendents of the Diana culture such as the Piano Conte group. In Central and Northern Italy, the Lagozza culture itself provides the transition to the Eneolithic. During the full Eneolithic, peninsular cultures include Gaudo in Campania, Andria in Puglia and Basilicata, Rinaldone in Lazio and Toscana, Vecchiano in northwestern Toscana, Ortucchio in the high central Apennines, and Conelle in Adriatic Central Italy. Several cultural groups are known in Northern Italy, including the Spilamberto group in Emilia, the Remedello group in the eastern Po Valley, and the Civate group in the Alps.

Although there is regional variation, there is a core of features which characterise the Neolithic–Copper Age transition.

Material Culture and Exchange

Pottery is one of the most obvious changes. Sometime between 4500 and 4000 BC, both surface-textured pots (including impressed, incised and stamped styles such as Impressed Ware, Stentinello and Matera Scratched

Ware) and painted wares (trichromes and Serra d'Alto) disappear. In their place arise Diana wares (sometimes called Diana-Bellavista) in the south and Sicily. In east-central Italy, the common style is a final version of Ripoli wares in which painted trichromes dwindle, leaving only dark burnished wares, and in Toscana and northern Italy Lagozza wares are widespread. The common denominator throughout is the replacement of gloriously ornate surfaces with plain, glossy ones, accompanied by a new forms, principally wide, shallow bowls but also in places including flasks, *askoi*, and certain handle forms (Figure 51). This striking change is found elsewhere with the Chassean in southern France, the Starcevo-Vinca transition in the Balkans, the Sesklo–Dimini transition in southern Greece, and other developments elsewhere. It is clear that, throughout Southern Europe, baroque was out; shiny was in.

Yet, paradoxically, this was essentially a local change. In virtually all regions, there are local precursors and transitional forms. Throughout peninsular Italy, even where painted finewares were typical, assemblages throughout the Neolithic had always contained a proportion of dark-surfaced, undecorated wares with carefully smoothed or burnished surfaces. As is clearest in the long Ripoli culture development, such vessels provided the origin of Late Neolithic and Copper Age surfaces. In Matera, Diana-Bellavista wares sometimes reproduce the form of local Serra d'Alto buff painted vessels but in grey undecorated pastes. In the Stentinello area and Lipari, Diana wares include an impasto version arising out of earlier plainwares and a red-slipped figulina version deriving from painted wares. Although the new Late Neolithic styles such as Diana may have occasionally spread as well-defined styles (for instance Diana finewares in the highland Abruzzo where there was very little previous tradition of figulina pottery), the general process was clearly convergent evolution via selection from preexisting repertoires. In other words, what spread or evolved in tandem was not pottery styles per se, but rather the general aesthetic principles for choosing a style, accompanied by the decision to make pots which looked like one's neighbours' rather than differing from them.

Technologically, making Diana pottery required higher temperatures, and it may have required enclosing structures or proto-kilns (Williams and Levi 2001): one example may be the circular daub ring a

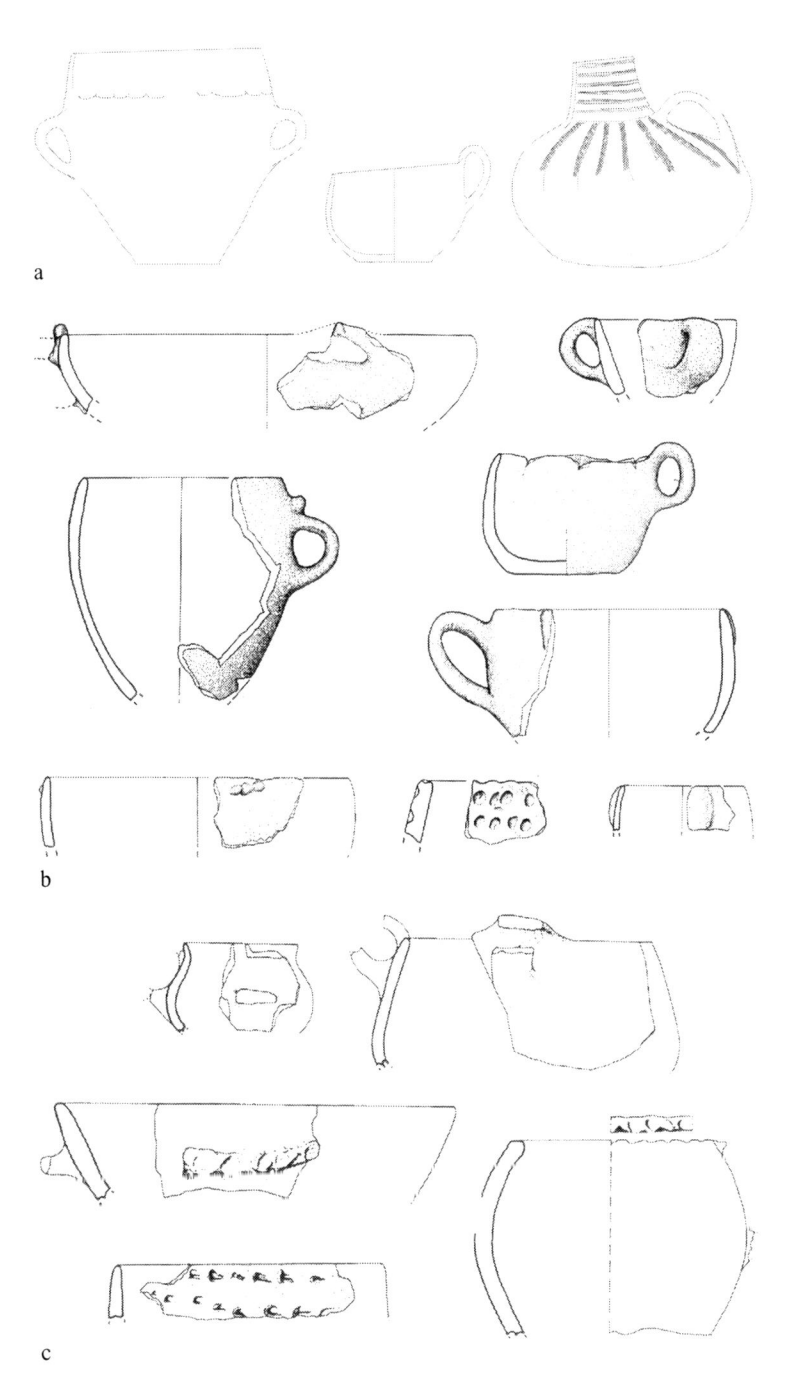

51. Copper Age pottery. (a) Pontecagnano, Campania (Bailo Modesti and Salerno 1998, courtesy of G. Bailo Modesti); (b) Maccarese, Lazio (Manfredini 2002, courtesy of A. Manfredini); and (c) Conelle di Arcevia, Marche (Cazzella and Moscoloni 1992, courtesy of A. Cazzella).

meter in diameter fired on the inside found at Umbro. Such structures, and the related know-how, may have derived from incipient experiments in metallurgy (Williams and Levi 2001).

Copper Age pottery repertories (Figure 51) continue to be based upon dark polished wares. There is a new range of common vessel forms including flasks, closed jars with raised necks, shallow bowls and askoi (globular oval jugs with an offset spout and prominent handle). Such decoration as occurs is typically based upon incision rather than painting and upon plastic decoration (except in the Sicilian Serraferlicchio culture), and decoration is typically rather spare. The basic attractiveness of the vessel seems to have depended primarily on its glossy, dark surface, and it has been suggested that some of these wares were intended to imitate metal vessels, although this seems improbable as no metal vessels to serve as prototypes are known from the Italian Eneolithic. Stylistically, the Copper Age is often seen as a return to regionally diverse styles after the broad horizons of the Late Neolithic and initial Eneolithic. This stands in contrast to the broad horizons of similarity in other things such as metalwork, and may relate principally to the particular meanings attached to pottery in this period.

Trade became more important from the Late Neolithic onwards, and also changed in scope. The Late Neolithic is the peak of the obsidian trade, with the stone reaching its furthest extent and greatest frequency. There are also new, standardised techniques for core reduction (Ammerman and Polglase 1993). Axes continue to be important, with several important new forms, including shaft-hole axes, axes with grooves for hafting which generically resemble "battle-axes" elsewhere in Europe, and polished stone "mace-heads."

Metals enter the scene, but very gradually. As elsewhere in Europe, the first experiments with copper happened in a firmly Neolithic context. The earliest copper use in Italy is found on Neolithic sites at Contrada Diana on Lipari and at Fossacesia and S. Maria in Selva in the Abruzzo, and about a dozen examples of copper smelting or artefacts are known from Neolithic contexts (Barfield et al. 2003; Skeates 1993). Copper sources are known in Liguria, the Trentino-Alto Adige, the Apuan Alps, and the Colline Metalliferine of southern Toscana, Sardinia, Calabria, and Sicily. Mines in Toscana and Liguria were worked in the Copper Age with wood and antler picks. It is only in the full Copper Age that metals found their way into common depositional contexts such as burials. It is hard to estimate whether the scarcity of copper in earlier Copper Age sites reflects a genuine scarcity. Most Copper Age sites yield little or no metal [Sicily has even been said to have a Copper Age without copper (Cazzella 1994)] and the use of skeumorphic substitutes such as flint daggers suggest a less than plentiful supply. On the other hand, Copper Age quarries in Liguria attest much more plentiful production than settlement evidence implies (Campana et al. 2006; Maggi and Pearce 2005), and fourth millennium sites with copper are widely scattered and sometimes far from ore sources (e.g., Pizzica Pantanello, Basilicata), which implies some widespread circulation. It therefore seems likely that metal was simply recycled and reworked rather than deposited in archaeologically recoverable contexts. One apparent effect of the introduction of metals was the final demise of the obsidian trade. The Copper Age obsidian crash is demonstrated both by the absence of the material on most Copper Age sites and on the shrinkage of settlement in the Aeolian islands, which have very few sites in this period.

In contrast to obsidian, flint continued to play an important role in the "age of metals." Flint mining continued in several areas. On the Gargano peninsula, where beds of high-quality flint are common, at least half a dozen mines operated during the Eneolithic (Di Lernia and Galiberti 1993; Palma di Cesnola and Vigliardi 1984; Tunzi Sisto 1990). Other flint mines were worked at Monte Tabuto, Sicily (Orsi 1898), and at Monte Lessini in the Alps (Barfield 1981). Although few attempts have been made to source flint, it would appear that throughout the Copper Age exotic material was used primarily for making prestigious lithic daggers and "Campignano" industry flaked stone axes. Other items which can be identified as exotic include marine shell, polished stone axes, and beads of marble and steatite. Marble and steatite are found primarily in the Apuan Alps and Liguria but were circulated throughout northwestern Italy (Barfield 1981; Cocchi Genick and Grifoni Cremonesi 1985; D'Ambrosio and Sfrecola 1990). Polished stone axes, often pierced as amulets, are as common in the Eneolithic as in earlier periods, particularly in Southern Italy, Sicily, and Malta (Skeates 1995).

Copper Age trade was motivated, at least in part, by weapon-related ideology (Figure 52). Metals were used in both axes and daggers. The trade in fine flint was probably linked to the manufacture of exquisitely pressure-flaked bifacial tools which show a level of ostentatious knapping skill unseen in Europe since the Solutrean. These include not only arrowheads, but also sometimes sizeable daggers.

Settlement and Productive Economy

Copper Age economy in Italy has always been discussed in terms of the rise of specialised pastoralism, but this is a highly debated issue, with pastoralism claimed to originate at many periods at or before early Classical times. Puglisi (1957) argued influentially that Bronze Age societies were essentially nomadic herders, and in culture historical syntheses, the Eneolithic was thought to have been brought into Italy by warlike shepherd peoples (Barker 1981). However, the antiquity of large-scale pastoralism has been seriously debated. Ancient authors use the idea of "pastoralism" to refer not only to an economic regime but other characteristics defining barbaric peoples such as the absence of towns (Shaw 1982–1983). Moreover, social barriers to long-range transhumance (such as negotiating access to very distant pastures) were probably not overcome until at least the Late Bronze Age, and large-scale transhumant pastoralists historically existed as specialised communities in the interstices of populous agricultural societies which provided them with grain and markets. Partly for these reasons, Barker (1981, 1989) and Sargent (1983) have argued that large-scale, long-range transhumance is a late consequence of urban commercial society, and that prehistoric transhumance was much more limited in scale.

Archaeological evidence on prehistoric pastoralism is slim. Skeletal evidence reveals a general decrease in dental disease in the Copper Age (a possible result of increased use of animal foods), a slight increase in stature and a decrease in signs of stress (Robb 1995). Vessels with perforated strainers at some Late Neolithic and Bronze Age sites have been interpreted as "milk boilers" similar to those used by shepherds in recent times. However, to date residue analysis has not confirmed the prehistoric use of dairying. Weaving apparatus such as loom weights and spindle whorls become far more common from around the end of the

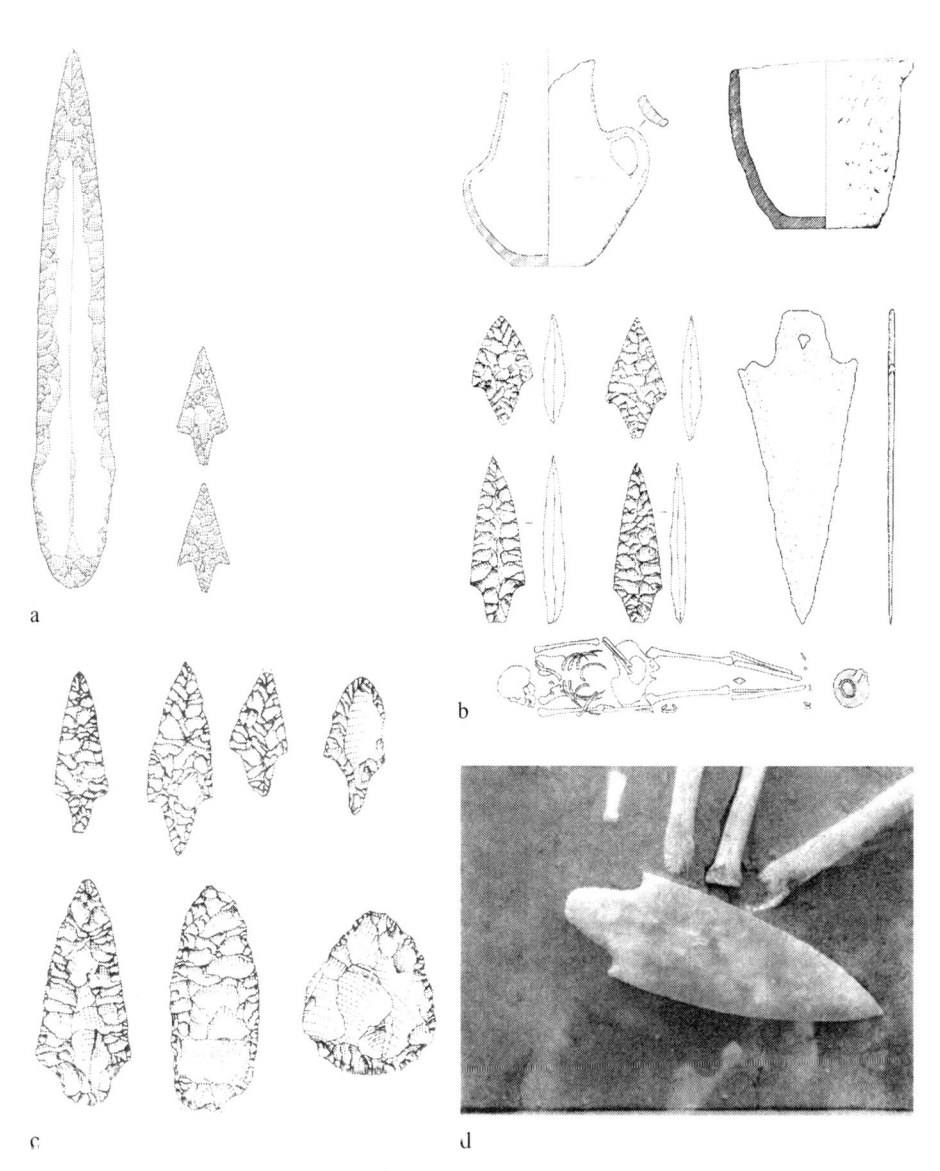

52. Copper Age weaponry. (a) Flint daggers and arrow points, Pontecagnano (Bailo Modesti and Salerno 1998, courtesy of G. Bailo Modesti); (b) Burial assemblage containing metal dagger, stone daggers, and arrow points, Spilamberto (Cazzella and Moscoloni 1992, courtesy of A. Cazzella); (c) Knives and arrow points, Moletta Patone di Arca (Cazzella and Moscoloni 1992, courtesy of A. Cazzella); and (d) Flint dagger, Remedello (Museo Civico, Reggio Emilia; photo: Robb).

a

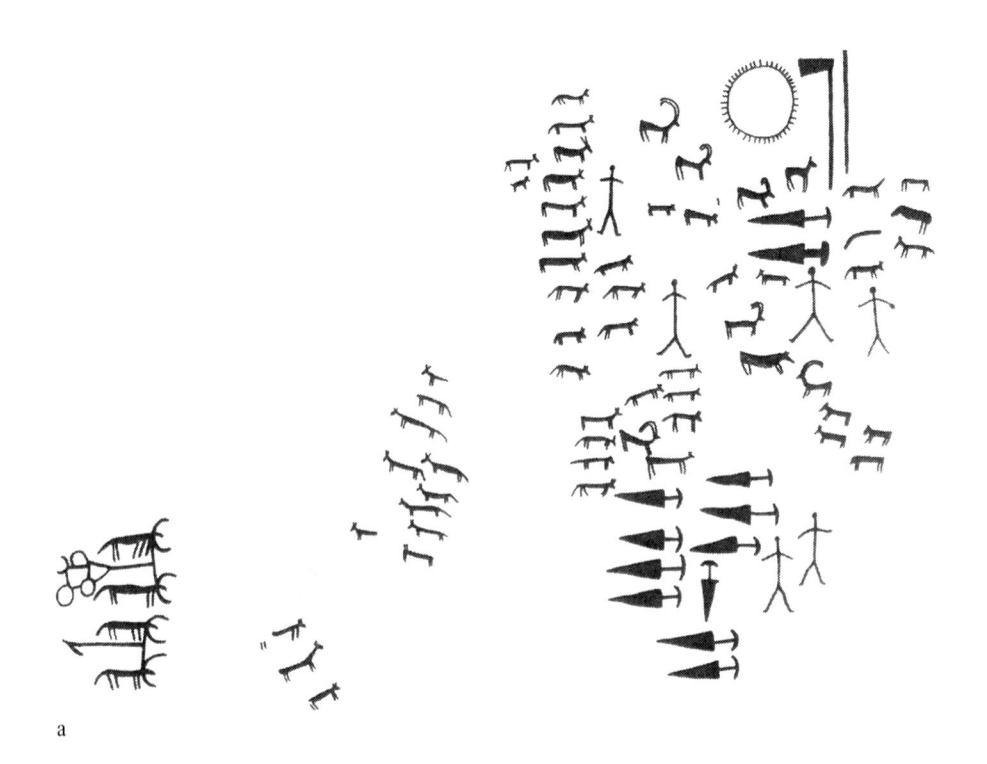

Neolithic onwards, for instance at Spilamberto at the Neolithic-Copper Age transition (Bagolini, Ferrari, and Steffè 1998). However, this does not confirm whether it was wool as opposed to flax which was spun. The first evidence for using animals for traction also comes from the Bronze Age, with depictions in Alpine rock carvings and with an actual wooden ard preserved at the lakeside village of Ledro. It has also been suggested that plow furrows under a Copper Age ceremonial site in the Alps were due to ritual plowing (Cardarelli 1992). Environmental reconstructions show that parts of Central and Northern Italy remained forested until at least the Bronze Age (Allegrucci et al. 1994; Balista and Leonardi 1985; Coltorti and Dal Ri 1985). Faunal samples in many areas show a clear increase in sheep and goats compared to cattle in the Late Neolithic (Tagliacozzo 1992). A few sites show increased use of pigs as well (for example, at Conelle where they made up 60 percent of the NISP). As a general rule, Copper Age samples show a slight increase in caprovines at the expense of cattle, particularly in cave sites, but variation is great.

53. Neolithic or Copper Age hunting and weapon art. (a) (opposite page) Cemmo statue-menhir, Valcamonica, note that this represents a palimpsest of imagery, probably including Bronze Age (plough motif) (Anati 1961, courtesy of E. Anati); (b) Naquane rock carvings, Valcamonica (Anati 1960, courtesy of E. Anati); and (c) Hunting scene, Porto Badisco cave paintings, Puglia (Graziosi 1974).

In some regions, hunting also increased in importance, for instance, in Copper Age Adriatic Central Italy. An increase in hunting is attested also by the rise of carefully pressure-flaked bifacial arrowheads and by representations of hunting in some rock art of the period. Such iconographic references suggest that, although increased hunting may have been related to the use of new highland areas, it also probably formed a prestigious and symbolically important activity for males (Figure 53).

The change in landscape use is clearer. In Puglia and the Materano, ditched villages rarely lasted long beyond about 5000 BC, to be replaced in the Serra d'Alto period apparently by less nucleated and delimited habitations, occasionally at the same villages [such as at the type site of Serra d'Alto (Lo Porto 1989)]. Diana period sites in these areas are far fewer (Tiné 1983; Whitehouse 1981). In eastern Calabria, Diana period sites are fewer, but also tend to be slightly larger as well (Hodder and Malone 1984; Morter 1992). Large sites on Lipari (Bernabò Brea and Cavalier 1960) and small dune sites in western Calabria (Ammerman 1985) are both probably related to the obsidian trade. Few other regions are well known. In general, throughout the Italian peninsula, fewer village sites are known for the Late and Final Neolithic; most known sites are either cave stations or funerary sites. In terms of architecture, few Diana period houses are known, though several have now been excavated [e.g., San Marco near Catania, (Maniscalco 1997; Maniscalco and Iovino 2004) and Mulino Sant'Antonio in Campania (Albore Livadie et al. 1987)]. A few Chassey-Lagozza houses are also known in Northern Italy (Bernabò Brea, Castagna, and Occhi 2003). Perhaps the most accurate way to characterise the change is simply as a final extension of the longstanding dispersed-hut tradition of settlement in areas where villages had been the norm. In compensation for the disappearance of villages, from the Diana period on, there is a common colonization of new environments, especially small islands and high mountains, a trend that continued into the Copper Age (see Chapter 3 in this book).

This pattern persists in many Eneolithic cultures. In Southern Italy, the Copper Age is known almost exclusively from cemeteries, isolated burials and caves, although Toppo Daguzzo, astride the trans-peninsula trade route on the Ofanto Valley, may have had a substantial village during this period. Almost no habitations have been excavated in Southern Italy, although a small hut with a horseshoe-shaped stone foundation, a hearth and a few pots was found at the Gaudo culture site of Contrada S. Martino (Talamo 1994). Habitation sites are equally poorly known for Tyrrhenian Central Italy (Cocchi Genick and Grifoni Cremonesi 1985; Peroni 1971), though a village of small huts has recently been excavated at Maccarese in Lazio (Manfredini 2002) and others are known around Rome (Anzidei and Carboni 2003). In Sicily, Copper Age settlement is characterised by longhouses, associated with a new pastoral use of highlands (McConnell 2003). On the eastern side of Central Italy, villages are well known: the type sites of both the Conelle and Ortucchio cultures are relatively large villages, the former located on a prominence and defended with a ditch. The Copper Age also sees an increased occupation of caves in the highlands of central Italy (Skeates 1991). In Northern Italy, data are similarly poor. A ditched village site was found adjacent to the cemetery at Remedello, but in general sites are small and imply rather brief occupations. Some were probably occupied seasonally or placed to take advantage of communication routes or local resources, such as copper, flint, or steatite (Cardarelli 1992).

Combining settlement, artefactual and faunal data, there is convincing evidence for an intensification of pastoralism from the Late Neolithic onwards, particularly in the colonization of uplands, the more intensive occupation of caves, and the attestation of spindle whorls and

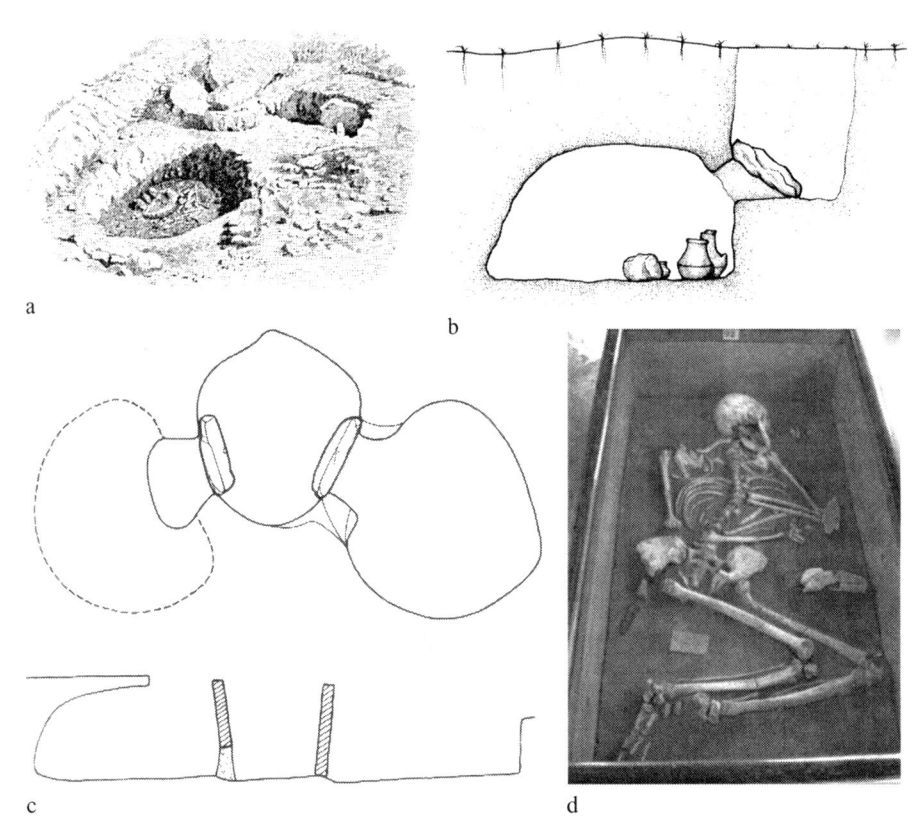

54. Copper Age burials. (a) Final Neolithic introduction of collective burials in stone cists, Masseria Bellavista, Taranto (Quagliati 1906); (b) Transitional Neolithic–Copper Age burials in small chamber tombs, Piano Vento, Sicily (redrawn after Castellana 1995); (c) Copper Age burials in small shaft-and-chamber tombs, Pontecagnano, Campania (Bailo Modesti and Salerno 1998, courtesy of G. Bailo Modesti); and (d) Single burial with status-related grave goods, Remedello (Museo Civico, Reggio Emilia; photo: Robb).

plows (Barker 1981). On the other hand, considerable evidence suggests that throughout Italian prehistory, animal products never displaced agriculture as the primary economic basis of society (Barker 1981; Barker 1985; Cazzella and Moscoloni 1992; Guidi 1992; Pellegrini 1992).

Burial, the Body, and Politics

The demise of villages is neatly paralleled by the rise of cemeteries. As the Neolithic period unfolds, experimentation with alternative forms of burial increases. In Serra d'Alto burials, both isolated burials and formal cemeteries (e.g., the Pulo di Molfetta) are known, and burials sometimes have a few grave goods. By Diana times, burial has been completely detached from settlements, and Diana burials are known in sometimes substantial cemeteries such as at Masseria Bellavista (Figure 54a). The most important Diana period innovation in burial is the collective tomb, pioneered in small stone cists which contained remains of several bodies, often with one articulated burial and rearranged bones or skulls of others [e.g., Masseria Bellavista (Quagliati 1906); Girifalco (Lucifero 1901)]. The cists sometimes contain red ochre and/or evidence of burning. Diana burials are highly varied, but the common denominator is secondary burial, which may have served as an occasion for communities to come together (Manfredini 2001).

Post-Neolithic burials develop tendencies inherent in the Final Neolithic (Figure 54). In both Sicily and peninsular Italy, Eneolithic burials appear to develop out of indigenous elements. To derive a Laterza, Gaudo, or Sicilian rock-cut tomb (Cazzella and Moscoloni 1992; Whitehouse 1972) from a Diana-Bellavista tomb, one needs only to deepen the cist into a shaft cut down into bedrock, and then add a side chamber, and this is in fact exactly what is seen at Arnesano, one of the latest Diana-Bellavista sites known. Late Neolithic burial sites are indeed difficult to distinguish from initial Copper Age sites in many areas. During the Copper Age, collective tombs were the general rule throughout peninsular Italy and Sicily, with burials known in crevices, within rock cut tombs, and within small stone cists or oven-shaped tombs. Regionally, burials show a great variety of styles (Bailo Modesti 2003, Cazzella 2003). Ochre is commonly found in graves, and was apparently applied directly to skulls at Ponte San Pietro and Sgurgola in Lazio. In both Gaudo and Rinaldone contexts, such tombs sometimes have an adult male with relatively plentiful goods as a central deposition. The two areas within which single burials are known include Conelle cemeteries in the Marche [e.g., Recanati (Galli 1950)] and Remedello cemeteries in the eastern Po valley (Bagolini 1981; Corrain 1963).

It is important to realise that these collective burials do not involve a single large tomb which draws in entire communities, but rather many small tombs in which sequential individual burials were made, each supplanting the last. They thus provide not a means of merging communities, as in Neolithic megalithic tombs elsewhere in Europe, but a grid individuating members of the community positionally in segments and temporal sequences. Socially, their affinity is not with Neolithic megalithic collective tombs but with contemporary and later Remedello, Corded Ware and Beaker cemeteries of individual burials organised with a clear horizontal structure.

What of the body and its representations? Very few figurines are known from Diana or contemporary contexts. It is unclear whether this reflects a real change in cultural practices, or merely a shift in excavated contexts from villages to caves and burial sites. Once into the Copper Age, the situation clearly changes (Figure 55). Except for a few odd, one-off figures such as the two pebbles carved with female features from Busonè, Sicily (Graziosi 1974), female figurines vanish. Two male figurines are known, from Piano Vento, Sicily (Castellana 1995) and Ortucchio in the Abruzzo (Radmilli 1997), though these are isolated occurrences rather than part of a connected pattern.

Instead, figurines are increasingly supplemented or replaced by two other forms of representation. One is rock art. Rock painting is known from Porto Badisco (cf. Chapter 3), Levanzo and a few other poorly dated sites in the south and the central Apennines. Rock carvings are known from many places in the Alps; the greatest concentration is found in Valcamonica and Valtellina. A few rock carvings date to the Neolithic, but the real florescence begins in the Eneolithic (Anati 1961, 1977; Priuli 1985). For the next two millennia, the dominant iconography in art represents daggers, axes, stags and other animals, sometimes arranged in large scenes with dozens of repeating images. Some rock compositions appear to be laid out to represent a schematic anthropomorphic design similar to the stelae found at this period in the Alto Adige and in Switzerland (Figure 55e). These stelae and the rock compositions sometimes have a "solar disc" in the head region, a necklace ornamented with a double-spiral, and various daggers and axes. The repertory of imagery shifts with time; new Bronze and Iron Age elements probably include ploughs, carts, battle scenes, warriors mounted on horses, and strange "topographic" compositions thought to be a kind of map. Throughout later prehistory, however, weapons continue to be a common and stereotyped representation.

The other new genre of body representation is monumental statuary. The earliest examples of this are two small stone statues of human heads on an undifferentiated, ungendered, cylindrical body, from widely separated Late Neolithic sites in Puglia (Arnesano)(Lo Porto 1972) and near Verona (Sant'Anna di Alfaedo) (Graziosi 1974). Although the Arnesano and Alfaedo statues, at 35 and 31 cm, respectively, are hardly monumental, they are significantly larger than any Neolithic figurines and clearly form a transition between hand-held statuary and human representations which were presumably stationary or fixed in place. Slightly later, the Copper Age sees the appearance of stelae with cosmological or human attributes (Ambrosi 1972; Fedele 1990; Graziosi 1974). These early examples from Lagundo and Valcamonica combine cosmological symbols, representations of artefacts such as weapons, pendants and necklaces, and animals in a vaguely anthropomorphic form, but they are soon supplanted by a much more standardised human form in a series such as the Lunigiana stelae. Statue-stelae are basically flat rectangular stone slabs with a human head and upper torso carved in a rigid and stylised bas relief; often recognizable and datable types of weapon and ornament are shown. This begins a tradition of stelae which lasts through the Iron Age in Italy and is clearly related to contemporary stelae in France, Spain, and elsewhere in Europe. Statue-stelae throughout Europe utilise a much more standardised template for representing the human body, which relates to a more standardised conception of social actors (see below). The stelae are almost always gendered through symbols such as necklaces and weapons; these images are mutually exclusive and ornaments are associated strongly with breasts (Ambrosi 1972, 1988; Whitehouse 1992).

The stelae's function is unknown, and as most have been found accidentally during construction work or plowing, contextual evidence is badly lacking. They seem to have been erected in open countryside between settlements, sometimes in groups; one such group has been excavated at Osimo (Fedele 1990). They sometimes mark transit routes such as passes, and as "stones of memory" (Maggi 2001) they may have marked territories or cleared areas where humans intervened in the landscape. One interpretation, predictably, has been that the females represent the Mother Goddess and are derived from Eastern Mediterranean prototypes, although the males represents supernatural heroes or

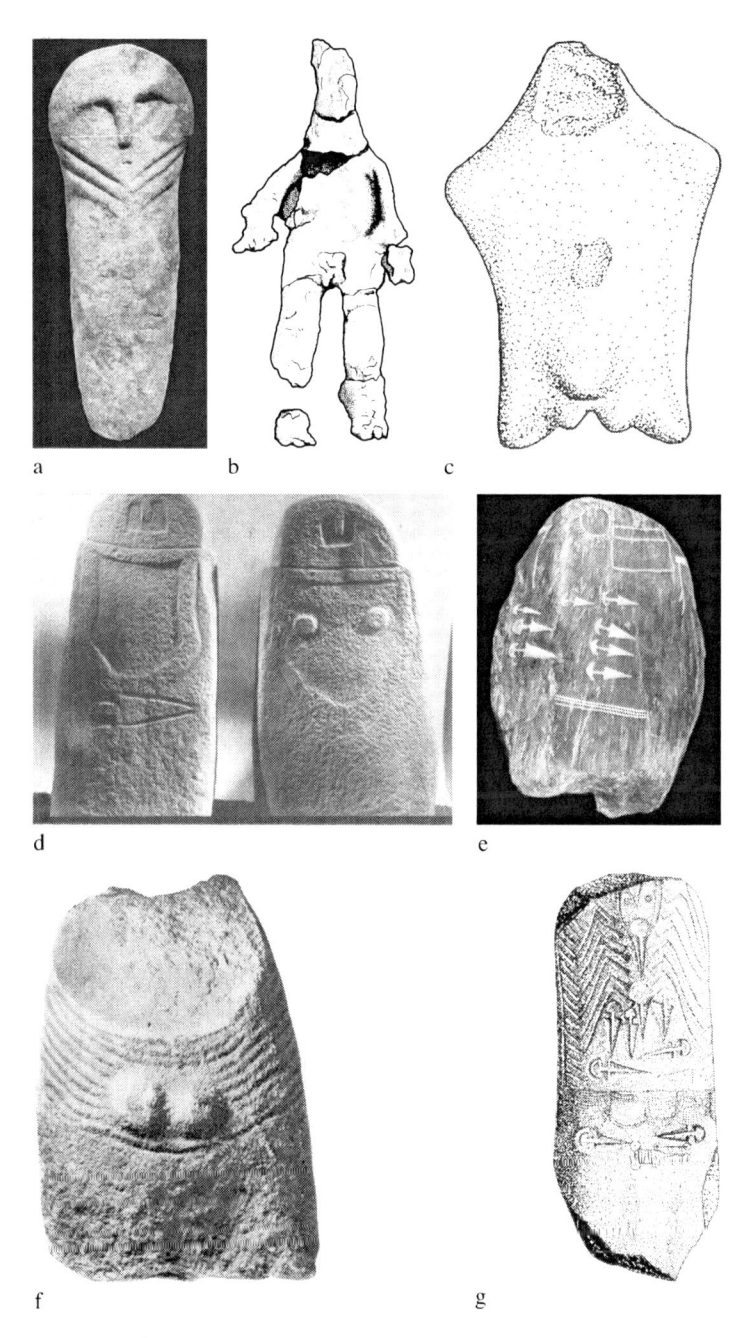

55. Copper Age human representations. (a) Stone statue from final Neolithic tomb, Arnesano, Puglia (Graziosi 1974); (b) Large male clay figurine from ritual deposition, Piano Vento, Sicily (redrawn after Castellana 1995); (c) Male figurine, Ortucchio, Fucino basin, Abruzzo (Irti 1992, courtesy of U. Irti); (d) Male and female statue-stelae, Lunigiana (Museo Civico, La Spezia; photo: Robb); (e) Menhir-stela, Bagnolo, Valcamonica (Graziosi 1974); (f) Female statue-stela, Lagundo (Graziosi 1974); and (g) Male statue-stela, Lagundo (Graziosi 1974). Not to scale.

309

solar deities (Formentini 1991; Laviosa Zambotti 1938). Ambrosi (1972) proposed that the Lunigiana stelae represented tutelary spirits or ancestors associated with places, and Peroni (1971) interprets them as ancestral figures. They show both a concern for monumentalisation of the human form, probably for political reasons as ancestors (Keates 2000), and consistent gender attributes which will remain stable through at least through the Bronze Age and in some cases right down to the historic period – weapons for males, and breasts and necklaces for females.

Iconography is not the only evidence for changes in the body around the end of the Neolithic. Although actual skeletal evidence is too sparse to tell much, grave goods show new patterns. In the Late Neolithic, grave goods are too infrequent to be very informative. Grave goods from all peninsular Copper Age cultures include arrowheads, spear points, and daggers of copper, bronze, flint, and bone. Projectile points became elaborated and finely worked, and pressure-flaked daggers represent the apogee of Holocene flint working as an art form. In Northern Italy, weapons were deposited with burials in some Copper Age cultures, particularly the Remedello culture of the Po Valley, as well as for most Bronze Age cultures. This stands in sharp contrast to the Neolithic, and begins a tradition of weaponry as grave goods which lasts through the Iron Age. Although collective inhumations mar the associations between individuals and grave goods in much of Italy, Remedello culture cemeteries normally mirror the association between males and weaponry encountered in stelae.

Late Neolithic and Copper Age political structure cannot be called politically or economically stratified. There is little convincing evidence for the accumulation of wealth or material capital (such as mortuary differentiation, architectural differentiation, or large scale irrigation and land improvement) or political centralization (such as settlement hierarchies, within-site architectural differentiation, full-time craft specialization). The same is true for aspects of ideological control such as large-scale ceremonial architecture, for instance. Instead, we see generally uniform burial goods, combined with the circulation of exotic materials and prestige goods. Eneolithic society was thus characterised by a developed economy for the circulation of prestige goods and by little formal political and economic stratification. For this reason, aside from occasional speculation upon sporadic burials with many grave goods such as the "capo tribù" from Gaudo (Barker 1981), virtually all prehistorians who have considered the question have dubbed Eneolithic and earlier Bronze Age societies tribes of some form (Cazzella and Moscoloni 1985; Cazzella and Moscoloni 1992; Guidi 1992, 2000; Peroni 1979).

The Great Simplification

This sequence of change resists the common frames archaeologists have tried to build around it. There is too much continuity to represent any large-scale replacement of population. Nor does it lend itself to any clear narrative about increasing social hierarchy, or for that matter, decreasing hierarchy. Rather, a complex picture emerges when the changes outlined above are characterised in social rather than archaeological terms.

Social Production and Intensifying Pastoralism

Why intensify pastoralism? There is no evidence at all that Neolithic populations had reached a density which required the development of new sources of food. Indeed, given the relative space needs of the different productive activities, the most direct way to reap more calories per square kilometer would simply be to herd, hunt and gather less and farm more (see Chapter 3 in this book).

Intensification is the adoption of technology and practices which allow a higher overall level of production. As any computer-user knows, new "labor-saving" technologies often do not actually reduce the total amount of time or work, but allow one to produce more overall output; you still type all day, but with the software upgrade you can now insert dynamically linked pictures in your footnotes! Intensification is thus more likely to happen under conditions when there is a strong social impetus to produce more, rather than simply to reduce labor: a "pull" rather than "push" situation. Nowhere is this clearer than in the Neolithic. With the possible exceptions of plowing and woolly sheep, no productive technology was available at the end of the Neolithic that had not already been known for at least a millennium before. The key limiting factor on how much and what was produced in the Neolithic was not land for farming or for pasture, particularly as many highland tracts were still uncolonised. Instead, the limit to growth was probably the amount of labor which could be mobilised for production purposes. Ethnographically, tribespeople tend not to overproduce beyond a certain safety margin (Sahlins 1968, 1972). The barrier lies in the ethic of generosity: people who amass a surplus are expected to redistribute it, and accumulators run the risk of ostracism and social sanctions. Indeed, in a world in which security and identity derive primarily from social relationships rather than from the accumulation of capital, this may be the best strategy as well; there is little outside the immediate social game to accumulate for. The circulation of goods within the community is also embedded in social relations; instead of "pure ownership" in which a producer has an absolute right to dispose of surplus, a producer finds that goods are already subject to strong expectations as to how they will be used within a complex web of debts and obligations, each with norms for proper mode, goods and time of payment.

One precondition for intensification, then, is an increased demand for overproduction, and this both happens in response to, and requires, new forms of social relationship. This underlies the simultaneous development of a prestige goods economy and various intensifications such as plow agriculture and pastoralism throughout prehistoric Europe. Yet this does not in itself explain why pastoralism particularly should be the medium of this intensification in Italy. There are a number of practical reasons why a given product should be intensifiable. Some products are self-limiting. Hunted game, though it was symbolically valued, tends to have diminishing returns in the face of increased exploitation. Although vines and olives are known in prehistoric Italy (Hopf 1991), intensive polyculture requires domesticated versions, political centralization guaranteeing the long-term security of orchards, and developed transportation, roads or markets. Moreover, the symbolic associations of a product are also important in motivating production for exchange. Given these restrictions, the two most obvious possibilities for intensification were small or localised valuables tradable over long distances and animals. Traceable networks in metals and stone may have been paralleled by other networks in, salt, fish, game, or other specialised craft items, such as pots, bows, stone axes, and containers. Textiles probably also afforded an easily transported, regionally differentiable product whose value would reflect additional labor put into manufacturing.

Pastoralism, in contrast, was a direct development of Neolithic habitus, the meanings of foods. In Chapter 4, we argued that different Neolithic foods carried different social meanings, with grain associated with household solidarity and meat with intergroup relatedness. If so, this would explain why the focus of Copper Age intensification was pastoralism: the novel development of the animal economy and its products to relate people into more extended social networks rested upon a much more ancient cultural preference.

Place and Relatedness

Some clue to the nature of new social relations is given by Late Neolithic and Copper Age landscapes. The cultural structuring of space is a way of creating physical history, concrete embodiments of beliefs about the nature of the social group, and its origin. As discussed above, among the most striking features of the Late Neolithic is the transformation of the architectural landscape. The Early and Middle Neolithic landscape was a landscape of villages and hamlets; the Late, and Final Neolithic, landscape was a "landscape of the dead," not only for archaeologists but probably also for Neolithic people in some meaningful sense as well.

In the Early and Middle Neolithic, both in areas of nucleated villages and in areas of dispersed settlements, the emphasis was upon the architectural definition of the community, and the placement of burials helped to define the history of the group as isomorphic with that of the village. This implies that the primary means of ascribing group identity and structuring interaction was coresidence, which coincided with a constructed common history centering on the village. In the Late Neolithic and the Eneolithic, the shift to a highly dispersed settlement pattern coincides with the rise of formal cemeteries. Such cemeteries provided space-fixing and time-stretching practices: for the first time burial structures in some cultures were visible above ground, and customs such as skull conservation and multiple burial became widespread. It is in this connection that the interpretations of stelae as ancestral figures marking a historicised landscape make sense.

In the Late Neolithic, the tie between coresidence and sharing a common history and identity split apart. The causes may have been many. Intensified production systems may have favored dispersed settlements in some regions, and new intervillage relations may have allowed them by providing cross-cutting alliances and systems of compensation as a means of containing raiding and feuding, a social substitute for the physical protection of nucleated groups living behind ditches and palisades (Feil 1987). Moreover, genealogy offered several advantages over coresidence in a dynamic system of exchange and alliance, principally its flexibility and ability to integrate much wider groups. At the same time, mapping the group's history via a structured assemblage of individual burials or small group tombs allows people to focus their relations via specific individuals or kin groups (Barrett 1994; Thomas 1999). Co-residence was relatively static and inflexible way of relating people. In contrast, genealogical structures less rigidly tied to settlements would have been flexibly extendible through the "discovery" of kin links, more easily remodeled to suit present contingencies, and more conducive to useful alliances via intermarriage. They made close relatedness spatially extendible in a way coherent with the extension of settlement discussed above. In an atmosphere in which competitive exchange was increasingly important to status, such manipulation may have been a key to making long-range contacts and to mobilizing labor and production for exchange. Access to scattered pastures, accumulating contributions for ceremonial exchanges and finding useful kin in neighboring societies may have been among the benefits.

In this context, communal tombs served as physical repositories of the common history of the group, a function formerly served by the village itself, burials and all. As a spatial means of defining society, they worked on two levels. Within the landscape, their position probably related a group's identity to its territory, giving it roots. Within the cemetery, the segmentary structure created by the nesting of earlier compounds within ditched villages was recreated, with the varied communal tombs bearing an analogous structural relation to the whole cemetery. The result was collective history activated as strategic idiom; a dynamic innovation rooted in timeless tradition (Robb 1994).

Gendered Bodies

These changes were clearly gendered, a fact reflected in a long archaeological tradition of linking them to male power. Traditional archaeological narratives characterised the "Indo-Europeans" and Copper Age pastoralists in general as patriarchical and warlike (Gimbutas 1991). Economic versions link the social role of Copper and Bronze Age males with their role in plowing (Ehrenberg 1989; Sherratt 1981), though it is clear neither why gender status should be derived principally from economic tasks, nor why such tasks should be gendered as they are. Postprocessualists, seeing gender as situational, multiple and nuanced, have generally avoided the question of broad-scale, "essentialising" change in gender ideologies. Yet, gender symbols and roles often form a part of the widespread vocabulary of ethnographic culture areas (Mediterranean peasant societies in Europe provide a classic example); they provide the essential matter which can be contested and reinterpreted. Treherne's (1995) discussion of the Bronze Age "warrior's beauty" provides a rare broad-brush interpretation of gender in later European prehistory.

For Copper Age Italy, gender symbolizations are both abundant and clear. Grave goods assemblages and stelae in particular suggest that human bodies were dichotomised into standard male and female types. The picture is much clearer and more familiar to us than that for the Neolithic, a fact reflected historically in the layers of interpretations which have claimed fourth and third millennia Europe as a founding ancestor for modern Europe. For males, weapons are the key symbol (Robb 1994). They were relevant to many contexts. They must have been carried or worn in daily life as a sort of male jewelry. They required participation in trade, to procure exotic metals and perhaps to exchange finished products, which might account for wide regional similarities in their form. They formed an important element defining a body in death in funerary assemblages. Where rock art is found, it often represents males with weapons, or even more frequently, merely the weapons themselves, evidently able as a single motif to summarise powerful meanings. Weapons normally form the only diacritic identifying males in stelae. Although weapons were presumably used for hunting or violence on occasion, the weapon's status as a key symbol is also apparent in the widespread appearance of possibly nonfunctional weapons [such as early copper daggers too soft to actually use as piercing weapons (Holloway 1974) and skeumorphs of flint and even bone (Barfield 1986)]. The association of maleness, weapon use and hunting probably had a long Neolithic pedigree, and Neolithic social life surely involved armed conflict (see Chapter 2 in this book); what is novel is the foregrounding of the use of weaponry in interhuman conflict as a social idiom.

Other, less apparently related fields of activity become genderised as well. In post-Neolithic times, cranial trauma becomes markedly more common in males than in females (Robb 1997), and the vast majority of trepanned individuals were males (Germanà and Fornaciari 1992). Significantly, although some genres of ritual unrelated to male prestige symbolism generally went defunct – the most notable example is the disappearance of small female figurines – genres which flourished in this period were symbolically tied to male prestige symbols; for instance, the Alpine petroglyphs.

One coherent reading of this evidence is in terms of a structural inequality based on gender ideology, an unbalanced opposition in which males were the principal reproducers of social value – in Collier and Rosaldo's (1981) phrase, "Man the Hunter and Woman" (Robb 1994). As Whitehead (1987, pp. 259–60) points out, ideologies of male potency often equate "the capacity for creating social connections through exchange and the power to convey 'life' or 'vitality.'" Weapons would have served to mediate relations in a range of male domains such as hunting, fighting, and exchange. Yet, there are at least three grounds for questioning such an interpretation. First, the deceptive familiarity of Copper and Bronze Age gender symbols makes it dangerously easy to map modern gender assumptions onto these periods – for instance, to assume that weapons pertain to important political processes while ornaments were "merely for display," or that women were automatically dependent upon males to obtain traded valuables. Second, there is no evidence for systematic material inequality between genders. Females are equally represented in burial contexts and stelae, and they are defined with valuables such as metal ornaments which are equally inserted into contexts of display and exchange. Finally, assuming pervasive gender inequalities may misrepresent the relations between the regional and the local, between structural possibilities and experienced actualities. To use Mediterranean ethnography as an example once again, even in societies with explicit discursive dogmas of gender inequality such as the famous Mediterranean "honor and shame" complex (Peristiany 1966), people may reinterpret such structures to question and contest these and to create alternative forms of authority (Bell 1974, Delamont 1995). Gender ideologies which ascribe special value to males are present in many tribal societies. Yet, many classic ethnographic examples of these, such as the Gebusi (Knauft 1985) and the Etoro (Kelly 1993), lack features of Late Neolithic and Eneolithic society such as economic intensification, high intervillage communication and extensive trade networks. Stereotypical Big Man societies of the Central Highlands often have less extensive gender antagonism, as expressed through avoidance taboos, beliefs about female impurity and contamination, and elaborate male initiation rites, than smaller, less dynamic Eastern Highlands Great Man societies (Feil 1987; Jorgenson 1991).

Agency, Aesthetics, and the Organization of Value: A New Synaesthesia

Rather than evidencing a new, pervasive gender hegemony, what the Late Neolithic and Copper Age evidence really demonstrates is the emergence of new ways of organizing persons; males with their weapons stand as the clearest example, but females also exhibit new, cross-context symbolisms linking activities such as spinning, economic roles, aesthetic creation (e.g., in dress and in cloth production), the body (in ornamentation) and social value.

During the Early and Middle Neolithic, it was argued above (see Chapters 2 and 6 in this book), the absence of eminent social persons in the archaeological record is not because people were unvalued, nor that their activities were unimportant. Rather, the disparate forms of value or prestige created through different activities were not organised around unitary kinds of value associated with social prominence. This was associated with an aesthetic reflex to create difference, evident in the heterarchies of pottery design, in fragmented local communities of ritual practice, and in multiple ways of configuring representations of the human body.

From the Late Neolithic, the situation shifts. Rather than value being ranged in incommensurate domains, there is the emergence of idioms of value which spanned many fields of action. Symbolic life in the Copper Age appears to have been organised around a handful of redundant, mutually reinforcing symbols which turn up in many different contexts. Hunting, warfare and violence have already been mentioned as contexts of weapon use. Trade is another one: as noted, one of the most prominent characteristics of Final Neolithic and Eneolithic society is a greatly increased level of trade and exchange. Economic production was at least partly geared to the procurement of exotic, prestigious goods such as obsidian, flint, greenstone axes, metals and possibly perishable goods; these goods appear to have been circulated and consumed rather than accumulated as permanent wealth. Pastoralism formed part of the pattern. Neolithic herds were social valuables whose circulation defined social units and the relations between them and whose consumption marked occasions of political relatedness. The spatial broadening of relatedness evident in Late Neolithic and Copper Age pastoralism is echoed in broader relations of trade and, through burial, affinity.

What emerges, therefore, is a new, generalised form of prestige or value which spans and binds together many fields of action, and which provides the clear standard of valuation evident in grave assemblages in this period both in Italy and across Europe. It is a form of personhood in which fields of action such as hunting, violence, and participating in extended networks of trade and labor are not kept apart but merged into a generalised social "centrality"; leaders of this period may have played a role as "relationship brokers" among kin, fellow villagers, and trading partners. As an evolutionary change, this did not necessarily involve the invention of new gender ideologies or sources of value, nor yet the rise of hierarchy. It is paradoxical to regard it even as the "emergence of individuals," because it creates a class of people who are fundamentally much more uniform than their Neolithic predecessors need have been. Indeed, the introduction of a cross-context social currency substituted, for Neolithic heterarchy, a combination of structurally simpler social relations with potentially more complex social strategies. By making value from different fields of activity potential equivalent, it allowed agents to compete for parity [in Fried's (1967, p. 79) apt phrase], a new form of heterarchy which laid the basis for future hierarchies.

As organizing principles for social action, these worked through the bodies of agents. The standardised bodily templates for stelae evident across Northern Italy from the Copper Age on suggest a much more uniform and formulaic way of seeing the body, in which the lower body was elided and relations between the upper body and head were more or less fixed. The use of material items such as ornaments and weapons to denote specific kinds of bodies implies that bodies were basically unfinished until completed through the addition of goods produced socially through exchange. Moreover, the essential valuables of the new system – weapons and ornaments – were items whose relationship with their users generated gestures, attitudes, and social personae; they imply a hexis (Bourdieu 1977), a habitus enacted through an entire system of bodily comportment.

A different aspect of habitus, though still bodily, is seen with aesthetic reflexes underlying things like pottery design. Late Neolithic and Copper Age vessels are not made with less skill, effort or technical success than earlier pots, but they aim at a different aesthetic. It is no accident that Diana pottery from Sicily to the Abruzzo is distinguished by stereotypical handles which can be typologised by beginners at twenty paces. Lagozza pottery is uniform across much of central and northern Italy, and even in the Copper Age, groups such as Gaudo and Rinaldone nevertheless share a general surface appearance and set of vessel forms. Earlier pottery aimed to create difference. The fundamental aesthetic transformation of the Late Neolithic and Copper Age is that plain burnished surfaces establish a single, common standard of valuation, with a criterion of competence and adequacy rather than individuation. The creation of similarity we see in pot decoration is mirrored by increasingly extensive long-distance trade centered around a handful of widely recognised valuables, the spread of uniform kits of burial goods, and the emergence of more unitary principles of relating people, such as the genealogical links implied by new cemeteries of secondary burials.

But pottery decoration does not provide a simple or functional reflection of politics. They span what must have been distinct ethnic groups – a sort of anti-ethnic pottery (if localizable anywhere archaeologically, Copper Age ethnicity should probably be looked for in burial and ritual practices). Nor, as pots of everyday use in egalitarian societies, can they be seen as restricted, prestigious symbolizations of value. Instead, it is probably most useful to see pottery decoration simply on its own terms, as an aesthetic reflex, a visual analogue for a specific way of, literally, seeing social value. Reflective brilliance is often seen as a visual correlate of social prominence (Saunders 2002). Here, perhaps, we draw a linkage between social prominence and the reflective play of light, something uncommon in both the natural world and the matte-surfaced Neolithic visual panorama, but part of European tradition ever since (Keates 2002). According to this logic, the important aspect of metals was their materiality. Beyond their visual qualities and their socially embedded chains of procurement and exchange discussed above, metals' malleability and transformability meant that, like a generalised human value, they could be refashioned and circulated among different forms and contexts in a way impossible with highly channeled material productions such as obsidian. There may also have been specialised knowledge and belief surrounding their transformations; we know nothing of this for Copper Age Italy, but rich ethnographic data from Africa and the New World shows that metallurgy is often laden with dense cosmological and gendered symbolisms (Herbert 1994; Hosler 1995; Reid and MacLean 1995). Metals were thus, in Gell's (1992) term, a "technology of enchantment" which helped usher in a new sensory-social world. In aesthetic reflexes linking colours, gestures and means of social categorization, the basis was laid for a new synaesthesia. Together with metals, Late Neolithic and Copper Age pots usher in the Age of Shine.

Processes of Change

Always in Transition

Frustrating as we may find it, there was no simple "before" and "after," no on-off switch or single point of transition. The archaeological data summarised above have to be sorted out into at least three distinct moments of change. First, some changes appear to begin in the early-to-mid-fifth millennium (e.g., between Early-Middle Neolithic groups and Serra d'Alto groups). These include the abandonment of villages, a rising interest in trade, and sporadic burial innovation. Second, with this as a gradual ramp, many of the most fundamental changes happen in the Late Neolithic, in the later fifth and earlier fourth millennium:

interregional trade, an increase in pastoralism, a change in aesthetic reflexes manifested in pottery, new settlement and new burial practices such as collective tombs. Finally, from about the mid-fourth millennium, metals definitively supplant traditional exchanged items such as obsidian, grave goods appear, and collective burial becomes the norm almost everywhere in Italy.

Along with such changes (which must have proceeded with different tempos in different areas) there were fundamental continuities of tradition. Almost all basic economic and technological practices continued throughout this period with only changes in emphasis. Societies throughout this span continued to lack coercive apparatus and ecological circumscription, a fact which curtailed their variation within the "tribal envelope" (see final section below). Many sites, particularly in caves, show continuous occupation across much of the span. Precursors can be found for almost every innovation. For example, Copper Age social weaponry is prefigured by the Neolithic Porto Badisco rock art of archers hunting; weapon use provides a continuous thread, though the shift from representing people using weapons to hunt to foregrounding actual conflict was surely an important change. The common use of red ochre in Late Neolithic and Copper Age burials descends from its uses on Neolithic habitation sites. Copper Age burials visibly descend from Late Neolithic ones, much as Late Neolithic burials owe much to Middle Neolithic ones. Similarly, traditional Neolithic trade goods such as obsidian and stone axes persisted until the end of the Neolithic, well after other important changes were well underway.

What we see, between about 5000 and 3000 BC is thus not a flip from black to white, but rather movement through a spectrum in which each colour has visible continuities with colours on either side of it. Change happened in degrees, without abrupt ruptures, even when the aggregate transformation over long epochs was dramatic. As this suggests, we must problematise the notion of transition, which is normally defined teleologically as part of an "origins" story of reaching a final state. It is the frame we construct which defines the Late Neolithic as transitional between the Early-Middle Neolithic and the Copper Age, rather than (say) seeing the Early-Middle Neolithic as "transitional" between the Mesolithic and the Late Neolithic. To put it another way, Italian prehistory was *always* in transition. Moreover, we must consider the human scale of time. The "Late Neolithic" lasted from sometime in the later fifth millennium to sometime in the earlier fourth millennium, an overall duration of at least 600 years and at most a millennium. The tradition of archaeological storytelling summarised in designations such as "Late Neolithic" and "Final Neolithic" almost compels us to see it as a transitional, dynamic phase of change, an unstable bridge between two enduring ways of life. But this "transitional" period was close to as long as the periods it linked. In human terms, this is around eighteen to twenty-four generations; in social time of memory and group continuity, it was a stable, normal eternity.

This pattern of change has important implications for how we try to explain the changes. It makes any migration theory of change improbable, unless we imagine the migrants arriving in carefully staged phases bearing different parts of their culture over at least a millennium. In fact, this applies to virtually any explanation which requires that the major changes be concurrent; it thus makes any simple monocausal interpretation of the change unlikely. On the other hand, the pattern of protracted, gradual changes building upon each other, interlaced with continuities and difficult to divide into neat periodisations, is entirely consonant with the model of long term change as historical practice presented above.

Re-Reading the Sequence

Without a single prime mover, explaining these changes requires understanding the interplay of social reproduction, the circumstances of action, and the cumulative consequences of action. Needless to say, if, by some archaeological miracle, the data were adequate to this task, it would be a huge project in itself; what is presented here is essentially a theoretical model of how the process may have unfolded which is consonant with the evidence reviewed above.

Early-Middle Neolithic Italian society was reproduced through many fields of action, different routes to value (see Chapter 6 in this book). It is likely that this pattern extended to modes of leadership as well; multiple forms of leadership coexist as alternative strategies in most tribal societies (Godelier 1991; Lemonnier 1991; Liep 1991). It was also suggested above that different forms of value deriving from a range of activities would have both existed in tension (for instance between those relating identity to locality and those deriving from trans-local sources) and would have been integrated within biographies, institutions, and chains of activity. The result was a pattern of Neolithic life remarkably stable through at least a millennium.

Such a system was resistant to change in many ways, but susceptible to being destabilised in others. Our account of the initial phase of change is based upon areas of village-based settlement, as the period 5000–4500 BC is too poorly researched in areas of dispersed settlement. The two key changes are the abandonment of villages, and an increasing interest in trade. These were related: ethnographic comparisons in Melanesia show a close linkage between generalised leadership, dispersed settlement, extended trade systems, exchange, and the containment of conflict via institutions such as compensation payments and peacemaking, even when the symbolism of fighting becomes more widespread and socially prominent (Feil 1987; Knauft 1987, 1991). If villages, and particularly ditched villages, suggest endemic hostility and the need for defense, leaving such villages would involve more developed ways to mediate and negotiate relations between groups. The fascinating aspect of this period of incipient change, however, is the attempt to maintain continuity evident in three spheres of activity. One is an increasing intensity of idiosyncratic ritual activities in the course of the fifth millennium – the Grotta Scaloria lower cave, the Ipogeo Manfredi hunting cult, the figurines representing prominent beings at Cala Scizzo, the Grotta Pacelli, and Baselice, and an increasing cult use of caves in general. The second is pottery: even as spheres of interaction became more widespread, pottery continues the long tradition of ornate decoration; Serra d'Alto finewares, and trichromes elsewhere, represent the magnificent culmination of this tradition. Finally, abandoning villages strained the traditional system of constituting coidentity through association of places of residence and the buried dead. Experiments with alternative forms of burial in caves and cemeteries were a way of coping with this situation, and particularly in sites such as Serra d'Alto, Serra Cicora, and the Pulo di Molfetta: this is the principal period in which we see the striking pattern of burial at sites no longer occupied (see Chapter 3 in this book) – an innovation which maintained traditions of community in the face of changing settlement patterns.

The most florid aspects of the transition between the Middle and Late Neolithic, thus, can be understood as a system of Neolithic oppositions — between exchange and burial, between dispersed settlement and residential identity — creaking under the tension of change. But these changes also would have had other consequences: the increased polarization of local and translocal values, the increased relaxation of constraints on exchange, and the promotion of new and more flexible criteria for group relationship. These were the essential preconditions for Late Neolithic developments. The most important Late Neolithic development was the linkage of several fields of action into a coherent and enduring structure: pastoralism as a way of exploiting wider landscapes via spatially extended labor networks, meat as the culinary idiom of relatedness within this system, and genealogy as a way of constructing understandings of relatedness. Among the new idioms established was a redefined role for burial, which now served spatially extended rather than localised relatedness. The release from coresidence as a criterion for relatedness may have lifted a major barrier to the growth of spatially extensive economies. The casualties in this transfer of functions were traditional practices of the creation of relatedness via residential taskscapes and the creation of difference in aesthetic practices such as pottery decoration. The extension of similar aesthetic reflexes to formerly disparate fields of action such as pottery decoration suggests that change was not limited to one category of actors but shared generally.

However, in this "transitional" period some 600 years long, action still involved traditional media such as obsidian and greenstone, and value was not personalised in the figures of eminent males and females familiar from Copper Age burials and stelae. Rather, the situation may have been much as Strathern (Strathern 1991, p. 210) describes, with central figures leading by transforming themselves in to embodiments of the collective will of the group: "the agency we tend to attribute to Big Men as self-interest, political self-aggrandisement or striving for prestige is inadequately likened to possessive individualism in so far as that misses the transformation of the big man himself."

This time, however, action had more extensive and visible consequences. Environmentally, clearance, pastures and settlement in new areas would presumably have built up gradually through the later fifth and fourth millennia (see Chapter 3 in this book). There may also have been demographic, environmental, and economic consequences which our poor data for this period are inadequate to outline. As Sherratt (1984) and Gilman (1981) have pointed out, economic changes linked to intensification themselves exert transformative effects. One critical threshold might have occurred when demand for production began to cause transformations of scale. The increase of caprovines may have kicked herd size above the threshold at which further herd increase is rapid and dependable. Increased production of high-calorie pastoral products would likely result in better childhood survival and population growth. This in turn would require that once-optional levels of production be maintained constantly. The population as a whole, therefore, would find itself increasingly locked into an integrated economic system and the ideological system underwriting it.

Structurally, the principal result was that social action happened through a series of aligned and closely interrelated institutions rather than opposed or balanced ones: a configuration structurally simpler but more generalised, and appropriately underwritten by a more interconvertible idea of value – the "great simplification" discussed above, which supplanted former heterarchies in politics and aesthetics. An accompanying structural consequence was, apparently, a loss of alternative styles and strategies for doing things, the ambiguities and tensions of the former period. This may have been an important precondition in the personalization of value in the subsequent Copper Age. Another important development, through both pottery and the first experiments with metal, was the concept of aesthetic qualities such as shine, perhaps associated with social presentation according to a standard of interchangeable adequacy – a basic precondition for the widespread adoption of metals to symbolise and circulate this value.

By the mid-fourth millennium, all the preconditions were in place for the final, associated changes into Copper Age society: the substitution of metals for earlier valuables, the intensification of collective burial, and the gendered personalization of value attested in standard grave goods kits. Inasmuch as there was an endogenous trigger, it was probably the effects of substituting metals for stone as trade valuables. This visibly altered landscapes such as Lipari (see Chapter 7 above) and ore-bearing regions of Lazio, Toscana, and Liguria. More significantly, metals and stones were not decontextualised valuables. The shift from obsidian to metals supplanted a relatively low-profile genre of action in restricted contexts using a material whose use life was short and inherently limited with one which involved much more public, personal display used in more contexts, and which could be recast into many forms and circulated indefinitely. Such considerations in part explain why people may have actually made the switch from other valuables to metals, rather than simply rejecting metals: because the material characteristics of metals corresponded much more closely to the emerging concept of generalised social value.

Causality and Spread

The interpretation above offers, as explanation, a summary theoretical representation of this sequence, a story without obvious causal protagonists. It must be admitted that virtually no detailed environmental, demographic or economic reconstruction has been done for this period of Italian and Sicilian prehistory. This leaves a great lacuna in both our ability to find external triggers for social change and to observe its unforeseen environmental and economic consequences, which must surely have been substantial over the spans of time discussed here. This is undeniably a serious limitation. The only detailed environmental evidence available, from the Tavoliere, suggests that Late Neolithic and Copper Age climate was drier than in earlier periods, with coastal lagoons drying out. Such changes could have had serious effects on human life and, in this case, may have been related to the apparent Late Neolithic abandonment of the Tavoliere (Boenzi et al. 2001; Caldara, Pennetta, and Simone 2002).

Nevertheless, as discussed above, such "external" changes will have been refracted through local cultural structures. For example, crowding in areas such as the Tavoliere and the Adriatic lowlands would probably be experienced most directly not as an insufficiency of food but as a restricting of hunting areas or pastures and as difficulty in fulfilling social obligations requiring game and animals. Similarly, an increase in the unpredictability of crop success might have placed a greater premium upon extra-group relations as an insurance policy (Halstead and O'Shea

1982). In such circumstances, even a relatively minor environmental change, well below the threshold of archaeological visibility, may have been important. However, such changes may have varied greatly from region to region; the real question is why such variations, should have had the effects they did at the moments when they did. And this is a question about context which we can hope to answer.

As preliminary causal hypotheses, it is clear that different factors were effective at different points. The initial shift away from Middle Neolithic village life towards dispersed settlement and trade may have been spurred by a changing attitude towards intergroup exchange. The shift to the Late Neolithic way of life represents a gradual but much more thoroughgoing transformation and may be best characterised as the incremental accumulation of changes set in action several centuries earlier. The trigger for the development of specific characteristics of the Copper Age per se seems to have been the introduction of metals, though even here technology cannot be isolated as a simple, exogenous trigger for change. The path of change was shaped not mechanistically by the presence of inert ores, or voluntaristically by entrepreneurial humans, but by the relationship between humans and metals. In this view, metals, as a social commodity, were effectively called into existence by the kind of value associated with them, and as this occurred, they helped to redefine value and how value was represented and circulated. In other words, it was the materiality rather than technology of metals which was important in causing change.

If causality therefore resides not in people, material things, or environments, but in the relations between them, the same is true for relations between groups. Contact between groups has traditionally been invoked as a *deus ex machina* causing changes such as the spread of new ways of life. In reaction, recent Anglo-American archaeological theory has tended to reject contact as a factor (emphasizing indigenous agency in recent views of both Neolithicization and colonial contact). Yet, looking only within societies for the roots of change limits how far we can explain coordinated or convergent changes on broader scales. The answer lies in the mutual constitution of political relationships between communities, the fact that internally generated courses of action depend on knowledge and conditions partly set by those with whom one interacts. A simple parable is the famous "prisoner's dilemma" in game theory, in which two prisoners are cross-examined separately about crimes they have jointly committed, with lighter sentences for whomever cooperates with the police. If each trusts the other to maintain solidarity, their best strategy is to deny everything; if either mistrusts the other, each one's best strategy is to betray the other. Even beyond the artificial, maximizing logic of game theory, there are many other illustrations of this point. For instance, in the "tragedy of the commons," a common good such as a collective pasture or a clean environment will be shared as long as all parties agree that nobody can appropriate it for personal use. Once some parties begin to exploit a common good for private use, parties who fail to do so will lose out completely. The point is simple: some of the parameters of action are the knowledge or the expectations of how others will also act. It is the network of interactants which sets the conditions of action, and since how each interactant decides to act is based in part upon these conditions, a network spanning communities can change individual decisions within each community.

In the Neolithic world, altering the nature of trade, the supply of exotic items, the level of aggressive action, or the amount of crowding over spatially peripheral resources would alter conditions for the reproduction of value in neighboring societies. To take one scenario suggested by the sequence described above, suppose that, in Middle Neolithic village landscapes, exchange was a source of prestige and that tensions with other forms of action generated an impulse to amplify it, but that trade, and intergroup interaction generally, was limited by the expectation of hostility – a plausible scenario in light of evidence for an emphasis on local definition of group identity, defensive structures such as village ditches, and ethnographic analogues (Feil 1987). If then a neighboring group admits the possibility of stable and extended trade relations, this is likely to alter how people within the group decide to behave, and increased trade could spread rapidly. Shennan (1986) elaborates a scenario in which denser political interaction among communities might lead to the reorganization of internal patterns of authority. As an archaeological record, this process might leave a crescendo of ritual elaboration, followed by an apparent devolution or simplification coincident with widespread horizons of newly ideologised prestige goods (Shennan 1986).

Changes in the conditions of exchange and intergroup relations thus could have spread rapidly from group to group in a kind of chain reaction. As a mechanism of change, this may provide a model for the fourth millennium paradox of rapid, parallel changes spreading across vast areas among a matrix of small-scale, decentralised societies without migrations or any centralised or unicausal motor of change.

Coda: Malta – The Road Less Taken

The high point of Neolithic Malta, paradoxically, happens after the Neolithic is over (Evans 1971, 1976; Malone and Stoddart 1996; Malone and Stoddart 2004; Malone et al. 2007; Robb 2001; Stoddart et al. 1993; Trump 1966, 1981). The Maltese Islands are an archipelago of four small islands with a total of about 320 km^2 land area. They lie about 100 km south of Sicily – far enough to be a serious journey of a day or several days in a small, open boat, but close enough that regular crossings were made throughout the Neolithic (Figure 1). The islands were first settled by Sicilian villagers in the mid-sixth millennium, and for about two millennia, the Maltese Neolithic looks very much like that of Sicily and Southern Italy. But around 3600 BC, just as the Copper Age social transformations discussed above were setting in in Sicily and Italy, Malta suddenly launched on a completely unique developmental tangent. Between 3600 BC and 2400 BC – a period confusingly termed the "Neolithic" on Malta and the "Copper Age" in Sicily and Italy – Malta was the site of extravagant, unique and mysterious "temples." These are multi-roomed megalithic buildings with forecourts and clusters of internal rooms with stone tables or "altars" (Figure 56). Unlike almost all other European megalithic monuments, the Maltese temples are not funerary monuments; people were buried either in small rock-cut tombs or in the two extremely large and complex underground funerary complexes, the Hypogeum of Hal Saflieni near the Tarxien temples on Malta and the Brochtorff Circle at Xaghra on Gozo, each of which held thousands of bodies.

Explaining why Malta developed so differently from its close neighbors has never been easy. Most explanations emphasise Malta's isolated island setting, either as a fragile and easily over-exploited ecosystem or as a backwater where peculiar habits could develop. The archipelago's

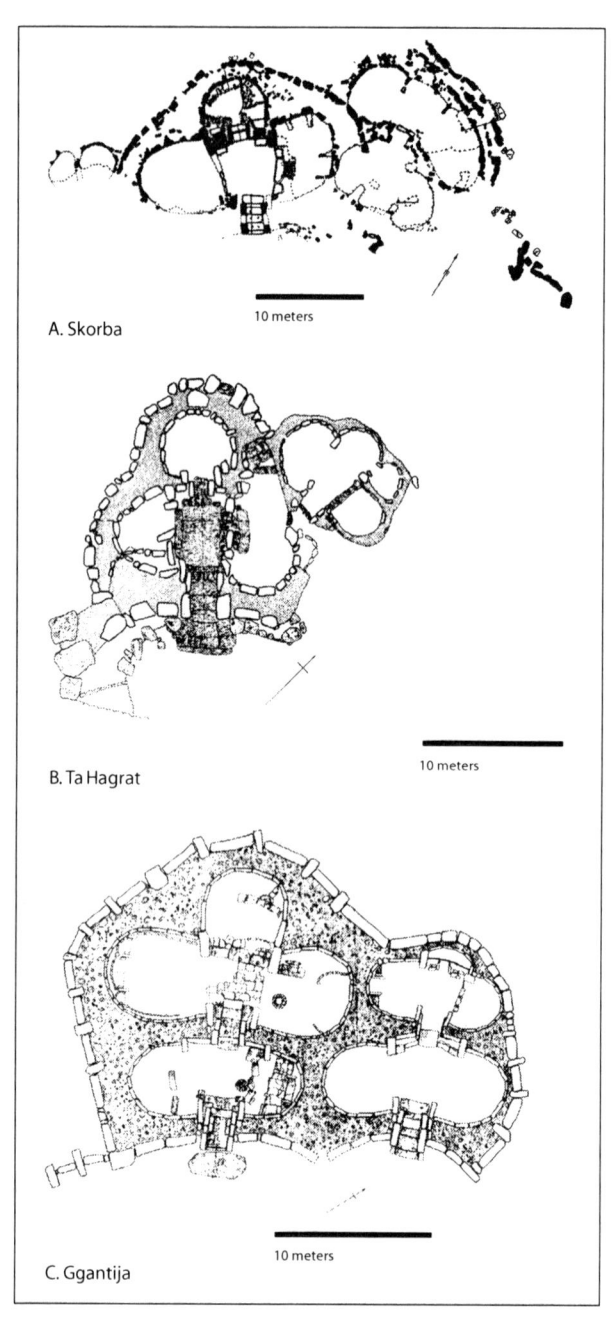

56. Malta and Gozo: megalithic temple plans. (Evans 1971). (a) Skorba; (b) Ta Hagrat; and (c) Ggantija.

isolation was certainly an important factor. Yet the remarkable megaliths cannot be ascribed solely to geography, for several reasons. There were two millennia of equally isolated Neolithic life prior to the "temple period" (as it is known) when Malta did not look very different from elsewhere in the Central Mediterranean, and when difference came, it came quickly, reaching its most florid level within a century or two. During the temple period, while ocean crossings certainly made communication with the mainland a highly structured and restricted business, there nevertheless remained considerable interaction, as attested by traded goods on Malta, and some practices, such as collective burial in rock-cut tombs, closely parallel contemporary developments on Sicily (Robb 2001; see Malone and Stoddart 2004 for an alternative view.)

During the temple period, Malta abundantly fulfills the criteria listed in Chapter 7 for a bounded social unit, and it is clear that the islands formed a bounded community, with the temples the most obvious symbols of local identity. As such, one interpretation of the temples is as loci of rites recreating the autochthonous origin of Maltese communities (Robb 2001). Socially, it is probable that leaders in Maltese communities formed a ritual elite (Bonanno 1996). Maltese ritual life is also distinguished by the abundant and elaborate use of human body imagery, particularly females and enigmatic genderless persons, in a way clearly descended from the general Central Mediterranean figurines tradition (see Chapter 2 in this book) but long after figurines have gone out of use everywhere else in the region except for Sardinia. (see Figure 57.)

Malta poses a problem in the development of difference. Why and how did it take such a different direction so abruptly? Although Malta merits extensive discussion for its own intrinsic interest, here Malta provides a fascinating example of the road less taken, in Robert Frost's phrase. Maltese "temple period" societies developed out of the common Central Mediterranean matrix, and most of their pronounced features – not merely their basic economy and technology, but also aspects such as the figurine tradition, the ritual use of ochre, and the ritual deposition of greenstone axes – originate directly in that tradition. But in this tiny archipelago, this tradition was developed in a completely different direction than elsewhere.

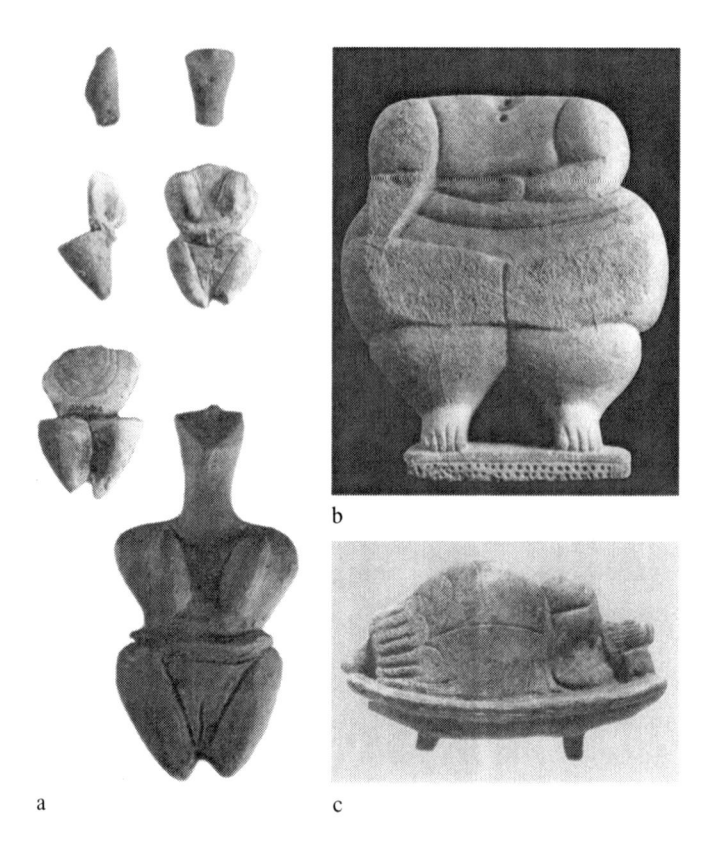

The model of Neolithic society presented above (see Chapter 6 in this book) is a balance, perhaps under tension, of fields of social action which provided alternative ways of exercising agency. In particular, exchange and related forms of action based on trans-local connections stood in opposition to burial, ritual, and related forms of action based on local origins and communities. In Sicily and peninsular Italy, by the Copper Age, this polarity had given way, with emerging spheres of generalised leadership symbolised by exchange and formerly opposed practices such as burial now redefined to support the new constellation of institutions. On Malta, the converse seems to have happened. Intensification was ideological, not economic. Leadership – which seems to have been distinctly more hierarchical as it was elsewhere – was ritual. Leaders seem not to have lived, nor died, differently from anyone else, but the control of secret ritual knowledge is implied

57. Malta and Gozo: human representations (Evans 1971). (a) Female figurines, Skorba temple; (b) Statue, Hagar Qim temple, note holes for attaching head; (c) "Sleeping Lady" figurine, Hal Saflieni hypogeum; (d) Carved stone phalli, Tarxien temples (not to scale).

d

by architectural features such as "oracle holes" in the temples and by the layering of access to temple spaces (Stoddart et al. 1993). Malta's island status may also have circumscribed mobility and capped available resources, contributing to the development of inequality. Perhaps the most interesting feature is the way in which continual contact with the mainland happened through a trade which served principally to provide materials such as ochre (Maniscalco 1989) for ritual sites and practices, effectively encapsulating a potentially competing institution within the hegemony of ritual (Robb 2001).

What caused this development is debated. Environmental causes may have contributed to social stress on the islands, and in such a small and singular case we can never rule out the happenstance of unique incidents. Malta's position as a resource-poor cul de sac in a period in which trade was becoming increasingly central to politics may have played a role. In any case, it is clear that the Maltese would have been aware of contemporary Sicilian societies, probably by visiting them directly, and hence aware of their own difference and identity. Given the common roots Malta shared with its neighbours and the speed with which Malta developed unique, identity-defining practices in the mid-fourth millennium, it seems likely that this difference was intentionally constructed, rather than simply evolving, perhaps in denial of, rather than in default of, close contact with nearby societies.

Malta, like Lipari, provides yet another example of the social history of unique places, a small community which chose, in the context of developing a local identity, a completely distinct route out of the general Neolithic background. History caught up with Malta, however, at the end of the temple period, when the new Tarxien Cemetery culture appeared with social characteristics very similar to contemporary Sicilian Bronze Age groups. The Tarxien culture differs radically, even to the point of implanting a cremation cemetery in the center of Malta's largest temple, and has always been interpreted as a takeover by hostile continental invaders. Whether or not this is true, Malta was back on the general track; its experiment in ideological intensification was over.

Wandering Through Tribespace: The Social Foundations of Prehistoric Italy

Archaeologists frequently justify their activities by claiming the deep time depth they can work in and the great ability this affords for tracking sequences of social change, but all too rarely do we actually make full use of this time depth to see what conclusions can be glimpsed in it. By way of conclusion, we here pull back from the close-up view to pan across the Central Mediterranean Neolithic, looking for what it can tell us about historical pattern and process.

I use the word "tribes" for convenience, to refer generically to these stateless societies, rather than as a technical term with a methodologically precise specification. Ethnographic research on all continents except Europe has established the amazing variety of such societies, and this has defied any straightforward attempt to place them in a single directed or "evolutionary" sequence [most famously, Service's evolutionary typology from bands to states (Service 1962)], or even to carry out the social classification such a linear sequence presupposes. One wild card in ethnological systematizations is colonial contact, which, through conquest, pacification, trade, missions, disease and demographic collapse, often restructured indigenous tribes almost completely, in many cases well before any ethnohistoric record of this process (Wolf 1982). Another limit is its lack of time depth: ethnohistory typically affords a century or less of a vision marred by the colonial encounter. Hence, ethnological sequences tend to be composed of random snapshots from many unrelated family albums, arranged in a sequence whose validity depends on the a priori belief that such ideal sequences do in fact exist. This is not to deny the value of ethnography for enlarging our ideas of cultural difference, nor the pattern of long-term directionality seen in world history at the largest scale. However, to understand how such a pattern may have come about, there is no ethnographic road map; archaeologists are on their own.

For archaeologists interested in the big picture, one of the most obvious lessons from Neolithic Italy is that there was no single way of life we can label as "Neolithic." At any moment before the Late Neolithic, there were several distinct ways of living. Several others followed the Late Neolithic transition before we encounter, millennia later in the mid-second millennium BC, something we would clearly recognise as a society of a different scale and nature. What the Italian sequence shows is the great degree to which tribal societies varied over deep time in a setting free from colonial contact. Moreover, this sequence, like that of later prehistoric Europe in general, cannot be wrestled into any simple framework of the "rise of complexity," a rising line punctuated by points when signs of political inequality, centralization, large-scale ritual and economic intensification all jump together. Instead, prehistoric Italians spent four or five millennia shifting about among qualitatively different kinds of tribal societies, without an easily legible teleological directionality.

The best way to conceptualise this situation is not as a series of "stages" but rather as movement within a tribal envelope whose limits were defined by basic parameters of the situation. On one hand, the beginning of the Neolithic marked a real boundary. Several institutions and conditions – sedentism, an economy based on domesticates, the expanded social role of material culture, rising population levels, among others – proved mutually reinforcing. They created a coherent way of life which tended to exclude alternatives and which made a return to loosely structured, highly mobile, low density forager groups a difficult and rare event. On the other hand, there were few exits from the tribal envelope: most change was self-limiting, and paths led back in, not out. For example, even with Late Neolithic and subsequent economies, the most basic challenge of intensification was to recruit labor. Without marked means of coercion, with production in many ways technologically rudimentary, and with centralised production and redistribution supplementing rather than substituting for basic domestic production of subsistence, there would have been little to strengthen followers' dependence upon a leader to the point at which compliance surpassed the bounds of obvious mutual advantage and developed into economic dependence. Such factors made change self-limiting and inequality largely ideological rather than political or economic. It is unsurprising that clearest case for social inequality in the Neolithic and Copper Age, on "temple period" Malta, is founded on the control of ritual knowledge rather than upon economic difference: if differential access to resources existed, it may have been sublimated through an extended participatory ritualism theoretically open to all to some degree, much as in Pueblos (Levy 1992). Elsewhere, intensification depended on enlisting labor through voluntary, mutual association, ties such as kinship bound similar persons together, and fission and movement were always available as ways of resisting potential hierarchy.

Within the long span between the beginning of the Neolithic and the Middle to Late Bronze Age – about four millennia in all – social change depended upon structuring principles of social reproduction which shaped possible trajectories within the envelope at each moment. My debt here Braithwaite (1984), Thorpe and Richards (1984), Shennan (1982), and Bradley (1984) will be obvious. These scholars pioneered relating historical processes to specific modes of social reproduction, for example reading the decline of megalithic traditions and the rise of individual burial in the British Late Neolithic–Early Bronze Age in terms of the replacement of a ritual-regulated mode of social reproduction with one based on prestige competition. A parallel approach has recently been developed in the American processual tradition with the characterization of ancient societies as predominantly following either "network" or "corporate" strategies for pursuing political power

(Blanton et al. 1996; Feinman 2001). What is useful here is the link between how social relations are reproduced and how history unfolds. For example, Thorpe and Richards (1984) argue convincingly that societies regulated by prestige competition are generally more unstable and expansionistic than societies regulated by ritual authority.

Reading the Italian sequence in these terms, the "social foundations of prehistoric Italy" (to generalise summarily) might include a number of pre-state phases:

- Early–Middle Neolithic (earlier sixth millennium to later fifth millennium): subsistence economy based on domesticates; settlement varying greatly, but social relations based upon the heterarchical production of difference, with identity conceptualised in terms of locality and co-residence.
- Late–Final Neolithic (later fifth to earlier fourth millennium): dispersed settlement with intensified pastoralism and occupation of highlands; identity conceptualised in terms of genealogically relatedness, expressed in burial; emergence of generalised forms of value linking multiple institutions (heterarchy based on potentially equal production of similarity).
- Copper Age and earlier Bronze Age (mid-fourth millennium to mid-second millennium): similar value structure, but more personalised expression with potentially prominent individuals thought of as apical ancestors of genealogical relations, emergence of clearly expressed dichotomy of genderised prestige. Metals emerge as most important traded item and way of conceptualizing material value; emphasis still on display or action rather than accumulation.
- Middle–Late Bronze Age and Iron Age (mid–late second millennium to early first millennium): highly varied, but sporadic attempts to form hierarchy, accompanied by shift from display to accumulation of valuables, increased range in metal uses and specialised production, new patron–client relationships and specialised trade-related sites (Peroni 1979).

In this sequence, Italy shows equally illuminating similarities and differences with the better-known European sequences such as Britain and Scandinavia. As elsewhere in Europe, the Italian sequence shows a clear transition to social relations based on generalised forms of prestige ushering in the Metal Ages, and a much more variable one sometime during or after the Middle Bronze Age towards a stratified society. Yet the differences between regions have significant implications for how we conceptualise prehistory:

1. It is striking how stable, and perhaps fundamentally conservative, quite different forms of society were, with many phases lasting half a millennium or more, and shading into each other in the spectrum effect noted above. Such stability is a major difference from sequences such as Britain and Scandinavia, in which parallel changes are compressed into a significantly shorter sequence. Time adds other complicating factors as well; for instance, megaliths, intimately associated with Neolithic social and cultural worlds in Britain and Scandinavia, do not seem to represent a general fact of all Neolithic societies, but rather a horizon which sweeps across European societies shortly after 4000 BCcal. In the Italian example, it appears to be not prestige competition per se but social hierarchy which increases the tempo of change, perhaps by supplying a vested interest in innovation rather than conservatism.
2. Although social change did not involve movement between discrete typologies of society, neither was it entirely free-form: there were limits on possible histories. For example, it is impossible to imagine a transition directly from the Neolithic to, say, the Middle Bronze Age as known from fortified coastal sites such as Coppa Nevigata (Cazzella and Moscoloni 1999) and elaborate burials such as Toppo Daguzzo (Cipolloni Sampò 1986); there is too little conceptual continuity. Yet a transformation from the Early–Middle Neolithic pattern to the Late Neolithic pattern involves a discrete number of important institutions; the same is true for the subsequent transition to the Copper Age, and thence to the Bronze Age, and so on.
3. Across Europe, histories are parallel but not identical. For example, there is very little evidence in Neolithic Italy for large-scale

ritual regulation of society; value was reproduced through daily activities. Hence even if Copper Age societies involved elements of prestige competition similar to Western European Beaker groups, the model of a ritual-prestige transition does not fit. Similarly, both Corded Ware (in Eastern and Central Europe) and Beakers (in Central and Western Europe) have been heralded as introducing individual identities negotiated through personalised use and display of valuables. However, the conceptual components of this change arose in several distinct phases in Italy, with a generalised prestige and a shift to burial to mediate social relationships in the Late Neolithic and the concept of personal prestige competition via display of valuables in the Copper Age. The point is that we need to eschew both the chimeric hope that one interpretation will fit everywhere if only we can specify the right one, and the myopic insistence that such distinct trajectories have nothing to do with other. Moreover, it is reductionist to argue simply that the Late Neolithic, the Copper Age, and the Beakers all represent societies marked by universal categories such as "network strategies" or prestige-goods economies. Rather, as with variations on a smaller scale above, such differences have to be seen as the regional workings-out of parallel structural possibilities. Such structural possibilities will draw upon unique local circumstances such as the presence or absence of particular resources such as obsidian or metals, and geographical factors such as access to communication and exchange routes. Moreover, such structural possibilities will be rooted in the cultural specifics of each society's predecessor rather than a general ideal type. The two opposed routes out of the Italian Neolithic in the Central Mediterranean were rooted not in a general ideal type but in the specific way in which earlier Neolithic society was constituted.

Yet balancing this divergence are moments of convergence, in which parallel developments and convergence reflect probable – not deterministic – common pathways (Sherratt 1984). One example is the paradox of Neolithic convergence, in which the "Neolithic package" as a widely found set of common institutions emerges in Asia, the Near East, Europe and Mesoamerica – but it emerges not as a cause of the agricultural origins but rather as consequence of it up to millennia later. Common patterns of elite behaviour in Iron Age societies at the margins of the Classical world provide another example. As another example, a system of social reproduction geared to the circulation of a male-oriented prestige both contained latent bases for inequality and partially specified the forms inequality would take when it emerged. With the activation of kinship to organise socially recreative activities such as production and exchange, structural differentiation was created. Within kinship segments, individuals were placed in genealogically central and peripheral positions, containing the seeds of a clientage system. As for the nature of inequality, competitive activity within the reciprocal norms of a small-scale society meant that the goal of political activity was primarily the conspicuous consumption and display of prestige goods, rather than the accumulation of wealth as capital. Given this, the sporadic rise of wealthy Middle Bronze Age elites, both in Italy and elsewhere in Europe, represents not the emergence of fundamentally different societies but rather the local realization of possibilities latent in a widespread ideological system.

Here, the opposition between ritual and prestige, on the pan-European scale, provides another example. It does not represent an opposition or necessary sequence between two discrete forms of society, but rather two of a limited numbers of directions in which Neolithic society could be intensified. Hence, in comparing the end of Stonehenge and the end of the Neolithic Maltese temples, we do not see a similar, general transition from ritual to prestige. Rather, we see examples, in specific historical trajectories which varied rather than repeated the same motions, of two of the relatively limited number of directions in which tribal societies in general could be intensified (Figure 58). One route leads to Malta, Stonehenge, and similar societies with ritual inequality, material equality, and general conservatism. The other path leads to much more egalitarian, "flatter" society, structurally simpler but with potential to be extended and elaborated into inequality greater than anything ever seen before.

THE GREAT SIMPLIFICATION

Italy: Iron Age wealth-based elites

Hierarchy based upon accumulation of value: wealth, class

hierarchy based upon different attainment of uniform value: Bronze age political elites

Malta: 4th millennium "temple" societies

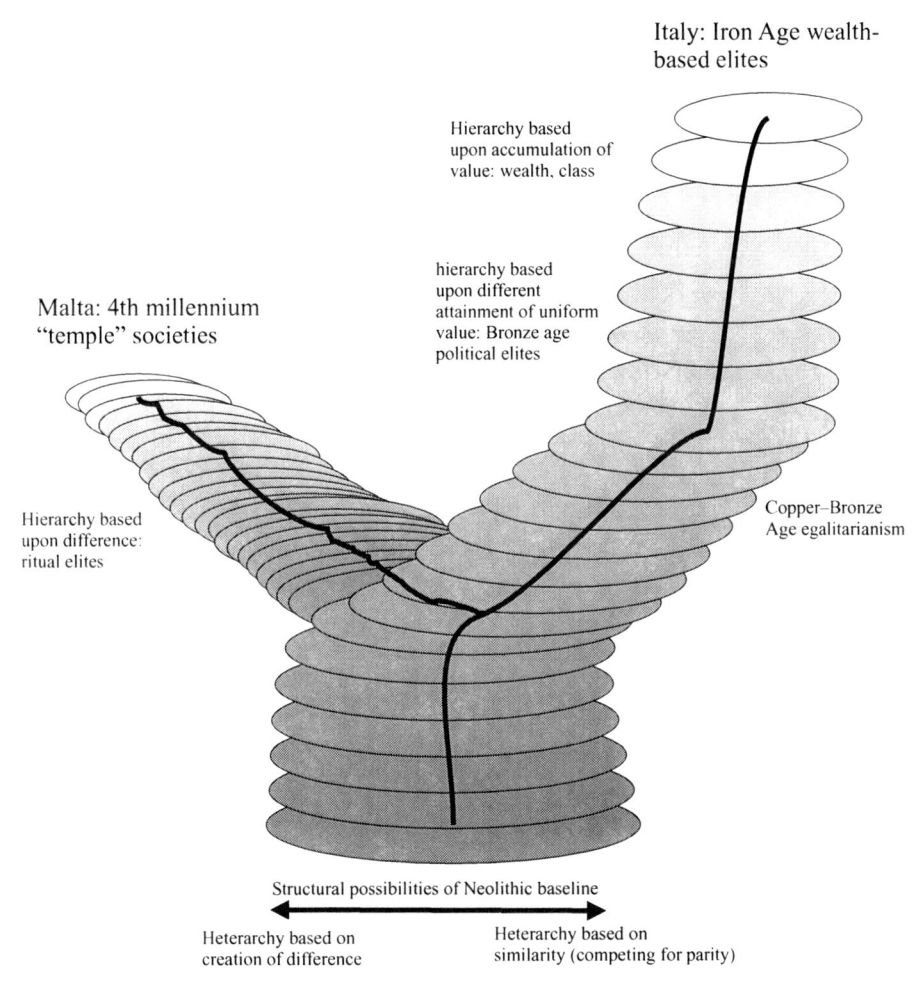

Hierarchy based upon difference: ritual elites

Copper–Bronze Age egalitarianism

Structural possibilities of Neolithic baseline

Heterarchy based on creation of difference

Heterarchy based on similarity (competing for parity)

58. Possible pathways for intensification; historical trajectory is movement within envelope of possibilities.

It is this phenomenon of structural convergence, periodically becoming predominant, which structures later European prehistory: many roads, few destinations, with transitions marking shifts from one stable world to another.

341

NOTES

ONE: THEORIZING NEOLITHIC ITALY

1. I am indebted to Clive Gamble for this illustration.
2. Small collective burials in rock-cut tombs and caves seem to appear in the late fifth and early fourth millennia, and the first real megaliths in the Central Mediterranean seem to date to the mid-fourth millennium BC (for instance the Maltese temples). Although the tendency in British theory has been to draw a fundamental link between the Neolithic and megaliths, from the Continental point of view, megaliths seem a horizon which spans Europe in the fourth millennium BC regardless of whether the societies involved are just turning Neolithic or have been so for several millennia and are now on the threshold of the Copper Age.

TWO: NEOLITHIC PEOPLE

1. Porto Badisco will be discussed as a cult cave in Chapter 3, and the dramatic changes in body representation in the Final Neolithic–Copper Age will be discussed in Chapter 7.
2. Interestingly, this standard tends to be applied inconsistently; although Neolithic figurines with pronounced buttocks are often considered female, the Iron Age Capestrano "warrior" with an equally pronounced posterior has always been considered male (Whitehouse 2001, pp. 90–91). Evidently the presence of weapons trumps lower body form in the taxonomy of gender assessment.
3. This figure is undoubtedly an underestimate, too, as "scattered" or "sporadic" bone is much less systematically reported and analysed than are articulated burials.
4. The contemporary use of an extremely similar way of representing females at Porto Badisco, at virtually the southernmost point of Adriatic Italy, and in Valcamonica high in the Alps, strongly implies that a similar symbolic notation must have been in use in archaeologically invisible ways in groups between these extremes. It would also imply some historical time depth extending back into the Neolithic, as a symbolism shared over very wide distances can hardly be imagined to arise or spread instantly.

THREE: THE INHABITED WORLD

1. Houses at La Marmotta (Fugazzola Delpino et al. 1993, Fugazzola 2001) and Capo Alfiere (Morter 1992) have been debated as potential ritual spaces, but the evidence both for and against this is tenuous. It is also possible, indeed likely, that ritual practices took place within houses without the edifices being defined specifically as ritual structures.

2   Interestingly, this mode of orientation, rather than absolute directions such as the cardinal compass points, still forms the colloquial way of referring to directions in Southern Calabria.

FOUR: DAILY ECONOMY AND SOCIAL REPRODUCTION

1   I am indebted to Rob Tykot for discussion of unpublished stable isotope data bearing upon this.
2   I am indebted to Rob Tykot for discussion of unpublished stable isotope data bearing upon this.
3   In one informal experiment at the Bova Marina Archaeological Project (Calabria), one liter (1,000 g) of sea water left in the July sun for a week yielded 55 g of salt in an irregular block dry to the touch. As the Central Mediterranean's salinity is between 0.35% and 0.4%, presumably about 15 g of this weight consisted of impurities and residual moisture.
4   These figures are for the NISP, or counts of specimens identified, rather than for the number of whole animals (MNI). MNI numbers are published for very few sites, but where they have been, they confirm this ratio of species. Although it is true sheep and goat bones are smaller and more subject to destruction than cow bones, the MNI for caprovines at Passo di Corvo is derived from mandible fragments, a relatively indestructible skeletal region far more commonly represented than long bones; this suggests that taphonomic bias is not a major factor in the relative proportion of species in the MNI.
5   I am indebted to Andrew Crosby and Yvonne Marshall for this information.

FIVE: MATERIAL CULTURE AND PROJECTS OF THE SELF

1   Whose classical location can, incidentally, be seen at the northern end of the Straits of Messina, figure 49.
2   The inference that Impressed Ware spread before the development of finewares is by very few dated excavations, though a few sites such as Favella in northern Calabria show a transition from archaic wares with all-over impressions to evolved wares with impressions organised in syntactical designs. However, the earliest finewares in each region show a marked regional variation which suggests that they are parallel, independent developments.
3   I am particularly indebted to Ruth Whitehouse for discussion of this issue.
4   I am indebted to Kostalena Michelaki for informative discussion of this operational sequence and pottery matters in general.
5   Indeed, in replicating Neolithic pots, we have found that different, apparently identical clay sources may yield vessels with distinctive odors and which give distinctive tastes to their contents (for instance, a clay outcrop high in sulfur); one imagines such knowledge may have been important in selecting raw materials.
6   We should also mention the so-called "Ripabianca burin," a long narrow burin with a distinct notch found at Early Neolithic sites in the upper Adriatic coast; its function is unknown although it has sometimes been interpreted as for use in opening shellfish (d'Errico 1987).
7   I am grateful to Helen Farr for extensive discussion of many ideas about the Lipari obsidian trade presented in this and the following sections.
8   I am indebted to John Clark for explaining this to me.
9   For example, Norman Douglas (1938) recorded that, while traveling around Calabria, "From a gentleman at Vaccarizza, I received a still more valuable present – two neolithic celts...they are supposed, as usual, to be thunderbolts, and I am also told that a piece of string tied to one of them cannot be burnt in a fire...." Beliefs of this kind dating to much earlier periods may explain why many Neolithic axes were found on the Sicilian Iron Age/Greek site of Morgantina (Leighton 1989).
10 Particularly in Northern Italy, the hafted area of axes was often left pecked roughly,

344

presumably so the haft would grip better. In future research, the presence of rough pecking on the hafted area may perhaps furnish a clue to the intended biographical pathway for such axes.

SEVEN: NEOLITHIC ITALY AS AN ETHNOGRAPHIC LANDSCAPE

1   All discussion to date (Fornaciari and Germanà 1992; Robb 1997) focuses upon healed pre-mortem trauma; no examination of peri-mortem trauma has been conducted.

2   I am indebted to V. Tinè for this information.

EIGHT: THE GREAT SIMPLIFICATION: LARGE SCALE CHANGE AT THE END OF THE NEOLITHIC

1   The term "Eneolithic" is used synonymously with "Copper Age" in Italian prehistory.

BIBLIOGRAPHY

Adams, D. (1986). *The hitchhiker's guide to the galaxy: A trilogy in four parts.* London: Heinemann.

Albore Livadie, C., R. Federico, F. Fedele, U. Albarella, F. De Matteis, and D. Esposito. (1987). Ricerche sull'insediamento tardo-neolitico di Mulino Sant'Antonio (Avella). *Rivista di Scienze Preistoriche* **41**:65–103.

Albore Livadie, C., and G. Gangemi. (1987). Nuovi dati sul neolitico in Campania. *Atti, Riunione Scientifica dell' I. I. P. P.* **26**:287–299.

Alexander, C. (2005). A Bayesian analysis of the radiocarbon evidence for the spread of the Neolithic in Italy. Cambridge, UK: M.Phil Thesis, Department of Archaeology, Cambridge University.

Allegrucci, F., E. Biondi, R. Fulton, R. Housley, C. Hunt, and S. Stoddart. (1994). Vegetation, land use and climate, in *Time, territory, and state: The archaeological development of the Gubbio basin.* Edited by C. Malone and S. Stoddart. Cambridge, UK: Cambridge University Press, pp. 34–58.

Amadei, A., and R. Grifoni Cremonesi. (1987). La Grotta all'Onda: Revisione ed inquadramento dei materiali. *Rassegna di Archeologia* **6**: 171–216.

Ambrosi, A. (1972). *Corpus delle statue-stele lunigianesi.* Collana Storica dell Liguria Orientale. Bordighera: Istituto Internazionale di Studi Liguri.

———. (1988). *Statue-stele lunigianesi.* Genova: Sagep.

Ammerman, A. J. (1985). *The Acconia survey: Neolithic settlement and the obsidian trade.* London: Institute of Archaeology.

Ammerman, A. J., and W. Andrefsky. (1982). Reduction sequences and the exchange of obsidian in Neolithic Calabria, in *Contexts for prehistoric exchange.* Edited by J. E. Ericson and T. K. Earle. New York: Academic, pp. 149–172.

Ammerman, A. J., and L. Cavalli-Sforza. (1984). *The Neolithic transition and the genetics of populations in Europe.* Princeton: Princeton University Press.

Ammerman, A. J., A. Cesana, C. Polglase, and M. Terrani. (1990). Neutron activation analysis of obsidian for two Neolithic sites in Italy. *Journal of Archaeological Science* **17**:209–220.

Ammerman, A. J., G. D. Shaffer, and N. Hartmann. (1988). A Neolithic household at Piano di Curinga, Italy. *Journal of Field Archaeology* **15**:121–140.

Ammerman, A. J., and C. Polglase. (1993). The exchange of obsidian at Neolithic sites in Italy, in *Trade and exchange in European prehistory.* Edited by C. Healy and C. Scarre. Oxford: Oxbow Books, pp. 101–107.

Anati, E. (1960). *La grande roche de Naquane* (Vol. 31). Mémoire. Paris: Archive de l'Institut de Paléontologie Humaine.

———. (1961). *Camonica Valley.* New York: Knopf.

———. (1977). Post-paleolithic stylistic changes in rock art as illustrated by the Valcamonica cycle, in *Form in indigenous art.* Edited by

P. Ucko. Canberra: Australian Institute of Aboriginal Studies, pp. 337–356.

André, J. (2003). La faune malacologique de Torre Sabea, in *Torre Sabea: Un Établissement du Néolithique Ancien en Salento*. Edited by J. Guilaine and G. Cremonesi. Rome: École Française de Rome, pp. 279–283.

Antoniazzi, A., B. Bagolini, G. Bermond Montanari, M. Massi Pasi, and L. Prati. (1987). Il neolitico di Fornace Cappuccini a Faenza e la Ceramica Impressa in Romagna. *Atti, Riunione Scientifica dell' I. I. P. P.* **26**:553–563.

Anzidei, A. P. (1987). Lo scavo dell'abitato neolitico di Quadrato di Torre Spaccata. *Atti, Riunione Scientifica dell' I. I. P. P.* **26**:681–689.

Anzidei, A. P., and G. Carboni. (2003). Strutture d'abitato di età neo-eneolitica nel territorio di Roma. *Atti, Riunione Scientifica dell' I. I. P. P.* **35**:797–801.

Appadurai, A. (Ed.). (1988). *The social life of things*. Cambridge, UK: Cambridge University Press.

Aranguren, B., and A. Revedin. (1998). Il giacimento mesolitico di Perriere Sottano (Ramacca, CT). *Bullettino di Paletnologia Italiana* **89**:31–72.

Bagolini, B. (1981). *Il neolitico e l'età del rame: ricerca a Spilamberto e S. Cesario, 1977–1980*. Bologna: Tamari.

Bagolini, B., G. Barker, P. Biagi, L. Castelletti, and M. Cremaschi. (1987). Scavi nell'insediamento neolitico di Campo Ceresole (Vhò di Piadena, Cremona): 1974–1979. *Atti, Riunione Scientifica dell' I. I. P. P.* **26**:455–466.

Bagolini, B., and G. Cremonesi. (1987). Il processo di Neolitizzazione in Italia. *Atti, Riunione Scientifica dell' I. I. P. P.* **26**:21–30.

Bagolini, B., A. Ferrari, and G. Steffè. (1998). Il recente Neolitico di Spilamberto (Modena). *Bullettino di Paletnologia Italiana* **89**:93–200.

Bagolini, B., and R. Grifoni Cremonesi. (1994). Il Neolitico italiano: Facies culturali e manifestazioni funerarie. *Bullettino di Paletnologia Italiana* **85**:139–170.

Bailey, D. W. (2005). *Prehistoric figurines: Representation and corporeality in the Neolithic*. London: Routledge.

Bailo Modesti, G. (2003). Rituali funerari eneolitici nell'Italia peninsulare: L'Italia meridionale. *Atti, Riunione Scientifica dell' I. I. P. P.* **35**:283–297.

Bailo Modesti, G., and A. Salerno. (1998). *Pontecagnano II.5, La necropoli eneolitica: L'età del Rame in Campania nei villaggi dei morti*. Napoli: Istituto Universitario Orientale.

Balista, C., and G. Leonardi. (1985). Hill slope evolution: Pre- and proto-historic occupation in the Veneto, in *Papers in Italian archaeology IV: The Cambridge Conference* (Vol. I). BAR International Series. Edited by C. Malone and S. Stoddart. Oxford: British Archaeological Reports, pp. 135–152.

Barfield, L. (1981). Patterns of N. Italian trade, 5000–2000 B.C, in *Archaeology and Italian Society*. International Series. Edited by G. Barker and R. Hodges. Oxford: British Archaeological Reports, pp. 27–51.

———. (1986). Chalcolithic burials in Northern Italy: Problems of social interpretation. *Dialoghi di Archeologia* **4**:241–248.

Barfield, L., M. Bernabò Brea, R. Maggi, and A. Pedrotti. (2003). Processi di cambiamento culturale nel neolitico dell'Italia settentrionale. *Atti, Riunione Scientifica dell' I. I. P. P.* **35**:665–685.

Barker, G. (1975). Prehistoric territories and economies in Central Italy, in *Palaeoeconomy*. Edited by E. Higgs. Cambridge, UK: Cambridge University Press, pp. 111–175.

———. (1981). *Landscape and society: Prehistoric central Italy*. New York: Academic Press.

———. (1985). *Prehistoric farming in Europe*. Cambridge, UK: Cambridge University Press.

———. (1989). The archaeology of the Italian shepherd. *Proceedings of the Cambridge Philological Society* **215**:1–19.

Barley, N. (1989). *Not a hazardous sport*. London: Penguin.

———. (1990). *Native land*. London: Penguin.

Barra, A., R. Grifoni Cremonesi, F. Mallegni, M. Piancastelli, A. Vitiello, and B. Wilkens. (1992). La Grotta Continenza di Trasacco: i livelli a ceramiche. *Rivista di Scienze Preistoriche* **42**:31–100.

Barrett, J. (1994). *Fragments from antiquity: An archaeology of social life in Britain, 2900–1200 BC*. Oxford: Blackwell.

———. (2001). Agency, the duality of structure, and the problem of the archaeological record, in *Archaeological theory today*. Edited by I. Hodder. Oxford: Polity, pp. 140–164.

Barth, F. (1987). *Cosmologies in the making: A generative approach to cultural variation in inner New Guinea*. Cambridge, UK: Cambridge University Press.
———. (2002). An anthropology of knowledge. *Current Anthropology* **43**:1–18.
Bell, R. (1974). *Fate and honor, family and village: Demographic and cultural change in rural Italy since 1800*. Chicago: University of Chicago Press.
Bender, B. (1978). Gatherer–hunter to farmer: A social perspective. *World Archaeology* **10**: 204–222.
Berger, P. L., and T. Luckmann. (1967). *The social construction of reality: A treatise in the sociology of knowledge*. Harmondsworth: Penguin.
Bernabò Brea, L. (1946). *Gli scavi nella caverna delle Arene Candide. Parte I: Gli strati con ceramiche*. Bordighera: Istituto di Studi Liguri.
———. (1947). Esplorazione archeologica dell'isola e scavo di una stazione neolitica al Piano Quartera. *Notizie di Scavi* **72**:222–230.
———. (1947). Tomba neolitica di Malfa. *Notizie di Scavi* **72**:220–221.
———. (1954). La Sicilia prehistorica y sus relaciones con oriente e con la peninsula Iberica. *Ampurias* **16**:135–235.
———. (1957). *Sicily before the Greeks*. London: Thames and Hudson.
———. (1987). Il neolitico delle Isole Eolie. *Atti, Riunione Scientifica dell' I. I. P. P.* **26**:351–360.
Bernabò Brea, L., and M. Cavalier. (1956). Civiltà preistoriche delle Isole Eolie e del territorio del Milazzo. *Bullettino di Paletnologia Italiana* **66**:7–98.
———. (1957). Stazioni preistoriche delle Isole Eolie. *Bullettino di Paletnologia Italiana* **66**:97–151.
———. (1960). *Meligunìs Lipàra. Volume I. La stazione preistorica della contrada Diana e la necropoli preistorica di Lipari*. Pubblicazioni del Museo Eoliano di Lipari. Palermo: S. F. Flaccovio.
———. (1968). *Meligunìs Lipàra, Volume III: Stazioni preistoriche delle isole Panarea, Salina e Stromboli*. Publications of the Museo Eolio. Palermo: Flaccovio.
———. 1980. *Meligunìs Lipàra, Volume IV: l'acropoli di Lipari nella preistoria*. Publications of the Museo Eolio. Palermo: Flaccovio.
———. (1991). *Isole Eolie: vulcanologia archeologia*. Lipari: Oreste Ragusi Editore.

———. (1995). *Meligunìs Lipàra. Volume VIII: Salina (ricerche archeologiche 1989–1993)*. Publications of the Museo Eolio. Palermo: Flaccovio.
Bernabò Brea, M. (1987). Il popolamento neolitico della Val Trebbia (PC). *Atti, Riunione Scientifica dell' I. I. P. P.* **26**:565–573.
Bernabò Brea, M., D. Castagna, and S. Occhi. (2003). Le strutture dell'abitato Chassey-Lagozza a S. Andrea di Travo (PC). *Atti, Riunione Scientifica dell' I. I. P. P.* **35**:785–789.
Biagi, P. (2003). A review of the Late Mesolithic in Italy and its implication for the Neolithic transition, in *The widening harvest: The Neolithic transition in Europe: Looking back, looking forward*. Edited by A. J. Ammerman and P. Biagi. Boston: Archaeological Institute of America, pp. 133–156.
Biagi, P., R. Maggi, and R. Nisbet. (1987). Primi dati sul neolitico della Liguria orientale. *Atti, Riunione Scientifica dell' I. I. P. P.* **26**:523–532.
Bianco, S., and M. Cipolloni Sampò. (1987). Il neolitico della Basilicata. *Atti, Riunione Scientifica dell' I. I. P. P.* **26**:301–320.
Biancofiore, F. (1965). I nuovi dipinti preistorici della Lucania. *Rivista di Antropologia* **52**:103–109.
Biddittu, I., N. Bruni, M. Cerqua, T. Mattioli, and A. Riva. (2004). Ritrovamenti neolitici e dell'Età del Rame nell'altopiano silano. *Atti, Riunione Scientifica dell' I. I. P. P.* **37**:761–764.
Bigazzi, G., S. Meloni, M. Oddone, and G. Radi. (1991). Nuovi dati sulla diffusione dell'ossidiana negli insediamenti preistorici italiani, in *Papers of the Fourth Conference of Italian Archaeology, Volume 3: New developments*. Edited by E. Herring, R. Whitehouse, and J. Wilkins. London: Accordia Research Centre, pp. 8–18.
Bigazzi, G., and G. Radi. (1981). Datazione con le tracce di fissione per l'identificazione della provenienza dei manufatti di ossidiana. *Rivista di Scienze Preistoriche* **36**:223–250.
Bistolfi, F., and I. Muntoni. (1997). Lo scavo delle area A, B, D, E, in *Casale del Dolce: Ambiente, Economia, e Cultura di una comunità preistorica del Valle del Sacco*. Edited by A. Zarattini and L. Petrassi. Roma: Soprintendenza Archeologica per il Lazio, pp. 59–159.
Black-Michaud, J. (1986). *Sheep and land: The economics of power in a tribal society*. New York: Cambridge University Press.

Blanton, R. E., G. M. Feinman, S. A. Kowalewski, and P. N. Peregrine. (1996). A dual-processual theory for the evolution of Mesoamerican civilization. *Current Anthropology* **37**:1–14.

Blitz, J. H. (1993). Big pots for big shots: Feasting and storage in a Mississippian community. *American Antiquity* **58**:80–96.

Boenzi, F., M. Caldara, M. Moresi, and L. Pennetta. (2001). History of the Salpi lagoon-sabhka (Manfredonia Gulf, Italy). *Il Quaternario* **14**:93–104.

Bogucki, P. (1988). *Forest farmers and stockherders: Early agriculture and its consequences in north-central Europe*. Cambridge, UK: Cambridge University Press.

———. (2000). How agriculture came to north-central Europe, in *Europe's first farmers*. Edited by T. D. Price. Cambridge, UK: Cambridge University Press, pp. 197–218.

Bökönyi, S. (1977/1982). The early neolithic fauna of Rendina. *Origini* **11**:237–249.

———. (1983). Animal remains from the test excavations, in *Studi sul Neolitico del Tavoliere della Puglia*. International Series 160. Edited by S. Cassano and A. Manfredini. Oxford: British Archaeological Reports, pp. 237–249.

Bonanno, A. (1996). Temple megalithism vs. funerary megalithism: the case of the Maltese Islands. *XIII International Congress of Prehistoric and Protohistoric Sciences (Forlì, Italy, 8–14 September 1996) Colloquia* **9**:103–107.

Bonato, M., F. Lorenzo, A. Nonza, G. Radi, C. Tozzi, M. Weiss, and B. Zamagni. (2000). Le nuove ricerche a Pianosa: gli scavi del 1998. in *Les Premier Peuplements Olocenes de l'Aire Corso-Toscane/Il Primo Popolamento Olocenico dell'Area Corso-Toscana*. Edited by C. Tozzi and M. Weiss. Pisa: Edizioni ETS, pp. 91–132.

Bourdieu, P. (1977). *Outline of a Theory of Practice*. Cambridge, UK: Cambridge University Press.

Bradford, J. (1949). "Buried landscapes" in Southern Italy. *Antiquity* **23**:58–72.

Bradley, R. (1984). *The social foundations of prehistoric Britain*. London: Longmans.

———. (1991). Ritual, time, and history. *World Archaeology* **23**:209–219.

———. (1998). *The significance of monuments: On the shaping of human experience in Neolithic and Bronze Age Europe*. London: Routledge.

———. (2000). *An archaeology of natural places*. London: Routledge.

Bradley, R., and M. Edmonds. (1993). *Interpreting the axe trade: Production and exchange in Neolithic Britain*. Cambridge, UK: Cambridge University Press.

Braithwaite, M. (1984). Ritual and prestige in the prehistory of Wessex, c.2200–1400 BC: A new dimension to the archaeological evidence, in *Ideology, power, and prehistory*. Edited by D. Miller and C. Tilley. Cambridge, UK: Cambridge University Press, pp. 93–110.

Bringsvaerd, T. A. (1976). The man who collected the First of September, 1973, in *The book of fantasy*. Edited by J. L. Borges, A. B. Casares, and S. Ocampo. New York: Carroll and Graf, pp. 77–80.

Brock, S., and C. Ruff. (1988). Diachronic patterns of change in structural properties of the femur in the prehistoric American Southwest. *American Journal of Physical Anthropology* **75**:113–127.

Broodbank, C. (1993). Ulysses without sails: Trade, distance, power, and knowledge in the early Cyclades. *World Archaeology* **24**:315–331.

Brown, K. (1991). A passion for excavation: Labour requirements and possible functions for the ditches of the "villaggi trincerati" of the Tavoliere, Apulia. *Journal of the Accordia Research Center* **2**:7–30.

———. (2003). Aerial archaeology of the Tavoliere: The Italian Air Photographic Record and the Riley Archive. *Journal of the Accordia Research Center* **9**: 123–146.

Brück, J. (1999). Houses, lifecycles, and deposition on Middle Bronze Age settlements in Southern England. *Proceedings of the Prehistoric Society* **65**:145–166.

Brumfiel, E. M. (1991). Weaving and cooking: Women's production in Aztec Mexico, in *Engendering archaeology*. Edited by J. Gero and M. Conkey. Oxford: Blackwell, pp. 224–251.

Bulgarelli, G. M., L. D'Erme, and E. Pellegrini. (2003). L'insediamento neo-eneolitico di Poggio Olivastro (Canino – VT): le strutture. *Atti, Riunione Scientifica dell' I. I. P. P.* **35**:803–806.

Burton, J. (1984). Quarrying in a tribal society. *World Archaeology* **16**:234–247.

Butler, J. (1993). *Bodies that matter: On the discursive limits of "sex."* London: Routledge.

Caldara, M., L. Pennetta, and O. Simone. (2002). Holocene evolution of the Salpi lagoon (Puglia, Italy). *Journal of Coastal Research* **36** (Special Issue):124–133.

Campana, N., R. Maggi, M. Pearce, and C. Ottomano. (2006). Quanto rame? stima della produzione mineraria del distretto di Sestri Levante fra IV e III millennio a.c. *Atti, Riunione Scientifica dell' I. I. P. P.* **39**: in press.

Campetti, S., G. Giachi, and L. Perrini. (2003). Tracce di sostanze collanti su cuspidi litiche provenienti da Grotta dell'Onda e dal Lago di Massaciuccoli (Lucca): analisi composizionali. *Atti, Riunione Scientifica dell' I. I. P. P.* **35**:999–1004.

Canci, A. (1998). Lesioni del cranio in resti scheletrici umani di epoca neolitica rinvenuti presso l'Arma dell'Aquila (Finale Ligure, Savona). *Bullettino di Paletnologia Italiana* **89**:81–92.

Canci, A., and E. Marini. (2003). La suddivisione dei ruoli nelle attività di sussistenza durante il Neolitico medio: I risultati di uno studio paleobiologico. *Atti, Riunione Scientifica dell' I. I. P. P.* **35**:1103–1108.

Cann, J. R., and C. Renfrew. (1964). The characterization of obsidian and its application to the Mediterranean region. *Proceedings of the Prehistoric Society, 1964* **30**:111–133.

Canuto, M., and J. Yaeger (Eds.). (2000). *The archaeology of communities: A new world perspective.* London: Routledge.

Carancini, G., and R. Guerzani. (1987). Gli scavi nella Grotta Pavolella presso Cassano allo Jonio (CS). *Atti, Riunione Scientifica dell' I. I. P. P.* **26**:783–792.

Cardarelli, A. (1992). L'età dei metalli nell'Italia settentrionale, in *Italia preistorica*. Edited by A. Guidi and M. Piperno. Rome: Laterza, pp. 366–420.

Cardini, L. (1970). Praia a Mare: relazione degli scavi 1957–1970. *Bullettino di Paletnologia Italiana* **79**:31–59.

Cardosa, M. (1996). Castello di Bova Superiore (Reggio Calabria): Nuovi dati sulla prima età del Bronzo nella Calabria meridionale ionica, in *L'antica età del Bronzo in Italia: Atti del Congresso di Viareggio, 9–12 gennaio 1995*. Edited by D. Cocchi Genick. Viareggio: Franco Cantini/Museo A. C. Blanc, pp. 592–593.

Carnieri, E., and B. Zamagni. (2000). La malacofauna marina di Pianosa, Cala Giovanna Piano, in *Les premier peuplements olocenes de l'aire Corso-Toscane/Il primo popolamento olocenico dell'area Corso-Toscana*. Edited by C. Tozzi and M. Weiss. Pisa: Edizioni ETS, pp. 117–122.

Cassano, S., A. Cazzella, A. Manfredini, and M. Moscoloni. (1987). *Coppa Nevigata e il suo territorio: testimonianze archeologiche dal VII al II millennio a.C.* Roma: Edizioni Quasar.

Cassano, S., and A. Manfredini. (1983). *Studi sul Neolitico del Tavoliere della Puglia*. International Series. Oxford: British Archaeological Reports.

———. (1990). Rinvenimento di una sepoltura Serra d'Alto a Masseria Candelaro: Scavo 1990. *Atti Convegno Nazionale sulla Preistoria, Protostoria e Storia della Daunia* **12**:31–36.

Cassano, S., A. Manfredini, G. Carboni, N. Marconi, and I. Muntoni. (2003). Il villaggio neolitico di Masseria Candelaro (FG): una premessa archeologica. *Atti, Riunione Scientifica dell' I. I. P. P.* **35**:813–818.

Cassano, S., I. Muntoni, and C. Conati Barbaro. (1995). *Dall'argilla al vaso: Fabbricazione della ceramica in una comunità neolitica di 7000 anni fa.* Rome: Museo delle Origini.

Castellana, G. (1995). *La necropoli protoeneolitica di Piano Vento nel territorio di Palma di Montechiaro*. Agrigento: Regione Sicilia Assessorato Regionale Beni Culturali Ambientali e Pubblica Istruzione.

Castelletti, L. (1996). Mele e pere selvatiche (Malus sylvestris e Pyrus sp.) carbonizzate, in *La Grotta Sant'Angelo sulla Montagna dei Fiori (Teramo)*. Edited by T. Di Fraia and R. Grifoni Cremonesi. Pisa: Istituti Editoriali e Poligrafici Internazionali, pp. 295–303.

Castelletti, L., E. Castiglioni, L. Leoni, and M. Rottoli (1998) Resti botanici dai contesti del Neolitico medio-recente. *Bullettino di Paletnologia Italiana* **89**:191–200.

Castelletti, L., L. Costantini, and C. Tozzi. (1987). Considerazioni sull'economia e l'ambiente durante il neolitico in Italia. *Atti, Riunione Scientifica dell' I. I. P. P.* **26**:37–55.

Castignino Berlinghieri, E. (2003). *The Aeolian Islands: Crossroads of Mediterranean maritime*

routes. International Series Vol. 1181. Oxford: British Archaeological Reports.
Catlin, G. (1973). *Letters and notes on the manners, customs, and conditions of North American Indians* (Vol. 1). New York: Dover.
Cavalier, M. (1971). Il riparo della Sperlinga di S. Basilio (Novara di Sicilia). *Bullettino di Paletnologia Italiana* **80**:7–63.
———. (1985). Nuovi rinveninenti sul Castello di Lipari. *Rivista di Scienze Preistoriche* **40**:223–254.
Cavanagh, W. G. (2004). WYSIWYG: Settlement and territoriality in Southern Greece during the Early and Middle Neolithic periods. *Journal of Mediterranean Archaeology* **17**:165–189.
Cazzella, A. (1994). Dating the "Copper Age" in the Italian peninsula and adjacent islands. *European Journal of Archaeology* **2**:1–19.
———. (2003). Rituali funerari eneolitici nell'Italia penisulare: l'Italia centrale. *Atti, Riunione Scientifica dell' I. I. P. P.* **35**:275–282.
Cazzella, A., and M. Moscoloni. (1985). Dislevelli culturali nel Mediterraneo centro-orientale fra terzo e secondo millennio a.C, in *Studi di paletnologia in onore di Salvatore M. Puglisi*. Edited by M. Liverani, A. Palmieri, and R. Peroni. Rome: Università di Roma "La Sapienza," pp. 531–547.
———. (1992). *Neolitico ed eneolitico. Popoli e civiltà dell'Italia antica.* Rome: Biblioteca di Storia Patria.
———. (1999). Coppa Nevigata: risulatati degli scavi in extensione 1983–1997, in *Ipogei della Daunia: Preistoria di un Territorio*. Edited by A. M. Tunzi Sisto. Foggia: Claudio Grenzi Editore, pp. 102–107.
Chapman, J. (2000). *Fragmentation in archaeology: Peoples, places, and broken objects in the prehistory of south-eastern Europe*. London: Routledge.
———. (2002). Colourful prehistories: The problem with the Berlin and Kay colour paradigm, in *Colouring the past: the significance of colour in archaeological research*. Edited by A. Jones and G. MacGregor. Oxford: Berg, pp. 45–72.
Chapman, R. (2003). *Archaeologies of Complexity*. London: Routledge.
Childe, V. G. (1957). *The dawn of European civilization*. New York: Knopf.

Cipolloni Sampò, M. (1982). Gli scavi nel villaggio neolitico di Rendina (1970–76): relazione preliminare. *Origini* **11**:183–323.
———. (1986). Le tombe di Toppo Daguzzo (Basilicata nord-orientale): considerazioni sulle comunità della media età del Bronzo nel sud-est italia, in *Traffici micenei nel Mediterraneo*. Edited by M. Marazzi, S. Tusa, and L. Vagnetti. Taranto: Istituto per la storia e l'archeologia della Magna Grecia, pp. 27–35.
———. (1992). Il Neolitico nell'Italia meridionale e in Sicilia, in *Italia Preistorica*. Edited by A. Guidi and M. Piperno. Roma: Laterza, pp. 334–365.
Clendinnen, I. (2003). *Ambivalent conquests: Maya and Spaniard in Yucatan, 1517–1570*. (2nd ed.). Cambridge, UK: Cambridge University Press.
Cocchi Genick, D., and R. Grifoni Cremonesi. (1985). *L'età dei metalli nella Toscana nord-occidentale*. Pisa: Pacini Editore.
Collier, J., and M. Rosaldo. (1981). Politics and gender in simple societies, in *Sexual meanings: The cultural construction of gender and sexuality*. Edited by S. Ortner and H. Whitehead. Cambridge, UK: Cambridge University Press, pp. 275–329.
Coltorti, M., and L. Dal Ri. (1985). Human impact on the landscape: some examples from the Adige valley, in *Papers in Italian Archaeology IV: the Cambridge Conference*, vol. I. BAR International Series. Edited by C. Malone and S. Stoddart. Oxford: British Archaeological Reports, pp. 105–134.
Conati Barbaro, C., C. Lemorini, A. Ciarico, and S. Sivilli. (2003). Attività produttive nel villaggio neolitico di Masseria Candelaro: L'apporto dell'indagine tecnologica e funzionale dell'industria litica. *Atti, Riunione Scientifica dell' I. I. P. P.* **35**:819–824.
Conkey, M., and S. Williams. (1991). Original narratives: The political economy of gender in archaeology, in *Gender at the crossroads of knowledge: feminist anthropology in the postmodern era*. Edited by M. di Leonardo. Berkeley: University of California Press, pp. 102–139.
Coote, J. (1992). "Marvels of everyday vision:" The anthropology of aesthetics and the cattle-keeping Nilotes, in *Anthropology, Art, and Aesthetics*. Edited by J. Coote and A. Shelton. Oxford: Clarendon, pp. 245–273.

Corrain, C. (1963). I resti scheletrici umani della stazione eneolitica di Remedello (Brescia). *Atti dell'Istituto Veneto di Scienze, Lettere ed Arti* **121**:165–208.

Costabile, F. (1972). La stazione neolitica di Prestarona in comune di Canolo. *Klearchos* **53–56**:5–27.

Costantini, L., L. C. Biasini, and A. Lentini. (2003). Indagini archeobotaniche sugli intonaci neolitici di Torre Sabea, in *Torre Sabea: un Établissement du Néolithique Ancien en Salento*. Edited by J. Guilaine and G. Cremonesi. Rome: École Française de Rome, pp. 234–246.

Coubray, S. (1997). Analisi preliminare dei macroresti vegetali, in *Casale del Dolce: Ambiente, Economia, e Cultura di una comunità preistorica del Valle del Sacco*. Edited by A. Zarattini and L. Petrassi. Roma: Soprintendenza Archeologica per il Lazio, pp. 273–281.

Cremonesi, G. (1965). Il villaggio di Ripoli alla luce dei recenti scavi. *Rivista di Scienze Preistoriche* **20**:85–155.

———. (1976). *La Grotta dei Piccioni di Bolognano nel quadro delle culture dal neolitico all'età del bronzo in Abruzzo*. Pisa: Giardini.

———. (1988). Osservazioni su alcune strutture in abitati neolitici dell'Italia meridionale. *Origini* **14**:83–99.

Cremonesi, G., and C. Tozzi. (1987). Il Neolitico dell'Abruzzo. *Atti, Riunione Scientifica dell' I. I. P. P.* **26**:229–238.

Crown, P. L. (2001). Learning to make pottery in the prehispanic American Southwest. *Journal of Anthropological Research* **57**:451–470.

Csordas, T. (1999). The body's career in anthropology, in *Anthropological Theory Today*. Edited by H. Moore. Cambridge, UK: Polity, pp. 172–205.

Cuda, M. T., and R. Murgano. (2004). Il sito neolitico di Sovereto di Nicotera (RC). *Atti, Riunione Scientifica dell' I. I. P. P.* **37**:163–174.

Curci, A., and A. Tagliacozzo. (2003). Aspetti economici e culturali nel villaggio neolitico Masseria Candelaro (Manfredonia – FG): l'analisi faunistica della "grande struttura." *Atti, Riunione Scientifica dell' I. I. P. P.* **35**:825–828.

D'Ambrosio, B., and S. Sfrecola. (1990). Le collane eneolitiche e del Bronzo Antico della Liguria: materie prime e fonti di approvvigionamento. *Rivista di Scienze Preistoriche* **41**:331–344.

D'Amico, C., M. Minale, E. Starnini, and P. Trentini. (2003). L'officina di produzione di asce in pietra levigata di Rivanazzano (PV): dati archeometrici e catena operativa, nota preliminare. *Atti, Riunione Scientifica dell' I. I. P. P.* **35**:981–986.

d'Errico, F. (1987). Technologie et fonction du burin de Ripabianca dans le cadre culturel du néolithique ancien de l'Italie septentrionale. *Anthropologie* **91**:411–431.

d'Ottavio, F. (2001). La caratterizzazione chimica della selce delle miniere preistoriche del Gargano: proposta di un metodo archeometrico basato sulle analisi chimiche eseguite con la tecnica strumentale ICP-AES. *Origini* **23**:111–143.

Dahl, G., and A. Hjort. (1976). *Having herds: Pastoral herd growth and household economy*. Stockholm Studies in Social Anthropology. Stockholm: Department of Social Anthropology, University of Stockholm.

Davidson, I. (1989). Escaped domestic animals and the introduction of agriculture to Spain, in *The walking larder: patterns of domestication, pastoralism and predation*. Edited by J. Clutton-Brock. London: Unwin Hyman, pp. 59–71.

Dawson, H. (2005). *Island Colonisation and Abandonment in Mediterranean Prehistory*. London: Ph.D. Thesis, Institute of Archaeology, University College London.

de Certeau, M. (2002). *The Practice of Everyday Life*. Berkeley: University of California Press.

De Lucia, A., D. Ferri, A. Geniola, C. Giove, M. Maggiore, N. Melone, V. Pesce Delfino, P. Pieri, and V. Scattarella. (1977). *La comunità neolitica di Cala Colombo presso Torre a Mare, Bari*. Bari: Società per lo Studio di Storia Patria per la Puglia.

Deetz, J. (1977). *In small things forgotten: The archaeology of early North American life*. New York: Doubleday.

Deith, M. (1987). La raccolta dei molluschi nel Tavoliere in epoca preistorica, in *Coppa Nevigata e il suo territorio: testimonianze archeologiche dal VII al II millennio a.C.* Edited by S. Cassano, A. Cazzella, A. Manfredini, and M. Moscoloni. Rome: Quasar, pp. 101–108.

———. (1989). Shellfish gathering and site function: a case study from Neolithic Apulia. *ArchaeoZoologia* **3**:163–176.

Delamont, S. (1995). *Appetites and identities: an introduction to the social anthropology of western Europe*. London: Routledge.

Delano Smith, C. (1979). *Western Mediterranean Europe: A historical geography*. New York: Academic.

———. (1983). L'ambiente, in *Passo di Corvo e la civiltà neolitica del Tavoliere*. Edited by S. Tinè. Genova: Sagep, pp. 11–22.

DeMarrais, E., L. J. Castillo, and T. K. Earle. (1996). Ideology, materialization, and power strategies. *Current Anthropology* **37**:15–31.

Dering, P. (1999). Earth-oven plant processing in Archaic period economies: An example from a semi-arid savannah in south-central North America. *American Antiquity* **64**:659–674.

di Lampedusa, G. T. (1960). *The Leopard*. New York: Pantheon.

Di Lernia, S., and A. Galiberti. (1993). *Archeologia mineraria della Selce nella preistoria*. Firenze: All'insegna del Giglio.

Díaz-Andreu, M., and T. Champion. (1996). *Nationalism and archaeology in Europe*. London: UCL Press.

Dietler, M. (1996). Feasts and commensal politics in the political economy: food, power, and status in prehistoric Europe, in *Food and the status quest*. Edited by P. Wiessner and W. Schiefenhövel. Oxford: Berghahn, pp. 87–126.

Dietler, M., and B. Hayden. (2001). Digesting the feast: good to eat, good to drink, good to think, in *Feasts: archaeological and ethnographic perspectives on food, politics and power*. Edited by M. Dietler and B. Hayden. Washington, DC: Smithsonian, pp. 1–22.

———. (2001). *Feasts: archaeological and ethnographic perspectives*. Washington, DC: Smithsonian.

Dobres, M.-A. (2001). *Technology and social agency: Outlining a practice framework for archaeology*. Oxford: Blackwell.

Dobres, M.-A., and J. Robb. (Eds.). (2000). *Agency in archaeology*. London: Routledge.

———. (2005). "Doing" agency: introductory remarks on methodology. *Journal of Archaeological Method and Theory* **12**:159–166.

Dobres, M.-A., and J. E. Robb. (2000). Agency in Archaeology: Paradigm or Platitude? in *Agency in Archaeology*. Edited by M.-A. Dobres and J. Robb. London: Routledge, pp. 3–17.

Donahue, R. (1991). Desperately seeking Ceres: a critical examination of current models for the transition to agriculture in Mediterranean Europe, in *Transitions to agriculture in prehistory*. Monographs in World Archaeology. Edited by A. Gebauer and T. D. Price. Madison: Prehistory Press, pp. 73–81.

Dornan, J. L. (2002). Agency and archaeology: Past, present, and future directions. *Journal of Archaeological Method and Theory* **9**:303–329.

Douglas, N. (1938). *Old Calabria*. New York: Oxford University Press.

Ducci, S., P. Perazzi, and A. Ronchitelli. (1987). Gli insediamenti neolitici abbruzzesi con ceramica impressa di Tricalle (CH) e Fontanelle (PE). *Rassegna di Archeologia* **6**:65–142.

Earle, T., and J. Ericsson. (1977). *Exchange systems in prehistory*. New York: Academic.

Edmonds, M. (1999). *Ancestral geographies of the Neolithic: Landscape, monuments and memory*. London: Routledge.

Ehrenberg, M. (1989). *Women in prehistory*. Norman: University of Oklahoma Press.

Ehrenreich, R. M., C. L. Crumley, and J. Levy. (1995). *Heterarchy and the analysis of complex societies*. (Vol. 6), Archaeological Papers. Washington, DC: American Anthropological Association.

Evans-Pritchard, E. (1940). *The Nuer*. Oxford: Clarendon.

Evans, J. (1971). *Prehistoric Antiquities of the Maltese Islands*. London: Athlone.

———. (1976). Archaeological evidence for religious practices in the Maltese Islands during the Neolithic and Copper Ages. *Kokalos* **22**:130–146.

Evett, D. (1975). A preliminary note on the typology, functional variability and trade of Italian Neolithic ground stone axes. *Origini* **7**:35–54.

Farr, R. H. (2001). Cutting Through Water: An Analysis of Neolithic Obsidian from Bova Marina, Calabria. MA Dissertation, University of Southampton.

———. (2006). Seafaring as social action. *Journal of Maritime Archaeology* **1**:1–15.

Farr, R. H., and J. Robb. (2005). Substances in Motion: Neolithic Mediterranean "Trade." in *The archaeology of Mediterranean prehistory*. Edited by E. Blake and A. B. Knapp. Oxford: Blackwell, pp. 24–45.

Fedele, F. (1990). *L'altopiano di Ossimo-Borno nella preistoria: ricerche 1988–1990*. Capo di Ponte: Edizioni del Centro.

Feil, D. (1987). *The evolution of highland Papua New Guinea societies*. Cambridge, UK: Cambridge University Press.

Feinman, G. (2001). Corporate/network: a new perspective on leadership in the American Southwest, in *Hierarchies in action: Cui bono*. Edited by M. Diehl. Carbondale: Center for Archaeological Investigations, Southern Illinois University, pp. 152–180.

Feinman, G. M., and J. Neitzel. (1984). Too many types: an overview of prestate societies in the Americas. *Advances in Archaeological Method and Theory* 7:39–84.

Fiorentino, G., M. La Torre, I. Muntoni, D. Pierattini, M. Picsciello, and F. Radina. (2003). Dinamiche di crollo e ricostruzione dell'alzato di capanna: approccio integrato all'analisi degli intonaci dell'insediamento del Neolitico antico di Balsignano (Modugno, Bari). *Atti, Riunione Scientifica dell' I. I. P. P.* **35**:807–812.

FitzGerald, E. (1957). *The Rubaiyat of Omar Khayyam*. Garden City: Doubleday.

Flannery, K. (1976). *The early Mesoamerican village*. New York: Academic.

———. (1999). Process and agency in early state formation. *Cambridge Archaeological Journal* **9**:3–12.

Forenbaher, S., and P. Miracle. (2005). The spread of farming in the Eastern Adriatic. *Antiquity* **79**:514–528.

Formentini, R. (1991). L'immagine femminile nelle statue-menhirs, in *Second Deyà International Conference of Prehistory: Recent developments in Western Mediterranean prehistory: Archaeological techniques, technology and theory*, vol. 2, BAR International Series. Edited by W. Waldren, J. Ensenyat, and R. Kennard. Oxford: Tempus Reparatum, pp. 365–385.

Formicola, V. (1983). Stature in Italian prehistoric samples with particular reference to methodological problems. *Homo* **34**:33–47.

Fornaciari, G. (1979). Lesione traumatica su una calotta dell'Eneolitico dell'Isola di Elba. *Quaderni di Scienze Antropologiche* **3**:28–36.

Foucault, M. (1977). *Discipline and punish: The birth of the prison*. London: Allen Lane.

Fowler, C. (2004). *The archaeology of personhood*. London: Routledge.

Francalacci, P. (1989). Dietary reconstruction at Arene Candide Cave (Liguria, Italy) by means of trace-element analysis. *Journal of Archaeological Science* **16**:109–124.

Frayer, D. (1981). Body size, weapon use and natural selection in the European Upper Paleolithic and Mesolithic. *American Anthropologist* **83**:57–63.

Fried, M. (1967). *The evolution of political society*. New York: Random House.

Fugazzola Delpino, M. A. (2001). La piccola "dea madre" del Lago di Bracciano. *Bullettino di Paletnologia Italiana* **91–92**:27–46.

Fugazzola Delpino, M. A., G. D'Eugenio, and A. Pessina. (1993). "La Marmotta" (Anguillara Sabazia, RM): Scavi 1989 – un abitato perilacustre di età neolitica. *Bullettino di Paletnologia Italiana* **84**:181–342.

Fugazzola Delpino, M. A., A. Manfredini, F. Martini, G. Radi, L. Sarti, and M. Silvestrini. (2003). Insediamenti e strutture neolitiche ed eneolitiche dell'Italia centrale. *Atti Riunione Scientifica dell' I. I. P. P.* **35**:93–112.

Fugazzola Delpino, M. A., and M. Mineo. (1995). La piroga neolitica del lago di Bracciano, La Marmotta 1. *Bullettino di Paletnologia Italiano (Rome)* **86**:197–266.

Fugazzola Delpino, M. A., and V. Tinè. (2003). Le statuine fittili femminili del Neolitico Italiano: iconografia e contesto culturale. *Bullettino di Paletnologia Italiana* **93–95**:19–51.

Galaty, J. (1989). Cattle and cognition: aspects of Maasai practical reasoning, in *The walking larder: Patterns of domestication, pastoralism and predation*. Edited by J. Clutton-Brock. London: Unwin Hyman, pp. 215–230.

Galiberti, A. (1987). La miniera preistorica della Defensola (Vieste): note preliminare. *Atti, Riunione Scientifica dell' I. I. P. P.* **26**:721–732.

———. (1999). La miniera della Defensola, in *Ipogei della Daunia: Preistoria di un Territorio*. Edited by A. M. Tunzi Sisto. Foggia: Claudio Grenzi Editore, pp. 30–33.

Galli, E. (1950). Nuove scoperte nella necropoli di "Fonte Noce" presso Recanati. *Bullettino di Paletnologia Italiana* **8**:1–19.

Gardner, A. (2004). *Agency uncovered: Archaeological perspectives on social agency, personhood, and being human*. London: UCL Press.

Gathercole, P., and D. Lowenthal. (Eds.) (1990). *The politics of the past*. London: Routledge.

Geertz, C. (1973). *The interpretation of cultures.* New York: Basic Books.
Gell, A. (1992). The technology of enchantment and the enchantment of technology, in *Anthropology, Art and Aesthetics.* Edited by J. Coote and A. Shelton. Oxford: Blackwell, pp. 40–67.
———. (1998). *Art and agency: An anthropological theory.* Oxford: Clarendon Press.
Geniola, A. (1987). La cultura di Serra d'Alto nella Puglia centrale. *Atti, Riunione Scientifica dell' I. I. P. P.* **26**:771–781.
———. (1992). *Marcianese: il villaggio Rossi: entità del neolitico medio arcaico abruzzese.* Lanciano: Itinerari.
Geniola, A., V. Camerini, and G. Lionetti. (1995). *Villaggi trincerati Neolitici negli agri di Matera, Santeramo, Laterza.* Matera: Grafiche Paternoster.
Geniola, A., and F. Ponzetti. (1987). Ricerche sul neolitico delle murge altamurane. *Atti, Riunione Scientifica dell' I. I. P. P.* **25**:209–221.
Geniola, A., and A. Tunzi Sisto. (1980). Espressioni cultuali e d'arte nella Grotta di Cala Scizzo presso Torre a Mare (Bari). *Rivista di Scienze Preistoriche* **35**:125–146.
Germanà, F., and G. Fornaciari. (1992). *Trapanazioni, craniotomie e traumi cranici in Italia dalla preistoria all'età moderna.* Pisa: Giardini.
Germanà, F., F. Mallegni, C. de Pompeis, and D. Ronco. (1990). Il villaggio neolitico di Villa Badessa (Pescara): aspetti paletnologici, antropologici e paleopatologici. *Atti, Società Toscana di Scienze Naturali* **97**:271–310.
Gero, J. (1991). Genderlithics: Women's role in stone tool production, in *Engendering Archaeology.* Edited by M. Conkey and R. Tringham. Oxford: Blackwell, pp. 163–193.
Giampietri, A., and C. Tozzi. (1989). L'industria litica del villaggio di Ripa Tetta (Lucera). *Atti Convegno Nazionale sulla Preistoria, Protostoria e Storia della Daunia* **11**:57–78.
Giannitrapani, M. (2002). *Coroplastica Neolitica antropomorfa d'Italia: Simboli ed iconografie dell'arte mobiliare quaternaria post-glaciale.* International Series (Vol. 1020). Oxford: British Archaeological Reports.
Giddens, A. (1979). *Central problems in social theory: Action, structure, and contradiction in social analysis.* Berkeley: University of California Press.
———. (1984). *The constitution of society.* Berkeley: University of California Press.
Gillespie, S. D. (2001). Personhood, agency, and mortuary ritual: A case study from the ancient Maya. *Journal of Anthropological Archaeology* **20**:73–112.
Gilman, A. (1981). The development of social stratification in Bronze Age Europe. *Current Anthropology* **22**:1–24.
———. (1991). Trajectories towards social complexity in the later prehistory of the Mediterranean, in *Chiefdoms: Power, economy, ideology.* Edited by T. Earle. New York: Cambridge University Press, pp. 146–168.
Gimbutas, M. (1991). *The civilization of the Goddess: The world of Old Europe.* San Francisco: Harper and Row.
Glass, M. (1991). *Animal production systems in Neolithic Central Europe.* BAR International Series. Oxford: Tempus Reparatum.
Gnoli, G., and J.-P. Vernant. (1982). *La mort, les morts dan les sociétés anciennes.* Cambridge, UK and Paris: Cambridge University Press/Editions de la Maison des Sciences de l'Homme.
Godelier, M. (1986). *The making of great men: Male domination and power among the New Guinea Baruya.* Cambridge, UK: Cambridge University Press.
———. (1991). An unfinished attempt at reconstructing the social processes which may have prompted the transformation of great-men societies into big-men societies, in *Big men and great men: Personifications of power in Melanesia.* Edited by M. Godelier and M. Strathern. Cambridge, UK: Cambridge University Press, pp. 275–304.
Godelier, M., and A. Strathern. (1991). *Big men and great men: Personifications of power.* Cambridge, UK: Cambridge University Press.
Gosden, C. (1994). *Social being and time.* London: Blackwell.
Gosden, C., and Y. Marshall. (1999). The cultural biography of objects. *World Archaeology* **31**:169–178.
Gravina, A. (1975). Fossati e strutture ipogeiche dei villaggi neolitici in agro di S. Severo. *Attualità Archeologiche* **1**:14–34.
Graziosi, P. (1974). *L'arte preistorica in Italia.* Firenze: Sansoni.

———. (1975). Nuove manifestazioni d'arte mesolitica e neolitica nel Riparo Gaban presso Trento. *Rivista di Scienze Preistoriche* **30**:237–278.

———. (1980). *Le pitture preistoriche di Porto Badisco*. Firenze: Martelli.

Gregg, S. (1988). *Foragers and farmers: Population interaction and agricultural expansion in prehistoric Europe*. Chicago: University of Chicago Press.

Grifoni Cremonesi, R. (1992). Il Neolitico nell'Italia Centrale e in Sardegna, in *Italia preistorica*. Edited by A. Guidi and M. Piperno. Roma: Laterza, pp. 306–333.

———. (2003). Sepolture neolitiche dell'Italia centro-meridionale e loro relazioni con gli abitati. *Atti, Riunione Scientifica dell' I. I. P. P.* **35**:259–274.

Grifoni Cremonesi, R., F. Mallegni, and A. Tramonti. (2003). La sepoltura del Neolitico antico di Torre Sabea, in *Torre Sabea: un Établissement du Néolithique Ancien en Salento*. Edited by J. Guilaine and G. Cremonesi. Rome: École Française de Rome, pp. 96–105.

Grifoni Cremonesi, R., and A. Radmilli. (2001). La grotta Patrizi al Sassi di Furbara (Cerveteri, Roma). *Bullettino di Paletnologia Italiana* 91–92:63–120.

Grifoni Cremonesi, R., C. Tozzi, and M. Weiss. (2000). Il Neolitico antico dell'area corso-toscana, in *Les Premier Peuplements Olocenes de l'Aire Corso-Toscane/Il Primo Popolamento Olocenico dell'Area Corso-Toscana*. Edited by C. Tozzi and M. Weiss. Pisa: Edizioni ETS, pp. 259–271.

Guidi, A. (1992). Le età dei metalli nell'Italia centrale e in Sardegna, in *Italia preistorica*. Edited by A. Guidi and M. Piperno. Rome: Laterza, pp. 420–470.

———. (2000). *Preistoria della complessità sociale*. Bari: Laterza.

Guilaine, J. (Ed.). (1993). *Dougne. Derniers chasseurs-collecteurs et premiers éleveurs de la Haute-Vallée de l'Aude*. Toulouse: Centre d'Anthropologie des Sociétés Rurales.

Guilaine, J., and G. Cremonesi. (1987). L'habitat néolithique de Trasano (Matera, Basilicate). Premiers résultats. *Atti, Riunione Scientifica dell' I. I. P. P.* **26**:707–719.

———. (Eds.). (2003). *Torre Sabea: Un Établissement du Néolithique Ancien en Salento* (Vol. 315). Collection de l'École Française de Rome. Rome: École Française de Rome.

Guzzardi, L., M. R. Iovino, and A. Rivoli. (2003). L'organizzazione del villaggio neolitico di Vulpiglia presso Pachino (Siracusa). *Atti, Riunione Scientifica dell' I. I. P. P.* **35**:845–849.

Hagerstrand, T. (1977). *Culture and ecology: four time-geographic essays*. Lund: Lund Universitets Kulturgeografiska Institutionen.

Hallam, B., S. Warren, and C. Renfrew. (1976). Obsidian in the western Mediterranean: characterization by neutron activation analysis and optical emission spectroscopy. *Proceedings of the Prehistoric Society* **42**:85–110.

Halstead, P. (1981). Counting sheep in Neolithic and Bronze Age Greece, in *Pattern of the past: studies in honour of David Clarke*. Edited by I. Hodder, G. Isaac, and N. Hammond. Cambridge, UK: Cambridge University Press, pp. 307–339.

———. (1989). The economy has a normal surplus: economic stability and social change among early farming communities of Thessaly, Greece, in *Bad year economics*. Edited by P. Halstead and J. O'Shea. Cambridge, UK: Cambridge University Press, pp. 68–80.

———. (1994). The North–South divide: Regional paths to complexity in prehistoric Greece, in *Development and decline in the Mediterranean*. Edited by C. Mathers and S. Stoddart. Sheffield: J. R. Collis Publications, pp. 195–219.

Halstead, P., and J. O'Shea. (1982). A friend in need is a friend indeed: Social storage and the origins of ranking, in *Ranking, resource, and exchange*. Edited by C. Renfrew and S. Shennan. Cambridge, UK: Cambridge University Press, pp. 92–99.

Hamilakis, Y. (1998). Eating the dead: Mortuary feasting and the politics of memory in the Aegean Bronze Age societies, in *Cemetery and Society in the Aegean Bronze Age*. Edited by K. Branigan. Sheffield: Sheffield Academic Press, pp. 115–132.

———. (1999). Food technologies, technologies of the body: The social context of wine and oil production and consumption in Bronze Age Crete. *World Archaeology* **31**: 38–54.

Hamilakis, Y., M. Pluciennik, and S. Tarlow. (Eds.). (2002). *Thinking through the body: archaeologies of corporeality*. London: Kluwer/Plenum Academic.

Hardy, K., and P. Sillitoe. (2003). Material perspectives: Stone tool use and material culture among the Wola, Papua New Guinea. *Internet Archaeology* 14.

Hastorf, C. A. (1991). Gender, space and food in prehistory, in *Engendering Archaeology*. Edited by M. Conkey and J. Gero. Oxford: Blackwell, pp. 132–161.

Hatch, E. (1989). Theories of social honor. *American Anthropologist* 91:341–353.

Hayden, B. (1990). Nimrods, Piscators, Pluckers, and Planters: The emergence of food production. *Journal of Anthropological Archaeology* 9:31–69.

Hegmon, M., and S. Kulow. (2005). Painting as agency, style as structure: Innovations in Mimbres pottery designs from Southwest New Mexico. *Journal of Archaeological Method and Theory* 12:313–334.

Helms, M. (1983). *Ulysses' sail*. Princeton: Princeton University Press.

———. (1998). *Access to origins: affines, ancestors, and aristocrats*. Austin: University of Texas Press.

Herbert, E. W. (1994). *Iron, gender, and power: Rituals of transformation in African societies*. Bloomington: Indiana University Press.

Hirth, K. (Ed.) (2003). *Mesoamerican lithic technology: Experimentation and interpretation*. Salt Lake City: University of Utah Press.

Hobsbawn, E., and T. Ranger. (1993). *The invention of tradition*. Cambridge, UK: Cambridge University Press.

Hodder, I. (1990). *The domestication of Europe*. London: Basil Blackwell.

Hodder, I., and C. Cessford. (2004). Daily practice and social memory at Çatalhöyük. *American Antiquity* 69:17–40.

Hodder, I., and C. Malone. (1984). Intensive survey of prehistoric sites in the Stilo region, Calabria. *Proceedings of the Prehistoric Society* 50:121–150.

Holloway, R. (1974). *Buccino*. Rome: de Luca.

———. (1975). Buccino: the Early Bronze Age village of Tufariello. *Journal of Field Archaeology* 2:11–81.

Holmes, K., and R. Whitehouse. (1998). Anthropomorphic figurines and the construction of gender in Neolithic Italy, in *Gender and italian archaeology: Challenging the stereotypes*. Edited by R. Whitehouse. London: Accordia Research Center, pp. 95–126.

Hopf, M. (1991). South and Southwest Europe, in *Progress in Old World palaeoethnobotany*. Edited by W. Van Zeist, K. Wasylikowa, and K.-E. Behre. Rotterdam: Balkema, pp. 241–277.

Horden, P., and N. Purcell. (2000). *The corrupting sea: A study of Mediterranean history*. Oxford: Blackwell.

Hosler, D. (1995). Sound, color, and meaning in the metallurgy of ancient West Mexico. *World Archaeology* 27:100–115.

Houston, S., and K. Taube. (2000). An archaeology of the senses: perception and cultural expression in ancient Mesoamerica. *Cambridge Archaeological Journal* 10:261–294.

Hurcombe, L. (1992). New contributions to the study of the function of Sardinian obsidian artifacts, in *Sardinia in the Mediterranean: A footprint in the sea*. Edited by R. H. Tykot and T. K. Andrews. Sheffield: Sheffield Academic Press, pp. 83–97.

Iacopini, A. (2000). Il sito neolitico di Casa Querciolaia (Livorno). *Rassegna di Archeologia* 17:127–178.

Ingold, T. (2000). *The perception of the environment: Essays on livelihood, dwelling, and skill*. London: Routledge.

Ingravallo, E. (1999). Le cose della preistoria, in *Fonti di Informazione e Contesto Archeologico: Manufatti Ceramici e Neolitizazzione Meridionale*. Edited by E. Ingravallo. Galatina: Mario Congedi, pp. 9–20.

———. (2001). Il sito neolitico di Serra Cicora (Nardò, LE): note preliminari. *Origini* 26:87–118.

Irti, U. (1992). Due statuette preistoriche dal Fucino. *Atti, Riunione Scientifica dell' I. I. P. P.* 28:433–440.

Jarman, M., and D. Webley. (1975). Settlement and land use in Capitanata, Italy, in *Palaeoeconomy*. Edited by E. Higgs. Cambridge, UK: Cambridge University Press, pp. 177–231.

Johnson, M. (1989). Conceptions of agency in archaeological interpretation. *Journal of Anthropological Archaeology* 8:189–211.

———. (2000). The medieval castle and the fashioning of agency, in *Agency in Archaeology*.

Edited by M.-A. Dobres and J. Robb. London: Routledge, pp. 213–231.
Jones, A., and G. MacGregor. (Eds.). (2002). *Colouring the past: the significance of colour in archaeological research.* Oxford: Berg.
Jones, G. B. D. (1987). *Apulia.* London: Society of Antiquaries.
Jones, R. (1989). Hunters of the dreaming: some ideational, economic, and ecological parameters of the Australian Aboriginal productive system. in *Production systems in the Pacific.* Edited by D. Yen and J. Mummery. Canberra: Department of Prehistory, Australian National University, pp. 25–55.
Jorgenson, D. (1991). Big men, great men and women: alternative logics of difference, in *Big men and great men: personifications of power in Melanesia.* Edited by M. Godelier and M. Strathern. Cambridge, UK: Cambridge University Press, pp. 256–272.
Joyce, R. (2000). Girling the girl and boying the boy: The production of adulthood in ancient Mesoamerica. *World Archaeology* 31:473–483.
Joyce, R., and J. Lopiparo. (2005). Doing agency in archaeology. *Journal of Archaeological Method and Theory* 12:365–374.
Kaiser, T., and S. Forenbaher. (1999). Adriatic sailors and stone knappers: Palagruza in the 3rd millenium BC. *Antiquity* 73:313–24.
Kamp, K. A. (2001). Prehistoric children working and playing: A case study in learning ceramics. *Journal of Anthropological Research* 57:427–450.
Keates, S. (2000). The ancestralization of the landscape: Monumentality, memory, and the rock art of Copper Age Vai Camonica, in *Signifying place and space: World perspectives in rock art and landscape.* International Series (Vol. 902) Edited by G. Nash. Oxford. British Archaeological Reports, pp. 83–102.
———. (2002). The flashing blade: copper, colour, and luminosity in North Italian Copper Age society, in *Colouring the past: The significance of colour in archaeological research.* Edited by A. Jones and G. MacGregor. Oxford: Berg, pp. 109–126.
Kelly, R. (1985). *The Nuer conquest: Structure and development of an expansionist system.* Ann Arbor: University of Michigan Press.

———. (1993). *Constructing inequality: the fabrication of a hierarchy of virtue among the Etoro.* Ann Arbor: University of Michigan Press.
Kensinger, K. (1989). Hunting and male domination in Cashinahua society, in *Farmers as hunters: The implications of sedentism.* Edited by S. Kent. Cambridge, UK: Cambridge University Press, pp. 18–26.
Kent, S. (1989). Cross-cultural perceptions of farmers as hunters and the value of meat, in *Farmers as hunters: The implications of sedentism.* Edited by S. Kent. Cambridge, UK: Cambridge University Press, pp. 1–17.
Knauft, B. (1985). *Good company and violence: Sorcery and social action in a lowland New Guinea society.* Berkeley: University of California Press.
———. (1987). Reconsidering violence in simple human societies: Homicide among the Gebusi of New Guinea. *Current Anthropology* 28:457–499.
———. (1991). Violence and sociality in human evolution. *Current Anthropology* 32:391–428.
———. (1993). *South coast New Guinea cultures: History, comparison, dialectic.* New York: Cambridge University Press.
Kuhn, S. L. (1995). *Mousterian lithic technology: An ecological perspective.* Princeton: Princeton University Press.
La Rocca, F. (2005). *La Miniera Pre-Protostorica di Grotta della Monaca (Sant'Agata di Esaro, Cosenza).* Roseto (Cosenza): Centro Regionale di Speleologia "Enzo dei Medici."
La Rosa, V. (1987). Un nuovo insediamento neolitico a Serra del Palco di Milena (CL). *Atti, Riunione Scientifica dell' I. I. P. P.* 26:801–808.
Langella, M., M. Boscaino, S. Coubrai, A. Curci, A. M. De Francesco, and M. R. Senatore. (2003). Baselice (Benevento): Il sito pluristratificato neolitico di torrente Cervaro. *Rivista di Scienze Preistoriche* 59:259–336.
Latour, B. (2005). *Reassembling the social: an introduction to actor-network-theory.* Oxford: Clarendon.
Laviosa Zambotti, P. (1938). Le civiltà preistoriche e protostoriche dell'Alto Adige. *Monumenti Antichi dei Lincei* 37:9–578.
Leighton, R. (1989). Ground stone tools from Serra Orlando (Morgantina) and stone axe studies in Sicily and Southern Italy. *Proceedings of the Prehistoric Society* 55:135–159.

———. (1992). Stone axes and exchange in south Italian prehistory: New evidence from old collections. *Journal of the Accordia Research Center* **3**:11–40.

———. (1999). *Sicily before History*. London: Duckworth.

Leighton, R., and J. Dixon. (1991). Alcune considerazioni sulle asce levigate in Italian Meridionale ed in Sicilia, in *Papers of the Fourth Conference of Italian Archaeology, Volume 3: New developments*. Edited by E. Herring, R. Whitehouse, and J. Wilkins. London: Accordia Research Centre, pp. 19–28.

———. (1992). Jade and greenstone in the prehistory of Sicily and Southern Italy. *Oxford Journal of Archaeology* **11**:179–200.

Lemonnier, P. (1991). From great men to big men: peace, substitution and competition in the Highlands of New Guinea, in *Big men and great men: Personifications of power in Melanesia*. Edited by M. Godelier and M. Strathern. Cambridge, UK: Cambridge University Press, pp. 7–27.

———. (1992). *Elements for an anthropology of technology*. Anthropological Papers. Ann Arbor: Museum of Anthropology, University of Michigan.

Leone, M. (1984). Interpreting ideology in historical archaeology: using the rules of perspective in the William Paca Garden in Annapolis, Maryland, in *Ideology, power, and prehistory*. Edited by D. Miller and C. Tilley. Cambridge, UK: Cambridge University Press, pp. 25–35.

Levi, P. (1988). *The Drowned and the Saved*. New York: Vintage.

Levy, J. E. (1992). *Orayvi revisited: social stratification in an "egalitarian" community*. Santa Fe: School of American Research.

Lewthwaite, J. (1987). Three steps to leaven: applicazione del modello di disponibilità al neolitico italiano. *Atti, Riunione Scientifica dell' I. I. P. P.* **26**:90–101.

Liep, J. (1991). Great man, big man, chief: a triangulation of the Massim, in *Big men and great men: Personifications of power in Melanesia*. Edited by M. Godelier and M. Strathern. Cambridge, UK: Cambridge University Press, pp. 28–47.

Lillios, K. (1999). Symbolic artifacts and spheres of meaning: groundstone tools from Copper Age Portugal, in *Material symbols: Culture and economy in prehistory*. Edited by J. E. Robb. Carbondale, Illinois: Center for Archaeological Investigations, Southern Illinois University, pp. 173–187.

———. (1999b). Objects of memory: the ethnography and archaeology of heirlooms. *Journal of Archaeological Method and Theory* **6**:235–262.

Lilliu, G. (1999). *Arte e religione della Sardegna prenuragica*. Sassari: Carlo Delfino editore.

Lindenlauf, A. (2004). Dirt, cleanliness, and social structure in ancient Greece, in *Agency uncovered: Archaeological perspectives on social agency, power and being human*. Edited by A. Gardner. London: UCL Press, pp. 81–106.

Livi-Bacci, M. (1999). *The population of Europe*. Oxford: Blackwell.

Lo Porto, F. (1972). La tomba neolitica con idola di pietra di Arnesano. *Rivista di Scienze Preistoriche* **27**:357–372.

———. (1978). La preistoria del Materano alla luce delle ultime ricerche. *Atti, Riunione Scientifica dell' I. I. P. P.* **20**:275–294.

———. (1989). *L'insediamento neolitico di Serra d'Alto nel Materano*. Rome: Giorgio Bretschneider.

Lowenthal, D. (1985). *The past is a foreign country*. Cambridge, UK: Cambridge University Press.

Lucas, G. (2004). *The archaeology of time*. London: Routledge.

Lucifero, A. (1901). Girifalco. *Rivistia Italiana di Scienze Naturali*:115.

Lupton, D. (1996). *Food, the body, and the self*. London: Sage.

Maggi, R. (2001). Pietre della memoria, in *Studie di Preistoria e Protostoria in onore di Luigi Bernabò Brea*. Edited by M. C. Martinelli and U. Spigo. Lipari: Museo Archeologico Regionale Eoliano, pp. 175–186.

Maggi, R., and M. Pearce. (2005). Mid-fourth-millennium copper mining in Liguria, north-west Italy: the earliest known copper mines in western Europe. *Antiquity* **79**:66–77.

Malafouris, L. (2005). The cognitive basis of material engagement: Where brain, body, and culture conflate, in *Rethinking materiality: the engagement of mind with the material world*. Edited by E. DeMarrais, C. Gosden, and C. Renfrew. Cambridge, UK: McDonald Institute for Archaeological Research, pp. 53–62.

Malinowski, B. (1922). *Argonauts of the western Pacific*. Routledge: London.

Mallory, J. (1987). Lagnano da Piede: an Early Neolithic village on the Tavoliere. *Origini* **13**:193–290.

———. (1989). *In search of the Indo-Europeans*. London: Thames and Hudson.

Malone, C. (1985). Pots, prestige and ritual in Neolithic southern Italy. *Papers in Italian archaeology IV: The Cambridge conference, Cambridge, 1985.* International series 244 Oxford: British Archaeological Reports, pp. 118–151.

———. (1994). The transition to agriculture, in *Time, territory, and state: The archaeological development of the Gubbio basin*. Edited by C. Malone and S. Stoddart. Cambridge, UK: Cambridge University Press, pp. 67–80.

Malone, C., and S. Stoddart. (1996). Maltese and Mediterranean megalithism in the light of the Brochtorff Circle. *XIII International Congress of Prehistoric and Protohistoric Sciences (Forlì, Italy, 8–14 September 1996) Colloquia* **9**:109–114.

———. (2004). Towards an island of mind? in *Explaining social change: studies in honour of Colin Renfrew*. Edited by J. Cherry, C. Scarre, and S. Shennan. Cambridge, UK: McDonald Institute for Archaeological Research, pp. 93–102.

Malone, C., S. Stoddart, D. Trump, A. Bonanno, and A. Pace. (Eds.). (2007). *Mortuary ritual in prehistoric Malta: The Brochtorff Circle at Xaghra excavations (1987–1994)*. Cambridge, UK: McDonald Institute for Archaeological Research.

Manfredini, A. (2001). Rituali funerari e organizzazione sociale: Una rilettura di alcuni dati della facies Diana in Italia meridionale, in *Studie di Preistoria e Protostoria in onore di Luigi Bernabò Brea*. Edited by M. C. Martinelli and U. Spigo. Lipari: Museo Archeologico Regionale Eoliano, pp. 71–88.

———, (Ed.). (2002). *Le dune, il lago, il mare: Una comunità di villaggio dell'età del Rame a Maccarese*. Firenze: Istituto Italiano di Preistoria e Protostoria.

Manfredini, A., and I. Muntoni. (2003). Gli spazi del vivere: Funzioni e cronologia delle strutture d'abitato dell'insediamento neolitico di Casale del Dolce (Anagni – FR). *Atti, Riunione Scientifica dell' I. I. P. P.* **35**:187–198.

Mangili, G. (1954). I reperti ossei della Grotta Patrizi (Sasso Furbara): Il cranio trapanato. *Rivista di Antropologia* **41**:52–67.

Maniscalco, L. (1989). Ocher containers and trade in the Central Mediterranean Copper Age. *American Journal of Archaeology* **93**:537–541.

———. (1997). l'insediamento preistorico presso Le Salinelle di San Marco (Paternò), in *Prima Sicilia: alle origini della società siciliana* (Vol. 1). Edited by S. Tusa. Palermo: Ediprint, pp. 193–197.

Maniscalco, L., and M. R. Iovino. (2004). La Sicilia Orientale e la Calabria Centro-Meridionale nel Neolitico. *Atti, Riunione Scientifica dell' I. I. P. P.* **37**:189–201.

Mann, T. (1952). *The Magic Mountain*. New York: Random House.

Marino, D. (1993). Il neolitico nella Calabria centro-orientale: Ricerche 1974–1990. *Annali della Facoltà di Lettere e Filosofia dell'Università degli Studi di Bari* **35–36**:21–101.

Marx, K. (1978). Preface to A Contribution to the Critique of Political Economy, in *The Marx–Engels Reader*. Edited by R. Tucker. New York: W. W. Norton, pp. 3–6.

Marx, K., and F. Engels. (1978). The German ideology, in *The Marx-Engels reader*, 2nd edition. Edited by R. Tucker. New York: Norton, pp. 146–201.

McCall, J. C. (1999). Structure, agency, and the locus of the social: Why post-structural theory is good for archaeology, in *Material symbols: Culture and economy in prehistory*. Edited by J. E. Robb. Carbondale, Illinois: Center for Archaeological Investigations, Southern Illinois University, pp. 16–21.

McConnell, B. E. (2003). Insediamenti dell'altopiano ibleo e l'architettura dell'Età del Rame in Sicilia. *Atti, Riunione Scientifica dell' I. I. P. P.* **35**:225–238.

McVicar, J., C. Backway, G. Clark, and R. Housley. (1994). Agriculture, in *Time, territory, and state: The archaeological development of the Gubbio basin*. Edited by C. Malone and S. Stoddart. Cambridge, UK: Cambridge University Press, pp. 94–105.

Meillassoux, C. (1981). *Maidens, meal, and money*. New York: Cambridge University Press.

Mello, E. (1983). Indagini scientifiche per l'individuazione della provenienza dei manufatti di ossidiana, in *Passo di Corvo e la civiltà neolitica del Tavoliere*. Edited by S. Tinè. Genova: Sage, pp. 122–124.

Merleau-Ponty, M. (1962). *Phenomenology of perception*. London: Routledge.

Meskell, L., and R. Joyce. (2003). *Embodied lives: Figuring ancient Maya and Egyptian experience*. London: Routledge.

Michelaki, K. (2006). *Household economies: Ceramic production and consumption among the Maros villagers of Bronze Age Hungary*. International Series, 1503. Oxford: British Archaeological Reports.

Milisauskas, S. (1983). *European prehistory*. New York: Academic.

———. (Ed.). (2002). *European Prehistory: a Survey*. New York: Kluwer Academic/Plenum.

Miller, D. (Ed.). (2005). *Materiality*. Durham: Duke University Press.

Mintz, S. (1994). Eating and being: What food means, in *Food: multidisciplinary perspectives*. Edited by B. Harriss-White and R. Hoffenberg. Oxford: Blackwell, pp. 102–115.

Modjeska, N. (1991). Post-Ipomoean modernism: the Duna example, in *Big men and great men: personifications of power in Melanesia*. Edited by M. Godelier and M. Strathern. Cambridge, UK: Cambridge University Press, pp. 234–255.

Morphy, H. (1992). From dull to brilliant: The aesthetics of spiritual power among the Yokgnu, in *Anthropology, art, and aesthetics*. Edited by J. Coote and A. Shelton. Oxford: Clarendon, pp. 181–208.

Morter, J. (1992). Capo Alfiere and the Middle Neolithic period in eastern Calabria, southern Italy. Ph.D. dissertation, University of Texas, Austin.

Morter, J., and J. Robb. (1998). Space, gender, and architecture in the southern Italian Neolithic, in *Gender and Italian archaeology: Challenging the stereotypes*. Edited by R. Whitehouse. London: Accordia Research Center, pp. 83–94.

Mosso, A. (1908). La stazione preistorica di Coppa Nevigata presso Manfredonia. *Monumenti Antichi dei Lincei* **19**:305–396.

Muntoni, I. M. (2003). *Modellare l'argilla: Vasai del neolitico antico e medio nelle murge pugliesi*. Firenze: Istituto Italiano di Preistoria e Protostoria.

———. (2004). Analisi archeometriche sulle ceramiche impresse di Favella: Caratterizzazione delle materie prime e tecnologia di manufattura. *Atti, Riunione Scientifica dell' I. I. P. P.* **37**:703–709.

Mussi, M. (2001). *Earliest Italy: An overview of the Italian Paleolithic and Mesolithic*. New York: Kluwer Academic/Plenum.

Naroll, R. (1962). Floor area and settlement population. *American Antiquity* 27:587–588.

Nelson, S. M. (1997). *Gender in archaeology: Analyzing power and prestige*. Walnut Creek: Altamira.

———. (2002). *In pursuit of gender: Worldwide archaeological approaches*. Walnut Creek: Altamira.

Nicoletti, F. (1997). Il commercio preistorico dell'ossidiana nel mediterraneo ed il ruolo di Lipari e Pantelleria nel più antico sistema di scambio, in *Prima Sicilia: alle origini della società siciliana*. Edited by S. Tusa. Palermo: Regione Siciliana, pp. 259–273.

Nicoletti, G. (2004). L'insediamento neolitico di Ceraso (Acri – CS). *Atti, Riunione Scientifica dell' I. I. P. P.* **37**:737–742.

O'Hare, G. (1990). A preliminary study of polished stone artefacts in prehistoric southern Italy. *Proceedings of the Prehistoric Society* **56**:123–152.

O'Shea, J. M. (1996). *Villagers of the Maros*. New York: Plenum.

Olsen, B. (2003). Material culture after text: Remembering things. *Norwegian Archaeological Review* **36**:87–104.

Orsi, P. (1890). Stazione neolitica di Stentinello. *Bullettino di Paletnologia Italiana* **16**:177–200.

———. (1898). Miniere di selce e sepolcri eneolitici a Monte Tabuto e Monte Racello presso Comiso (Siracusa). *Bullettino di Paletnologia Italiana* **24**:165–206.

———. (1921). Megara Hyblaea. *Monumenti Antichi dei Lincei* **27**:109–150.

———. (1924). Villaggio trincerato dell'età della pietra scoperto a Megara Hyblaea. *Bullettino di Paletnologia Italiana* **44**:214–220.

Ortiz, A. (1969). *The Tewa world: Space, time, being, and becoming in a Pueblo society*. Chicago: University of Chicago Press.

Ortner, S. (1972). On key symbols. *American Anthropologist* **75**:1338–1346.

———. (1984). Theory in anthropology since the sixties. *Comparative Studies in Society and History* **1**:126–166.

Palma di Cesnola, A., and A. Vigliardi. (1984). Il neo-eneolitico del promontorio del Gargano, in *La Daunia antica dalla preistoria all'altomedioevo*. Edited by M. Mazzei. Milano: Electa, pp. 55–74.

Pandolfi, L., and B. Zamagni. (2000). La pietra verde in Toscana: i dati sulle analisi delle provenienze, in *Les Premier Peuplements Olocenes de l'Aire Corso-Toscane/Il Primo Popolamento Olocenico dell'Area Corso-Toscana*. Edited by C. Tozzi and M. Weiss. Pisa: Edizioni ETS, pp. 245–248.

Papadopoulos, J. K. (2000). Skeletons in wells: towards an archaeology of social exclusion in the ancient Greek world, in *Madness, disability, and social exclusion: The archaeology and anthropology of "difference."* Edited by J. Hubert. London: Routledge, pp. 96–118.

Papathanassopoulos, G. A. (1996). *Neolithic culture in Greece*. Athens: N.P. Goulandris Foundation.

Parker Pearson, M. (1999). *The archaeology of death and burial*. Sutton: Stroud.

Parker Pearson, M., and C. Richards. (1994). *Architecture and order: approaches to social space*. London: Routledge.

Patrizi, S., A. Radmilli, and G. Mangili. (1954). Sepoltura ad inumazione con cranio trapanato nella Grotta Patrizi, Sasso Furbara. *Rivista di Antropologia* **41**:33–68.

Patroni, G. (1902). Un villaggio siculo presso Matera. *Monumenti Antichi dei Lincei* **8**:417–520.

Pauketat, T. R. (2001). Practice and history in archaeology: An emerging paradigm. *Anthropological Theory* **1**:73–98.

Pellegrini, E. (1992). Le età dei metalli nell'Italia meridionale e in Sicilia, in *Italia preistorica*. Edited by A. Guidi and M. Piperno. Roma: Laterza, pp. 471–516.

Pennacchioni, M. (2003). Navigazione, commercianti e materie prime. *Atti, Riunione Scientifica dell' I. I. P. P.* **35**:1053–1058.

Peristiany, J. (1966). *Honor and shame: The values of Mediterranean society*. Chicago: University of Chicago Press.

Perlès, C., and K. D. Vitelli. (1999). Craft specialization in the Neolithic of Greece, in *Neolithic society in Greece*. Edited by P. Halstead. Sheffield: Sheffield Academic Press., pp. 96–107

Peroni, R. (1971). *L'età del Bronzo nella penisola Italiana*. Firenze: Olschki.

———. (1979). From Bronze Age to Iron Age: Economic, historical, and social considerations, in *Italy before the Romans*. Edited by D. Ridgway and F. Ridgway. New York: Academic, pp. 7–30.

Pesce Delfino, V., V. Scattarella, A. De Lucia, D. Ferri, and C. Giove. (1979). Tomba megalitica a camera del III millennio in Rutigliano (Bari): triplice deposizione. *Antropologia Contemporanea* **2**:453–457.

Petrequin, P. (1996). Management of architectural woods and variations in population density in the fourth and third millennia BC (Lakes Chalain and Clairvaux, Jura, France). *Journal of Anthropological Archaeology* **15**:1–19.

Pfaffenberger, B. (1992). Social anthropology of technology. *Annual Review of Anthropology* **21**:491–516.

Phillips, P. (1992). Western Mediterranean obsidian distribution and the European Neolithic, in *Sardinia in the Mediterranean: A footprint in the sea*. Edited by R. H. Tykot and T. K. Andrews. Sheffield: Sheffield Academic Press, pp. 71–82.

Pluciennik, M. (1997). Historical, geographical, and anthropological imaginations: Early ceramics in Southern Italy, in *Not so much a pot, more a way of life, Oxbow Monographs*. Edited by C. Cumberpatch and P. Blinkhorn. Oxford: Oxbow, pp. 37–56.

———. (1998). Representations of gender in prehistoric Southern Italy, in *Gender and Italian archaeology: Challenging the stereotypes*. Edited by R. Whitehouse. London: Accordia Research Center, pp. 57–82.

Pollard, J. (2001). The aesthetics of depositional practice. *World Archaeology* **33**:35–333.

Pred, A. (1990). *Making histories and constructing human geographies: The local transformation of practice, power relations, and consciousness*. Boulder: Westview.

Price, T. D. (2003). The arrival of agriculture in Europe as seen from the North, in *The widening harvest: The Neolithic transition in Europe: Looking back, looking forward*. Edited by A. J. Ammerman and P. Biagi. Boston: Archaeological Institute of America, pp. 273–295.

Priuli, A. (1985). *Incisioni rupestri della Valcamonica*. Torino: Priuli and Verlucca.

Puglisi, S. (1957). *La civiltà apenninica: origine delle comunità pastorale in Italia*. Firenze: Olshki.

Quagliati, Q. (1906). Tombe neolitiche in Taranto e nel suo territorio. *Bullettino di Paletnologia Italiana* **32**:17–49.

———. (1936). *La Puglia preistorica*. Rome: Società per la Storia Patria per la Puglia.

Quarta, G., M. D'Elia, E. Ingravallo, I. Tiberi, and L. Calcagnile. (2005). The Neolithic site of Serra Cicora: Results of the AMS radiocarbon dating. *Radiocarbon* **47**:207–210.

Radi, G. (1987). Scavo preliminare a Fonte di San Callisto (L'Aquila). *Rassegna di Archeologia* **6**:143–170.

———. (2000). La distribuzione dell'ossidiana in Toscana nel neolitico antico, in *Les Premier Peuplements Olocenes de l'Aire Corso-Toscane/Il Primo Popolamento Oloccenico dell'Area Corso-Toscana*. Edited by C. Tozzi and M. Weiss. Pisa: Edizioni ETS, pp. 249–252.

Radi, G., and B. Wilkens. (1989). Il sito a ceramica impressa di Santo Stefano (Ortucchio, L'Aquila): Notizia preliminare. *Rassegna di Archeologia* **8**:97–116.

Radina, F. (1999). La ricerca archeologica nell'insediamento neolitico di Balsignano (Modugno, Bari), in *Fonti di informazione e contesto archeologico: Manufatti ceramici e neolitizazzione meridionale*. Edited by E. Ingravallo. Galatina: Mario Congedi, pp. 93–103.

———. (2003). Le ricerche archeologiche, in *Modellare l'argilla: Vasai del neolitico antico e medio nelle murge pugliesi*. Edited by I. Muntoni. Firenze: Istituto Italiano di Preistoria e Protostoria, pp. 81–96.

Radmilli, A. (1974). Dal Paleolitico all'Età del Bronzo, in *Popoli e culture dell'Italia antica, Volume 1*. Edited by A. Radmilli. Rome: Biblioteca di Storia Patria, pp. 69–404.

———. (1997). *I Primi agricoltori in abruzzo: Il neolitico*. Pescara: Editrice Italica.

Randle, K., L. Barfield, and B. Bagolini. (1993). Recent Italian obsidian analyses. *Journal of Archaeological Science* **20**:503–509.

Rappaport, R. (1979). *Ecology, meaning, and religion*. Berkeley: North Atlantic Press.

Redding, R. (1981). Decision making in subsistence herding of sheep and goats in the Middle East. Ph.D. dissertation, University of Michigan.

Reid, A., and R. MacLean. (1995). Symbolism and the social contexts of iron production in Karagwe. *World Archaeology* **27**:144–161.

Rellini, U. (1923). La Grotta delle Felci a Capri. *Monumenti Antichi dei Lincei* **29**:305–406.

———. (1934). La più antica ceramica dipinta d'Italia. Roma: Collana Meridionale Editrice.

Renfrew, C. (1975). Trade as Action at a Distance: Questions of Integration and Communication, in *Ancient civilization and trade*. Edited by J. Sabloff and C. Lamberg-Karlovsky. Albuquerque: University of New Mexico Press, pp. 3–59.

———. (1976). Megaliths, territories, and populations, in *Acculturation and continuity in Atlantic Europe*. Edited by S. De Laet. Brugge: De Tempel, pp. 198–220.

Renfrew, C., and J. E. Dixon. (1976). Obsidian in western Asia: A review, in *Problems in economic and social archaeology*. Edited by G. G. Sieveking, I. H. Longworth, and K. E. Wilson, London: Duckworth, pp. 137–150.

Rice, P. (1987). *Pottery analysis: A sourcebook*. Chicago: University of Chicago Press.

Ridola, D. (1924). Le grandi trincee preistoriche di Matera, I. *Bullettino di Paletnologia Italiana* **44**:97–122.

———. (1925). Le grandi trincee preistoriche di Matera, II. *Bullettino di Paletnologia Italiana* **45**:85–98.

———. (1926). Le grandi trincee preistoriche di Matera, III. *Bullettino di Paletnologia Italiana* **46**:135–174.

Robb, J. (1991). Neolithic skeletal remains from the Grotta Scaloria: The 1979 excavations. *Rivista di Antropologia* **69**:111–124.

———. (1994). The Neolithic of peninsular Italy: Anthropological synthesis and critique. *Bullettino di Paletnologia Italiana* **85**:189–214.

———. (1994). Burial and social reproduction in the Peninsular Italian neolithic. *Journal of Mediterranean Archaeology* **7**:29–75.

———. (1994). Gender contradictions: Moral coalitions and inequality in prehistoric Italy. *Journal of European Archaeology* **2**:20–49.

———. (1995). From gender to class: Inequality in prehistoric Italy. Ph.D. dissertation, University of Michigan, Ann Arbor.

———. (1997). Intentional tooth removal in Neolithic Italian women. *Antiquity* **71**:659–669.

———. (1997). Violence and gender in early Italy, in *Troubled times: osteological and archaeological evidence of violence*. Edited by D. L.

Martin and D. Frayer. New York: Gordon and Breach, pp.108–141.

———. (2001). Island identities: ritual, travel, and the creation of difference in Neolithic Malta. *European Journal of Archaeology* **4**:175–202.

———. (2001). Why do we find "Late Neolithic" burials in "Middle Neolithic" villages?" Paper presented at the International Union of Prehistoric and Protohistoric Sciences, Liege.

———. (2002). Time and biography, in *Thinking through the Body: Archaeologies of Corporeality*. Edited by Y. Hamilakis, M. Pluciennik, and S. Tarlow. London: Kluwer Academic, pp. 153–171.

———. (2003). *Bova Marina Archaeological Project survey and excavations: Preliminary report, 2003 season.* Cambridge, UK: Department of Archaeology, Cambridge University.

———. (2004). The extended artifact and the monumental economy: A methodology for material agency, in *Rethinking materiality: The engagement of mind with the material world.* Edited by E. DeMarrais, C. Gosden, and C. Renfrew. Cambridge, UK: McDonald Institute for Archaeological Research, pp. 131–139.

———. (2004). Il Neolitico dell'Aspromonte. *Atti, Riunione Scientifica dell' I. I. P. P.* **37**:175–188.

Robb, J., and F. Mallegni. (1994). Anthropology and paleopathology of human remains from Catignano (Pescara, Italy). *Rivista di Antropologia* **72**:197–224.

Robb, J., F. Mallegni, and D. Ronco. (1991). New human remains from the southern Italian Neolithic: Ripa Tetta and Latronico. *Rivista di Antropologia* **69**:125–144.

Robb, J., and P. Miracle. (2007). Beyond "migration" versus "acculturation": new models for the spread of agriculture, in *Going over: The Mesolithic-Neolithic transition in Western Europe.* Edited by A. Whittle and V. Cummings. London: British Academy, pp. 97–113.

Robb, J., and R. Tykot. (2003). Ricostruzione tramite analisi GIS di aspetti marittimi e sociali nello scambio dell'ossidiano durante il Neolitico. *Atti, Riunione Scientifica dell' I. I. P. P.* **35**:1021–1025.

Robb, J., and D. Van Hove. (2003). Gardening, foraging and herding: Neolithic land use and social territories in Southern. *Antiquity* **77**:241–254.

Robertshaw, P. (1989). The development of pastoralism in East Africa, in *The walking larder: Patterns of domestication, pastoralism and predation.* Edited by J. Clutton-Brock. London: Unwin Hyman, pp. 207–214.

Romito, M. (1987). Un insediamento neolitico a Palinuro. *Atti, Riunione Scientifica dell' I. I. P. P.* **26**:691–695.

Ronchitelli, A. (1983). L'industria litica dell'area B, in *Passo di Corvo e la civiltà neolitica del Tavoliere.* Edited by S. Tinè. Genova: Sagep, pp. 101–121.

Rosaldo, R. (1980). *Ilongot headhunting: A study in society and history, 1885–1974.* Palo Alto: Stanford University Press.

———. (1986). Ilongot hunting as story and experience, in *The anthropology of experience.* Edited by V. W. Turner and E. M. Brunes. Urbana: University of Illinois Press, pp. 97–138.

Roscoe, P. (2000). New Guinea leadership as ethnographic analogy: A critical review. *Journal of Archaeological Method and Theory* **7**:79–126.

Rottoli, M. (1993). "La Marmotta" (Anguillara Sabazia (RM), scavi 1989. Analisi paletnobotaniche: prime risultanze. *Bullettino di Paletnologia Italiana* **84**:305–315.

———. (2001). Zafferanone selvatico (Carthamus lanatus) e cardo della Madonna (Silybum marianun), piante raccolte o coltivate nel Neolitico antico a "La Marmotta"? *Bullettino di Paletnologia Italiana* **91–92**:47–62.

Rowly-Conwy, P. (1997). The animal bones from Arene Candide: Final report, in *Arene Candide: a functional and environmental assessment of the Holocene sequence.* Edited by R. Maggi. Rome: Il Calamo, pp. 153–277.

Runnels, C. (2003). The origins of the Greek Neolithic: A personal view, in *The widening harvest: The Neolithic transition in Europe: Looking back, looking forward.* Edited by A. J. Ammerman and P. Biagi. Boston: Archaeological Institute of America, pp. 121–132.

Russell, N. (1998). Cattle as wealth in Neolithic Europe: Where's the beef? in *The archaeology of value.* International Series (Vol. 730). Edited by D. W. Bailey. Oxford: British Archaeological Reports, pp. 42–54.

———. (1999). Symbolic dimensions of animals and meat at Opovo, Yugoslavia, in *Material Symbols: Culture and economy in prehistory*. Edited by J. Robb. Carbondale, Illinois: Center for Archaeological Investigations, Southern Illinois University, pp. 153–172.

Russell, N., and L. Martin. (2000). Trashing rubbish, in *Towards reflexive method in archaeology: The example at Çatalhöyük*. Edited by I. Hodder. Cambridge, UK: McDonald Institute for Archaeological Research, pp. 57–69.

Rye, O. S. (1981). *Pottery technology: Principles and reconstruction*. Washington, DC: Smithsonian.

Sahlins, M. (1963). Poor man, rich man, big man, chief: Political types in Melanesia and Polynesia. *Comparative Studies in Society and History* **5**:285–303.

———. (1968). *Tribesmen*. Engelwood Cliffs, Prentice-Hall.

———. (1972). *Stone Age economics*. Chicago: Aldine.

———. (1981). *Historical metaphors and mythical realities*. Ann Arbor: University of Michigan Press.

———. (1985). *Islands of history*. Chicago: University of Chicago Press.

Saitta, D. J., and R. H. McGuire. (1998). Dialectics, heterarchy, and Western Pueblo social organization. *American Antiquity* **63**:334–336.

Salvadei, L., and R. Macchiarelli. (1983). Studi antropologici, in *Studi sul Neolitico del Tavoliere della Puglia*. International Series 160. Edited by S. Cassano and A. Manfredini. Oxford: British Archaeological Reports, pp. 253–264.

Salvadei, L., and E. Santandrea. (2003). Condizioni di vita e stato di salute nel campione neolitico di Masseria Candelaro (FG). *Atti, Riunione Scientifica dell' I. I. P. P.* **35**:829–834.

Sammartino, F. (1990). Insediamenti neolitici e della prima età dei metalli in località La Puzzolente (Livorno): un'officina per la lavorazione della steatite. *Rassegna di Archeologia* **9**:153–182.

Sargent, A. (1983). Exploitation territory and economy in the Tavoliere of Apulia, in *Studi sul Neolitico del Tavoliere della Puglia*. International Series 160. Edited by S. Cassano and A. Manfredini. Oxford: British Archaeological Reports, pp. 223–236.

———. (1983). Neolithic plant remains, in *Studi sul Neolitico del Tavoliere della Puglia*. International Series 160. Edited by S. Cassano and A. Manfredini. Oxford: British Archaeological Reports, pp. 250–252.

Sarti, L., C. Corridi, F. Martini, and P. Pallecchi. (1991). Mileto: un insediamento Neolitico della ceramica a linee incise. *Rivista di Scienze Preistoriche* **43**:73–154.

Sarti, L., F. Martini, M. Magi, E. Cioppi, M. Mazzini, M. L. Bernabei, R. Birtolo, B. Foggi, G. Mazzoni, R. Franchi, and P. Pallecchi. (1985). L'insediamento Neolitico di Neto di Bolasse (Sesto Fiorentino, Firenze). *Rassegna di Archeologia* **5**:63–118.

Saunders, N. J. (2002). The colours of light: Materiality and chromatic cultures of the Americas, in *Colouring the past: The significance of colour in archaeological research*. Edited by A. Jones and G. MacGregor. Oxford: Berg, pp. 209–226.

Service, E. (1962). *Primitive social organisation*. New York: Random House.

Sewell, W. (1992). A theory of structure: Duality, agency and transformation. *American Journal of Sociology* **98**:1–29.

Shaffer, G. D. (1983). Neolithic building technology in Calabria, Italy. Ph.D. dissertation, State University of New York, Binghamton.

———. (1985). Architectural resources and their effect on certain neolithic settlements in Southern Italy, in *Papers in Italian Archaeology IV: The Cambridge conference*. BAR International Series. Edited by C. Malone and S. Stoddart. Oxford: British Archaeological Reports, pp. 101–117.

———. (1993). Archaeomagnetic study of a wattle and daub building collapse. *Journal of Field Archaeology* **20**:59–75.

Shanks, M., and C. Tilley. (1987). *Social theory and archaeology*. Albuquerque: University of New Mexico Press.

Shaw, B. (1982–1983). "Eaters of flesh, drinkers of milk:" The ancient Mediterranean ideology of the pastoral nomad. *Ancient Society* **13–14**:5–31.

Shennan, S. (1982). Ideology, change and the European Bronze Age, in *Symbolic and structural archaeology*. Edited by I. Hodder. Cambridge, UK: Cambridge University Press, pp. 155–161.

———. (1986). Interaction and change in third millennium BC Western and Central Europe, in *Peer polity interaction and socio-political change*. Edited by C. Renfrew and J. Cherry. New York: Cambridge University Press, pp. 137–148.

———. (1989). *Archaeological approaches to cultural identity*. London: Routledge.

Shepard, A. O. (1956). *Ceramics for the archaeologist*. Washington, DC: Carnegie Institution of Washington.

Sherratt, A. (1981). Plough and pastoralism: Aspects of the secondary products revolution, in *Pattern of the past: Studies in honor of David Clarke*. Edited by I. Hodder, G. Isaac, and N. Hammond. Cambridge, UK: Cambridge University Press, pp. 261–305.

———. (1984). Social evolution: Europe in the Later Neolithic and Copper ages, in *European social evolution: Archaeological perspectives*. Edited by J. Bintliff. Bradford: Bradford University Press, pp. 123–134.

———. (1997). Cups that cheered: The introduction of alcohol to prehistoric Europe, in *Economy and society in prehistoric Europe: Changing perspectives*. Edited by A. Sherratt. Edinburgh: Edinburgh University Press, pp. 376–402.

Shilling, C. (2003). *The body and social theory*. (2nd ed.). London: Sage Publications.

Sillitoe, P. (1988). *Made in Niugini: Technology in the Highlands of New Guinea*. London: British Museum.

———. (1997). The earth oven, in *The anthropologist's cookbook*. (2nd ed.). Edited by J. Kuper. London: Kegan Paul, pp. 224–231.

Simone, L. (1982). Il villaggio neolitico della Villa Comunale di Foggia. *Origini* 11:129–182.

Sinclair, A. (1995). The technique as symbol in Late Glacial Europe. *World Archaeology* 27:50–62.

Singer, I. B. (1973). *The fools of Chelm and their history*. New York: Farrar, Straus & Giroux.

Skeates, R. (1991). Caves, cult and children in Neolithic Abruzzo, Central Italy, in *Sacred and Profane*. Edited by P. Garwood, D. Jennings, R. Skeates, and J. Toms. Oxford: Oxford University Committee for Archaeology, pp. 122–134.

———. (1992). Thin-section analysis of Italian neolithic pottery, in *Papers of the Fourth Conference of Italian Archaeology. Volume 3: New developments in Italian archaeology*. Edited by E. Herring, R. Whitehouse, and J. Wilkins.

London: Accordia Research Center, pp. 29–34.

———. (1993). Early metal use in the central Mediterranean region. *Accordia Research Papers* 4:5–48.

———. (1994). Ritual, context, and gender in Neolithic south-eastern Italy. *Journal of European Archaeology* 2:199–214.

———. (1995). Animate objects: A biography of prehistoric 'axe-amulets' in the central Mediterranean region. *Proceedings of the Prehistoric Society* 61:279–301.

———. (1998). The social life of Italian Neolithic painted pottery, in *The archaeology of value*. International Series (Vol. 730). Edited by D. W. Bailey. Oxford: British Archaeological Report, pp. 131–141s.

———. (2002). The social dynamics of enclosure in the Neolithic of the Tavoliere, south-east Italy. *Journal of Mediterranean Archaeology* 13:155–188.

———. (2003). Radiocarbon dating and interpretations of the Mesolithic-Neolithic transition in Italy, in *The widening harvest: The Neolithic transition in Europe: Looking back, looking forward*. Edited by A. J. Ammerman and P. Biagi. Boston: Archaeological Institute of America, pp. 157–187.

Sofaer, J. (Ed.). (2000). *Children and material culture*. London: Routledge.

Soprintendenza Archeologica della Basilicata. (1976). *Il Museo Nazionale Ridola di Matera*. Matera: Edizioni Meta.

Sorensen, M. L. (2000). *Gender archaeology*. Oxford: Polity.

Sorrentino, C. (1983). La fauna, in *Passo di Corvo e la civiltà neolitica del Tavoliere*. Edited by S. Tinè. Genova: Sagep, pp. 149–158.

———. 1984. Lo studio della fauna di Tirlecchia. *Rivista di Scienze Preistoriche* 39:73–84.

Spataro, M. (2002). *The first farming communities of the Adriatic: Pottery production and circulation in the early and middle Neolithic*. Quaderni 9. Trieste: Società per la Preistoria e Protostoria della Regione Friuli – Venezia Giulia.

Spindler, K. (1994). *The man in the ice*. London: Weidenfeld and Nicolson.

Stark, M. (1998). *The archaeology of social boundaries*. Washington, DC: Smithsonian.

Steensberg, A. (1980). *New Guinea gardens: a study of husbandry with parallels in prehistoric Europe.* London: Academic.

Stevanovic, M. (1997). The age of clay: The social dynamics of house destruction. *Journal of Anthropological Archaeology* **16**:334–395.

Stoddart, S., A. Bonanno, T. Gouder, C. Malone, and D. H. Trump. (1993). Cult in an island society: Prehistoric Malta in the Tarxien period. *Cambridge Archaeological Journal* **3**:3–19.

Strathern, A., and M. Lambek. (1998). Embodying sociality: Africanist-Melanesianist comparison, in *Bodies and Persons: Comparative Perspectives from Africa and Melanesia.* Edited by A. Strathern and M. Lambek. Cambridge, UK: Cambridge University Press, pp. 1–25.

Strathern, M. (1988). *The gender of the gift: Problems with women and problems with society in Melanesia.* Berkeley: University of California Press.

———. (1991). One man and many men, in *Big men and great men: Personifications of power in Melanesia.* Edited by M. Godelier and M. Strathern. Cambridge, UK: Cambridge University Press, pp. 197–214.

Striccoli, R. (1988). *Le culture preistoriche di Grotta Pacelli (Castellana Grotte, Bari).* Brindisi: Schena Editore.

Taçon, P. (1991). The power of stone: Symbolic aspects of stone use and tool development in western Arnhem-land, Australia. *Antiquity* **65**:192–207.

Tagliacozzo, A. (1992). I mammiferi dei giacimenti pre-e protostorici italiani: Un inquadramento paleontologico e archeozoologico, in *Italia preistorica.* Edited by A. Guidi and M. Piperno. Rome: Laterza, pp. 68–102.

———. (1993). Archeozoologia della Grotta dell'Uzzo, Sicilia. *Bullettino di Paletnologia Italiana* **84** (supplemento), (II):1–278.

———. (1997). Dalla caccia alla pastorizia: La domesticazione animale, le modificazioni economiche tra il mesolitico ed il neolitico e l'introduzione degli animali domestici in Sicilia, in *Prima Sicilia: alle origini della società siciliana* (Vol. 1). Edited by S. Tusa. Palermo: Ediprint, pp. 237–248.

Tagliacozzo, A., and I. Fiore. (1997). Analisi dei resti ossei faunistici di una struttura neolitica (Fossa 116) dell' area E, in *Casale del Dolce: ambiente, economia, e cultura di una comunità preistorica del Valle del Sacco.* Edited by A. Zarattini and L. Petrassi. Roma: Soprintendenza Archeologica per il Lazio, pp. 227–247.

Talalay, L. (1993). *Deities, dolls and devices: Neolithic figurines from Franchthi Cave, Greece.* Bloomington: Indiana University Press.

———. (2004). Heady business: skulls, heads, and decapitation in Neolithic Anatolia and Greece. *Journal of Mediterranean Archaeology* **17**:139–163.

Talamo, P. (1994). La capanna di Contrada S. Martino a Taurasi (AV), in *L'ultima pietra, il primo metallo.* Pontecagnano: Museo Nazionale dell'Agro Picentino, pp. 70–73.

Thomas, J. (1999). *Understanding the Neolithic.* London: Routledge.

———. (2003). Thoughts on the "repacked: Neolithic revolution. *Antiquity* **77**:67–75.

Thorpe, I. (1996). *The origins of agriculture in Europe.* London: Routledge.

Thorpe, I., and C. Richards. (1984). The decline of ritual authority and the introduction of beakers into Britain, in *Neolithic studies.* British Series 133. Edited by R. Bradley and J. Gardiner. Oxford: British Archaeological Reports, pp. 67–78.

Tilley, C. (1994). *A phenomenology of landscape: Places, paths, and monuments.* Oxford: Berg.

———. (1996). *An ethnography of the Neolithic.* Cambridge, UK: Cambridge University Press.

Tinè, S. (1962). Successione delle culture preistoriche in Calabria alla luce dei recenti scavi in provincia di Cosenza. *Klearchos* **4**:38–43.

———. (1964). La grotta di S. Angelo III a Cassano Ionio. *Atti e Memorie della Società della Magna Grecia* **5**:11–55.

———. (1983). *Passo di Corvo e la civiltà neolitica del Tavoliere.* Genova: Sagep.

———. (1988). Il Neolitico, in *Storia della Calabria Antica.* Edited by S. Settis. Reggio Calabria: Gangemi, pp. 39–63.

———. (1992). *Bova Survey 1992.* Genova: Istituto Italiano di Archeologia Sperimentale.

Tinè, S., and E. Isetti. (1980). Culto neolitico delle acque e recenti scavi nella Grotta Scaloria. *Bullettino di Paletnologia Italiana* **82**:31–70.

Tinè, V. (2004). Il Neolitico in Calabria. *Atti, Riunione Scientifica dell' I. I. P. P.* **37**:115–144.

———. (2007). *Favella: un villaggio neolitico della Sibaritide* (Vol. 2). *Studi di Paletnologia*. Rome: Museo Pigorini.

Tinè, V., and E. Natali. (2005). Grotta San Michele di Saracena (CS): la campagna di scavo 2003, in *Preistoria e Protostoria della Calabria 1: Scavi e ricerche 2003*. Edited by B. Ambrogio and V. Tinè. Pellaro: Gruppo Archeologico Pellarese., pp. 17–28

Todisco, L., and D. Coppola. (1980). *Ceramica Neolitica nel Museo di Bisceglie*. Bari: Dedalo.

Torrence, R. (1986). *Production and exchange of stone tools: Prehistoric obsidian in the Aegean*. Cambridge, UK: Cambridge University Press.

Tozzi, C., and G. Tasca. (1989). Ripa Tetta. *Atti Convegno Nazionale sulla Preistoria, Protostoria e Storia della Daunia* **11**:39–54.

Tozzi, C., and L. Verola. (1990). La campagna di scavo 1990 a Ripatetta (Lucera, Foggia). *Atti Convegno Nazionale sulla Preistoria, Protostoria e Storia della Daunia* **12**:37–48.

Tozzi, C., and M. Weiss. (Eds.). (2000). *Les Premier Peuplements Olocenes de l'Aire Corso-Toscane/Il Primo Popolamento Olocenico dell'Area Corso-Toscana*. Pisa: Edizioni ETS.

Tozzi, C., and B. Zamagni. (2000). Il Neolitico antico nella Toscana settentrionale (Valle del Serchio), in *Les Premier Peuplements Olocenes de l'Aire Corso-Toscane/Il Primo Popolamento Olocenico dell'Area Corso-Toscana*. Edited by C. Tozzi and M. Weiss. Pisa: Edizioni ETS, pp. 57–70.

———. (2001). Una statuetta fittile dal villaggio neolitico di Catignano (Pescara): nota preliminare. *Rivista di Scienze Preistoriche* **51**:465–469.

———. (2003). *Gli scavi nel villaggio Neolitico di Catignano, 1971–1980*. Firenze: Istituto Italiano di Preistoria e Protostoria.

Treherne, P. (1995) The warrior's beauty: The masculine body and self-identity in Bronze Age Europe. *Journal of European Archaeology* **3**:105–144.

Trigger, B. G. (1969). *The Huron: Farmers of the north*. New York: Holt, Rinehart and Winston.

———. (1978). *Handbook of North American Indians, Volume 15: Northeast*. Washington, DC: Smithsonian.

Tringham, R., B. Brukner, T. Kaiser, K. Borojevic, L. Bukvic, P. Steli, N. Russell, M. Stevanovic, and B. Voytek. (1992). Excavations at Opovo, 1985–1987: Socioeconomic change in the Balkan Neolithic. *Journal of Field Archaeology* **19**:351–386.

Trump, D. (1966). *Skorba: excavations carried out on behalf of the National Museum of Malta, 1961–1963*. London: Society of Antiquaries.

———. (1981). Megalithic architecture in Malta, in *Antiquity and man: Essays in honour of Glyn Daniel*. Edited by J. D. Evans, B. Cunliffe, and C. Renfrew. London: Thames and Hudson, pp. 128–140.

Tunzi Sisto, A. (1990). Nuova miniera preistorica sul Gargano. *Atti Convegno Nazionale sulla Preistoria, Protostoria e Storia della Daunia* **12**:63–71.

———. 1999. *Ipogei della Daunia: Preistoria di un Territorio*. Foggia: Claudio Grenzi Editore.

Turner, V. (1974). *Dramas, fields, and metaphors: Symbolic action in human society*. Ithaca: Cornell University Press.

———. (1988). *The anthropology of performance*. New York: PAJ.

Tusa, S. (1993). *La Sicilia nella preistoria*. (2nd ed.) Palermo: Sellerio.

———. (1997). Origine della società agro-pastorale, in *Prima Sicilia: Alle origini della società siciliana* (Vol. 1). Edited by S. Tusa. Palermo: Ediprint, pp. 173–191.

———. (Ed.). (1997). *Prima Sicilia: Alle origini delle società siciliana*. Palermo: Ediprint.

Tusa, S., and I. Valente. (1994). La ricerca archeologica in Contrada Stretto-Partanna: il fossato/trincea Neolitico, in *La preistoria del Basso Belice e della Sicilia meridionale nel quadro della preistoria siciliana e mediterranean*. Edited by S. Tusa. Palermo: Società Siciliana per la Storia Patria, pp. 177–195.

Twiss, K. (Ed.). (2007). *We were what we ate: The archaeology of food and identity*. Carbondale: Center for Archaeological Investigations, Southern Illinois University.

Tykot, R. H. (1997). Characterization of the Monte Arci Obsidian sources. *Journal of Archaeological Science* **24**:467–479.

———. (1998). Mediterranean Islands and Multiple Flows: The sources and exploitation of Sardinian obsidian, in *Archaeological obsidian studies*. Edited by M. S. Shackley. New York: Plenum Press, pp. 67–82.

Tykot, R. H., and A. J. Ammerman. (1997). Mediterranean obsidian provenance studies. *Antiquity* **71**:1000–1006.

Ucko, P. (1969). Ethnography and archaeological interpretation of funerary remains. *World Archaeology* **1**:262–280.

Van Hove, D. (2003). *Imagining Calabria: A GIS Approach to Neolithic Landscapes*. Ph.D. dissertation, University of Southampton.

Vida Navarro, M. C. (1992). Warriors and weavers: Sex and gender in Early Iron Age graves from Pontecagnano. *Journal of the Accordia Research Center* **3**:67–100.

Vigne, J.-D. (2003). L'exploitation des animaux à Torre Sabea: Nouvelles analyses sur les débuts de l'élevage en Méditerranée centrale et occidentale, in *Torre Sabea: un Établissement du Néolithique Ancien en Salento*. Edited by J. Guilaine and G. Cremonesi. Rome: École Française de Rome, pp. 325–359.

Villa, P., C. Bouville, J. Courtin, D. Helmer, E. Mahieu, P. Shipman, G. Belluomini, and M. Branca. (1986). Cannibalism in the Neolithic. *Science* **233**:431–437.

Villari, P. (1995). *Le fauna della tarda preistoria nella Sicilia orientale*. Siracusa: Ente Fauna Siciliana.

Vinson, S. (1975). Excavations at Casa S. Paolo: 1971–1972. *American Journal of Archaeology* **79**:49–66.

Vitelli, K. D. (1995). Pots, potters, and the shaping of Greek Neolithic society, in *The emergence of pottery: Technology and innovation in ancient societies*. Edited by W. K. Barnett and J. W. Hoopes. Washington, DC: Smithsonian Institution Press, pp. 55–64.

Von Eles Masi, P., and G. Steffè. (1987). Primi risulatati delle ricerche nell'insediamento neolitico di Lugo di Romagna (Ravenna). *Atti, Riunione Scientifica dell' I. I. P. P.* **26**:595–602.

Wagstaff, M., and C. Gamble. (1983). Island resources and their limitations, in *Melos: an island polity*. Edited by C. Renfrew and M. Wagstaff. Cambridge, UK: Cambridge University Press, pp. 95–105.

Warren, S. E., and J. G. Crummett. (1985). Chemical analysis of Calabrian obsidian, in *The Acconia survey: Neolithic settlement and the obsidian trade*. Institute of Archaeology Occasional Publications. Edited by A. J. Ammerman. London: Institute of Archaeology, University of London, pp. 107–114.

Wason, P. (1994). *The archaeology of rank*. Cambridge, UK: Cambridge University Press.

Watson, A. (2001). Composing Avebury. *World Archaeology* **33**:296–314.

Weiss, K. M. (1973). *Demographic models for anthropology*. Volume 27. Society for American Archaeology Memoirs. Washington, DC: Society for American Archaeology.

Weller, O. (2002). The earliest rocksalt exploitation in Europe: A salt mountain in the Spanish Neolithic. *Antiquity* **76**:317–318.

Whitehead, H. (1987). Fertility and exchange in New Guinea, in *Gender and kinship: Essays toward a unified theory*. Edited by J. Collier and S. Yanagisako. Palo Alto: Stanford University Press, pp. 244–267.

Whitehead, N. (1992). Tribes make states and states make tribes: Warfare and the creation of colonial tribes and states in northeastern South America, in *War in the tribal zone: expanding states and indigenous warfare*. Edited by R. Ferguson and N. Whitehead. Santa Fe: School of American Research Press, pp. 127–150.

Whitehouse, R. (1969). The neolithic pottery sequence in Southern Italy. *Proceedings of the Prehistoric Society* **35**:267–310.

———. (1972). The rock-cut tombs of the Central Mediterranean. *Antiquity* **46**:275–281.

———. (1981). Prehistoric settlement patterns in Southeast Italy, in *Archaeology and Italian Society*. International Series. Edited by R. Hodges and G. Barker. Oxford: British Archaeological Reports, pp. 157–165.

———. (1984). Social organization in the Neolithic of Southern Italy, in *The Deyà Conference of prehistory*. International Series 229 (iv). Edited by W. Waldren. Oxford: British Archaeological Reports, pp. 1109–1133.

———. (1992). Tools the manmaker: The cultural construction of gender in Italian prehistory. *Accordia Research Papers* **3**:41–53.

———. (1992). *Underground religion: Cult and culture in prehistoric Italy*. London: Accordia Research Center.

———. (2001). Exploring gender in prehistoric Italy. *Papers of the British School at Rome* **68**:49–96.

Whittle, A. (1996). *Europe in the Neolithic: the creation of new worlds*. Cambridge: Cambridge University Press.

———. (2003). *The archaeology of people: Dimensions of Neolithic life*. London: Routledge.

Whittle, A., and V. Cummings. (Eds.). (2007). *Going over: The Mesolithic-Neolithic transition in Western Europe*. London: British Academy.

Wiessner, P., and W. Schiefenhövel. (1996). *Food and the status quest: An interdisciplinary perspective*. Oxford: Berg.

Wiessner, P., and A. Tumu. (1998). *Historical vines: Enga networks of exchange, ritual and warfare in Papua New Guinea*. Washington, DC: Smithsonian Institution Press.

Wilkens, B. (1989). Il cervo dal Mesolitico all' Età del Bronzo nell' Italia centro-meridionale. *Rassegna di Archeologia* 8:63–95.

Williams, J. L. (1980). A petrological examination of the prehistoric pottery from the excavation in the Castello and Diana plain of Lipari, in *Meligunìs Lipára, Volume IV: L'acropoli di Lipari nella preistoria*. Edited by L. Bernabò Brea and M. Cavalier. Palermo: Flaccovia, pp. 845–868.

Williams, J. L., and S. Levi. (1995). The characterisation of Neolithic Stentinellian pottery fabrics from the Aeolian Islands and the type site of Stentinello near Syracuse, Sicily, in *Meligunìs Lipára. Volume VIII: Salina (ricerche archeologiche 1989–1993)*. Edited by L. Bernabò Brea and M. Cavalier. Palermo: Flaccovia, pp. 138–163.

———. (2001). Archeometria della ceramica eoliana: nuovi risultati, sintesi, e prospettive, in *Studie di Preistoria e Protostoria in onore di Luigi Bernabò Brea*. Edited by M. C. Martinelli and U. Spigo. Lipari: Museo Archeologico Regionale Eoliano, pp. 265–304.

Winn, S., and D. Shimabuku. (1988). *The heritage of two subsistance strategies: Preliminary report on the excavations at the Grotta Scaloria, Southeastern Italy, 1978*. Halifax, Nova Scotia: Saint Mary's University.

Wobst, H. (1974). Boundary conditions for Paleolithic social systems: A simulation approach. *American Antiquity* **39**:147–178.

———. (1978). The archaeo-ethnology of hunter-gatherers or the tyranny of the ethnographic record in archaeology. *American Antiquity* **43**:303–309.

Wolf, E. (1982). *Europe and the people without history*. Berkeley: University of California Press.

Wood, J. W., G. R. Milner, H. Harpending, and K. Weiss. (1992). The osteological paradox: Problems in inferring prehistoric health from skeletal samples. *Current Anthropology* **33**:343–370.

Yeats, W. B. (1962). *Selected poems and two plays of William Butler Yeats*. New York: Collier.

Zarattini, A., and L. Petrassi. (Eds.). (1997). *Casale del Dolce: Ambiente, economia, e cultura di una comunità preistorica del Valle del Sacco*. Rome: Soprintendenza Archeologica per il Lazio.

———. (1997). Il valore dell'ossidiana e le vie terrestri: Ipotesi dopo i primi risultati della fluorescenza ai raggi x, in *Casale del Dolce: Ambiente, economia, e cultura di una comunità preistorica del Valle del Sacco*. Edited by A. Zarattini and L. Petrassi. Roma: Soprintendenza Archeologica per il Lazio, pp. 191–207.

Zilhão, J. (2003). The Neolithic transition in Portugal and the role of demic diffusion in the spread of agriculture across West Mediterranean Europe, in *The widening harvest: The Neolithic transition in Europe: Looking back, looking forward*. Edited by A. J. Ammerman and P. Biagi. Boston: American Institute of Archaeology, pp. 207–226.

Zohary, D., and M. Hopf. (1993). *Domestication of plants in the Old World*. Oxford: Clarendon.

Zvelebil, M., and P. Rowly-Conwy. (1986). Foragers and farmers in Atlantic Europe, in *Hunters in transition: Mesolithic societies of temperate Eurasia and their transition to farming*. Edited by M. Zvelebil. Cambridge, UK: Cambridge University Press, pp. 67–93.

INDEX

ablation (intentional tooth removal), 38, 203
Abruzzo, 32, 60, 87, 97, 114, 127, 137, 167, 296, 298, 307, 319
Acconia, 78, 81, 83, 86, 88, 90, 199, 264, 272, 274
Acquasalsa, Masseria, 92
activity areas, 86, 90
activity, skeletal markers of, 37, 68
Aeolian Islands (Isole Eolie), 253
agency, 6–7. *See* social reproduction.
  of material things, 18, 19, 245, 246
Albania, 25
Alicudi, 281
Alps, 24, 25, 28, 44, 60, 112, 127, 200, 205, 207, 260, 295, 298, 299, 302, 307, 343
Apennines, 25, 28, 32, 114, 115, 135, 254, 261, 265, 270, 271, 295, 307
Aquila, Arma dell', 39, 40
Aquilone, Masseria, 130
archaeomagnetism, 88
Arene Candide, 49, 54, 123, 128, 276
Ariano Irpino, 254
Arnesano, 44, 54, 55, 306, 308
Arpi, 187
art, prehistoric. *See* figurines; Porto Badisco; stelae; Valcamonica
  Copper and Bronze Age rock art, 307
  rock art, 43, 68, 110, 128
art, prehistoric, 44, 52
art, prehistoric Italian, 43
Aspromonte, 113, 114, 116, 213, 253
Attiggio, 126
axes, 37, 40, 69, 81, 84, 86, 104, 112, 113, 205, 206, 207, 208, 209, 210, 211, 212, 213, 214, 215, 216, 217, 228, 229, 231, 232, 235, 236, 244, 256, 258, 260, 298, 299, 300, 307, 313, 318, 344, 344
  artefact biographies of, 214–218
  contextual deposition of, 208–214
  forms, variation and use of, 205–206
  raw material use, 206
  shaft-hole, 298
  small forms (axe-amulets, axettes), 206, 208, 210, 214, 215, 217, 228
  summary, 226

Balsignano, 78, 87, 88, 95
Barth, Fredrik, 15, 17, 43, 53, 178, 180, 294
Baselice, 47, 51, 54, 56, 258, 323
Basilicata, 25, 33, 77, 91, 97, 113, 115, 116, 165, 169, 183, 184, 190, 209, 223, 261, 272, 275, 280, 295, 299
bear, 124, 229
Beatrice Cenci, Grotta della, 114
Bell Beakers, 288
Bellavista, Masseria, 60, 171, 228, 306
Berbentina, 126
Big Men, 71, 249, 324
biography, artefact, 18, 50, 146, 204, 226, 235, 248
  axes, 214–218
  houses, 87–90
biography, human, 13, 35, 64, 65, 67, 222, 234, 246, 248
  and identity, 237–239
boats, 41, 255, 256, 267, 329
bodily modification, Neolithic. *See* ablation; tattooing; trepanation
body, 11–13
  Copper Age iconography, 310
  summary of Neolithic evidence, 221–222

Bottom, weaver, 219
Bourdieu, Pierre, 5, 8, 10, 11, 12, 86, 110, 154, 290, 319
Bova Marina. *See* Umbro; Penitenzeria
Bova, Castello di, 113
bow, 60, 69, 109, 189, 313
Bracciano, Lake, 55, 129, 255, 266, 267
Bradford, John, 76, 261
Brochtorff Circle at Xaghra, 329
Bronze Age, 12, 39, 43, 45, 69, 70, 72, 73, 89, 113, 123, 131, 134, 139, 157, 206, 227, 240, 241, 266, 270, 282, 300, 310, 311, 315, 316, 334, 336, 337, 338, 340
burial, Copper Age, 307
burial, Neolithic, 56–67
  and biography, 63
  disarticulated, 57
  exposure, 60
  in and around villages, 95–98
  manpiulation or curation of skulls, 58
  mass burials, 61
  ritual, 60
  summary, 222
  traditions, 56
Busonè, 307
butchery, 156, 203

caches, 86, 95, 204, 208, 214, 216
Cala Colombo, 58, 126
Cala Scizzo, 46, 54, 56, 258, 323
Cala Tramontana, 97
Calabria, 25, 33, 34, 46, 51, 54, 61, 80, 91, 97, 99, 104, 105, 108, 112, 113, 114, 115, 125, 147, 165, 167, 170, 175, 180, 181, 187, 188, 189, 190, 193, 196, 199, 201, 207, 209, 211, 215, 223, 225, 227, 258, 259, 261, 264, 268, 271, 272, 273, 274, 275, 278, 279, 280, 281, 284, 292, 298, 303, 344, 344, 344
  social networks, Stentinello pottery and obsidian trade, 269–275
Campania, 113, 115, 139, 140, 167, 170, 188, 193, 207, 223, 254, 258, 264, 280, 295, 304
Campignano axes, 207, 208, 210, 299
Campo Ceresole (Vhò), 53, 77, 127
Candelaro, Masseria, 80, 95, 96, 97, 123, 126, 189
cannibalism, 123
canoes. *See* boats
Capo Alfiere, 78, 87, 104, 126, 130, 131, 132, 169, 182, 190, 208, 210, 211, 216, 264, 272, 343
Capo d'Acqua, 126

Capri, 132, 169, 227
carnivores, 61, 69, 124, 125, 152, 155, 224
Casa Gazza, 150, 174
Casa Lopez, 278
Casa Querciola, 257
Casa San Paolo, 58, 96
Casa Soverito, 264
Casale del Dolce, 58, 60, 77, 90, 135, 140, 146
Casatico, 126
Castellaro Vecchio, 187, 278, 279, 282, 284
Çatal Hüyük, 264
Catania, 113, 180, 253, 264, 304
Catignano, 37, 38, 39, 40, 42, 48, 49, 50, 53, 54, 66, 78, 80, 86, 87, 124, 126, 149, 151, 152, 208
Catlin, George, 250, 251
cattle (cows), 12, 33, 84, 127, 134, 137, 138, 139, 140, 141, 142, 143, 144, 145, 146, 147, 153, 155, 156, 224, 231, 239, 263, 302, 344
causality, 326, 327
causation, 291, 293, 295
caves, 38, 44, 56, 58, 60, 62, 63, 67, 68, 69, 76, 108, 109, 110, 128, 226, 264, 272, 302, 303, 304, 307, 321, 323, 343, 343
c-ditches, 84, 91, 92, 95, 147, 262
chaîne opératoire, 17, 81, 121, 172, 204, 222, 225, 236, 243
change, social, 20–22, 27, 157
  European Copper and Bronze Age, general changes, 287–290
  explanations of, 286
  historical practice, 290–291
  long-term trajectory of Central Mediterranean prehistory, 334–341
  nature of Copper Age transition, 320–322
  reconstruction of Copper Age transition, 322–326
  scale and time depth, 291–295
Charybdis, 160
Chelm, 286
chiefdoms, 70, 240
children and childhood, 37, 39, 40, 41, 60, 62, 65, 66, 85, 109, 136, 221, 222
Chiozza di Scandiano, 54
circumcision, 203
clay, 38, 46, 48, 50, 54, 55, 60, 77, 79, 81, 82, 83, 84, 86, 88, 89, 129, 132, 133, 137, 149, 150, 165, 173, 174, 176, 177, 179, 183, 184, 188, 197, 228, 236, 278, 280, 281, 283, 344
Colle Santo Stefano, 137, 142

colour, 132, 136, 146, 153, 156, 174, 175, 186, 200, 202, 203, 205, 206, 224, 227, 228, 229, 230, 320
communities of practice, 14
conservatism, 106, 181, 293, 338, 340
Continenza, Grotta, 60, 109
conversation, 8, 238
cooking, 86, 90, 120, 121, 135, 149, 150, 151, 152, 153, 156, 163, 237
Coppa Nevigata, 60, 123, 130, 338
Copper Age sites and cultures
  Andria, 295
  Civate, 295
  Conelle, 295, 302, 304, 306
  Gaudo, 295, 304, 306, 311, 319
  Ortucchio, 50, 142, 295, 304, 307
  Rinaldone, 295, 306, 319
  Serraferlicchio, 298
  Spilamberto, 135, 295, 302
  Vecchiano, 295
coppicing, 105
Corazzo di Soverito, 97, 98
Corded Ware, 288, 289, 307, 339
corporate and network strategies, 240, 336
Corsica, 112, 255
cribra orbitalia, 36
Croatia, 193, 256
crops and plant foods
  barley, 75, 129, 130, 153, 245
  beans, 130, 132
  lentils, 130, 132, 153
  peas, 130, 132, 153
  spelt, 129, 130
  vetches, 132, 153
  wheat, 32, 114, 129, 131, 132, 153
Crotone, 116, 188, 210, 211, 264, 271, 272, 273
cuisine, 13, 120, 121, 122, 136, 146, 152, 153, 154, 155, 156, 224, 230
cult sites, 107, 108, 109, 110, 113, 226, 323
culture history, 4, 5, 161, 162, 165, 186, 288, 300

dairy products, 134, 139, 143, 146, 148, 153, 288, 300
Dalmatia, 23, 193, 260
daub, wattle and, 33, 77, 78, 80, 81, 82, 83, 85, 88, 89, 90, 104, 129, 133, 174, 222, 229, 282, 296
demography, 37, 40, 41, 139, 142
  regional population structure, 252–254
depositional practices, 9, 50, 54, 58, 60, 63, 67, 80, 86, 94, 105, 106, 170, 196, 205, 208, 213, 214, 216, 222, 226, 235, 331

di Lampedusa, Giuseppe, 286, 294
Diana, Contrada, 137, 149, 152, 169, 171, 276, 282, 284, 298
difference, creation of, 55, 62, 72, 74, 118, 178, 180, 181, 184, 186, 238, 241, 242, 243, 244, 253, 258, 317, 319, 331, 333, 337
Diga di Occhito, 39, 59, 61, 259
Dimini, 171, 296
dimorphism, 37, 68, 110
ditches and ditched villages, 28, 33, 42, 50, 59, 61, 64, 70, 76, 78, 79, 85, 91, 92, 93, 95, 96, 97, 98, 146, 147, 223, 234, 235, 259, 261, 262, 281, 283, 303, 304, 314, 323, 328
dogs, 87, 124, 125, 139, 142, 152, 153, 155, 229
domesticated animals. See cattle; dogs; donkey; horse; pigs; sheep and goats; pastoralism
donkey, 137
down the line exchange, 198

earth ovens, 150, 151, 152, 153, 224
earthquakes, 292
economy, Neolithic
  subsistance needs and land use, 98–102
  egalitarian, 35, 70, 72, 186, 319, 340
Emilia Romagna, 202
enchainment, 18, 236
Enga, 253, 269, 292
Engels, Friedrich, 4, 20
environment and environmental change, 127, 247, 265, 287, 290, 292, 302, 324, 326, 327, 333
Etna, Mount, 33, 113, 207
European Copper and Bronze Age, general changes, 287–290
Evans-Pritchard, E. E., 159, 269
evolution, social. See change, social
exchange. See trade and exchange
exotic items, 162, 190, 198, 200, 299, 310, 318

fat, 87, 135, 136, 145, 197
Favella, 42, 47, 51, 54, 80, 88, 134, 344
feasting. See food and foodways, Neolithic
Felci, Grotta delle, 109, 132, 169, 227
field of action, 7, 13, 14, 15, 16, 17, 20, 21, 22, 51, 72, 120, 156, 177, 178, 220, 226, 235, 236, 238, 241, 242, 243, 244, 248, 259, 289, 294, 318, 322, 324, 326

field of discourse. *See* field of action
figurines, 43, 46, 221
    Copper Age, 307
    deposition of, 50
    material characteristics of, 46
    typology, 52
    use of, 48
Filicudi, 112, 253, 278, 284
fish and fishing, 44, 123, 124, 152, 153, 155, 200, 224, 267, 313
Flannery, Kent V., 3, 6, 86
flavours, 133, 136, 146, 153, 154, 155, 156, 224, 231
flint, 60, 86, 112, 132, 187, 188, 189, 190, 191, 197, 199, 200, 202, 207, 211, 225, 256, 261, 278, 281, 299, 300, 304, 310, 316, 318
fondi di capanne, 80, 83
Fontanarosa Uliveto, 97, 98
Fontbregua, 123
Fonte Chiarano, 114
Fonte San Callsto, 127
Fonteviva, 39, 183
food and foodways
    social embeddedness of, 122
food and foodways, Neolithic
    domestic animal choices, 137–142
    flavours, colours and tastes, 133–137
    foods rarely or never used, 122–129
    hunting, 125–129
    meat consumption, social embeddedness of, 144–148
    Neolithic cuisine as generative map, 152–157
    role of grains and legumes, 129–133
    sociality of herds, 142–144
    summary, 223–225
    wild resources. *See* fruits and nuts, game, gathered plants, hunting,
Fornace Cappuccini, 262
Fossa delle Felci, 281
Fossacesia, 80, 298
Foucault, Michel, 10, 11, 18, 220, 294
fox, 33, 60, 124, 125, 229
fragmentation, 18, 48, 50, 58, 208, 210, 216, 217, 235
France, 128, 163, 171, 193, 256, 296, 308
frequentation, 10, 100, 104, 110, 118, 223, 234, 243, 248
fruits and nuts, gathered, 100, 134, 135, 137, 153, 266
Fucino, 32, 114, 137, 142, 253, 265

Gaban, Riparo, 49, 53, 60
Gabellotto Gorge obsidian source, Lipari, 187
Gaione, 195, 202, 258
game, 124, 128, 129, 265
Gargano Peninsula, 112, 187, 188, 189, 191, 256, 299
gathered plants, 135, 138, 153, 197, 224, 229
gathering.
gender, 50–52
    and figurines, 50–52
    and spatiality, 110, 112
    Copper Age gender ideology, 315–317
    Copper Age symbolisms, 310
    in burials, 62
    Neolithic, 70
genre of action. *See* field of action
Giddens, Anthony, 5, 6, 11, 98, 247
Girifalco, 58, 258, 306
Gozo, 101, 112, 253, 329
grain. *See* crops and plant foods
Great Men, 240
Greece, 25, 27, 61, 163, 268, 296
grey zone, 7
grinding and grinding stones, 28, 60, 81, 84, 86, 132, 133, 148, 173, 200, 227, 228, 236, 262, 278, 283
Gubbio, 127, 253, 265
Gulliver, 21

habitus, 5, 11, 13, 55, 110, 154, 156, 226, 243, 248, 249, 289, 290, 293, 294, 313, 319
Hagerstrand, Torsten, 11, 98, 230, 231
Hal Saflieni, 210, 212, 329
heirlooms, 18, 204
herds and herding. *See* pastoralism; food and foodways, Neolithic.
Herxheim, 96
heterarchy, 15, 71, 239–244, 317, 318, 325, 337
hexis, 12
hierarchy, 15, 70, 71, 72, 74, 222, 239, 240, 275, 288, 310, 311, 318, 336, 337, 338
history and historical process. *See* change, social
honey, 87, 100, 135, 137, 153, 187
Hopi, 260, 269, 294
horses, 137, 288
houses
    social importance, 75
houses and households, Neolithic, 80
    house construction as embedded technology, 81–85

intentional destruction of houses, 87–90
social uses of houses, 86–87
summary, 222
human bone, use of, 58, 60, 64, 65, 95, 96
human nature, 4
hunting, 14, 37, 42, 43, 44, 45, 69, 100, 104, 109, 110, 127, 128, 139, 224, 240, 241, 243, 254, 288, 303, 315, 316, 318, 321, 323, 326
significance of in Neolithic, 125–129

Ice Man (Ötzi), 22, 38, 40, 60, 203
Indo-Europeans, 288, 315
inequality, 242, 316, 333, 335, 336, 340
inhabitation, 76
intensification, 287, 288, 304, 311, 312, 313, 317, 325, 332, 334, 335, 336
Copper Age, 311–313
Ipogeo Manfredi (Santa Barbara), 110, 126, 128, 323
Iron Age, 43, 44, 45, 58, 73, 136, 307, 308, 310, 337, 340, 343, 344
islands, 25, 100, 112, 116, 134, 163, 188, 194, 223, 253, 255, 264, 278, 279, 280, 281, 284, 299, 304, 329, 331, 333
Istria, 163

Jericho, 264

key symbols, 11, 16
kilns, 90, 150, 174, 296
knowledge, 9, 10, 15, 16, 17, 20, 21, 43, 46, 53, 66, 68, 85, 87, 102, 107, 109, 118, 121, 135, 155, 156, 174, 176, 178, 180, 184, 185, 197, 200, 204, 223, 225, 226, 230, 231, 234, 238, 243, 244, 246, 248, 256, 259, 260, 262, 320, 327, 332, 336, 344

La Defensola, 112, 188, 199
La Marmotta, 49, 55, 129, 135, 136, 255, 266, 267, 343
La Puzzolente, 257
La Quercia, Masseria, 80
Lagnano da Piede, 86, 126, 140, 141, 169, 183
Lagozza di Besnate, 266
Lagundo, 308
lake villages, 55, 82, 266
landscape, 9–11
Italian, 32

landscape, Copper Age, 313–314
landscape, Neolithic, 116–118
and natural places, 112–116
avoidance of high mountains, 116
economy and frequentation, 98–102
kinds of sites, 76
summary, 222–223
temporality of, 102–107
Lazio, 25, 140, 167, 193, 266, 271, 295, 304, 306, 325
learning, 22, 66, 176, 177
Ledro, 131, 302
Leone, Grotta del, 9, 109
Levanzo, 43, 44, 307
life expectancy, 40, 41
life tables, 40
lifespan, 40. See biography
Liguria, 25, 37, 39, 54, 114, 123, 163, 257, 264, 298, 299, 325
Linearbandkeramik (LBK), 84, 89, 96, 99, 206, 264
Lipari, 101, 112, 113, 149, 167, 169, 171, 187, 188, 189, 190, 192, 193, 194, 196, 198, 199, 202, 225, 253, 256, 274, 275, 276, 277, 278, 279, 280, 281, 282, 283, 284, 285, 296, 298, 303, 325, 334, 344
social history of, 276–285
Lipari, Acropolis, 276, 280, 284
lithics
blades and bladelets, 60, 123, 187, 189, 190, 191, 196, 197, 199, 201, 202, 204, 206, 225, 243, 273, 282
debitage, 189
Neolithic formal typology, 189
Neolithic intensity of use, 189, 191
Neolithic lithic economy, 186–192
Neolithic obsidian trade. See obsidian
Neolithic, summary, 226
pressure flaked, 201, 300, 303, 310
regional variations in raw material use, 190
Lombardia, 266
Lugo di Ravenna, 263

Maccarese, 137, 304
mace-heads, 298
Maddalena di Muccia, 126
Madonna delle Grazie, 39, 60
Madonna, Grotta della, 108, 272
Malerba, 97, 133
Malta, 23, 25, 28, 44, 56, 101, 112, 124, 131, 165, 167, 171, 180, 181, 193, 210, 212, 230, 253, 256, 260, 269, 270, 271, 299, 329, 331, 333, 334, 336, 340, 343

INDEX

Malta (cont.)
   historical development of temple culture, 329–334
Manfredonia, 108, 109, 136
Marche, 53, 76, 114, 207, 265, 306
Marcianese, 80, 87, 95, 209
Marx, Karl, 4, 5, 20
Marxist models for 4th–3rd millennium change, 288
Mastrodonato, Masseria, 183
Matera, 76, 91, 92, 96, 97, 165, 167, 169, 174, 180, 181, 182, 184, 262, 271, 295, 296
materiality, 8, 14, 46, 176, 237, 248, 320, 327
mating networks, 42
Matrensa, 97, 262
meat. *See* food and foodways
Megara Hyblaea, 96, 97, 262
Melanesia, 68, 73, 152, 206, 323
memory, 9, 10, 13, 15, 41, 42, 63, 64, 65, 66, 67, 95, 104, 106, 117, 155, 178, 222, 235, 263, 293, 308, 322
Mesolithic, 25, 26, 27, 28, 113, 114, 123, 124, 128, 157, 192, 223, 265, 269, 321
Messina, Straits of, 185, 189, 256, 271, 279, 344
metals, 192, 287, 288, 298, 299, 300, 312, 315, 318, 320, 321, 325, 327, 337, 339
   bronze, 43, 310
   copper, 229, 298, 304, 310, 316
middens, 50, 64
Mileto, 149, 150, 151
milk. *See* dairy products
milk boilers, 300
mines and quarries, 80, 81, 89, 112, 136, 188, 189, 193, 199, 207, 298, 299
mobility, 26, 36, 37, 67, 68, 110, 236, 243, 260, 263, 333
Monte Arci, 188, 192, 193, 194, 202
Monte Bego, 45, 131
Monte Grande, 54
Monte Pelato, Lipari, 276
Monti Iblei, 112, 188, 190, 256
Monti Lessini, 112, 188
mountains, use of, 116
Mulino Sant'Antonio, 195, 304
Murgecchia, 96, 97
Murgia Timone, 92, 96

Native Americans, 254, 294
navigation and seafaring, 255, 278, 284
Neolithic, Italian, general description, 28
Neolithic, origins and spread of, 24, 25

Neto di Bolasse, 127
New Archaeology. *See* processualism
New Guinea, 136, 145, 151, 190, 250, 253, 291, 292, 294
normality, 20, 22, 157, 161, 226, 236, 292
Nuer, 159, 269
nutrition, 120, 121

obsidian, Neolithic trade in, 258
   cultural motivations for, 204
   prestige goods explanations, 200, 201
   social role, 202, 203
   sources and circulation, 192–197
   summary, 226
   technological explanations, 199
   time-space embeddedness, 203
ochre, 53, 55, 69, 80, 146, 197, 199, 227, 229, 230, 236, 256, 283, 306, 321, 331
olive, 32, 114, 130, 134, 135
Onda, Grotta all', 124, 211
origins research, 286, 321
ornaments, 33, 43, 69, 124, 128, 216, 257, 288, 307, 308, 316, 317, 319
Orsi, Paolo, 77, 262, 282, 283, 299
Ortucchio, 50, 142, 295, 304, 307

Pacelli, Grotta, 46, 54, 56, 126, 127, 140, 141, 210, 258, 323
Palaeolithic, 36, 55, 108, 221, 267
Palagruza, 112, 255
Palinuro, 193
Panarea, 281
Pantelleria, 112, 188, 193, 194, 202, 255
Passo di Corvo, 47, 48, 53, 57, 58, 59, 61, 90, 92, 96, 126, 130, 140, 141, 147, 169, 183, 184, 187, 195, 208, 209, 262, 344
pastoralism, 38, 134, 137–144, 148, 158, 203, 224, 283, 287, 300, 304, 311, 312, 313, 318, 321, 324, 337
   Copper Age developments, 300–303
   social context of Copper Age herding, 311–313
Patrizi, Grotta, 38, 60, 62, 69, 109, 210
pavements, cobbled, 283
Pavolella, Grotta, 61, 259
Peleponnese, 268
Penitenzeria, 33, 34, 41, 47, 50, 51, 54, 80, 88, 90, 99, 102, 103, 104, 105, 172, 173, 174, 175, 176, 177, 178, 179, 180, 182, 184, 196, 197, 208, 209, 228, 264
Perriere Sottano, 192
personhood, 11, 12, 15, 51, 52, 204, 221, 318
Piano Conte, 282, 295

378

INDEX

Piano di Cerreto, 114
Piano Vento, 44, 50, 97, 307
Pianosa, 123, 209
Piccioni, Grotta dei, 109, 126, 210
Pienza, 126, 130
pigs, 33, 100, 128, 134, 137, 138, 139, 140, 141, 142, 143, 145, 146, 147, 151, 153, 155, 289, 291, 302
Pipistrelli, Grotta dei, 169
pits, 58, 64, 80, 83, 87, 90, 132, 149, 150, 151, 173, 283
Pizzica Pantanello, 209, 299
plows and plowing, 44, 131, 134, 288, 302, 305, 308, 311, 312, 315
Poggio Olivastro, 50
political structure
  Copper Age, 310
  Neolithic, 70–73
  Neolithic, and difference, 239–244
Pollino, 113, 275
Ponte San Pietro, 306
population, 26, 34, 40, 223
Porto Badisco, 43, 44, 66, 68, 69, 108, 109, 128, 307, 321, 343, 343
Posta Villano, 92
post-processualism, 4, 120, 163, 241, 315
pottery, 170
  figulina, 48, 228, 272, 296
  finewares, 98, 162, 163, 165, 170, 171, 174, 176, 182, 186, 271, 296, 323, 344
  painted wares, 44, 48, 53, 80, 83, 97, 108, 109, 162, 169, 170, 171, 174, 176, 180, 181, 182, 184, 228, 229, 242, 272, 275, 279, 280, 281, 296
pottery styles and periods
  bichrome wares, 98, 169, 280
  Cardial Wares, 25, 163, 275
  Catignano, 48, 167, 170
  Chassey-Lagozza, 28, 113, 167, 171, 295, 296, 304, 319
  Diana-Bellavista, 28, 57, 69, 97, 98, 112, 113, 167, 171, 172, 186, 276, 279, 282, 295, 296, 306, 319
  Ghar Dalam, 167, 271
  Grey Skorba, 171
  Impressed Ware, 48, 53, 97, 163, 167, 169, 180, 183, 272, 275, 280, 295, 344
  La Quercia, 170, 182
  Linear (Sasso, Fiorano), 167, 271
  Matera Scratched, 97, 165, 169, 180, 184, 295
  meandro-spiralic, 279, 284
  Passo di Corvo, 167, 170
  Red Skorba, 171

Ripoli, 28, 113, 167, 171, 181, 296
Scaloria, 184
Serra d'Alto, 48, 54, 97, 98, 108, 113, 128, 162, 167, 170, 193, 262, 272, 279, 281, 296, 303, 306, 323
Stentinello, 53, 97, 98, 113, 165, 167, 169, 175, 178, 179, 180, 181, 185, 271, 272, 279, 280, 281, 295, 296
trichrome, 98, 162, 167, 169, 183, 230, 279, 280
VBQ (Vaso a Bocca Quadrata), 53, 54, 167, 271
pottery, Copper Age, 295–298
pottery, Neolithic, 225
  chaîne opératoire and creative process, 172–178
  local knowledge and perception of, 184–185
  social history of, 163–172
  stylistic decoration and geographical patterning, 178–184
  stylistic hybrids, 182
  traditions of interpretation, 161–163
power, 7, 15, 18, 109, 116, 161, 220, 239, 315, 316, 336
Pozzi del Piano, 109
Prato Don Michele, 163
prestige. *See* value
prestige competition, 70, 72, 74, 201, 241, 336, 338, 339
processualism, 4, 62, 70, 120, 162, 198, 239, 271, 336
projects, 14, 15, 19, 22, 35, 102, 231, 236, 237, 241, 243, 245, 247, 259, 265
Pueblos, 84, 106, 294, 336
Puglia, 23, 25, 28, 32, 33, 43, 59, 60, 61, 75, 76, 80, 87, 91, 97, 108, 109, 110, 112, 116, 123, 128, 165, 167, 171, 181, 182, 184, 187, 188, 190, 193, 195, 207, 210, 242, 254, 258, 259, 261, 263, 267, 271, 272, 280, 295, 303, 308
Pulo di Molfetta, 306, 323
pulses. *See* crops and plant foods
Punto del Milazzese, 281

Quadrato di Torre Spaccato, 86
querns. *See* grinding and grinding stones
Quinzano, 211, 262

Recanati, 306
reeds, 77, 80, 81, 82, 83, 133
regional analysis and scale, 251–252
regional differences, Neolithic, 260–269
relationship brokers, 318

379

Remedello, 295, 304, 306, 307, 310
Ridola, Domenico, 77, 92, 262
Rinicedda (Rinella), 278, 279
Ripa Tetta, 40, 58, 59, 61, 78, 82, 91, 112, 126, 150, 174
Ripabianca di Monterado, 48, 126
Ripoli, 49, 53, 76, 90, 97, 124, 126, 127, 262
Rivanazzano, 205

Salina, 112, 253, 278, 281, 284
salt, 136, 153
Samari, 58
Sammardenchia, 54
San Calogero, Grotta di, 47, 54
San Marco, 113, 127, 130, 304
San Martino, 97
San Martino, Contrada, 304
San Mauro, 140
San Michele, Grotta, 272, 274
Sant'Angelo, Grotta (Abruzzo), 135
Sant'Angelo, Grotta (Calabria), 272
Sant'Anna di Alfaedo, 44, 54, 55, 308
Santa Maria in Selva, 127, 298
Santa Tecchia, Masseria, 123, 127, 130
Sardinia (Sardegna), 23, 25, 44, 112, 188, 192, 193, 194, 201, 255, 298, 331
Scaloria, Grotta, 60, 108, 109, 123, 128, 210, 212, 323
Scamuso, 130
Scandinavia, 24, 26, 28, 260, 338
Schifata, Masseria, 210
Schletz, 61
Scylla, 160
secondary products, 134, 288
senses, archaeology of the, 13, 230
Serra Cicora, 75, 97, 98, 258, 323
Serra d'Alto, 76, 97, 169, 183, 262, 303, 323
Serra del Palco, 86, 104
Sesklo, 171, 296
settlement size, 34, 42, 90
settlement, Copper Age, 304
settlement, Neolithic
  dispersed, 264–265
  East-West divide, 268
  highlands, 266
  lake villages, 266
  of unique places, 276
  variation, 91
  villages, 261–263
Sgurgola, 306
sheep and goats, 33, 127, 128, 134, 138, 139, 140, 141, 142, 144, 146, 147, 153, 155, 229, 281, 302, 311, 344

shell, 33, 123, 125, 128, 173, 200, 228, 229, 230, 299
shellfish, 123, 124, 153, 155, 224, 344
shine, gleam (visual quality), 229, 320, 325
Sibari, 116, 272, 274, 275
Sicily (Sicilia), 23, 25, 28, 33, 43, 44, 46, 51, 54, 55, 75, 76, 86, 91, 96, 97, 108, 112, 113, 122, 123, 128, 165, 167, 170, 179, 181, 182, 185, 186, 188, 192, 193, 199, 201, 206, 223, 225, 254, 255, 256, 260, 261, 262, 264, 266, 269, 270, 271, 273, 276, 278, 279, 280, 281, 284, 295, 296, 298, 299, 304, 306, 307, 319, 329, 331, 332
sickle gloss, 189
Sila, 113, 210, 213, 272
similarity, creation of. *See* difference, creation of
Siracusa, 112, 146, 180, 188, 262, 281
skeletons, human, 12, 36, 37, 38, 39, 40, 48, 57, 61, 65, 68, 74, 110, 206, 221, 222, 228, 243, 259, 300, 310, 344
skill, 11, 15, 16, 83, 156, 170, 174, 175, 177, 191, 197, 201, 225, 241, 243, 255, 256, 300, 319
Skorba, 131, 167, 208
skulls, 38, 39, 58, 64, 67, 87, 95, 110, 124, 222, 259, 306, 313
social centrality, 65, 318
social reproduction, 6, 9, 11, 19, 20, 22, 42, 70, 71, 72, 74, 157, 178, 218, 220, 236, 241, 244, 246, 248, 289, 290, 293, 322, 328, 336, 340
South Tyrol, 38
spatiality, 9–11, 230–236
  of exchange, 256, 258
  of food, 156
  of gender, 110
  of house-building, 83
  of pottery, 184–185
Sperlinga di San Basilio, 113, 266
Spilamberto, 135, 295, 302
spindle whorls, 300, 304
spondylus, 200, 201
stability, 20, 143, 157, 237, 247, 287, 295, 338
stable isotopes, 37, 143, 224
stature, 36, 300
stelae, statue-stelae, and statue-menhirs, 43, 45, 206, 308, 310, 314, 315, 316, 319, 324
  Alpine, 43, 44, 307
  Daunian, 43

Lunigiana, 43, 44, 68, 308, 310
Villanovan, 43
Stentinello, 76, 96, 123, 137, 140, 262
Stilo, 190
stone, 12, 50, 55, 57, 100, 102, 112, 132, 149, 188, 190, 194, 200, 202, 207, 229, 298, 306, 308, 312
stone and geological resources
   amphibolite, 205
   basalt, 206, 207
   flint, 60, 86, 112, 132, 187, 188, 189, 190, 191, 197, 199, 200, 202, 207, 211, 225, 256, 261, 278, 281, 299, 300, 304, 310, 316, 318
   igneous rock, 112, 207
   jasper, 200, 256
   lava, 200
   marble, 200, 256, 299
   metamorphic rock, 112, 205, 206, 207, 211
   quartz and quartzite, 60, 202, 211, 229
   steatite, 55, 200, 257, 267, 299, 304
stone tools. *See* lithics
stress, skeletal, 37
Stretto di Partanna, 281
string, 82, 191, 231, 344
Stromboli, 112, 113, 276, 281
structuralism, 5, 12, 154, 240
strutturi di combustione, 80, 149, 151, 224, 283
synaesthesia, 230, 317, 320
systematics, 225

Talheim, 61
Tarxien, 329, 334
Tarxien Cemetery, 334
taskscape, 10, 20, 107, 118, 144, 154, 156, 234, 236, 324
tattoos, 38, 203
Tavoliere, 26, 32, 42, 76, 81, 91, 92, 95, 96, 101, 123, 146, 147, 170, 188, 189, 191, 253, 257, 261, 262, 326
tea, 119
technology of enchantment, 320
temples, Maltese, 329, 331, 334, 336, 340, 343
temporality, 9–11, 230–236
   of food, 156
   of pottery, 172
Thessaly, 28, 268
thick description, 23, 157
thin-section studies, 162, 184
time markings, 234
time-space geography, 98, 230

Tirlecchia, 97, 127, 169
Toppo Daguzzo, 304, 338
Torre Canne, 130
Torre Sabea, 104, 123, 127, 146
Toscana, 23, 114, 167, 195, 206, 211, 257, 264, 271, 275, 295, 296, 298, 325
traction. *See* plows and plowing
trade. *See* obsidian
trade and exchange, 72, 110, 191, 198, 214, 236, 241, 243, 256, 257, 258, 259, 278, 284, 312, 314, 316, 318, 319, 327, 328, 329
tragedy of the commons, 328
Trasano, 38, 97, 150, 174, 262
trauma, skeletal, 38, 39, 60, 206, 259, 316, 345
travel, 9, 110, 114, 156, 193, 220, 223, 236, 252, 254, 255, 259, 274, 275, 278, 279
Tremiti Islands, 163, 255
Trentino-Alto Adige, 298
trepanation, 38, 39, 56, 60, 67, 69, 203, 222, 235
tribes, 2, 70, 239, 250, 253, 311, 334
Tricalle, 79
Troina, 113
Tunisia, 188, 193
Tuppo dei Sassi, 109, 128
Tuscan Archipelago, 112, 123, 255
type fossils, 165, 170
tyranny of the ethnographic record, 287

Umbria, 167
Umbro, 99, 106, 125, 172, 173, 174, 180, 187, 208, 209, 215, 227, 228, 298
use-wear analysis, 48, 189, 199, 207
Uzzo, Grotta dell', 123, 124, 130, 266

Valcamonica, 43, 44, 69, 307, 308, 343
Valente, Masseria, 40, 126, 281
Valle Sbernia, 188
Valtellina, 307
value, 71, 72, 146, 240, 241, 242, 317, 318
   Copper Age value, personhood and aesthetics, 317–320
Vannaro, Grotta, 126
Vhò, 49, 53, 54, 127
Villa Badessa, 40, 97, 211
village size, 90
villages, 76, 261–263
   burial and villages as ancestral places, 95–98
Villaggio Leopardi, 127
violence, 38, 39, 69, 94, 221, 315, 318

volcanos, 118
Vulcano, 112, 113, 276, 278, 281
Vulpiglia, 97, 123, 128, 199, 262

warfare and raiding, 41, 42, 61, 64, 71, 89, 94, 118, 223, 240, 241, 243, 252, 258, 259, 291, 293, 314, 318
water, 81, 83, 89, 93, 108, 110, 139, 173, 197, 255, 276, 280, 344
weapons, 12, 201, 206, 226, 258, 288, 307, 308, 310, 315, 316, 317, 319, 321, 343

weaving, 24, 300
wild resources. *See* fruits and nuts, game, gathered plants, hunting
wild zones, 110, 129, 137
Windmill Hill, 96
Wola, 106, 190, 197
wood and timber, 37, 82, 84, 89, 116, 172, 173, 199, 229, 258, 266, 283, 299
woodland management, 82, 105

Yeats, William Butler, 1, 4, 247